D0211904

Praeger Handbook on Understanding and Preventing Workplace Discrimination

Praeger Handbook on Understanding and Preventing Workplace Discrimination

Volume 1
Legal, Management, and Social Science Perspectives

Volume 2
Best Practices for Preventing and Dealing with Workplace Discrimination

REFERENCE BOOK
Not to be taken from the
Library

Praeger Handbook on Understanding and Preventing Workplace Discrimination

Volume 1

Legal, Management, and Social Science Perspectives

Michele A. Paludi, Carmen A. Paludi, Jr., and Eros R. DeSouza, Editors

Foreword by D. Gayle Loftis

 PRAEGER

AN IMPRINT OF ABC-CLIO, LLC
Santa Barbara, California • Denver, Colorado • Oxford, England

m61.r

WISSER MEMORIAL LIBRARY

Ref.

HD4903.5

.U58

P72

2011

v.1

c.1

Copyright 2011 by Michele A. Paludi, Carmen A. Paludi, Jr., and Eros R. DeSouza

All rights reserved. No part of this publication may be reproduced, stored in a
retrieval system, or transmitted, in any form or by any means, electronic,
mechanical, photocopying, recording, or otherwise, except for the inclusion
of brief quotations in a review, without prior permission in writing from
the publisher.

Library of Congress Cataloging-in-Publication Data

Praeger handbook on understanding and preventing workplace discrimination /
Michele A. Paludi, Carmen A. Paludi, Jr., and Eros R. DeSouza, editors.
   v. cm.
   Includes bibliographical references and index.
   Contents: v. 1. Legal, management, and social science perspectives—v. 2. Best practices
for preventing and dealing with workplace discrimination.
   ISBN 978-0-313-37974-1 (hardcopy : alk. paper)—ISBN 978-0-313-37975-8 (ebook)
   1. Discrimination in employment—United States. 2. Discrimination in employment—United
States—Prevention. I. Paludi, Michele Antoinette. II. Paludi, Carmen A. III. DeSouza, Eros.
IV. Title: Handbook on understanding and preventing workplace discrimination.
   HD4903.5.U58P72 2011
   658.3008—dc22   2010012556

ISBN: 978-0-313-37974-1
EISBN: 978-0-313-37975-8

15 14 13 12 11   1 2 3 4 5

This book is also available on the World Wide Web as an eBook.
Visit www.abc-clio.com for details.

Praeger
An Imprint of ABC-CLIO, LLC

ABC-CLIO, LLC
130 Cremona Drive, P.O. Box 1911
Santa Barbara, California 93116-1911

This book is printed on acid-free paper ∞

Manufactured in the United States of America

You never really understand a person until you consider things from his point of view—until you climb inside of his skin and walk around in it.
—Harper Lee, *To Kill a Mockingbird*

We hope this handbook will assist employers and employees alike, especially managers and corporate leaders who are empowered to prevent workplace discrimination.
—Michele A. Paludi and Carmen A. Paludi, Jr.

For Mark Smith:
Spouse, lover, and friend.
Thank you for all your support, especially during times of stress.
—Eros R. DeSouza

Volume 1 Contents

Foreword

Discrimination occurs in many forms. It is not a new issue, just one about which the public has become more aware. Unfortunately, awareness of its existence does not equate with an understanding of the multitudes of ways that persons and organizations can engage in discrimination, react to discrimination, or respond to an allegation of discrimination against a person or organization. Retaliation for making the complaint, whether the claim is found to be justified or not, has become even more common in recent years.

The investigation of claims of discrimination or retaliation requires an understanding of more than just how to ask a question. How should an employer train the workforce to be sensitive to discrimination, to prevent it, and to deal with such an allegation when made? Do the reactions and damages claimed by the plaintiffs have any basis in social science or studies?

As an attorney who has worked on numerous such cases over the last thirty years, both in state and federal courts, it has become clear to me that more understanding of "the nature of the beast" is required. Education in the subject matter and the processes that operate in both the prevention and elimination of discriminatory or hostile workplaces is needed not only for the legal practitioner, but also for the individuals who are in the trenches of the workplace. The costs for business and government when prevention and elimination are not seriously undertaken by the employer are significant. They include emotional damages and medical care for the victim, distraction of the employer's employees from their business in order to participate in litigation discovery and testimony, and counsel fees for defense as well as for the successful plaintiff. Furthermore, seldom is there only one victim. The uneducated and untrained duplicate their errors repeatedly, and the costs may even escalate due to the failure to address obvious problems of discrimination in the workplace. Frequently, the offender creates a pool of victims even if the victims may not be aware of each other's existence.

I have been fortunate to work with Dr. Michele A. Paludi, who has demonstrated to me that understanding discrimination and working to eliminate it requires more than just a knowledge of how to litigate for damage that has occurred, and that a victim of discrimination is not alone in the social science that has addressed this subject. The chapters compiled by the editors in this work can serve as a reference for every human resource office and law firm that must deal with these subjects. It is to be hoped that the greater understanding that can be derived from works such as this can ultimately result in money being spent by businesses to train and educate for prevention, rather than as damages and attorneys' fees to victims.

We can only aspire to that day.

D. Gayle Loftis, Esq.
Hackensack, New Jersey

Acknowledgments

Michele A. Paludi and Carmen A. Paludi, Jr.

> Sexual, racial, gender violence, and other forms of discrimination and violence in a culture cannot be eliminated without changing culture.
> —Charlotte Bunch

Charlotte Bunch's sentiment is echoed throughout this handbook on workplace discrimination. The contributors to this handbook have taught courses in, conducted research on, and written about workplace discrimination in their respective disciplines. Many contributors have been advocates on behalf of civil rights legislation by working with clients; local, state, and federal agencies; legislators; the courts; the Equal Employment Opportunity Commission; and the United Nations. We have been honored to have collaborated with the esteemed contributors to this handbook. They have greatly increased our understanding and appreciation of workplace discrimination preventative strategies.

Special thanks are due to Jeff Olson and Brian Romer and their colleagues at Praeger for encouraging us to edit this handbook.

We thank our families for their support during the preparation of this handbook. We are reminded of how no protections from discrimination were provided to our fathers, Michael Paludi and Carmen Paludi, Sr., for the many years that they worked at General Electric as skilled laborers. Our fathers' stories of how co-workers were treated, shared with us when we were just children, and before the passage of Title VII of the 1964 Civil Rights Act, continue to fuel our passion to help employers and employees treat each other with respect and dignity.

During the preparation of this handbook, we mourned the passing of Carmen Paludi, Sr. Excerpts from his eulogy continue to establish the basis and motivation for this edited volume:

> Tom Brokow aptly referred to pop's generation as the "Greatest Generation." He said that these are "men and women whose everyday lives of duty, honor, achievement, and courage gave us the world we have today." . . .
>
> The son of immigrant parents, he [Carmen] was raised in the tenement houses on Weaver Street (Schenectady, New York). He learned that the color of your skin, your nationality, or your religion didn't matter. African American, Slovak, Polish, Italian, Jew, Irish, all grew up in the tenements and neighborhoods during the depression, and learned to rely on one another to survive. He taught us the value of all people without prejudice. . . .
>
> So if his is the "Greatest Generation," and if the next generation is supposed to do better than the previous one, then pop, while here no longer, continues to challenge all of us to move forward and be better.

It was during this "greatest generation" that many of the efforts to recognize workplace discrimination began, and much of the legislation was introduced and organizations and policies formed to mitigate it. Our generation continues to address these challenges. This book is for Carmen, Sr., and Michael. Their memories live on.

Eros R. DeSouza

I thank my spouse, Mark Smith, for his moral support during the preparation of this handbook. In addition, I offer my special thanks to Dr. Frances P. McNiece, my mentor since graduate school and spiritual mother who is watching over me from her special place in heaven. Lastly, I owe my early training in community psychology to Dr. Gordon Allport, whose writings about the uniqueness of each individual and his seminal work on the nature of prejudice—and how to combat it through a "one world" perspective that may potentially bind all of humanity—continue to be an inspiration to me.

Introduction to Volume 1

Education is important because, first of all, people need to know that discrimination still exists. It is still real in the workplace, and we should not take that for granted.

—Alexis Herman

In 2005, Paul Haggis wrote and directed the movie, *Crash,* which asked its viewers to consider the complexities of tolerance. The movie's synopsis included the following description:

A Brentwood housewife and her DA husband. A Persian store owner. Two police detectives who are also lovers. An African- American television director and his wife. A Mexican locksmith. Two car-jackers. A rookie cop. A middle-aged Korean couple. . . . They all live in Los Angeles. And during the next 36 hours, they will all collide. . . . Diving headlong into the diverse melting pot of post-9/11 Los Angeles, this compelling urban drama tracks the volatile intersections of a multi-ethnic cast of characters' struggles to overcome their fears as they careen in and out of one another's lives. In the gray area between black and white, victim and aggressor, there are no easy answers. . . . CRASH boldly reminds us of the importance of tolerance as it ventures beyond color lines . . . and uncovers the truth of our shared humanity. (Celebrity Wonder, 2005)

Crash left unaswered more questions than it answered for its viewers, for example:

- What are the origins of discrimination?
- What prevents individuals from challenging their prejudices about race, ethnicity, age, national origin, disability, and sex?
- How can institutions, such as workplaces, in this society assist individuals in overcoming stereotypes and prejudices about co-workers who are "different" from themselves because of religion, race, national origin, sex, and sexual orientation?
- Under which conditions is race stereotyping likely to occur?

This handbook addresses these questions. The questions stem from our consulting work with academic institutions and businesses as well as from our understanding of the following cases related to workplace discrimination, which received prominent attention in the national media during the preparation of this handbook:

1. In 2009, President Obama signed the Lily Ledbetter Fair Pay Act of 2009. This act allows employees to claim back pay for a period of up to two years before the filing of the claim with the Equal Employment Opportunity Commission. In addition, the act is retroactive, with an effective date of May 28, 2007.
2. On September 25, 2008, President George W. Bush signed a bill amending the Americans with Disabilities Act, which became effective on January 1, 2009.
3. In June 2008, the Supreme Court ruled in favor of 28 employees who lost their jobs during cutbacks at a federal research laboratory in upstate New York, Knolls Atomic Power Laboratory. Twenty-seven of the employees were at least 40 years old, the age at which protections begin under the Age Discrimination in Employment Act.
4. In March 2008, 15 African American and Latino airport employees in Dallas settled a lawsuit for $1.9 million. They alleged that their white co-workers created a hostile work environment by intimidating them with swastikas, nooses, and other racist symbols.
5. In August 2008, Video Only, a home-electronics retailer in Seattle, Washington, was ordered by a Portland judge to pay $630,000 to employees at one of its stores in Jantzen Beach. The employees alleged religious and racial slurs, including a doll with its face and hair painted black, which was hogtied and hung by a nail in a break room.

6. In November 2008, a federal district court judge in Arizona entered a consent decree for nearly $2 million and remedial relief to resolve a class-based religious bias lawsuit against the University of Phoenix and Apollo Group, Inc. The suit alleged discrimination against non-Mormon employees.

7. In September 2008, Faiza Abu, who was employed at the Best Western Airport Executel in Sea Tac, Washington, refused to take off her hijab, a Muslim head scarf, when her manager informed her the hijab did not work with their new uniforms. She wore the hijab because of religious reasons. According to the lawsuit, Shawn Walters, Ms. Abu's manager stated: "Either you're going to take it off or I'm going to fire you."

    Ms. Abu stated: "I didn't take it off—and he fired me."

8. On October 8, 2008, the U.S. Supreme Court heard arguments in *Crawford v. Metro Gov't of Nashville and Davidson County, Tenn.* Vicky Crawford had cooperated in an internal investigation of sexual harassment filed against a human resources director, Gene Hughes. Hughes received no discipline. However, Crawford and three other employees who cooperated with the investigation were fired.

WORKPLACE DISCRIMINATION LEGISLATION

Under Title VII of the Civil Rights Act of 1964, the Americans with Disabilities Act, and the Age Discrimination in Employment Act, it is illegal to discriminate in any aspect of employment, including the following:

- Hiring and Firing
- Compensation, Assignment, or Classification of Employees
- Transfer, Promotion, Layoff, or Recall
- Job Advertisements
- Recruitment
- Testing
- Use of Company Facilities
- Training and Apprenticeship Programs
- Fringe Benefits
- Pay, Retirement Plans, and Disability Leave

In addition to federal legislation, states prohibit discrimination as well (see Volume 1, Appendix B). For example, New York enacted SONDA legislation, the Sexual Orientation Non-Discrimination Act, which prohibits discrimination on the basis of actual or perceived sexual orientation. California, Massachusetts, New Hampshire, New Jersey, and Vermont have similar legislation with respect to sexual orientation.

As another example of state-protected categories, Oregon includes marital status. New Jersey and California added gender identity as a protected category. New Jersey also includes domestic partnership status and atypical hereditary cellular or blood trait as protected categories. Rhode Island and Missouri include AIDS testing as a protected category. Louisiana includes sickle-cell trait as a protected category. As a final example, political affiliation is a protected category in the District of Columbia.

Discriminatory practices under federal and some state laws also include the following:

* Harassment on the basis of race, color, religion, sex, national origin, disability, or age
* Retaliation against an individual for filing a charge of discrimination
* Participation in an investigation or opposing discriminatory practices
* Employment decisions based on stereotypes or assumptions about the abilities, traits, or performance of individuals of a certain sex, race, age, sexual orientation, religion, or ethnic group, or individuals with disabilities
* Denial of employment opportunities to a person because of marriage to, or association with, an individual of a particular race, religion, or national origin, or an individual with a disability, including HIV/AIDS

HOSTILE WORK ENVIRONMENTS

Behavioral examples of discriminatory treatment include the following: racial slurs or epithets, unwelcome sexual advances, sexual graffiti, telling jokes pertaining to protected categories, sexually suggestive posters and engaging in threatening, and intimidating or hostile acts toward an individual because that person belongs to or is associated with any protected categories.

A hostile work environment may exist for employees when (1) verbal and or nonverbal behavior in the workplace occurs because of an individual being a member of a protected category, (2) the behavior is unwanted and unwelcome, and (3) the behavior is severe or pervasive enough to unreasonably affect the employee's work environment. In addition, a hostile work environment can be created by an individual's peers; it does not have to occur only between individuals of unequal power in the workplace. Furthermore, the hostile environment must be more than trivial; it has to affect the conditions on an employee's work. Hostile work environments can occur although the individuals are of the same race, sex, age, sexual orientation, and so on.

"REASONABLE CARE" IN PREVENTING WORKPLACE DISCRIMINATION

Employers have a legal responsibility to prevent hostile work environments by exercising "reasonable care" through an effective and enforced policy statement, effective and enforced investigatory procedures, and training programs on discrimination and hostile work environments for all members of the workplace. California, Connecticut, and Maine have mandated training, for example, on sexual harassment. California also has defined what it considers to be a qualified trainer—that is, an individual who "either through formal education and training or substantial experience can effectively lead in person (training) or webinars" (Johnson, 2005).

Furthermore, all employers must investigate complaints of discrimination when a complaint is filed and when a supervisor or manager is told of the discrimination, even if this individual is not the official designated complaint officer and even if the complaint is not made in an "official" manner. Thus, once the employer knows, the requirement of responsive action begins. The employer knows when an employee with organizational authority is made aware of the alleged complaint.

The Equal Employment Opportunity Commission (EEOC) demands that investigations be completed promptly, confidentially, and with impartiality. Employers must take measures to ensure that the employee who was subjected to the hostile work environment is "made whole," the legal term for being put into the position they would have been had the harassment not occurred. Once the remedy is undertaken, it is vital that the employee who experienced a hostile work environment know that her or his employer will continue to monitor the situation and pay attention to actions taken with regard to her or his employment situation.

RATIONALE FOR THIS HANDBOOK

Despite these guidelines for investigating complaints of discrimination and establishing preventative measures, statistics indicate that employers may not be properly implementing antidiscrimination laws in their

Table 1
EEOC Complaints of Workplace Discrimination, 2009

Protected Category	Number of Complaints Filed with EEOC in 2009
Age	22,778
Disability	21,451
Equal Compensation	942
National Origin	11,134
Pregnancy	6,196
Race/Color	33,579
Religion	3,386
Retaliation	33,613
Sex	28,028
Sexual Harassment	12,696

Source: EEOC 2010.

Note: Statistics regarding complaints of genetic information discrimination were not available for 2009; this form of discrimination became illegal in November 2009.

organizations. Individuals may seek resolution through the EEOC after they have exhausted internal procedures. In January 2010, the EEOC published its report dealing with the number of charges of workplace discrimination filed with this agency in 2009 (see Table 1).

These statistics and the cases summarized at the beginning of this Introduction underscore problems that exist in U.S. workplaces. Employees experience (1) harassment and discrimination because they are members of protected classes, and (2) retaliation for bringing to their employers' attention their perceived discrimination or harassment. Thus, assistance is required for organizations, including their human resource managers and presidents, to understand how to prevent and deal with workplace discrimination and harassment.

This two-volume handbook seeks to accomplish this goal. Volume 1 of *The Praeger Handbook on Workplace Discrimination* provides an overview of workplace discrimination through an examination of federally protected categories, including age, disability, equal compensation, genetic information, national origin, pregnancy, race/color, religion, sex, and sexual harassment. In addition, the volume includes a discussion of retaliation. Furthermore, Volume 1 offers guidance on state laws that prohibit discrimination and harassment because of individuals' sexual orientation. An overview of state protected classes is presented. The role of the EEOC in seeking resolution for complaints of discrimination and harassment is also discussed. Volume 1 also presents chapters on employers' legal responsibilities to prevent workplace discrimination and to investigate complaints brought to their attention.

Volume 2 offers strategies related to "reasonable care" in terms of preventing workplace discrimination through policies, procedures, and training programs. These strategies are grounded in case law, management theory, and empirical research in the social sciences that are discussed in Volume 1. Resources such as Web sites and organizations devoted to workplace discrimination issues are also provided for the reader.

Chapters in both volumes are written by noted attorneys, human resource managers, scholars, consultants, and academicians who have published extensively in the area of workplace discrimination. Attention is paid to scholarly research, case law, and human resource practices for implementing the law and management theories in the workplace with respect to each type of discrimination. It is a goal of this handbook that the strategies for policies, procedures, and training programs stimulate additional research, advocacy, and legislation in the area of workplace discrimination.

Schingel (2006) noted, with respect to the movie *Crash:* "Until we as a society can take the time to understand the roots of discrimination and take a good look at our own thought patterns, we'll never move forward."

In keeping with Schingel's sentiment, the major goal of this handbook is to provide companies with the tools necessary to prevent as well as deal with all types of discrimination in the workplace.

REFERENCES

Celebrity Wonder. (2005). *Synopsis.* Retrieved September 6, 2009, from http://www.celebritywonder.com/movie/2005_Crash.html.

EEOC (Equal Employment Opportunity Commission). (2010). Retrieved April 18, 2010, from http://www.eeoc.gov.

Johnson, M. (2005). California requires sexual harassment training. *Legal Report,* January-February. Retrieved April 18, 2010, from http://www.usc.edu/ schools/medicine/faculty_staff-resource/equity/calif.pdf.

Schingel, R. (2006). *How the movie Crash illustrates race and ethnic relations in America.* Retrieved September 6, 2009, from http://www.associatedcontent.com/article/18187.

1

Age Discrimination

Jennifer L. Martin

> Leave safety behind. Put your body on the line. Stand before the people
> you fear and speak your mind—even if your voice shakes. When you least
> expect it, someone may actually listen to what you have to say. Well-
> aimed slingshots can topple giants.
>
> —Maggie Kuhn

Robert Butler coined the term ageism in 1969, and he demonstrated its
similarities with discrimination based on race and sex. As Butler states,
"Ageism can be seen as a process of systematic stereotyping of and
discrimination against people because they are old, just as racism and
sexism accomplish this with skin color and gender" (as cited in Cohen,
2001, p. 576). Ageism has been defined as prejudice that stems from
"erroneous beliefs, stereotypes, and discriminatory behavior directed at
older people" (Rupp, Vodanovich, & Crede, 2006, p. 1339), and according to Copper, it is the "negative social response to different stages in
the process of aging and it is a political issue" (2009, p. 106). Research
indicates that ageism is more prevalent than sexism or racism, and age
discrimination lawsuits tend to be more costly than suits involving sexual and racial discrimination (Rupp et al., 2006). Between the years of
1988 and 1995, the average age discrimination lawsuit cost companies
$219,000. This chapter will discuss research and legal issues regarding

issues of ageism and age discrimination in the workplace as well as potential solutions to combat these problems for both individuals and organizations.

There are more than 16 million Americans age 55 and over who are either working or looking for work. Older workers are obtaining new jobs at a rate of 4.1 percent annually, which is more than double the rate of the general population. Older workers make up 10 percent of the American workforce, but 22 percent of the nation's job growth (GO60.com). This percentage will only increase (Lee, Czaja, & Sharit, 2009). So, we must deal with the attitudes and perceptions causing ageism or the prevalence of ageism will only increase as well. More research is necessary into the causes and potential solutions for organizations.

According to Steinberg, Donald, Najman, and Skerman (1996), "Ageism is characterized by a widely held set of beliefs about the personal qualities and abilities of the elderly and by a set of institutional practices which give support to and maintain ageist stereotypes. This appears to be particularly so in the workforce" (p. 154). Ageism can involve jokes, disrespect, or stereotypes based on age, disability, or other characteristics. According to Roscigno, Mong, Byron, and Tester (2007), "Such patterns are manifested by a culture consumed with 'youth,' passed to individuals through socialization and enacted within institutions and organizations" (p. 314). Popular culture is preoccupied with and elevates all things youthful; this preoccupation does much to exacerbate ageism. For example, bouts of forgetfulness are often deemed "senior moments," no matter the age of the individual. Billions of dollars are spent annually on maintaining a youthful appearance through the use of antiaging products, surgery, miracle diets, and other antidotes to aging. Although these media expectations primarily target women, men are facing increasing pressures to maintain youthful appearances. The result of this youth obsession is that older individuals often are not as revered for their knowledge and experience as they were in previous generations. Age bias negatively can affect older workers by creating barriers to entry for many occupations. Ageism, in general, including exposure to ageist discourse, negative attitudes based on age, and discrimination based on age, has many negative consequences for older workers, including a decrease in self-efficacy, job satisfaction and performance, decreased job involvement and commitment, and increased stress (Rupp et al., 2006).

Discriminatory actions are the logical extension of discriminatory attitudes. Thus, the phenomenon of ageism can lead to discrimination against older workers. According to Warr (1994), age discrimination exists when, "individuals are refused employment, dismissed from jobs, paid less, or denied promotions, training, or other benefits because of their age" (as cited in Redman & Snape, 2002, p. 357). Workplace discrimination based on age often stems from negative stereotypes of older workers. A common stereotype of older workers is that with age comes decreased work performance, which then can lead to negative self-fulfilling prophecies. Research, however, indicates that chronological age has little to do with job performance (Rupp et al., 2006). According to Rupp et al., older workers tend to receive lower ratings on performance than do younger workers based on subjective supervisor ratings; the performance errors of older workers are likely to be seen as a result of age (that is, as a result of stable factors such as the loss of memory). Younger workers, on the other hand, are given time to improve on performance errors through formal assistance. In sum, expectation has much to do with how ageist attitudes and discrimination can begin and perpetuate. According to Redman and Snape (2002), negative appraisals may trump actual performance for older workers, thus causing a "silver ceiling."

Ageism can be disguised by employers and in organizational policy in a variety of ways. These coded messages include stating that an employee "costs too much," "has been with the organization too long," "lacks the skills to adapt to new technologies," "lacks energy," "does not keep up with the times," and other criticism. The manifestations of these attitudes can include the refusal to hire or promote, the altering of benefits for older workers, limiting training of older workers so that they are less able to stay current (thus fulfilling the expectation already set up for them by ageist attitudes), and limited job responsibilities. Moreover, older workers may be encouraged to retire early. In other words, many older workers are not valued for their level of knowledge and extensive life experience; instead, they often are viewed as replaceable. Older workers are commonly encouraged to retire early and thought to be less "essential" to the workforce (Steinberg et al., 1996). According to Steinberg et al., 1996, "Industry groups, unions, training institutions and the media all have roles to play in correcting misinformation about older workers. This could, in turn, make a significant contribution in helping to reduce negative stereotyping of older people in general" (p. 185). The organization can do much to change perceptions about the value of older workers to the workforce in general, as will be shown.

A recent study (see Segrave, 2001, as cited in Rupp et al., 2006) found that an organization consisting of workers who were all 50 years of age or older experienced 18 percent higher productivity, 16 percent lower turnover of workers, 40 percent decreased absenteeism, and 60 percent decreased inventory loss. The reason for these findings may be attributed to the fact that the majority of workers in the organization studied were considered to be older workers, and because of this, the workplace was less subject to ageist attitudes; workers thus were more content and felt they were in a safe environment. Although expectations for older workers tend to be lower than for younger workers, research indicates that no correlation exists between productivity and age. According to Pillay, Kelly, and Tones (2006), older workers appear to be less flexible and productive for a variety of reasons: "older workers were less likely to want to retire early than younger workers and were interested in less physically demanding jobs, which is a significant shift in terms of the stereotypical views that older workers are resistant to change" (p. 301).

Although no correlation exists between aging and performance, ageist stereotypes do exist that connect aging with a decrease in workplace performance; for example, negative perceptions can include the belief that older workers are less efficient and possess lower performance capabilities (McMullin & Shuey, 2006). Much of the age discrimination that occurs in the workplace stems from attribution errors, which then lead to stereotypes. Stereotypes of older workers include inflexibility, disorganization, and inadaptability: in sum, older workers are slow to learn, and difficult to teach (Roscigno et al., 2007). These stereotypes exist for a variety of reasons. Some older workers have spent longer periods of time doing one particular job (historically, the job market tended to be more static), and thus it becomes more difficult for these workers, when compared with their younger counterparts, to adapt quickly to a new task. Older workers may face greater obstacles when it comes to entering the workforce because of these stereotypes (Rupp et al., 2006). These stereotypes can lead to generalizations about older workers as a group, thus creating a vicious cycle in which ageist attitudes prevail and age discrimination can result. Employer perceptions about older workers have influenced hiring, training, promotion, and retention; additionally, most employers do not institute policies for the recruitment or retention of older workers (McMullin & Shuey, 2006).

Displacement is another common phenomenon stemming from ageism and age discrimination that older workers face. Displacement of older workers often is seen as fiscally responsible to employers for it is cheaper to hire younger workers in their place. As Roscigno et al. (2007) state, "The consequences, particularly for higher skilled older workers, have been significant job displacement over the past 20 years, involuntary exit from the labor market, and downward mobility upon re-employment" (p. 315). In addition, discriminatory treatment of older workers can create a "push" for them to leave a hostile working environment. This phenomenon is different from self-selection to leave an organization. According to Noonan (2005), older individuals either reenter the workforce or continue working despite passing retirement age include the following: the need to engage in meaningful activity, financial concerns, personal fulfillment, and issues of identity.

As the baby boom generation reaches retirement age, we see increasing changes in policies, programs, and supports in response to dwindling resources to provide monetary support for the expected generational increase in the number of retirees. In 2002, 61 million people over the age of 55 lived in the United States; researchers project an increase to 103 million by the year 2025, which will represent 30 percent of the population (Lee et al., 2009). To complicate matters, as the workforce ages, changes in the structure of the workplace itself are occurring, including technological advances and organizational structural changes that may make it more difficult for older workers to adapt. A major difference between 21st-century retirees and those of previous generations is that the retirees of today and of tomorrow expect to continue working in some capacity through their retirement years. The reasons for this include monetary reasons, maintaining mental health, and staying productive (AARP, 2007). According to Yeatts, Folts, and Knapp (2000), "For employers, resisting to adaptation means the added costs of hiring and training new employees and the loss of expertise that often is difficult to replace" (p. 566). Organizations can benefit from utilizing the knowledge of older workers.

PROTECTIONS AGAINST AGE DISCRIMINATION IN THE WORKFORCE

The United States has the longest history of antidiscrimination legislation among English-speaking countries. Despite this fact, U.S. society has much work to do in promoting positive images of older workers and older people in general, and in preventing ageism. The rights of workers age 40 and over are protected under the Age Discrimination in Employment Act of 1967 (ADEA). Congress found that—

(1) in the face of rising productivity and affluence, older workers find themselves disadvantaged in their efforts to retain employment, and especially to regain employment when displaced from jobs;

(2) the setting of arbitrary age limits regardless of potential for job performance has become a common practice, and certain otherwise desirable practices may work to the disadvantage of older persons;

(3) the incidence of unemployment, especially long-term unemployment with resultant deterioration of skill, morale, and employer acceptability is, relative to the younger ages, high among older workers; their numbers are great and growing; and their employment problems grave;

(4) the existence in industries affecting commerce, of arbitrary discrimination in employment because of age, burdens commerce and the free flow of goods in commerce.

The purpose of ADEA is to promote the employment of older workers based on their ability as opposed to their age, to prohibit arbitrary age discrimination in employment, and to help employers and workers solve issues arising from the impact of age on employment.

Moreover, according to ADEA, it is unlawful for an employer:

(1) to fail or refuse to hire or to discharge any individual or otherwise discriminate against any individual with respect to his [or her] compensation, terms, conditions, or privileges of employment, because of such individual's age;

(2) to limit, segregate, or classify his employees in any way which would deprive or tend to deprive any individual of employment opportunities or otherwise adversely affect his [or her] status as an employee, because of such individual's age; or

(3) to reduce the wage rate of any employee in order to comply with this chapter.

ADEA was amended by the Older Workers' Benefit Protection Act (OWBPA) in 1990 and 1998 to give workers increased protection, but it does not apply to companies with fewer than 20 employees or to independent contractors. However, many states have laws that prohibit age discrimination in smaller companies. Some professions, such as police and fire departments, are exempt from this legislation in terms of hiring and retirement (not for trainings or promotions).

In 1986, amendments to ADEA eliminated upper age limits to the law. In *Smith v. City of Jackson* (2005) the court found that older workers can sue their employers for "disparate impact" under the ADEA when organizational policies, which may appear neutral, have a more negative impact on older workers than on younger workers (see Leedom, 2006).

Additionally, the 1990 amendments to ADEA include a provision that protects the benefits of older workers, including pensions, insurance, and disability, making them commensurate with those of younger workers unless cost differences are significant. However, ADEA does not provide for compensatory damages for victims of age discrimination for emotional and physical harm.

WOMEN AND AGING

The phenomenon of ageism in U.S. society is exacerbated by other prejudices, such as those of class, race, and gender. For example, aging women experience a heightened sense of discrimination because of their gender. Because the standard of maintaining one's outward appearance is still greater for women, women may face more obstacles to aging than their male counterparts. U.S. culture is obsessed with youth and beauty. Women, however, are expected to maintain a higher standard and to sculpt, adorn, and maintain their bodies as projects. Because of these factors, when women age, they may face a different kind of discrimination based on their appearance, perceived diminished sex appeal, and other factors. As Copper (1986) states,

> The ageism that old women experience is firmly embedded in sexism—an extension of the male power to define, control values, erase, disempower, and divide. Woman-to-woman ageism is an aspect of the horizontal conflict that usurps the energies of the colonized—part of the female competition for the crumbs of social power. (p. 106–107)

Not only are women subject to heightened ageism and discrimination based on gendered appearance and perceived diminishing sex appeal, but also older women workers and leaders are excluded from the traditional power structure. According to Copper (1986),

> Patriarchal institutions are, without exception, designed to exclude the vision of old women. Most old women have little experience in leadership, influence, or even respect. Mostly, old women know how to serve. The roles reserved and expected of women in old age—grandmothers, self-effacing volunteers to the projects and priorities designed by others, or caretakers of old men—are custom fit to our powerless status. (p. 109)

Although this stereotype is changing, these attitudes persist such that older women in the workforce are deemed, whether officially or unofficially, workplace caretakers (or kin keepers). These women often are expected to do a variety of extra unpaid tasks, such as planning and preparing for special occasions and holidays, and preparing for celebratory events such as bosses' day (and other days of recognition), employee birthdays, and other parties.

To combat these attitudes and expectations, individual women must first change their perceptions of themselves and their worth. They must demand respect and workplace equity. According to Copper (1986), "The first step is for women to recognize that they have been programmed to hate old women and to deny them power. . . . Empowerment of women will come when we identify with women older than we are and not before" (p. 109). Once older women workers become empowered, they should then pass on these egalitarian attitudes through knowledge building and ensure that their organization is in compliance with antidiscrimination laws such as ADEA and Title VII. Title VII of the Civil Rights Act of 1964, in addition to ADEA, also can assist with the prevention of discrimination in the workforce, because older women workers and older minority workers often face multiple forms of discrimination.

JOB TRAINING

Although age discrimination in the workplace affects both younger and older workers, it disproportionately affects older workers, especially those over the age of 50 (Meenan, 1999). In a study conducted in the United Kingdon, Meenan, 1999 found that obtaining employment was the area that most affected older workers because of stereotypes, age limits in postings, and subtle discrimination such as listing job requirements as "newly qualified."

Walker (1999) discusses the incentives for organizations to institute practices and policies to combat ageism and age barriers. As Walker (1999) states, "In order to maintain a balanced labor market policy, and avoid intergenerational conflict, it is important not to excessively target initiatives on older workers. It also has to be recognized that some older workers do not want to return to work or stay employed" (p. 374). Training of workers can do much to lessen the problem of workplace discrimination based on age. Support from senior management and the human resource department, an organizational atmosphere that values training, buy-in from older workers themselves, open and constant communication, education of younger workers against stereotyping, monitoring and feedback, adjustments if need be, and assessments of program effectiveness all are important components of combating ageism in the workplace.

Additional antiageism measures should include provisions that all employees be trained in new technologies. Research indicates that older workers exhibit less mastery of training materials and take longer to train than younger workers (Lee et al., 2009). Many reasons, however, could explain these phenomena, such as perceptions about technology; self-fulfilling prophecies; attribution errors on the part of supervisors; negative perceptions on the part of the individual, their co-workers, and the employer; lack of support systems and mentoring; personal perceptions of self-efficacy; anxiety; and peceived benefits. More research is needed on the best methods of training used with older workers.

Lee et al. (2009) found that older workers often need flexibility and job training to feel comfortable in an organization. According to Hierro (2006), "the capacity to exercise power and the need for protection change in accordance with age and gender" (p. 342). For example, historically speaking, men begin their lives in positions of control over their surroundings more so than women. This changes as men and women age. In many cultures, women gain more status as they age. These cultural norms could be used by the organization. In the United States, even when older workers are valued for their knowledge and experience, they simultaneously are thought to be less flexible and less able to adapt to technology (Steinberg et al. 1996).

According to Yeatts et al. (2000), age is not the only reason for workplace complacency or knowledge obsolescence. The real issue is time of tenure, or time doing the same job, that inhibits flexibility and adaptability in the workplace. Unfortunately, length of tenure tends to be longer for older workers, which perpetuates the stereotype that older workers inherently cannot adapt to changes in the workplace or that their level of knowledge is becoming obsolete based on their lack of desire to learn or stay current.

As Yeatts et al. (2000) state, "Reestablishing the fit between an employee and a redesigned job is likely to be easier for employees who have multiple skills and abilities and a broad knowledge base" (p. 570). When occupations become redesigned, older workers do in fact have a more difficult time responding to these changes because they have been working successfully within the same routines for many years. Younger workers may not have yet developed similar successful patterns as yet, and thus appear to be more flexible, and adaptable to changes in the workplace environment, job duties, and so on (Yeatts et al., 2000).

In a summary of research, according to Gordon, Rozelle, and Baxter (1989), studies show that bias in hiring exists against older workers and female applicants. An evaluation of applicants, however, may accord with the age-related stereotype of a particular job, and the extent to which a position represents a position of management. Women may be at an automatic disadvantage (older women may be at a double disadvantage). For example, when trying to break into a field or position that is not considered to be traditionally "female," traditional expectations of the eventual employee to be hired still come to the minds of those who make these decisions. These expectations potentially penalize women and maintain the status quo. Again, ageism is exacerbated for female workers who already tend to possess greater challenges within the workplace; women tend to work in lower paying, less flexible occupations with lower status levels, a higher degree of supervision, and less autonomy (McMullin & Shuey, 2006).

According to McMullin and Shuey (2006), "There is a strong relationship between age and disability or to 'natural ageing.' If the latter is true, they may not believe that they need or qualify for workplace accommodations" (p. 831). McMullin and Shuey (2006) found that those who attributed their disability to age were less likely to feel a need for workplace accommodations; likewise, those workers who recognized a need for accommodations, and also attributed their disabilities to ageing, were unlikely to receive them. To complicate the effect of aging on employment, older workers with disabilities are faced with an even higher rate of discrimination, for many negative perceptions abound for people living with disabilities.

Because of the increasingly global economy, employers are beginning to desire more flexibility in terms of the ability to hire and fire, so that they may increase efficiency and reduce costs. This desired flexibility often includes employing and sustaining individuals who can maintain a flexible work schedule and adapt to ever-changing challenges, tasks, and job requirements. Because of this, all workers must meet the new challenges of the changing workforce.

Increasing globalization and changes in demography are influencing workplace organization in general; this is leading employers to change the way they do business. Employers are seeking greater productivity for lower compensation from workers, outsourcing jobs, and offering reduced benefits all in attempt to reduce costs. Rising health care costs and retirement benefits are exacerbating the problem of lower compensation. These same issues are causing the need for the worker to stay in the workforce longer: Many workers have to pay part or all of their health care costs, and reductions in pensions or retirement contributions from employers contribute to older workers remaining in the workforce even longer than they may desire.

According to the American Association for Retired Persons (AARP), many age-friendly companies offer employment to older workers. Some of the benefits that these organizations offer to older workers include an age-friendly culture, flexible scheduling (work days and hours), phased retirement, temporary work as a bridge to retirement, retiree health insurance, benefits for part-time work, percentage of health insurance premiums paid by company for family health care, tuition reimbursement, mentoring programs, age-related training for managers, preretirement planning, immediate 100 percent vesting on all company matches, and career counseling. Additional workplace incentives for older workers include advising programs for employees coping with family responsibilities, childcare centers open to grandchildren, education benefits, ergonomic workspaces, on-site eldercare classes, retiree prescription drug coverage, flexible benefits package, accrued sick time for dependent care, and home-computer purchase programs.

To combat ageist attitudes and workplace discrimination, all employees should be trained on the importance of possessing accepting attitudes. If a nonbiased workplace setting is desired, the organization must run training sessions to promote such an atmosphere. These trainings cannot be considered a one-time effort; they must be repeated and reinforced as deemed necessary, perhaps annually or biannually based on employee need and turnover. It is imperative that employers use research-based approaches to training.

ADDITIONAL STRATEGIES FOR COMBATING AGE DISCRIMINATION IN THE WORKPLACE

Older workers are a heterogeneous group. Thus, solutions to prevent age discrimination and to support older workers in the employment realm must be varied and diverse. Employers must be committed to providing a supportive work environment for employees of all ages. They should assess the organizational culture to determine whether age discrimination or ageism is part of the culture, and then they should review the needs of their staff regarding training and professional development needs. Part of this assessment should include a review of hiring and screening processes, benefits, and retirement policies. Employers should provide awareness training at all levels of the organization on discrimination and discriminataory practices, and all employees at all levels within the organization should be mandated to attend these sessions. Employers should make it clear that harassment and discrimination of any kind will not be tolerated in the organization.

Organizations can begin to combat discriminatory practices by adopting policies and procedures that create supportive work environments that value workers of all age levels and prevent the use of stereotypes. The organization should post all relevant antidiscrimination laws and policies in areas that are accessible by all. Antidiscrimination and harassment policies should include definitions of harassment (and examples of its many forms), remedies, reporting procedures, consequences for perpetrators, a description of the grievance process, and a nonretaliation statement for those who come forward to report either first- or second-hand accounts of discrimination. An ombudsman should be appointed to deal with grievances; this person should be accessible to all personnel and be provided with trainings as needed. Policies should include guidelines for promotions: Promotions should be based on ability or demonstrated potential; recruitment for employment and promotion should be fair; and where promotion opportunities arise, they should be advertised widely.

Organizational leaders must advocate for the reduction of stereotypes. All employees must be educated on the realities of aging. To combat age discrimination, organizations and governmental interventions must focus on all aspects of age, and not just on aging workers. All employees must be encouraged to speak up if they are experiencing age discrimination (or discrimination of any kind). Individual responsibility also should be stressed.

Human resource managers committed to the reduction of age discrimination can do the following: They can remove the date of birth portion from all job applications and, instead, focus on experience and qualifications. During interviews, they should ask only job-related questions and refrain from asking questions based on stereotypes. Human resource managers should use the same hiring criteria for all prospective employees. When using interview teams, they should ensure that the team is diverse (including diversity of ages of team members). Human resource managers should review age discrimination laws with all members of interview teams. They should not include age cutoffs for promotions or trainings, and should remove maximum hiring ages and mandatory retirement from organizational policies and procedures. Additionally, training and professional development of human resource managers is crucial to keep them informed of changes in laws and strategies to deal with older workers and with ageist attitudes in the workplace.

General managers should ensure the following: Training for all jobs is offered to all workers, that it is designed to capture all ages and styles of learning, and that training and development is provided specifically for older workers. Training should be preventative and proactive, rather than reactive. Trainings to prevent ageist attitudes and discriminatory behavior should be organized for all employees at all levels of the organization. Technological training programs should include periodic updates and be offered to all workers to include those who may not acquire these skills on their own. This may or may not disproportionately affect older workers. Support systems, such as mentoring and cross-age mentoring programs, should be in place for older workers in transition. Placing emplyees in mixed age-groups can be highly beneficial for both older and younger workers.

Best practices should be shared; organizations should pass on what has worked well for them. Best practices, new ideas, and innovative training programs can be posted on Web sites and shared within and between organizations.

Individuals can do much to reduce workplace discrimination based on age. The first step is becoming informed to be an advocate for one's own interests. Individuals can join organizations that lobby for these interests, such as AARP. Such organizations can raise awareness and keep both employees and employers apprised of changes in antidiscrimination law and foster nondiscriminatory work environments. Individuals can become activists by achieving awareness of ageist issues and passing this awareness on to others. In sum, older employees in the 21st-century workforce should be aware and keep apprised of any changes in laws, organizational policies, and procedures, and should pass on this awareness to others in an empowering manner. This is the first step in toppling giants.

REFERENCES

AARP (American Association for Retired Persons). (2007). *Perspectives of employers, workers, and policymakers in the G7 countries on the new demographic realities*. Retrieved March 20, 2009, from http://www. aarpinternational.org/usr_doc/intl_older_worker.pdf.

Cohen, S. (2001). The complex nature of ageism: What is it? Who does it? Who perceives it? The *Gerontologist, 41* (5), 576–577.

Copper, B. (2009). Voices: On becoming old women. In S. Shaw & J. Lee (Eds.), *Women's voices, feminist visions: Classic and contemporary readings* (4th ed., pp. 106–109). Boston, MA: McGraw Hill.

Filinson, R. (2008). Age discrimination legislation in the U.K.: A comparative and gerontological analysis. *Journal of Cross Cultural Gerontology, 23*, 225–237.

Go60.com. (n.d.). *Seniors aging well, wisely and successfully helping seniors improve with age.* Retrieved May 4, 2009, from http://www.go60.com.

Gordon, R. A., Rozelle, R. M., & Baxter, J. C. (1989). The effect of applicant age, job level, and accountability on perceptions of female job applicants. *The Journal of Psychology, 123* (1), 59–68.

Hierro, G. (2006). The ethical and legal aspects of age. In C. Sauvain-Dugerdil, H. Leridon, & N. Mascie-Taylor (Eds.), *Human clocks: The bio-cultural meanings of age* (pp. 338–349). New York: Peter Lang Publishing.

Huffman, M. L. (1999). Who's in charge? Organizational influences on women's representation in managerial positions. *Social Science Quarterly, 80* (4), 738–756.

Lee, C. C., Czaja, S. J., & Sharit, J. (2009). Training older workers for technology-based employment. *Educational Gerontology, 35*, 15–31.

Leedom, M. (2006, Winter/Spring). Smith v. City of Jackson: Disparate impact in age discrimination cases. *Richmond Journal of Law and the Public Interest*, 57–68.

Meenan, H. (1999). Age discrimination in the United Kingdom. *International Journal of Discrimination and the Law, 3*, 227–248.

McMullin, J. A., & Shuey, K. M. (2006). Ageing, disability, and workplace accommodations. *Ageing and Society, 26* (6), 831–847.

Noonan, A. E. (2005). "At this point now": Older workers' reflections on their current employment experiences. *International Journal of Aging and Human Development, 61* (3), 211–241.

Pillay, H., Kelly, K., & Tones, M. (2006). Career aspirations of older workers: An Australian study. *International Journal of Training and Development, 10* (4), 298–305.

Redman, T., & Snape, E. (2002). Ageism in teaching: Stereotypical beliefs and discriminatory attitudes towards the over-50s. *Work, Employment and Society 16* (2), 355–371.

Roscigno, V. J., Mong, S., Byron, R., & Tester, G. (2007). Age discrimination, social closure and employment. *Social Forces, 86* (1), 313–334.

Rupp, D. E., Vodanovich, S. J., & Crede, M. (2006). Age bias in the workplace: The impact of ageism and causal attributions. *Journal of Applied Social Psychology, 36* (6), 1337–1364.

Steinberg, M., Donald, K., Najman, J., & Skerman, H. (1996). Attitudes of employees and employers towards older workers in a climate of anti-discrimination. *Australian Journal on Aging, 15* (4), 154–185.

Walker, A. (1999). Combating age discrimination at the workplace. *Experimental Aging Research, 25,* 367–377.

Yeatts, D. E., Folts, W. E., & Knapp, J. (2000). Older workers' adaptation to a changing workplace: Employment issues of the 21st century. *Educational Gerontology, 26,* 565–582.

The United States Equal Employment Opportunity Commission. *The Age Discrimination in Employment Act of 1967.* Retrieved May 1, 2009, from http://www.eeoc.gov/policy/adea.html.

2

Disability Discrimination

Michele A. Paludi, Eros R. DeSouza, and Deanndra E. Dodd

> People didn't always see a person with a disability who had to use a ramp or elevator as people who have been given unnecessary privileges. But I run into that often now. People are saying, "Why do we have to go to great expense for these people?"
> —Major Owens (Brainy Quote.com, 2009)

In fiscal year 2009, the Equal Employment Opportunity Commission (EEOC) received 21,451 charges of disability discrimination. Charges included discriminatory treatment at work because of orthopedic and structural impairments of the back, nonparalytic orthopedic impairment, cancer, cumulative trauma disorder, kidney impairment, diabetes, alcoholism, Alzheimer's, anxiety disorder, tuberculosis, depression, manic depressive disorder, and allergies. Psychological disability charges filed with the EEOC made up approximately 30 percent of disability discrimination charges filed each year (Dalgin, 2001; EEOC, 2009). The complainants' employers were not able to resolve these charges, in keeping with Wooten and James (2005) research findings that organizations have difficulty in preventing discrimination against job applicants and employees with disabilities. Thus, individuals sought resolution from the EEOC, an enforcement agency created by the Civil Rights Act of 1964 that has the authority to investigate and conciliate complaints that allege a violation of law of employment discrimination. One-on-one correspondence between the person filing the incidence and reporting to the EEOC and the employer. Thus, the number of employees who file charges with the EEOC is an underestimate of the number of men and women with disabilities who experience disability discrimination or harassment in their workplaces.

This chapter is concerned with disability discrimination, specifically Title I of the Americans with Disabilities Act (ADA), which prohibits discrimination in all employment practices, including recruitment and selection, training and development, compensation, layoff, fringe benefits, leave and other terms, and conditions and privileges of employment. Research (Stefan, 2001) finds that individuals with disabilities experience discrimination in most if not all of these terms and conditions of employment. In this chapter, we discuss disability discrimination and harassment in employment. Disability discrimination is conduct directed at an employee or job applicant because of her or his mental or physical disability, which subjects her or him to differential treatment that limits his or her ability to participate in or benefit from services or privileges provided by the employer.

This chapter also addresses disability-based harassment (Jones, 2008; Tahvonen, 2003) of employees. Disability harassment is verbal or physical conduct that is directed at an individual because of his or her mental or physical disability that is sufficiently severe, pervasive, or persistent to have the purpose or effect of creating a hostile work environment (Weber, 2007).

This chapter also discusses physical and mental disabilities and offers research from the social sciences concerning stigma of employees with disabilities (Banks & Kaschak, 2003; Fishbein, 2002; Mezey, 2005; Stefan, 2002). We agree with Cook and Burke (2002) in their "new paradigm" of disability legislation with social science research. As they conclude, "social science can be used in more meaningful ways to understand both the intended and unintended consequences of federal policy" (p. 541). This chapter discusses the fact that, despite the ADA, applicants and employees still face discriminatory treatment in the workplace because of prejudice and discriminatory attitudes held by managers and co-workers (Bonnie & Monahan, 1997; Miceli, Harvey, & Buckley, 2001; Scheid, 2005).

In addition, we integrate gender and racial equity issues in disability rights (for a review, see Banks & Kaschak, 2003; Banks & Marshall, 2004). This chapter concludes with recommendations for employers to ensure ADA compliance, including policies, investigatory procedures, and training programs on the ADA, as well as ways to restructure workplaces to accommodate individuals with disabilities (Ward & Baker, 2005).

Bruyere, Erickson, and Ferrentino (2003) estimated that 19.3 percent of individuals in the United States are individuals with disabilities. A nationally representative face-to-face household survey conducted between 2001 and 2003 with respondents 18 years of age and older revealed that mental disorders are widespread in the United States, with 26 percent of Americans suffering from a diagnosable mental disorder in a given year (Kessler, Chiu, Demler, & Walters, 2005). Of these, 22 percent were classified as serious and 37 percent were classified as moderate (or 14 percent of the total population). Moreover, mental disorders are the major cause of disability in the United States for individuals between 15 and 44 years of age (World Health Organization, 2004). Research has further indicated that individuals with disabilities are less likely to be employed than individuals who are not disabled (Bruyere et al., 2003). We thus offer recommendations for proactive approaches to disability management, as recommended by the EEOC (2008) and Bruyere et al. (2003). We discuss the revised ADA as of January 1, 2009.

Although mental disorders reside within individuals, disability is a socially constructed phenomenon—that is, how society views people with disabilities significantly affects their well-being (Mason, Pratt, Patel, Greydanus, & Yahya, 2004). It is, however, important to distinguish disability from impairment. Disability refers to physical and psychosocial barriers in the sociopolitical environment, whereas impairment refers to a reduction in physical, sensory, or cognitive functioning within the person (Olkin, 1999). Throughout this chapter we use the term "employees with disabilities" rather than "disabled employees" to highlight that the employee is more than her or his disability. This terminology is in keeping with the American Psychological Association Guidelines to Reduce Bias in Language (1992) and with the disability rights movement (see Green, Davis, Karshmer, Marsh, & Straight, 2005).

THE AMERICANS WITH DISABILITIES ACT

The ADA was signed into law on July 26, 1992. The ADA is a civil rights law consisting of five titles. These titles are identified as follows:

- Title I prohibits employment discrimination against qualified individuals with disabilities.

- Title II prohibits discrimination in public services.
- Title III prohibits discrimination in public accommodations.
- Title IV prohibits telecommunications discrimination.
- Title V provides instructions to federal agencies involved in regulating and enforcing Titles I–IV.

The passage of the ADA evolved out of several research findings at the time, including the following: (1) approximately 50 million Americans had one or more physical or mental disability; (2) discrimination exists in housing, education, communication, health services, access to public services, and employment; and (3) legal recourse was lacking for individuals with disabilities who experienced discrimination. Mayerson (1992) noted the history of the ADA began with the independent living movement that challenged the then-prominent belief that individuals with disabilities needed to be institutionalized and instead worked toward having people with disabilities live in the community. Similar to the civil rights movement of the 1960s, the disability rights movement sought justice through the courts and through Congress. According to Mayerson (1992):

> From a legal perspective, a profound and historic shift in disability public policy occurred in 1973 with the passage of Section 504 of the 1973 Rehabilitation Act. Section 504, which banned discrimination on the basis of disability by recipients of federal funds, was modeled after previous laws which banned race, ethnic origin and sex based discrimination by federal fund recipients. . . . Enactment of Section 504 evidenced Congress' recognition that the inferior social and economic status of people with disabilities was not a consequence of the disability itself, but instead was a result of societal barriers and prejudices. (p. 1)

This chapter focuses on Title I, discrimination in employment. The ADA covers employers with 15 or more employees and applies to private employers, state and local governments, labor unions, and employment agencies. The ADA prohibits discrimination against all applicants or employees with disabilities.

The statute states:

> No covered entity shall discriminate against a qualified individual with a disability because of the disability of such individual in regard to job

application procedures, the hiring, advancement, or discharge of employees, employee compensation, job training, and other terms, conditions, and privileges of employment.

The ADA (EEOC, 2002) has defined "disability" in the following manner: "An individual with a disability is a person who: Has a physical or mental impairment that substantially limits one or more major life activities; Has a record of having such an impairment; or Is regarded as having such an impairment."

According to the ADA, a major life activity is any activity that a person can perform with little or no difficulty (for example, walking, seeing, hearing, speaking, breathing, learning, performing manual tasks, caring for oneself, working, sitting, standing, lifting, and reading). We provide additional detail for each part of this legal definition.

Has a physical or mental impairment that substantially limits one or more major life activities

The ADA applies to employees and applicants for employment who have impairments that substantially limit major life activities. "Impairment" is defined as any physiological disorder, cosmetic disfigurement, or anatomical loss affecting one or more of several body systems or any psychological disorder—for example, hearing impairment, performing manual tasks, visual impairment, epilepsy, and breathing problems. Individuals with a short-duration illness (for example, flu or sprained ankle), however, are not covered by the ADA.

Specific disabilities are not listed in the ADA. The act does list, however, conditions that should not be regarded as disabilities—for example, voyeurism, compulsive gambling, pyromania, bisexuality, homosexuality, and disorders from using illegal drugs.

In addition, the ADA does protect employees with intellectual disabilities—for example, individuals who have intelligence quotients below 70–75. The ADA lists specific learning disabilities as a physical or mental impairment. Learning is included in the ADA as a major life activity. "Learning disabilities" is a general term that refers to a heterogeneous group of disorders manifested by significant difficulties in the acquisition and use of listening, speaking, reading, writing, reasoning, or mathematical abilities (for a review of types of learning disabilities, see Price, Gerber, & Mulligan, 2003).

According to the EEOC (2004),

> An individual is considered to have an intellectual disability when: (1) the person's intellectual functioning level (IQ) is below 70-75; (2) the person has significant limitations in adaptive skill areas as expressed in conceptual, social, and practical adaptive skills; and (3) the disability originated before the age of 18.

"Adaptive skill areas" refers to basic skills needed for everyday life. They include communication, self-care, home living, social skills, leisure, health and safety, self-direction, functional academics (reading, writing, basic math), and work.

Intellectual disabilities will vary in degree and effect from person to person, just as individual capabilities vary considerably among people who do not have an intellectual disability. People should not make generalizations about the needs of persons with intellectual disabilities. In some instances, an intellectual disability will not be obvious from a person's appearance, nor will it be accompanied by a physical disability.

Has a record of having such an impairment

The ADA protects applicants and employees who have had a record of disabilities, for example, having recovered from a physical illness (such as cancer) or mental illness (such as manic depressive disorder).

Is regarded as having such an impairment

The ADA also covers applicants and employees who are regarded as having a limiting impairment even though the individual does not have such an impairment. Thus, this provision would protect a qualified individual being denied employment because an employer was concerned about the reactions of co-workers to this individual's disability, for example, disfigurement.

Wilson v. Phoenix Specialty Mfg. Co., Inc. (2008) illustrates the prong of the ADA that prohibits employers from discriminating against employees they "regard as" having a disability even if the employee is not disabled. In this case, Jimmy Wilson worked as a shipping supervisor at Phoenix Specialty Manufacturing Company, Inc. During a work meeting in 2001, Mr. Wilson experienced a major panic attack. He had been diagnosed with Parkinson's disease. After having his medications adjusted, Mr. Wilson was approved to return to work. After each visit Mr. Wilson had with his physician, Phoenix required Mr. Wilson to provide a report of his Parkinson's disease. In addition, management began avoiding Mr. Wilson. They refused to train him on new computer systems and denied his request for a 21-inch computer screen instead of the standard 17-inch screen. Eventually Phoenix eliminated Mr. Wilson's position, while creating similar positions in the company. Both the district court and appellate court found in Mr. Wilson's favor. The court held that Phoenix perceived Mr. Wilson as having a disability because management at the company ignored the physician's medical opinion that Mr. Wilson was capable of working.

ADDITIONAL ASPECTS OF THE ADA

"Relationship or Association" with an individual who has a disability

The ADA applies to individuals who are discriminated against because they have a known association or relationship with an individual with a disability. ADA includes this component in its coverage to protect job applicants and employees from stereotypic beliefs on the part of management or co-workers that association with an individual with a disability would impact their job performance. We address stereotypic beliefs about individuals with disabilities subsequently in this chapter.

Prevention of Retaliation   The ADA prohibits retaliation against an applicant or employee who has opposed the employers' practices that discriminate based on a physical or mental disability or who has participated in an investigation as a complainant, accused individual, or witness.

Reasonable Accommodation   The ADA does not state that because individuals have physical or mental disabilities they automatically qualify for a job. Rather, the act prohibits discrimination against "qualified individuals," individuals who, with or without a reasonable accommodation, can perform "essential functions" of the job. Functions are essential when they are the reason the job exists or because the function is so highly specialized that the individual hired for the job is hired for their expertise in performing the specialized functions.

A modification or adjustment is "reasonable" by law if it "seems reasonable on its face, i.e., ordinarily or in the run of cases." Thus, the request is reasonable if it appears to be plausible or feasible. A reasonable accommodation enables an applicant with a disability to have an equal opportunity to participate in the application process and to be considered for hire in an organization. In addition, a reasonable accommodation permits an employee with a disability the equal opportunity to enjoy the benefits and privileges of employment that employees without disabilities enjoy.

Reasonable accommodation may include, but is not limited to, the following (Blanck, Andersen, Wallach, & Tenney, 1994; EEOC, 2008; Foote, 2000):

- Making existing facilities used by employees readily accessible to and usable by employees with disabilities, for example, installing ramps, lowering water fountains, modifying bathroom facilities, increase natural lighting or full spectrum lighting, and setting up work locations away from noisy machinery.
- Acquiring or modifying equipment or devices, for example, text telephones, teletype (TTY), alternative keyboards, and Braille printers.
- Adjusting training pedagogies for employees with hearing or visual impairments.
- Providing qualified readers or interpreters during staff meetings or training programs.
- Providing both written and spoken instructions.
- Modifying employment tests.
- Providing breaks according to individual needs instead of a fixed schedule.
- Allowing permission to have beverages or food at workstations to mitigate the side effects of medications and so on.

Undue Hardship   The ADA states that employers must make reasonable accommodations for mental and physical disabilities unless the accommodation would impose an undue hardship on the organization. The ADA defines undue hardship as an "action requiring significant difficulty or expense when considered in light of factors such as an employer's size, financial resources, and the nature and structure of its operation" (EEOC, 2002, p. 2). According to Schroeder (2009), the following factors will determine whether an accommodation will yield an undue hardship for the employer:

- The cost and nature of the accommodation.
- The employer's financial resources.

- The nature of the organization (size, structure, composition).
- Accommodation costs previously incurred by the employer.

The EEOC maintains that most accommodations cost the employer $500.

ADA AND LEGAL OBLIGATIONS ON EMPLOYERS

The ADA imposes several legal obligations on employers (Blanck et al., 1994; Goodman-Delahunty, 2000), including the following:

- Employers must not make preemployment inquiries about an applicant's disability. Employers may, however, ask applicants about their ability to perform specific job functions.
- Job offers must be given before medical exams required for the position. Medical exams must be job related and consistent with the employer's business needs.
- If following a medical exam the employer rescinds a job offer, the applicant must be provided with the specific reason for the offer being rescinded.
- Employers must ensure job applications, interview questions and procedures, and job descriptions are free from discriminatory terms.
- Employers must make a reasonable accommodation to an applicant or employee unless the accommodation will result in undue hardship for the employer.

Furthermore, under the ADA, it is illegal to discriminate in any aspect of employment, including the following: hiring and firing; compensation, assignment, or classification of employees; transfer, promotion, layoff, or recall; job advertisements; recruitment; testing; use of company facilities; training and apprenticeship programs; fringe benefits; pay retirement plans; and disability leave or other terms and conditions of employment.

AMERICANS WITH DISABILITIES ACT AMENDMENTS ACT OF 2008

The moral test of government is how it treats those who are in the dawn of life . . . the children; those who are in the twilight of life . . . the elderly; and those who are in the shadow of life . . . the sick . . . the needy . . . and the disabled.

—Hubert H. Humphrey

On September 25, 2008, President Bush signed the Americans with Disabilities Act Amendments Act of 2008. This act became effective January 1, 2009, adding significant changes to the definition of "disability" (EEOC, 2008). For example, this act expands the definition of "major life activities" by including the following that previously had not been identified by EEOC: bending, communicating, and reading. In addition, the act includes major bodily functions, that is, "functions of the immune system, normal cell growth, digestive, bowel, bladder, neurological, brain, respiratory, circulatory, endocrine and reproductive functions." Furthermore, the act indicates that an impairment that is in remission or is episodic would still be considered a disability if the impairment would substantially limit the individual's major life activity when active.

This act also maintains that individuals covered only under the "regarded as" aspect of disability are not entitled to any reasonable accommodation. This act points out that "disability" must be interpreted broadly.

DISABILITY HARASSMENT

Claims under the ADA typically have focused on adverse employment decisions toward individuals with mental or physical disabilities. More recently, however, ADA has been addressing disability harassment, specifically, hostile work environments because of the employee's disability (Holzbauer & Berven, 1996; Johnson, 2008; Schroeder, 2009; Susser, 2005). According to the EEOC (2004):

> The ADA prohibits offensive conduct that is sufficiently severe or pervasive to create a hostile or abusive work environment. Acts of harassment may include verbal abuse, such as name-calling, behavior such as graphic and written statements, or conduct that is physically threatening, harmful, or humiliating. . . . To be actionable, conduct related to an employee's intellectual disability must be sufficiently severe or pervasive as to be both subjectively hostile and abusive (to the person) and to a reasonable person.

Thus, legally, a hostile work environment may exist with respect to an individual's disability when the following criteria apply:

- The employee is a qualified individual with a disability.
- Verbal or nonverbal behavior occurs because of an individual being a member of a protected class (for example, having a physical or mental disability).

- The harassment is unwanted or unwelcome.
- The harassment is severe or pervasive enough to unreasonably impact the employee's work environment.
- The employer knew or should have known of the harassment and failed to take prompt and remedial action.

Behaviorally, a hostile work environment for disability can include the following: posters, e-mail, cartoons, or pictures displayed in the work area that creates an offensive and intimidating environment for employees with disabilities; engaging in threatening, intimidating, or hostile acts toward an employee with a disability; actual denial of a job-related benefit to an employee with a disability; telling jokes pertaining to people with disabilities; making suggestive, obscene, or insulting sounds about individuals with disabilities; or mimicking an employee with a speech impediment. In addition, a hostile work environment for employees with disabilities includes inappropriate reference to disability, unwelcome discussion of the impact of disability, and refusal to work with and exclusion of people with disabilities from social events or staff meetings and training programs (Weber, 2007).

The case of *Flowers v. Southern Regional Physician Services, Inc.* (2001) illustrates disability harassment. Sandra Flowers was employed by Southern Regional Physician Services for two years and its predecessor for four years prior. Ms. Flowers was a medical assistant to a physician. They had a friendly relationship that changed when her supervisor learned that Ms. Flowers was HIV positive. Her supervisor stopped socializing with Ms. Flowers, refused to shake her hand, intercepted her telephone calls, eavesdropped on her conversations and hovered around her desk.

In addition, the supervisor submitted Ms. Flowers to four random drug tests within a one-week period. While her performance appraisals had been good before her supervisor learned of her health status, she was written up twice and put on a 90-day probation after the supervisor knew she was HIV positive. A few days before the probation ended, the supervisor wrote up Ms. Flowers and put her on another 90-day probation. The president of the company referred to Ms. Flowers as a "bitch" and said that he was "tired of her crap." Ms. Flowers was subsequently terminated.

Based on this evidence, a jury determined that Ms. Flowers had been subjected to disability harassment. The appeals court affirmed this lower court's decision and indicated that the ADA is intended to protect employees against harassment because of their inclusion in a protected category, in this case, an employee with a disability.

DISABILITY DISCRIMINATION AND HARASSMENT: THE VIEW FROM SOCIAL SCIENCE RESEARCH

> Congress acknowledges that society's accumulated myths and fears about disability and disease are as handicapping as are the physical limitations that flow from actual impairment.
>
> —William J. Brennan, Jr.

Disability Stereotyping

Despite the legislation concerning disability discrimination that has existed in the United States since 1992, individuals with disabilities still face enormous discrimination and harassment in the workplace because of stereotyping (Green et al., 2005; Wooten & James, 2005). Stereotypes refer to individuals' thoughts and cognitions that typically do not correspond with reality. Stereotypes occur when individuals are classified by others as having something in common because they are members of a particular group or category of people (for example, employees with physical disabilities, employees with mental disabilities). Psychological research has identified that stereotypes have the following four characteristics (Fiske & Stevens, 1993):

1. Groups that are targeted for stereotypes are easily identified and relatively powerless.
2. There is little agreement between the composite picture of the group and the actual characteristics of that group.
3. This misperception is difficult to modify even though individuals who hold stereotypes have interacted with individuals of the group who disconfirm the stereotypes.
4. This misperception is the product of a bias in individuals' information-processing mechanisms.

Disability stereotyping is a psychological process that describes individuals' structured set of beliefs about the personal attributes of people with disabilities (for example, incompetent, burdens, incapable of participating fully in all aspects of life, victims, nonsexual, or having an illness that can be contracted by contact at the workplace) (see Fine & Asch, 1998;

Goodman-Delahunty, 2009; Lasalvia & Tansella, 2008; Stone-Romero, 2005). Psychologists have identified an emotional component to stereotypic cognitions: prejudice as well as behavioral component to individuals' cognitions—that is, discrimination. Thus, individuals' statements and nonverbal gestures toward individuals with disabilities provide insight into their structured set of beliefs and emotions about people with disabilities (Bruyere et al., 2003).

Bruyere et al. (2003) contacted more than 1,000 members of the Society for Human Resource Management, the entire membership of the Washington Business Group on Health, and human resource personnel and equal employment opportunity personnel in federal agencies. They asked individuals about several human resource management functions including the following: reasonable accommodation, recruitment, preemployment screening, testing and new employee orientation, compensation, health benefits, disciplinary process, union relations and personnel training on the ADA, and the role of disability management programs in contributing to employees accepting individuals with disabilities. They noted that stereotyped attitudes are a "continuing barrier to the hiring and retention of people with disabilities" (Bruyere et al., 2003, p. 5).

As we discussed with respect to *Flowers v. Southern Regional Physician Services, Inc.* (2001), stereotypes are commonly expressed in the workplace with respect to individuals living with or affected by HIV-AIDS (Herek, 1998; Simon, 1998). Employers must not unlawfully discriminate against applicants or employees living with or affected by HIV or AIDS. HIV is a blood-borne virus and is spread only through intimate contact with blood, semen, vaginal secretions, and breast milk. Scientists continue to make new discoveries about HIV infection and AIDS, but one piece of information has never changed—how the disease spreads. Scientists have recognized this fact since 1982. The basic facts about HIV transmission and prevention are sound. Some employees still cling to stereotypes about HIV and AIDS, however, and express these stereotypes by avoiding employees known or assumed to have HIV or AIDS and extending this stereotyping to lesbians and gay men in general (Herek, 1998).

According to social science research (Fiske, 1993), stereotyping in the workplace is likely to be elicited (that is, a hostile work environment is set up) under the following conditions: (1) rarity (one or a few employees with a disability present), (2) priming (explicit comments, nonverbal gestures, pictures, posters, e-mails present in the workplace that make negative reference to individuals with disabilities), (3) participation in disability discrimination or harassment by supervisors, and (4) inadequate and ineffective policies to prohibit the verbal and nonverbal expression of disability stereotypes.

Stone and Colella (1996) offered a model for understanding the ways in which employees with disabilities are treated by managers and peers. Stone and Colella (1996) identified six aspects of stereotyping of employees with disabilities: social competence, task competence, concern for others, integrity, emotional adjustment, and potency. All of these aspects have been found to have a significant impact on employment decisions regarding the abilities of employees with disabilities. Once stereotypes have been formed, they are highly difficult to reverse, and consequently, unfounded beliefs about employees and applicants with disabilities persist, thus maintaining a hostile work environment for these individuals.

Stereotyping affects individuals' career development. Doren and Benz (2001) noted in their review of 34 empirical studies dealing with gender, disability, and employment outcomes from 1972 to 1998 that women who have disabilities are less likely to be employed than women without disabilities or men with or without disabilities. In addition, Doren and Benz (2001) found that women with disabilities earn less than men with disabilities and the wage gap increases with time. Women with disabilities also are likely to be employed in positions rated as having lower status and as part-time employees than men with disabilities. Finally, Doren and Benz (2001) found that women with disabilities do not remain at any one job as long as do men with disabilities. Thus, stereotypes get expressed behaviorally in discriminatory treatment of employees with disabilities in terms of wages, pay increases, and promotions. In addition, women of color with disabilities experience even more stereotyping than white women or men in general, illustrating the concept of "intersectionality," which explains the oppressions faced by people who are simultaneously members of more than one disenfranchised group (Banks & Marshall, 2004; Hill Collins, 2004/1986; hooks, 2004/1990).

STEREOTYPING OF JOB APPLICANTS WITH DISABILITIES

Research on stereotypes about job applicants with disabilities has reported that employers are reluctant to hire individuals with disabilities because of concerns related to increased cost, safety issues; legal liability; reactions of co-workers, vendors, clients, and other employers; and the need for increased supervision of employees with disabilities. Gouvier, Sytsma-Jordan, and

Mayville (2003) found discriminatory treatment in the hiring of individuals with disabilities. Larger organizations (having more than 100 employees) are more likely to hire individuals with disabilities (Bruyere et al., 2003). These same studies found that employers hold more negative stereotypes and are less likely to hire individuals with psychological disabilities or who have alcoholism (also see Corrigan et al., 2000; Corrigan, Watson, Warpinski, & Gracia, 2004; Lengnick-Hall, Gaunt, & Kulkami, 2008; Scheid, 2005; Stefan, 2001).

Stoddard, Jans, Ripple, and Kraus (1998) and Zsembik, Peek, and Peek (2000) found that the severity of the disability has the greatest impact on whether the individuals with disabilities will be employed. Approximately 25 percent of women and 28 percent of men with a severe disability are employed. With respect to less severe disabilities, 68 percent of women and 85 percent of men are employed. Thus, individuals with severe disabilities are more likely to live in poverty. Unemployment rates for individuals with disabilities are disproportionately higher than individuals without disabilities.

A recent report by deBoer (as cited in Rabin, 2009) indicated that cancer survivors have a 37 percent higher rate of joblessness than individuals who are healthier. deBoer commented that "this issue is so important to patients, because they often regard returning to work as indicative of complete recovery" (Rabin, 2009, p. 2). Employers who do not hire or promote individuals with disabilities are missing out on attracting and retaining top talent (Lengnick-Hall et al., 2008; Minton-Eversole, 2007).

Hunt and Hunt (2004) state that it is easier to implement structural changes (for example, replacing stairs with ramps and making bathrooms accessible) than to change people's attitudes toward individuals with disabilities. This inability to change attitudes is due to widespread stigma, which is defined as the application of a negative trait to a group or individual (Scheid, 2005). According to Scheid, persons with mental illness are stigmatized by the labels of disability and mental illness, and they are widely perceived as dangerous, irrational, slow, stupid, and unpredictable. It is no surprise that the stigma is greater toward persons with mental illness than toward those with physical disabilities (Corrigan et al., 2000), and such stigma is the main barrier to employment for people with mental disabilities (Mechanic, 1998; Scheid, 2005).

Feldman and Crandall (2007) found that three major dimensions account for social rejection of mentally ill individuals: (1) personal responsibility (it is the person's own fault for his or her mental illness), (2) dangerousness behavior (the mentally ill person is a threat to others), and (3) rarity (uncommon mental disorders have unknown risks associated with them). Other researchers (Angermeyer & Matschinger, 2003; Corrigan, Edwards, Green, Diwan, & Penn, 2001; Corrigan et al., 2002; Corrigan, Larson, & Kuwabara, 2007) also found that fear of dangerousness is linked to avoidance, which is a key factor leading to stigmatization and discrimination of persons with mental disorders.

The organizational climate can create attitudinal, behavioral, and physical barriers for workers with disabilities (Schur, Kruse, & Blanck, 2005). That is, attitudes shared by employers, supervisors, and co-workers have a dramatic impact on the hiring and employment experiences of workers with mental disabilities (Scheid, 2005; Schur et al., 2005). Employees with disabilities are entitled to accommodations, which may cause resentment by those without disabilities who often evaluate the just distribution of outcomes based on an equity rule, that is, a balance between outcomes or job rewards received and inputs or the job contributions made (Nichols, 2008; Schur et al., 2005). An employee with a disability who is being accommodated to do his or her job may be viewed as receiving extra rewards and making the job harder or less desirable for employees without disabilities, leading to perceptions of inequity or unfairness (Nichols, 2008; Schur et al., 2005). Those who take into consideration the needs of employees with disabilities are generally more likely to approve of accommodations for those with physical disabilities than for those with psychiatric disabilities, who are more likely to be blamed for their condition (Corrigan et al., 2007; Feldman & Crandall, 2007; Schur et al., 2005).

IMPACT OF DISABILITY DISCRIMINATION ON INDIVIDUALS AND WORKPLACES

Research on disability discrimination and harassment, similar to the literature on race and sexual harassment, has documented impacts on several areas of functioning, including the following: emotional and psychological, physiological or health related, career and work, social, and self-perception (Bahm & Forchuk, 2008; Banks & Ackerman, 2003; Green et al., 2005; Holzbauer & Berven, 1996; Stefan, 2002). Most individuals experience severe distress associated with discrimination and harassment. The symptoms become exacerbated when these individuals are in continued contact with the perpetrator and when they are retaliated against for complaining about disability discrimination or harassment to their employer. Longitudinal research indicates that the negative effects of disability discrimination are enduring and often are com-pounded by additional discrimination.

Examples of the emotional and psychological effects of disability dis-crimination and harassment include, but are not limited to, guilt, denial, withdrawal from social settings, shame, depression, fear, anger, anxiety, phobias, isolation, fear of crime, helplessness, frustration, shock, and decreased self-esteem. Physical and health-related effects of disability harassment and discrimination, include the following: headaches, tired-ness, respiratory problems, substance abuse, sleep disturbances, eating disorders, lethargy, gastrointestinal disorders, dermatological reactions, and inability to concentrate. In addition, empirical research has indicated that individuals who experience disability discrimination or harassment also experience a negative impact on their career goals and on their abil-ity to perform their job. These impacts include, but are not limited to, the following: changes in work habits, absenteeism, and changes in ca-reer goals.

The impact of disability discrimination and harassment on social and interpersonal relationships includes the following: withdrawal, fear of new people, lack of trust, changes in social network patterns, and rela-tionship difficulties.

Social science research has documented a strong relationship among discrimination, harassment, and negative psychological outcomes. In the Model of Harm (Fitzgerald, Drasgow, Hulin, Gelfand, & Magley, 1997), results indicate that it is generally what happens to a victim as a result of discrimination and harassment that is most prominently related to negative psychological outcomes, not previous victimization or health issues. In addition, other factors that must be taken into account include the frequency with which harassment and discrimination occurs and the status of the perceived harasser. These factors are objective responses to harassment and discrimination and thus operate independently of the harassment victim's vulnerability. In most cases, all of these symptoms affect the individual's disability, putting more stress on the individual and, consequently, the disability becomes more pronounced.

Effects of disability discrimination and harassment on the workplace include the following: decreased morale, increased absenteeism, increased turnover, and decreased productivity (Smith & Mazin, 2004).

Stefan (2002) also notes that employment discrimination against people with mental disabilities interfaces with discrimination based on sexual orientation, gender, and race or ethnicity. That is, sexual orientation harass-ment, sexual harassment, and race or ethnic harassment may cause or aggravate physical and psychiatric problems. Empirical research supports this conclusion by finding that racial or ethnic discrimination in the workplace is a risk factor for mental disorders among workers (Bhui et al., 2005).

DISABILITY MANAGEMENT IN THE WORKPLACE: HUMAN RESOURCE RESPONSES

Through personal accounts from individuals with disabilities, employers can learn about recommendations for disability management (Breakthrough UK, 2009):

> We want employers to know that they are employing an individual, not "the disability" or "the impairment." Support needs to be within the workplace and the person should not feel they are being a burden by requiring this support. Obviously performance is an issue but this will be achieved and excelled in the right circumstances. Employers need to understand how society disables people and think about their role in removing barriers that stop disabled people from progressing at work. Don't make assumptions about what a disabled person can't do. To negatively define is to negatively confine. To exclude. To disable. To discriminate.
>
> Employers wrongly assume that someone with a particular impairment will have certain access requirements which may be costly and time consuming. Not every disabled person needs specialist equipment, often it is just a case of working in a different way. (pp. 1–2).

This chapter has focused attention on institutional factors that contribute to employees reporting their experiences with disability discrimination and harassment. Our position is that workplaces should exercise "reasonable care" to ensure a discriminatory-free and retaliatory-free work environment for employees with physical and mental disabilities. This "reasonable care," adapted from the Supreme Court ruling in *Faragher v. Boca Raton* (1998) includes the following, at a minimum:

- Establish and disseminate an effective antidiscrimination and harassment policy dealing with physical and mental disabilities.
- Establish and disseminate effective investigative procedures.
- Facilitate training in disability discrimination and harassment in general and in the organization's policy and procedures specifically.

See chapter 13, Exercising "Reasonable Care": Policies, Procedures, and Training Programs, in this volume, which deals with organizations taking reasonable care in preventing workplace discrimination and harassment. The chapter provides an overview of components of effective policy statements, investigatory procedures, and training programs that include needs assessments and post-training evaluations. In addition, Paludi and Barickman (1998) offered a series of questions for workplaces to address when reviewing their sexual harassment policy for effectiveness. This list is adapted for disability discrimination and harassment. It serves as a human resource audit (Dessler, 2009; Smith & Mazin, 2004): Audits provide information for administrators on ways disability discrimination is operating in their organization. As Greenberg-Pophal (2008) stated, a human resource audit is "an analysis by which an organization measures where it currently stands and determines what it has to accomplish to improve its human resource function" (in Dessler, 2009; p. 412). Audit questions include the following:

1. Is there a policy statement for dealing with disability discrimination and harassment?
2. Does the policy prohibit discrimination/harassment from peers or it is limited to discrimination or harassment by managers?
3. Is the policy statement well publicized? Is it circulated periodically among all members of the company?
4. How do employees learn to whom they should report complaints?
5. Are remedies clear and commensurate with the level of discrimination or harassment?
6. Does the company have procedures to inform new employees about disability discrimination and harassment?
7. Does the company facilitate regular training programs on disability discrimination and harassment?
8. What services are available at the company to employees who have experienced disability discrimination or harassment?
9. Does the workplace foster an atmosphere of prevention by sensitizing individuals to the topic of disability discrimination and harassment?
10. Does the workplace provide services for employees with disabilities in the form of interpreters? Readers?
11. Does the employer postpone the medical exam until after a formal job offer is made? Are applicants aware of this procedure through the employees' handbook and other communications?
12. Does the employer follow state laws with respect to disability discrimination and harassment as well as federal law?

13. Has the employer modified its ADA policy to take into account the new ADAA effective January 1, 2009?

14. Are the employment tests nondiscriminatory for applicants with disabilities?

15. Are policies, procedures, and handbooks available in Braille and on audio tape?

16. Does the employer ensure that training sites are accessible to employees with disabilities?

Holly v. Clairson Indus., L.L.C. (2007) illustrates the necessity of ensuring that policy statements take into account special needs of employees with disabilities. Tommy Holly is a paraplegic confined to a wheelchair. He was regularly late for work because his disability required him to navigate his wheelchair around many obstacles en route to the time clock. For 15 years Mr. Holly's employer informally dealt with his disability-related tardiness. In addition, Mr. Holly always made up the time at breaks or after work. Mr. Holly's supervisor informed the human resource department that Mr. Holly's tardiness was not a problem so that this would not be seen negatively on his annual performance appraisal. Mr. Holly's supervisor also indicated that the tardiness did not affect how work was done in the Mold Shop Department, where Mr. Holly worked as a mold polisher.

After a change in management, however, the company instituted a no-fault tardiness policy. This new policy actually stated that ADA situations were not exempt from the policy. Each absence was identified as an "occurrence" of tardiness, a tardy arrival counted as one half of an occurrence. Employees who clocked in even one second after the shift began received a tardy. Following the receipt of 18 write-ups for tardiness, employees were immediately terminated. In addition, the new policy did not allow for managers to judge whether employees' excuses were credible or excusable.

Mr. Holly expressed concern about the policy to his manager, but nothing could be done and ultimately Mr. Holly was terminated. The Court determined that "timeliness" might not be an essential function of his job (which the new tardiness and absentee policy stated it was). The Court of Appeals also said that if it was not an essential function of his job, then it was a reasonable accommodation to allow his disability-related tardiness, of which he was only a few minutes late—usually because he had difficulty navigating his wheelchair around debris and tables left in the way of the time clock. The Court stated: "The very purpose of reasonable accommodation laws is to require employers to treat disabled individuals differently in some circumstances—namely, when different treatment would allow a disabled individual to perform the essential functions of his position by accommodating his disability without posing an undue hardship on the employer."

ADDITIONAL EMPLOYER CONSIDERATIONS

Organizations with flexible employment options report less stress for employees, lower absenteeism, higher morale, positive publicity, improved work satisfaction, and lower turnover rates. These organizations offer staffing over a wide range of hours, childcare hours that conform to work hours, and access to quality infant, child, and elder care (Anderson, 2009; Frone & Yardley, 1996; House, 2009; Paludi & Neidermeyer, 2007). Examples of flexible employment options include the following: flextime, job sharing, part-time work, telecommuting, intranet work, on-site childcare, on-site health services, time off and career break, compressed workweek, and elder-care referral services. Examples of such policies are found in Paludi and Paludi (2007). These flexible employment options have been found to be effective options for employees with disabilities (Anderson, 2009; EEOC, 2005; House, 2009).

For example, telecommuting can help employees with disabilities be more efficient and productive. Telecommuting or telework is a work arrangement in which an employee works from a remote work site away from the primary workplace or from home for a portion of the workday or workweek or pay period. Employees may send work to and communicate with the main office via telephone, computer, or fax. MITE and the Humphrey Institute of Public Affairs (in Anderson, 2009) found in their research with telework practices of 432 employers that the majority of telework-friendly employers offered this flexible work arrangement to employees who needed to better manage their disability.

These organizations reported several benefits for the company as a result of the option to telework, including retaining employees, reducing employee turnover and recruitment costs, and increasing their ability to respond to employees' unique needs. It is important that employers not provide flexible work arrangements to avoid in person contact with employees with disabilities. According to the EEOC (2005):

The ADA does not require an employer to offer a telework program to all employees. However, if an employer does offer telework, it must allow employees with disabilities an equal opportunity to participate in such a program. Changing the location where work is performed may fall under the ADA's reasonable accommodation requirement of modifying workplace policies, even if the employer does not allow other employees to telework. However, an employer is not obligated to adopt an employee's preferred or requested accommodation and may instead offer alternate accommodations as long as they would be effective.

It is recommended in the human resource management literature for employers to have a formal policy on telecommuting. A sample telecommuting policy may be found in Paludi and Paludi (2007). In addition, employers must review their job descriptions to ensure that statements of essential functions are identified as being performed at home as well as at the workplace.

As discussed earlier in this chapter, most individuals with mental disorders want to work and are able to work (Mechanic, Bilder, & McAlpine, 2002). To increase the number of persons with mental disorders in the workplace, studies indicate that the best approach is to place them directly into the workforce (that is, the place-train model), providing them with greater income, duration of employment, and better relationships with co-workers, and to do so without increasing the frequency of relapse (for a review of studies that examined the place-train model, see Corrigan & McCracken, 2005). It is also important to combat mental illness stigma in the workplace. There are three strategies to reduce the stigma of mental illness: (1) protest (framing stigma as a social injustice and suppressing stigmatizing attitudes about mental illness), (2) education (providing information about the myths and facts of mental illness), and (3) contact (enhancing interactions with individuals with mental illness) (see Corrigan & Penn, 1999).

Corrigan, River, et al. (2001) found that the protest strategy did not produce attitude change; however, education and contact strategies produced significant attitude change (that is, decreased stereotypes and prejudices about mental illness). Furthermore, Corrigan et al. (2002) found that education had some positive benefits, but contact with persons with mental illness produced the greatest consistent results. Of course, education and contact strategies can be implemented together, for example, education programs can be improved by face-to-face contact with persons with mental disorders (Corrigan & Penn, 1999). A recent approach that has emerged is imagined intergroup contact (that is, to mentally imagine a positive encounter with a stigmatized person), which provides an inexpensive, practical, and effective means of reducing intergroup anxiety and improving attitudes toward stigmatized groups and individuals. Imagined contact has significant potential for policy makers and educators seeking to increase social diversity in the workplace (Crisp & Turner, 2009). Whether this promising approach will be adopted by employers is unknown to date.

REFERENCES

American Psychological Association. (1992). *Guidelines for non-handicapping language in APA journals.* Retrieved March 1, 2009, from http://www.apastyle.org/disabilities.html.

Anderson, J. (2009). *Telecommuting: A work option for persons with disabilities.* Retrieved February 26, 2008, from http://www.mite.org/telecommut disabilities/telecommutdisabilities.html.

Angermeyer, M. C., & Matschinger, H. (2003). The stigma of mental illness: Effects of labelling on public attitudes towards people with mental disorder. *Acta Psychiatrica Scandinavica, 108,* 304–309.

Bahm, A., & Forchuk, C. (2008). Interlocking oppressions: The effect of a comorbid physical disability on perceived stigma and discrimination among mental health consumers in Canada. *Health and Social Care in the Community, 17,* 63–70.

Banks, M., & Ackerman, R. (2003). All things being unequal: Culturally relevant roads to empowerment. In F. Menz & D. Thomas (Eds.), *Bridging gaps: Refining the disability research agenda for rehabilitation and the Social Science Conference Proceedings.* Menomonie: University of Wisconsin-Stout, Stout Vocational Rehabilitation Institute, Research and Training Centers.

Banks, M., & Kaschak, E. (Eds.). (2003). *Women with visible and invisible disabilities: Multiple intersections, multiple issues, multiple therapies.* New York: Haworth Press.

Banks, M., & Marshall, C. (2004). Beyond the "triple whammy": Social class as a factor in discrimination against persons with disabilities. In J. Chin (Ed.), *The psychology of prejudice and discrimination: Combating prejudice and all forms of discrimination: Vol. 4. Disability, religion, physique and other traits* (pp. 95–110). Westport, CT: Praeger.

Bhui, K., Stansfeld, S., McKenzie, K., Karlsen, S., Nazroo, J., & Weich, S. (2005). Racial/ethnic discrimination and common mental disorders among workers: Findings from the EMPIRIC study of ethnic minority groups in the United Kingdom. *American Journal of Public Health, 95,* 496–501.

Blanck, P., Andersen, J., Wallach, E., & Tenney, J. (1994). Implementing reasonable accommodation using ADR under the ADA: The case of a white collar employee with bipolar mental illness. *Mental and Physical Disability Law Reporter, 18,* 458–464.

Bonnie, R., & Monahan, J. (Eds.). (1997). *Mental disorder, work disability, and the law.* Chicago: University of Chicago Press.

Brainy Quote.com. (2009). Retrieved October 20, 2009, from http://www. brainyquote.com/quotes/keywords/disability.html.

Breakthrough-UK. (2009). *Things disabled people want employers to know.* Retrieved March 1, 2009, from http://www.breakthrough-uk.com.

Bruyere, S., Erickson, W., & Ferrentino, J. (2003). Identity and disability in the workplace. *William and Mary Law Review, 44,* 1173–1196.

Cook, J., & Burke, J. (2002). Public policy and employment of people with disabilities: Exploring new paradigms. *Behavioral Sciences and the Law, 20,* 541–557.

Corrigan, P. (2004). How stigma interferes with mental health care. *American Psychologist, 59,* 614–625.

Corrigan, P. W., Edwards, A. B., Green, A., Diwan, S. L., & Penn D. L. (2001). Prejudice, social distance, and familiarity with mental illness. *Schizophrenia Bulletin, 27,* 219–225.

Corrigan, P. W., Larson, J. E., & Kuwabara, S. A. (2007). Mental illness stigma and the fundamental components of supported employment. *Rehabilitation Psychology, 52,* 451–457.

Corrigan, P. W., & McCracken, S. G. (2005). Place first, then train: An alternative to the medical model of psychiatric rehabilitation. *Social Work, 50,* 31–39.

Corrigan, P. W., & Penn, D. L. (1999). Lessons from social psychology on discrediting psychiatric stigma. *American Psychologist, 54,* 765–776.

Corrigan, P. W., River, L., P., Lundin, R. K., Penn, D. L., Uphoff-Wasowski, K., Campion, J., et al. (2001). Three strategies for changing attributions about severe mental illness. *Schizophrenia Bulletin, 27,* 187–195.

Corrigan, P., River, L., Lundin, R., Wasnowski, K., Campion, J., Mathisen, J., et al. (2000). Stigmatizing attributions about mental illness. *Journal of Community Psychology, 28,* 91–103.

Corrigan, P. W., Rowan, D., Green, A., Lundin, R., River, P., Uphoff-Wasowski, K., et al. (2002). Challenging two mental illness stigmas: Personal responsibility and dangerousness. *Schizophrenia Bulletin, 28,* 293–309.

Corrigan, P., Watson, A., Warpinski, A., & Gracia, G. (2004). Stigmatizing attitudes about mental illness and allocation of resources to mental health services. *Community Mental Health Journal, 40,* 297–307.

Crisp, R. J., & Turner, R. N. (2009). Can imagined interactions produce positive perceptions? Reducing prejudice through simulated social contact. *American Psychologist, 64,* 231–240.

Dalgin, R. (2001). Impact of Title I of the Americans with Disabilities Act on people with psychiatric disabilities. *Journal of Applied Rehabilitation Counseling, 32,* 45–50.

Dessler, G. (2009). *Fundamentals of human resource management.* Upper Saddle River, NJ: Prentice Hall.

Doren, B., & Benz, M. (2001). Gender equity issues in the vocational and transition services and employment outcomes experienced by young women with disabilities. In H. Rousso & M. Wehmeyer (Eds.), *Double jeopardy: Addressing gender equity in special education* (pp. 289–312). Albany, NY: State University of New York Press.

Equal Employment Opportunity Commission. (2002). *Disability discrimination.*

Equal Employment Opportunity Commission. (2004). *Questions & answers about persons with intellectual disabilities in the workplace and the Americans with Disabilities Act.*

Equal Employment Opportunity Commission. (2005). *Work at home/telework as a reasonable accommodation.*

Equal Employment Opportunity Commission. (2008). *Disability discrimination.*

Faragher v. City of Boca Raton, 524 U.S.C. 725 (1998).

Feldman, D. B., & Crandall, C. S. (2007). Dimensions of mental illness stigma: What about mental illness causes social rejection? *Journal of Social and Clinical Psychology, 26,* 137–154.

Fine, M., & Asch, A. (1988). *Women with disabilities: Essays in psychology, culture and politics.* Philadelphia, PA: Temple University Press.

Fishbein, H. (2002). *Peer prejudice and discrimination: The origins of prejudice.* Mahwah, NJ: Erlbaum.

Fiske, S. (1993). Controlling other people: The impact of power on stereotyping. *American Psychologist, 48,* 621–628.

Fiske, S., & Stevens, L. (1993). What's so special about sex? Gender stereotyping and discrimination. In S. Oskamp & M. Costanzo (Eds.), *Gender issues in contemporary society.* Newbury Park, CA: Sage.

Fitzgerald, L. F., Drasgow, F., Hulin, C. L., Gelfand, M. J., & Magley, V. J. (1997). The antecedents and consequences of sexual harassment in organizations: A test of an integrated model. *Journal of Applied Psychology, 82,* 578–589.

Flowers v. Southern Regional Physician Services, Inc., 247 F.3d 229 (5th Cir. 2001).

Foote, W. E. (2000). A model for psychological consultation in cases involving the Americans with disabilities act. *Professional Psychology: Research and Practice, 31* (2), 190–196.

Frone, M., & Yardley, J. (1996). Workplace family-supportive programmes: Predictors of employed parents' importance ratings. *Journal of Occupational and Organizational Psychology, 69,* 351–366.

Goodman-Delahunty, J. (2000). Psychological impairment under the Americans with Disabilities Act: Legal guidelines. *Professional Psychology: Research and Practice, 31,* 197–205.

Gouvier, W., Sytsma-Jordan, S., & Mayville, S. (2003). Patterns of discrimination in hiring job applicants with disabilities: The role of disability type, job complexity and public contact. *Rehabilitation Psychology, 48*, 175–181.

Green, S., Davis, C., Karshmer, E., Marsh, P., & Straight, B. (2005). Living stigma: The impact of labeling, stereotyping, separation, status loss and discrimination in the lives of individuals with disabilities and their families. *Sociological Inquiry, 75*, 197–215.

Herek, G. (1998). *Stigma and sexual orientation: Understanding prejudice against lesbians, gay men and bisexuals.* New York: Sage.

Hill Collins, P. (2004/1986). Learning from the outsider within: The sociological significance of black feminist thought. In S. Harding (Ed.), *The feminist standpoint theory reader: Intellectual & political controversies* (pp. 103–126). New York: Routledge.

Holly v. Clairson Indus, L.L.C., 492 F.3d 1247,1255 (11th Cir. 2007).

Holzbauer, J., & Berven, N. (1996). Disability harassment: A new term for a long-standing problem. *Journal of Counseling and Development, 74*, 478–483.

hooks, b. (2004/1990). Choosing the margin as a space of radical openness. In S. Harding (Ed.), *The feminist standpoint theory reader: Intellectual & political controversies* (pp. 153–159). New York: Routledge.

House, C. (2009). *Telecommuting as a reasonable accommodation for disabled employees.* Retrieved February 26, 2009, from http://www.lorman.com/newsletters/article.php?article.

Hunt, C. S., & Hunt, B. (2004). Changing attitudes toward people with disabilities: Experimenting with an educational intervention. *Journal of Managerial Issues, 16*, 266–280.

Johnson, H. (2008). Disability harassment. *Journal of Deaf Studies and Deaf Education, 13,* 302.

Jones, C. (2008). The future of disability harassment law in the workplace. *SAM Advanced Management Journal.* Retrieved April 18, 2009, from http://findarticles.com/p/articles/mi_hb6698/is_2_73/ai_n29445905/?tag=content;col1.

Kessler, R. C., Chiu, W. T., Demler, O., & Walters, E. E. (2005). Prevalence, severity, and comorbidity of 12-month DSM-IV disorders in the National Comorbidity Survey Replication. *Archives of General Psychiatry, 62*, 617–627.

Lasalvia, A., & Tansella, M. (2008). Fighting discrimination and stigma against people with mental disorders. *Epidemiological Psychiatry Sociology, 17,* 1–9.

Lengnick-Hall, M., Gaunt, P., & Kulkami, M. (2008). Overlooked and underutilized: People with disabilities are an untapped human resource. *Human Resource Management, 47*, 255–273.

Mason, A., Pratt, H. D., Patel, D. R., Greydanus, D. E., & Yahya, K. Z. (2004). Prejudice toward people with disabilities. In J. L. Chin (Ed.), *The psychology of prejudice and discrimination: Vol. 4. Disability, religion, physique, and other traits* (pp. 51–93). Westport, CT: Praeger.

Mayerson, A. (1992). *The history of the ADA: A movement perspective.* Retrieved February 26, 2009, from http//www.empowermentzone.com/ada_hist.txt.

Mechanic, D. (1998). Cultural and organizational aspects of application of the Americans with Disabilities Act to persons with psychiatric disabilities. *The Milbank Quarterly, 76*, 5–23.

Mechanic, D., Bilder, S., & McAlpine, D. D. (2002). Employing persons with serious mental illness. *Health Affairs, 21*, 242–253.

Mezey, S. (2005). *Disabling interpretations: The Americans with Disabilities Act in federal court.* Pittsburgh, PA: University of Pittsburgh Press.

Miceli, N., Harvey, M., & Buckley, M. (2001). Potential discrimination in structured employment interviews. *Employee Responsibilities and Rights Journal, 13*, 15–38.

Minton-Eversole, T. (2007). *Payoffs can be big for companies hiring people with disabilities.* Psychologically Healthy Workplace Program. Retrieved February 24, 2009, from http://www.phwa.org/resources/article.php?id=1219.

Nichols, J. L. (2008). The influence of coworker justice perceptions on worksite accommodations and the return to work of persons with disabilities. *Journal of Applied Rehabilitation Counseling, 39*, 33–39.

Olkin, R. (1999). *What psychotherapists should know about disability.* New York: Guilford Press.

Paludi, M., & Barickman, R. (1998). *Academic and workplace sexual harassment: A resource manual for prevention.* Albany: State University of New York Press.

Paludi, M., & Neidermeyer, P. (Eds.), (2007). *Work, life and family imbalance: How to level the playing field.* Westport, CT: Praeger.

Paludi, M., & Paludi, C. (2007). Integrating work/life: Resources for employees, employers, and human resource specialists. In M. Paludi & P. Neidermeyer (Eds.), (2007). *Work, life and family imbalance: How to level the playing field* (pp. 122–154). Westport, CT: Praeger.

Price, L., Gerber, P., & Mulligan, R. (2003). The Americans with Disabilities Act and adults with learning disabilities: The realities of the workplace: *Remedial and Special Education, 24,* 350–358.

Rabin, R. (2009, February 18). Cancer survivors struggle to find jobs, study finds. *New York Times.* Retrieved February 24, 2009, from http://www.nytimes.com/2009/02/18/health/18cancer.html.

Scheid, T. (2005). Stigma as a barrier to employment: Mental disability and the Americans with Disabilities Act. *International Journal of Law and Psychiatry, 28*, 670–690.

Schroeder, A. (2009). Disability discrimination in the workplace: An overview of the ADA. *Nolo.* Retrieved February 25, 2009, from http://www.nolo.com/article.cm/object/CB4EA68F-D2DD-4860.

Schur, L., Kruse, D., & Blanck, P. (2005). Corporate culture and the employment of persons with disabilities. *Behavioral Sciences and the Law, 23*, 3–20.

Simon, A. (1998). The relationships between stereotypes of and attitudes toward lesbians and gays. In G. Herek (Ed.), *Stigma and sexual orientation: Understanding prejudice against lesbians, gay men, and bisexuals.* New York: Sage.

Smith, S., & Mazin, R. (2004). *The HR answer book.* New York: AMACOM.

Stefan, D. (2001). *Unequal rights: Discrimination against people with mental disabilities and the Americans with Disabilities Act.* Washington, DC: American Psychological Association.

Stefan, S. (2002). *Hollow promises: Employment discrimination against people with mental disabilities.* Washington, DC: American Psychological Association.

Stoddard, S., Jans, L., Ripple, J., and Kraus, L. (1998). What occupations are held by people with a work disability who are employed? Chartbook on work and disability in the United States, 1998: An InfoUse report. Washington, DC: U.S. National Institute on Disability and Rehabilitation Research (NIDRR).

Stone, D., & Colella, A. (1996). A model of factors affecting the treatment of disabled individuals in organizations. *Academy of Management Review, 21,* 352–401.

Stone-Romero, E. (2005). Personality-based stigmas and unfair discrimination in work organizations. In R. Dipboye & A. Colella (Eds.), *Discrimination at work: The psychological and organizational bases* (pp. 255–280). Mahwah, NJ: Erlbaum.

Susser, P. (2005). *Disability discrimination and the workplace.* Portland, OR: BNA Books.

Tahvonen, H. (2003). Disability-based harassment: Standing and new standards for a "new" cause of action. *William and Mary Law Review, 44,* 1489.

Ward, A., & Baker, P. (2005). Disabilities and impairments: Strategies for workplace integration. *Behavioral Sciences and the Law, 23,* 143–160.

Weber, M. (2007). *Disability harassment.* New York: NYU Press.

Wilson v. Phoenix Specialty Mfg.Co., Inc. South Carolina, no. 06-1818 (2008).

Wooten, L., & James, E. (2005). Challenges of organizational learning: Perpetuation of discrimination against employees with disabilities. *Behavioral Sciences and the Law, 23,* 123–141.

WHO (World Health Organization). (2004). *The world health report 2004: Changing history, annex table 3: Burden of disease in DALYs by cause, sex, and mortality stratum in WHO regions, estimates for 2002.* Geneva: WHO.

Zsembik, B., Peek, M., & Peek, C. (2000). Race and ethnic variation in the disablement process. *Journal of Aging and Health, 12,* 229.

3

Equal Compensation Discrimination

William Gaeddert

The mandate that persons employed in substantially equal jobs should be paid the same has been a part of federal law since the passage of the Equal Pay Act of 1963. Further protections for equal compensation for U.S. workers has been provided by Title VII of the Civil Rights Act of 1964, the Age Discrimination in Employment Act of 1967, and Title I of the Americans with Disabilities Act of 1990. Some states, such as California, Minnesota, and New York have similar legislation. In all instances, the legislation mandates that equal pay be accorded to people working not just in jobs with the same titles, but rather jobs that are substantially equal in skill, effort, and responsibility requirements, that are performed under similar working conditions, and within the same establishment. Although there is a persistent difference in the earnings of full-time employed men and women, 70 percent of working women believe they are paid at the same rate as men, and 87 percent of men believe that women are paid at the same rates that they are (Gallup News Service, 2000). John Stossel (2005) opined that the marketplace is just and pay rates for men, women, and minorities are accurate measures of their contributions to organizations. Yet on January 29, 2009, President Obama signed the Lily Ledbetter Fair Pay Act of 2009, which will facilitate equal pay discrimination suits. Contrary to the perceptions of respondents to the Gallup poll, appreciable wage gaps still exist. The focus of this review will be on examining the degree to which the marketplace is truly just in setting wages for men, women, and minorities.

EARNINGS GAPS—DESCRIPTIVE CHARACTERISTICS

For full-time, employed men and women, the average disparity in earnings in the United States is approximately 33 percent (Bishaw & Semega, 2007). This overall gap varies by region, ranging from slightly less than 7 percent in the District of Columbia to 37 percent in Wyoming, with the greatest gaps tending to occur in the South and upper Midwest (Bishaw & Semega, 2007). The gap varies by industry as well, ranging from less than 3 percent in maintenance and repair occupations to nearly 50 percent in legal occupations, and it is substantially narrower in public sector organizations than in the private sector (Bishaw & Semega, 2007; Semyonov & Lewin-Epstein, 2009). A gender gap in earnings occurs in each racial and ethnic group identified by the U.S. Census Bureau, but this gap is narrower among racial minority groups (Bishaw & Semega, 2007; Greenman and Xie, 2008). Emelech and Lu (2004) found that black and Hispanic women are substantially disadvantaged in comparison with white males, and they found (as did Greenman & Xie, 2008) that the overall gender gap is greater among white persons.

Historical analyses of changes in earning gaps suggest that some narrowing of both racial and gender gaps occurred during the 1960s and 1970s, but it has stagnated since then (Hill & O'Neill, 1990; Jarrell & Stanley, 2004; Semyonov & Lewin-Epstein, 2009). However, Jarrell and Stanley's (2004) analysis suggests that the gender gap in wages continued to narrow at a rate of 0.6 percent per year during the decades following the 1970s, and Winslow-Bowe (2006) found that the proportion of couples with wives earning more than husbands increased from 16 percent in 1990 to 18 percent in 1994. Gender-based wage gaps are an international phenomenon, with some evidence that gaps are narrower in richer countries than in relatively disadvantaged countries (Mandel & Semyonov, 2005; Oostendorp, 2004).

SOURCES OF EARNINGS GAPS

The mere existence of gender and racial gaps in average earnings is not evidence of unfair discrimination in wages. Neoclassical economic theory would hold that such disparities are fair, and a natural outgrowth of rational economic decision making. In this type of demand-side explanation, differences in human capital (for example, education, skill levels) are accorded differential rates of pay. Therefore, research on these human capital explanations focus on the ways in which differences in such factors as education, training, and job tenure are used in rational ways to affect wages. Another demand-side explanation rooted in neo-classical economic theory (that is, statistical discrimination theory) suggests that earning gaps are the result of employers making rational decisions regarding the probability that members of particular groups will make significant contributions to the economic health of an organization. In this view, for example, women, owing to the need for their contributions to their families and children, would be expected to have less commitment to continuous work involvement, and therefore would be of lesser economic value to an organization than would men. In addition, this reasoning would lead to the sorting of women (and minorities) into occupations with lower skill and occupational attachment requirements. In these lines of research, characteristics of occupational groups that contain greater numbers of women and minorities have been identified and used to help explain the gaps.

Much of the research on these topics has focused on examining gender and racial gaps in earnings, with the assumption that unexplained portions of the gaps may be attributable to discrimination. To examine the possibility of nonrational influences (that is, discrimination) in determining wage structure, researchers typically examine earnings gaps between groups using multiple regression equations. Human capital factors or occupational characteristics, along with group identification, are used as predictor variables and earnings (typically log-transformed hourly wages) are used as dependent variables. These types of analyses rather stably have resulted in an estimate that about one-quarter of overall wage gaps are unexplained (Leicht, 2008). Some examples of these lines of research will be described. Other bodies of research focus on the role of gender differences in psychological characteristics with the aim of accounting for choices that may result in pay gaps, that is, focusing on supply-side considerations. This reasoning suggests that women's life choices lead them into occupations with lower demands and skill requirements and therefore lower pay. Finally, this chapter will review research focused specifically on the role of unfair discrimination in accounting for pay gaps.

HUMAN CAPITAL

In a rational marketplace, wages will be set in accordance with workers' ability to contribute to organizational success. Personal characteristics such as cognitive ability and level of education are seen to be important variables in this regard. Also, in this context, work history and labor force attachment are considered to be a part of the capital that workers provide an organization. Although extensive literature has been published in this area, only a few studies will be reviewed to provide a flavor of this type of research.

Using data from the National Longitudinal Survey of Youth Cohort (NLSY), Green and Ferber (2005) examined regression models that contained human capital variables, such as education and work experience, as well as personal characteristics such as cognitive ability (measures using scores on the Armed Forces Qualification Test) age, number of children, and marital status. Models including these variables left as much as 50 percent of the gender wage gap among whites unexplained. These variables also left up to 25 percent of racial gaps in wages unexplained. Farkas, England, Vicknair, and Kilbourne (1997) also found that differences in cognitive skills (using Armed Forces Qualification Test and data from NLSY) help explain racial differences in pay, but they do not account for gender differences within race. Alon and Haberfeld (2007) used NLSY data and focused especially on labor force attachment, which is the proportion of time spent annually in paid employment. They found that labor force attachment was associated with substantial differences in wages, and that women, particularly minority women, accumulated less labor force attachment than did men. Konstantopolous and Constant (2008) included the quality of the high school experience as a human capital issue. School quality added to prediction of wages for white males, but not for other groups (white females, black and Hispanic males and females). Importantly, they used quantile regression to examine gaps in wages at different points along the overall wage continuum. Although wage gaps exist at all earning levels, they were pronounced among those in the 90th percentile for earnings, a result that Konstantopolous and Constant (2008) attributed to a pernicious glass-ceiling effect. However, Renner, Rives, and Bowlin (2002) suggested that when the glass ceiling has been broken by top-level women executives, gender does not play a large role in compensation.

In addition to decomposing gender and racial wage gaps using human capital variables, some researchers have approached the question of wage discrimination focusing on cohort analyses. The assumption under-lying these analyses is that to the degree that equal opportunity laws and guidelines have made an impact, more recent cohorts of workers should experience a lesser wage gap than those of earlier cohorts. Much of the research mentioned above, which used NLSY data, included such analyses (Alon & Haberfeld, 2007; Farkas et al., 1997; Green and Ferber, 2005). Those studies do not supply evidence for substantial lessening of earnings gaps, over and above that based on human capital variables. Maume (2004) focused specifically on the decomposition of wage gaps for gender and race by cohort, comparing workers in their prime earning years (ages 25–49) in four cohorts spanning from the 1980s to 1992. Using fixed-effects regression analyses to fully control for possibly unmeasured human capital variables, Maume (2004) found consistent earnings gaps across cohorts, supporting a persistent inequality perspective, as opposed to a cohort perspective. Focusing specifically on the effects of the accumulation of human capital across a career, Tomaskovic-Devey, Thomas, and Johnson (2005) found a much flatter trajectory of accumulation of human capital for Hispanic men compared with white men. Again, persistent inequality of opportunities for training and advancement affect women and minorities throughout their careers.

Leicht (2008) reviewed sociological and economic research regarding earnings gaps conducted since the 1960s, providing an excellent summary of extant findings. He argued that the group gap approach, which has characterized studies to date, fails to take into account the growth of within group disparities in earnings and wealth. That is, increasing gaps between rich and poor in earnings and overall wealth may lead to erroneous conclusions when examining only differences in group averages for earnings. In this regard, Konstantopolous and Constant's (2008) use of quantile regression is worth noting, in particular, their finding that gender disparities are greater in higher paid groups of workers.

STATISTICAL DISCRIMINATION

Work in the United States is a gendered activity, and although some parity has been achieved in some occupations, substantial segregation remains within occupations (Bielby & Baron, 1986; Bishaw & Semega, 2008). Neoclassical economic theory suggests that gender-based divisions of labor within families leads women more than men to prepare for and enter occupations that have lower skill and commitment requirements (and thus lower pay). No similar assumption exists for examining racial gaps. Blau and Kahn (1999; 2000) have provided extensive analyses of human capital variables in conjunction with structural characteristics of occupations that contribute to wages (that is, the degree to which occupations are gendered), finding that although human capital variables account for some of the gaps in earnings, structural variables can account for up to 50 percent of the earnings gaps. England, Farkas, Kilbourne, and Dou (1988) using fixed-model regression analysis (in which participants serve as their own controls for unmeasured human capital variables) found no support for the human capital explanation. Rather, they interpreted their findings as indicating pay discrimination for both men and women working in female-dominated occupations. England, Hermsen, and Cotter (2000) measured both general education human capital as well as specialized vocational training to account for differences in wages in sex-segregated jobs and occupations, finding again that workers pay an earnings penalty for working in female-dominated occupations. Penner (2008), studying wage offers in relation to the market salary rate and adjusting for occupational category, found that the bulk of gender and race differences in wage offers was attributable to occupational sorting. That is, lower pay is a characteristic of occupations predominately filled by women and minorities. Bielby and Baron (1986) found that even within occupational classifications, gender segregation was observed (for example, no heavy lifting by women; finger dexterity jobs done by men). Their results suggest that occupation-level analyses are inadequate for studying sex segregation in labor, and that underlying structural bases for bias exist in occupational status (that is, the sex segregation that occurs even within occupational classifications). Gupta and Rothstein (2001) using regression analyses, showed that occupational segregation accounts for more than 50 percent of the wage gap in Denmark; however, even taking into account human capital variables, men and women earn different wages within job cells. Ostroff and Atwater (2003), after controlling for human capital variables, suggested that not only does a wage gap favoring men exist, but also managerial pay is lower when managers' referent groups are largely female, when subordinates are outside the prime age-group, and when peers and supervisors are younger. Carrington and Troske (1996) took a unique approach in their plant-level analysis of earnings gaps. Their analyses indicate that having greater numbers of women in a plant accounts for much more of the gender wage gap than do human capital variables. On the other hand, Aisenbrey and Bruckner (2008), using samples of West German workers, found that occupational segregation was apparent, but they did not account for the gender wage gap. A gap of about

30 percent was evident within occupations. Because statistical discrimination theory is rooted in the neoclassical assumption that women more than men will exhibit greater focus on their families than would men, it is not surprising that a "motherhood penalty" exists. For example, Budig and England (2001) calculated a wage penalty of at least 5 percent per child. Interestingly, the motherhood penalty is greater among married women, and women do not obtain career benefits of a nonemployed spouse (Kirchmeyer, 2006).

Statistical discrimination explanations rest on the assumption that labor markets rationally expect differential productivity on the part of women and men, so it is especially useful to examine the utility of that assumption. Tomaskovic-Devey and Skaggs (1999) used random sample of employees in North Carolina and found no consistent differences in productivity between groups. Rather, their data support "a model of job segregation through stereotyping and social closure by advantaged employees" (Tomaskovic-Devey & Skaggs, 1999, p. 339).

PSYCHOLOGICAL GENDER DIFFERENCES

Thus far, the literature reviewed has focused on demand-side characteristics of earnings gaps. A large literature concerns supply-side characteristics, in which gender differences in individual's predilections help determine the nature of their workforce participation. Aspects of these gender differences that have received attention in relation to their impact on earnings gaps include education and occupational aspirations, feelings of personal entitlement, and gender-role ideology. For example, Shauman (2009) examined education utilization (that is, the match between college major and occupation) in analyses of gender gaps in wages. Although the results were complex, generally speaking, males in male-dominated majors obtained a closer match between their education and occupation. Similarly, Zhang (2008) found that the degree of female dominance in a field (for example, health sciences versus business and engineering) in conjunction with variables, such as selectivity of baccalaureate institution, accounted for as much as 56 percent of the earnings gap between men and women. Roska (2005) also determined that college major, and therefore a career in a female-dominated area (such as human services), accounted for lower pay.

Major and colleagues (for a review, see Major, 1987) have produced a substantial body of research regarding gender differences in feelings of entitlement. Feelings of personal entitlement provide individuals with the sense that they deserve positive outcomes, such as higher pay. According to the entitlement perspective, this sense of deservingness could explain some aspects of earnings gaps, to the extent that feeling less entitled would lead women to expect lower wages and not to negotiate as assiduously as would men.

Major, McFarlin, and Gagnon (1984) found that when given the opportunity to set their own wage rates, women pay themselves less than do men and that women expect to receive lower starting salaries than do men. These effects, however, seem to be confined to the domain of work, rather than outcomes in relationships (Major, Bylsma, & Cozzarelli 1989). The finding that these effects occur with respect to work, rather than relationships, suggests that societal valuing of work over relationships underlies women's sense of deservingness for pay (Major, 1987). On the other hand, Desmarais and Curtis (2001) found that, among more recent samples of employees in Canada, there was little or no gender difference in feelings of entitlement. Both women and men reported feeling similarly underpaid. Individual differences in levels of occupational and career aspirations, however, can account for as much as 16 percent of the gender wage gap (Marini & Fan, 1997).

Consistent with the findings that gender role expectations may lead to lesser feelings of entitlement among women, some researchers have found that the degree to which men and women espouse traditional gender role ideology is associated with average wages. While controlling for human capital variables, regression analyses indicated that traditional gender ideology is negatively associated with wages for white women, and for black men and women, but not for white men. Studies by Keil and Christie-Mizell (2008) and Judge and Livingston (2008) confirmed the negative effects of traditional gender ideology on wages for women.

Although it may be tempting to argue that occupational segregation resulting in earnings gaps reflects the choices made by women and persons of color, the findings that wage differentials exist within occupational categories (Aisenbrey & Bruckner, 2008; Bielby & Baron, 1986) suggest otherwise. In addition, Alksnis, Desmarais, and Curtis (2008) showed that merely labeling jobs as feminine (for example, home economics versus industrial arts teacher) resulted in lower salary projections independent of ratings of the requirements of the jobs (compensable factors). Thus, women's work, regardless of ratings of the job requirements, was associated with lower pay.

UNFAIR DISCRIMINATION IN WAGES

Research regarding wage disparities has been unable to account for the entire gap in earnings between white men, and minorities and women. Analyses using fixed-effects models to account for unmeasured human capital variables (for example, England et al., 1988; Maume, 2004) are particularly powerful in demonstrating that some portion of wage gaps must be the result of unfair discrimination. With a reasonable estimate of the average unexplained gap being about 25 percent of the gap, a nontrivial gap of approximately 7 percent in average earnings must be attributable to unfair discrimination (compare Leicht, 2008).

The current legal and social climate in the United States suggests that most of the unfair discrimination in wages should be attributed to subtle and persistent factors, rather than overt "old-fashioned" racism and sexism (compare Dovidio & Gaertner, 1986). Sociological perspectives on such persistent discrimination (Leicht, 2008; Maume, 2004; Tomaskovic et al., 2005) suggest that privileged gatekeepers control access to the resources needed by women and minorities to attain parity with white men in the workplace. Such gatekeeping includes sorting women and minorities into low-paying occupations at the point of hire and limiting access to social support systems, such as mentors (compare Maume, 2004). In addition, the accumulation of the human capital (for example, training, education) needed to accomplish parity is seen as part of a social system that restricts opportunities for women and minorities (compare Tomaskovic et al., 2005).

Conversely, workplace discrimination cases suggest that at least some unfair discrimination is blatant and overt. For example, Ortiz and Roscigno (2009) considered more than 33,000 discrimination cases from a 15-year period beginning in 1988 using both quantitative and qualitative analyses of the cases. Their quantitative analyses indicated that discriminatory firings accounted for nearly 60 percent of the cases, likely due to the fact that such discriminatory behavior is obvious to the complainant, whereas discriminatory hiring practices, wage structures, and social gatekeeping would be less obvious. Such discriminatory firings, however, certainly would be associated with their workforce attachment, an important contributor to their human capital. Ortiz and Roscigno's (2009) qualitative analyses, conducted on a randomly selected subset of cases, indicate process differences in overt discrimination by race. White women's cases were more likely to focus on discriminatory firing based on their gender (for example, pregnancy related), whereas black women's cases tended to involve discriminatory firings based on more generally hostile environments. Ortiz and Roscigno (2009) provided examples of transcripts of hearings, which detail blatant mistreatment such as the following two examples (Ortiz & Roscigno 2009, p. 351):

> During the time that I worked (while pregnant) the atmosphere at the job was hostile. The Owner male, made derogatory comments about my pregnancy. Certain employees told another employee that if I returned to work after my pregnancy that they would leave the company. While I was out on maternity leave one girl in the office said that if I was not pregnant that she would beat me up.

Also consider the following example:

> I believe that I was discharged due to considerations of my race, Black, because Martha Gregory, White, Medical Biller, had excessive absences and was not discharged. I only missed two days while employed by Respondent and I successfully completed my probationary period. Between September 21, 1998 and December 1998, Moss called me an asshole, referred to me as a child and called me out of my name, but Moss never treated White employees this way. Two days after my discharge, Respondent replaced me with a White person. Prior to my discharge, I was never given an oral or written warning or a suspension.

Psychological perspectives on sexism and racism provide descriptions of the mechanisms that underlie both blatant and subtle expressions of prejudice, with an emphasis on the cognitive processes that generate the more subtle features of those behaviors. Researchers typically differentiate prejudice, which is thought to be a largely emotional reaction to members of a particular group, from discrimination, which generally is considered to be behavior based on prejudice. Underlying both is thought to be the operation of stereotypes, which are cognitive mechanisms used to organize information about easily identifiable groups. Stereotypes contain information pertinent to physical characteristics, ability levels, and personality traits. All three forms of bias reflect tendencies to make judgments based on group membership, rather than on specific, individual information.

A large body of literature has accumulated regarding the social psychology of stereotyping, prejudice, and discrimination since the publication of Gordon Allport's seminal book (Allport, 1954). One of the basic messages from this literature is that biases in thoughts and feelings occur, even among well-intentioned and seemingly unprejudiced people, in an automatic and nonconscious fashion (compare Devine, 2001; Fiske, 2002). Fiske (2002) described the outcomes of this phenomenon for the well-intentioned majority (estimated at perhaps 80 percent of people in Western cultures) as well as for the perhaps 10 percent who are blatantly biased. The blatantly biased are likely those featured in the examples provided by Ortiz and Roscigno (2009), whereas the moderate and well-intentioned could certainly be gatekeepers as described by Tomaskovic-Devey and Skaggs (1999), Maume (2004), and others.

According to Fiske (2002) and others (Devine, 2001), identification of an individual with a stigmatized group (minorities, women) automatically and unconsciously elicits stereotype-consistent thoughts, which lead to biased perceptions and judgments and which are expressed in a variety of everyday behaviors. This priming of stereotype-relevant biases can result in slips of the tongue and nervousness or anxiety in the company of the objects of the stereotypes. Seemingly chivalrous behavior toward women in the workplace also may be an outcome of the activation of stereotypes regarding women. And the tendency to award differential pay rates for male versus female occupations seen in Alksnis et al.'s (2008) study can be interpreted as a function of such stereotype activation. Among the well intentioned, however, stereotype activation can be controlled by metacognitive activity (the act of monitoring one's thought processes) and self-control (compare Devine, 1989; Fiske, 2002; Wheeler & Fiske, 2005). This control over the use of stereotype-relevant information, however, requires motivation to use cognitive resources (self-control and thought monitoring) and can be blocked by cognitive overload as well as by the perception of immediate threats. Even a well-meaning manager, if busy or otherwise distracted, easily could be expected to rely on stereotype-relevant biases in making employment offers. The identification of an individual as a member of an out-group (not like "me") as opposed to a member of an in-group (like "me") can have subtle effects on the judgments of even well-intentioned people. Members of in-groups are responded to more positively than are members of out-groups, and this tendency seems to be pronounced with regard to discretionary behavior. Thus, for the well intentioned, the effect of in-group versus out-group responses generally takes the form of withholding positive affect and rewards from out-group members, rather than conspicuously negative actions directed at members of the out-group. Finally, among the well intentioned, racial and gender biases can be ambivalent, reflecting both positive yet vaguely derogatory feelings, such as benevolent or chivalrous sexism directed toward traditional women (Fiske, 2002). The most common overall effect of such subtle biases among the well intentioned is unintentional exclusion of individuals about whom stereotypes are held. And, such exclusionary behavior can have unsubtle effects on the targets of the exclusion. Logel et al. (2009) showed that interacting with mildly sexist males produced anxiety (stereotype threat) that was manifest in poorer performance on a stereotyped activity. Among extremists, biases are much simpler to identify compared with the well intentioned. Their biases are overt, direct, and conscious, often resulting in clearly discriminatory behavior and aggression (Fiske, 2002).

Biernat (2003), in her shifting standards model of the effects of stereotypes, provides evidence for other and far-reaching effects of stereotypes. The shifting standards model makes an important distinction between stereotype-relevant judgments based on within-category comparisons (subjective perspective) as opposed to cross-category comparisons (a common-rule perspective). In subjective comparisons, the behavior or performance of an individual is judged in comparison with others in the same category. Using this perspective, for example, a woman's athletic prowess would be judged in relation to other women, rather than in relation to standards that cut across genders. The 1992 film *White Men Can't Jump* is based to some degree on this premise. That is, part of the plot revolves around opponents' surprise when a white basketball hustler is able to play as well as his black partner. Use of subjective comparisons could result in a variety of subtle discriminatory workplace behaviors. For example, a black applicant might make a short list for new hires based on subjective comparisons (his application was the best among the black applicants), yet the black application might not be offered employment based on a common-rule perspective that, based on stereotypes, devalues his competence. Similarly, starting salaries may be biased based on the application of subjective and common-rule comparison standards.

CONCLUSION AND SUGGESTIONS

John Stossel (2005), oddly enough, was wrong. A meaningful gap does exist in the earnings of U.S. workers, some of which cannot be attributed to the workings of a fair marketplace. Unfair discrimination in wages exists, and well-documented mechanisms, both sociological and psychological in nature, underlie the discrimination. Employers, however, can take concrete steps to ensure that pay scales, and hiring and promotion practices, are legal and nondiscriminatory. These steps are considered to be an integral component of best practices in human resource management. Paludi et al. (2009) have provided a set of recommendations that outline these steps and the National Committee on Pay Equity (2009) has prepared a 10-point audit for organizations to use in assessing their practices (see http://www.pay-equity.org/cando-audit.html).

In essence, these steps involve the development of systematic recruitment and promotion systems, transparent wage structures, and monitoring organizational climate and culture. The development of job titles and job descriptions that accurately reflect the duties, responsibilities, and skill requirements of jobs is a necessary component of ensuring fair and legal recruitment procedures, promotion policies, and wage equality. Conducting job evaluations and preparing wage audits that take into account both external pay equity and internal pay equity are useful and important. The external pay equity audits should consider the fact that some job categories and some groups of people have been underpaid traditionally, and the internal pay equity audits should be prepared to allow for comparisons of wage structures for women and people of color with men and white employees.

Monitoring the organizational climate and culture through regular employee surveys is a first step in generating a climate in which wage transparency is valued and in which nondiscriminatory hiring and promotion practices are encouraged. These surveys should be anonymous and should be designed to consider the perspectives of all employees. If employee survey results indicate that particular demographic groups or persons in particular job categories perceive themselves to be undervalued or underpaid, job evaluation data and wage audits should be examined, undertaken, or updated. Results of the audits should be disseminated widely as part of a climate of transparency in employment practices. Changes in wage structure, if suggested by the data, can be implemented, and recruitment and promotion practices can be reviewed for their utility and legality.

Unfair discrimination in wages do exists, and this discrimination may be fostered inadvertently even by well-intentioned individuals. Using best practices in human resource management with careful attention to objective data and employee perceptions can ameliorate the negative effects of the discrimination and support fair and legal compensation practices.

REFERENCES

Aisenbrey, S., & Bruckner, H. (2008). *European Sociological Review, 24*, 633–649.

Alksnis, C., Desmarais, S., & Curtis, J. (2008). Workforce segregation and the gender wage gap: Is "women's" work valued as highly as "men's"? *Journal of Applied Psychology, 38*, 1416–1441.

Allport, G. (1954). *The nature of prejudice*. Reading, MA: Addison Wesley.

Alon, S., & Haberfeld, Y. (2007). Labor force attachment and the evolving wage gap between white, black, and hispanic young women. *Work and Occupations, 34*, 369–398.

Bielby, W. T., & Baron, J. N. (1986). Men and women at work: Sex segregation and statistical discrimination. *The American Journal of Sociology, 91*, 759–799.

Biernat, M. (2003). Toward a broader view of social stereotyping. *American Psychologist, 58*, 1019–1027.

Bishaw, A., & Semega, J. (2008). *Income, earnings, and poverty data from the 2007 American Community Survey* (American Community Survey Reports, ACS-09). Washington, DC: U.S. Census Bureau.

Blau, F. D., & Kahn, L. M. (1999). Analyzing the gender pay gap. *The Quarterly Review of Economics and Finance, 39*, 625–646.

Blau, F. D., & Kahn, L. M. (2000). Gender differences in pay. *The Journal of Economic Perspectives, 14*, 75–99.

Budig, M., & England, P. (2001). The wage penalty for motherhood. *American Sociological Review, 66*, 204–225.

Carrington, W. J., & Troske, K. R. (1996). *Sex segregation in U.S. Manufacturing*. Washington, DC: U.S. Census Bureau, Economic Planning and Coordination Division.

Christie-Mizell, C. A. (2006). The effects of traditional family and gender ideology on earnings: Race and gender differences. *Journal of Family and Economic Issues, 27*, 48–70.

Desmarais, S., & Curtis, J. (2001). Gender and perceived income entitlement among full-time workers: Analyses for Canadian national samples, 1984–1994. *Basic and Applied Social Psychology, 23* 157–168.

Devine, P. G. (1989). Stereotypes and prejudice: Their automatic and controlled components. *Journal of Personality and Social Psychology, 56*, 5–18.

Devine, P. G. (2001). Implicit prejudice and stereotyping: How automatic are they? Introduction to the special section. *Journal of Personality and Social Psychology, 81*, 757–759.

Dovidio, J. F., & Gaertner, S. L. (Eds.). (1986). *Prejudice, discrimination, and racism*. San Diego, CA: Academic Press.

Emelech, Y., & Lu, H. (2004). Race, ethnicity, and the gender poverty gap. *Social Science Research, 33*, 158–182.

England, P., Farkas, G., Kilbourne, B. S., & Dou, T. (1988). Explaining occupational sex segregation and wages with findings from a model with fixed effects. *American Sociological Review, 53,* 544–558.

England, P., Hermsen, J. M., & Cotter, D. A. (2000). The devaluation of "women's work": A comment on Tam. *The American Journal of Sociology, 105,* 1741–1751.

Farkas, G., England, P., Vicknair, K., & Kilbourne, B. S. (1997). Cognitive skill, skill demands of jobs, and earnings among young European American, African American, and Mexican American workers. *Social Forces, 75,* 913–938.

Fiske, S. T. (2002). What we know now about bias and intergroup conflict, the problem of the century. *Current Directions in Psychological Science, 11,* 123–128.

Gallup News Service. (2000). Most working women deny discrimination in their pay. Retrieved April 18, 2009, from http://www.gallup.com/poll/3262/Most-Working-Women-Deny-Gender-Discrimination-Their-Pay.aspx.

Green, C. A., & Ferber, M. A. (2005). Do detailed work histories help to explain gender and race/ethnic wage differentials. *Review of Social Economy, 63,* 397–402.

Greenman, E., & Xie, Y. (2008). Double jeopardy? The interaction of gender and race on earnings in the United States. *Social Forces, 86,* 1217–1244.

Gupta, N. D., & Rothstein, D. S. (2001). *The impact of worker and establishment-level characteristic on male-female wage differentials: Evidence from Danish matched employee-employer data.* (Working Paper 347). Washington, DC: U.S. Department of Labor, Bureau of Labor Statistics.

Hill, M. A., & O'Neil, J. E. (1990). *A study of intercohort change in women's work patterns and earnings.* Washington, DC: U.S. Department of Labor, Bureau of Labor Statistics.

Jarrell, S. B., & Stanley, T. D. (2004). Declining bias and gender wage discrimination? A meta-regression analysis. *The Journal of Human Resources, 39,* 828–838.

Judge, T., & Livingston, B. (2008). Is the gap more than gender? A longitudinal analysis of gender, gender role orientation and earnings. *Journal of Applied Psychology, 93,* 994–1012.

Keil, J., & Christie-Mizell, C. (2008). Beliefs, fertility and earnings of African American, Hispanic and non-Hispanic White mothers. *Hispanic Journal of Behavioral Sciences, 30,* 299–323.

Kirchmeyer, C. (2006). The different effects of family on objective career success across gender: A test of alternative explanations. *Journal of Vocational Behavior, 68,* 323–346.

Konstantopolous, S., & Constant, A. (2008). The gender gap reloaded: Are school characteristics linked to labor market performance? *Social Science Research, 37,* 374–385.

Leicht, K. T. (2008). Broken down by race and gender? Sociological explanations of new sources of earnings inequality. *American Review of Sociology, 34* 237–255.

Logel, C., Walton, G. M., Spencer, S. J., Iserman, E. C., von Hippel, W., & Bell, A. E. (2009). Interacting with sexist men triggers social identity threat among female engineers. *Journal of Personality and Social Psychology, 96,* 1089–1103.

Major, B. (1987). Gender, justice, and the psychology of entitlement. In P. Shaver & C. Hendrick (Eds.), *Review of personality and social psychology: Vol. 7. Sex and gender* (pp. 124–148). Newbury Park, CA: Sage.

Major, B., Bylsma, W. H., & Cozzarelli, C. (1989). Gender differences in distributive justice preferences: The impact of domain. *Sex Roles, 21,* 487–497.

Major, B., McFarlin, D. B., & Gagnon, D. (1984). Overworked and underpaid: On the nature of gender differences in personal entitlement. *Journal of Personality and Social Psychology, 47,* 1399–1412.

Mandel, H., & Semyonov, M. (2005). Family policies, wage structures, and gender gaps: Sources of earnings inequality in 20 countries. *American Sociological Review, 70,* 949–967.

Marini, M. M., & Fan, P. (1997). The gender gap in earnings at career entry. *American Sociological Review, 62,* 588–604.

Maume, D. T. (2004). Wage discrimination over the life course: A comparison of explanations. *Social Problems, 51,* 505–527.

National Committee on Pay Equity. (2009). *Employer pay equity self-audit.* Retrieved April 17, 2009, from http://www.pay-equity.org/cando-audit.html.

Oostendorp, R. H. (2004). *Globalization and the gender wage gap* (World Bank Policy Research Working Paper 256). Washington, DC: World Bank.

Ortiz, S. Y., & Roscigno, V. J. (2009). Discrimination, women, and work: Processes and variations by race and class. *Sociological Quarterly, 50,* 336–359.

Ostroff, C., & Atwater, L. E. (2003). Does whom you work with matter? Effects of referent group gender and age composition on managers' compensation. *Journal of Applied Psychology, 88,* 725–740.

Paludi, M., Martin, J. L., Pauldi, C., Boggess, S., Hicks, K., & Speech, L. (2009). Pay equity as justice: United Sates and international perspectives. In M. Paludi (Ed.), *Feminism and women's rights worldwide: Vol. 3. Feminism and human rights.* Santa Barbara, CA: Praeger.

Penner, A. M. (2008). Race and gender differences in wages: The role of occupational sorting at the point of hire. *Sociological Quarterly, 49,* 597–614.

Renner, C., Rives, J. M., & Bowlin, W. F. (2002). The significance of gender in explaining senior executive pay variations: An exploratory study. *Journal of Managerial Issues, 3,* 331–345.

Roska, J. (2005). Double disadvantage or blessing in disguise? Understanding the relationship between college major and employment sector. *Sociology of Education, 78,* 207–232.

Semyonov, M., & Lewin-Epstein, N. (2009). The declining earnings' gap in United States: Multi-level analysis of males' earnings 1960-2000. *Social Science Research, 38*, 296–311.

Shauman, K. A. (2009). Are there sex differences in the utilization of educational capital among college-educated workers? *Social Science Research, 38,* 535–571.

Stossel, J. (2005). *The wage gap: Give me a break.* Retrieved April 15, 2009, from http://townhall.com/columnists/JohnStossel/2005/06/22/the_wage_gap,_give_me_a_break.

Tomaskovic-Devey, D., Thomas, M., & Johnson, K. (2005). Race and the accumulation of human capital across the career: A theoretical model and fixed-effects application. *The American Journal of Sociology, 111*, 58–89.

Tomaskovic-Devey, D., & Skaggs, S. (1999). An establishment level test of the statistical discrimination hypothesis. *Work and Occupations, 26*, 422–445.

Wheeler, M. E., & Fiske, S. T. (2005). Controlling racial prejudice social-cognitive goals affect amygdala and stereotype activation. *Psychological Science, 16*, 56–63.

Winslow-Bowe, S. (2006). The persistence of wives' income advantage. *Journal of Marriage and Family, 68*, 824–842.

Zhang, L. (2008). Gender and racial gaps in earnings among recent college graduates *The Review of Higher Education, 32*, 51–72.

4

Genetic Information Discrimination

Michele A. Paludi

It is absolutely essential that in this time of fantastic scientific advances and discovery, [genetic] information be used for the purpose of preventing, treating, and healing diseases, and not as a basis for discrimination.

—Senator Christopher Dodd

By signing this executive order, my goal is to set an example and pose a challenge for every employer in America, because I believe no employer should ever review your genetic records along with your resume.

—President Bill Clinton

No individual should have to choose between the benefits of genetic testing and keeping a job or health insurance. In some cases, fear of genetic discrimination can be as destructive as traditional discrimination. . . . And the more individuals fear discrimination, they less willing they will be to participate in clinical trial studies that may require genetic testing . . . the very kind of research that could help all of us live longer, healthier lives.

—Debra L. Ness, National Partnership for Women and Families

In 2001, the Equal Employment Opportunity Commission (EEOC) filed suit against Burlington Northern & Santa Fe Railroad for secretly testing their employees for hereditary neuropathy with liability to pressure palsies, a rare genetic condition that causes carpal tunnel syndrome (Hereditary Neuropathy Pressure Palsies, 2009). This syndrome is a repetitive-motion disorder affecting the wrist, affecting more than 40,000 United States employees and costing employers more than $60 million annually in medical claims (DiLuigi, 2000). The railroad acknowledged that they performed this testing on employees who had filed claims or internal reports of carpal tunnel syndrome to determine whether the disorder was caused by their jobs.

During this testing, the railroad's physicians also screened for other medical conditions, including alcoholism and diabetes. Employees were not informed that they were undergoing genetic testing. An employee who refused to cooperate in the testing was threatened with loss of his job. The EEOC suit alleged that the railroad violated the Americans with Disabilities Act (see Paludi, DeSouza, & Dodd, chapter 2 in this volume) by engaging in genetic testing of its employees without their consent. EEOC mediated with the railroad and settled for $2.2 million.

This case was the first genetic information discrimination case brought by the EEOC. Genetic discrimination refers to the discrimination "against an individual or a member of an individual's family solely on the basis of that individual's genotype" (Hodge, 2004; Krumm, 2002). As of December 2009, no genetic-employment discrimination cases had been brought into state or federal courts. Some states had enacted legislation protecting employees from genetic discrimination, including California, Connecticut, New Jersey, and New York. Until the passage of the Genetic Information Nondiscrimination Act (GINA), no federal law had protected against genetic discrimination. Hailed by Sen. Edward Kennedy as "the first civil rights bill of the 21st century" (cited in Wikipedia, 2009), GINA was signed into law on May 21, 2008. According to the EEOC (2009a):

> GINA was enacted, in large part, in recognition of developments in the field of genetics, the decoding of the human genome, and advances in the field of genomic medicine. Genetic tests now exist that can inform individuals whether they may be at risk for developing a specific disease or disorder. But just as the number of genetic tests increase, so do the concerns of the general public about whether they may be at risk of losing access to health coverage or employment if insurers or employers have their genetic information. . . . Congress enacted GINA to address these concerns, by prohibiting discrimination based on genetic information and restricting acquisition and disclosure of such information. (p. 1)

This chapter (1) outlines the focus of GINA, especially as it applies to workplace discrimination; (2) offers social science research on genetic information discrimination in the workplace; and (3) provides recommendations for employers to prevent and deal with genetic information discrimination.

GINA: GENETIC INFORMATION NONDISCRIMINATION ACT

Health Insurance Discrimination

GINA includes Title I, an amendment to part of the Employee Retirement Income Security Act, the Public Health Service Act, and the Internal Revenue Code, which deals with the use of genetic information in health insurance. In essence, the legislation prohibits group health plans and insurers from denying coverage to an individual or charging higher premiums because of a genetic predisposition to having a disease or disorder (EEOC, 2009a). Title I became effective in May 2009.

Ossa (2004), Malpas (2008), and the Council for Responsible Genetics (2009) reported that hundreds of genetic information discrimination cases in health insurance have been identified despite no litigation to date. For example, the Council for Responsible Genetics (2009) reported genetic testing results that indicated a young boy had Fragile X syndrome.[1] The family's insurance company dropped the boy's health coverage, insisting that this syndrome was a preexisting condition.

Genetic disabilities, however, are not preexisting conditions; genetic testing indicates only the possibility of developing an illness or disability in the future. Thus, while scientists have identified genetic markers for several diseases, including cancer, diabetes, Alzheimer's disease, Huntington's disease, cystic fibrosis, and psychiatric illnesses (Bertram et al., 2000; Dinwiddie, Hoop, & Gershon, 2004; Morren, Rijken, Baanders, & Bensing, 2007; Sobel & Cowan, 2000), genetic tests do not always indicate if and when individuals will develop the disease, when they will experience symptoms of a disease, the severity of the disease, or whether the disease will affect an individual's work history (National Workrights Institute, 2009).

Employment Discrimination

Title II of GINA, which became effective on November 21, 2009, prohibits employers of 15 or more employees from using genetic information in all aspects of employment, including recruitment and hiring, training, promotion, and compensation. Title II is thus akin to other protected categories discussed in this volume with respect to employer coverage, prohibitive practices, retaliation, confidentiality, and strategies to prevent and deal with genetic information discrimination (for "reasonable care," see chapters 13 and 14 in this volume). According to the EEOC (2009b):

> The law forbids discrimination on the basis of genetic information when it comes to any aspect of employment, including hiring, firing, pay, job assignments, promotions, layoffs, training, fringe benefits, or any other term or condition of employment. *An employer may never use genetic information to make an employment decision because genetic information doesn't tell the employer anything about someone's current ability to work.* (p. 1)

According to Title II, employers:

1. Must not request information from job applicants or employees regarding their genetic information.
2. Are banned from requiring applicants and employees to take a genetic test unless it is for protecting the individual's safety.
3. Are prohibited from using genetic information about a family member of a job applicant or employee.
4. Must not retaliate against an applicant or employee because this individual was a party to a complaint of genetic discrimination (for example, filed a complaint with their employer or participated as a witness in an investigation conducted by the employer).
5. Must not obtain genetic information from applicants or employees.
6. Must not disclose any genetic information about job applicants or employees.
7. Must prohibit harassment because of employees' genetic information, including a hostile work environment caused by jokes pertaining to genetic disorders, slurs, or epithets, or engaging in threatening, intimidating, or hostile acts toward an individual because they have or their family member has a genetic disorder.

Title II does not preempt state laws on genetic information discrimination (EEOC, 2009b). The EEOC defines "genetic information" as any results of genetic tests of an applicant or employee or of their family member or a disease in the individual's family. The EEOC (2009a) identifies the following exceptions to their prohibition against employers obtaining genetic information from job applicants or employees: When genetic information is—

1. Acquired as part of the process for the Family and Medical Leave Act (U.S. Department of Labor, 2009) in which an employee requests leave for caregiving responsibilities for themselves or a family member.

2. Obtained as part of a wellness program offered by the employer.

3. Acquired by the employer through publicly available documents, for example, newspapers, that he or she has not searched specifically to obtain information about employees' or job applicants' genetic information.

4. Obtained through inadvertently overhearing a discussion concerning the illness of an employee's family member.

5. Acquired through DNA testing for law enforcement purposes but that may be used for quality control purposes only.

6. Acquired through an employer's legally required genetic monitoring program that is in effect to monitor the impact of toxic substances in the workplace.

In these cases, the employer must maintain confidentiality concerning the private information obtained. In addition, employers must maintain a separate medical file from the employee's personnel file to keep confidentiality paramount. This requirement is similar to requirements under the American with Disabilities Act (see Paludi, DeSouza, & Dodd, chapter 2 in this volume). Research by Roberts et al., (2005) indicated that employees perceive their genetic information as more sensitive than other health care information provided to their employer. In addition, these employees reported that they perceive that disclosing genetic information has more potential negative consequences to their employment than other health issues. Their concerns are related to stereotypes individuals hold regarding genetic information and the implication of a potential illness on work productivity and medical costs to the employer, issues that are addressed in the next section of this chapter.

GENETIC INFORMATION: STEREOTYPING, PREJUDICE, AND DISCRIMINATION

As discussed by contributors to this volume (for example, DeFour & Paludi, chapter 5; Paludi, Ellens, & Paludi, chapter 8), stereotypes refer to individuals' thoughts and cognitions that do not correspond with reality (Feinberg, 2000). Stereotypes are organized mental frameworks that helps individuals process information. One aspect of this process is the formation of categories (Katz, 2003). These categories or "schemas" allow us not to have to take each new situation as a new one; we can incorporate the situation into our existing schemas.

Stereotypes occur in the workplace when employees are classified by others as having something in common because they are members of a particular group. Genetic information stereotyping is a process that describes an individual's structured set of beliefs about the personal attributes of individuals with or associated with individuals who have genetically related diseases. There is an emotional component to stereotypic cognitions: prejudice and behavioral components to an individual's cognitions, that is, discrimination and harassment. Individuals' statements and nonverbal gestures toward individuals provide insight into their cognitions about genetic information. Behavioral examples of hostile work environments for employees as a result of genetic information discrimination include slurs or epithets, graffiti, telling jokes pertaining to the genetic disease, obscene and insulting sounds, posters, e-mail, cartoons, and pictures displayed in the work area that create an offensive and intimidating environment, as well as engaging in threatening, intimidating, or hostile acts toward an employee because he or she belongs to or is associated with a genetic disease.

Thus, stereotypes are expressed behaviorally in discriminatory treatment of employees with perceived or actual genetic diseases in terms of wages, pay increases, retention, and promotions. Krumm (2002) offered the following examples of genetic discrimination in the workplace:

> A 24-year-old-woman has been excelling at her job as a social worker. She attends a conference at which Huntington's Disease[2] is discussed. At that time, she disclosed that she is at risk for developing the disease. Shortly thereafter, she is fired. (p. 492)
>
> A man applies for a job with the government. Though he is qualified for the position, the government refuses to hire him because his brother has Gaucher disease.[3] The government reasons that if his brother has the disease, this man also must be a carrier of the disorder. (p. 492)

In 2001, the American Management Association (cited in Human Genome Project, 2009) surveyed businesses in the United States and identified that employers accessed genetic information about job applicants and employees by conducting genetic tests for sickle cell anemia[4] and Huntington's disease. In addition, employers reported conducting workplace susceptibility testing that included genetic testing. Twenty percent of the employers requested family medical histories of their employees. Studies such as this one contribute to individuals' fears that they may experience discrimination with respect to the terms and conditions of their employment. As Miller (reported in National Partnership for Women and Families, 2004) stated: "there is both hard and anecdotal information indicating that employees' fears are not baseless, and that the problem will only get worse as technology develops" (p. 5).

For example, Adya (2005) found genetic information affected hiring recommendations, promotions, retention and other job related factors. Penziner et al., (2007) studied perceptions of genetic discrimination and stigmatization among individuals who had completed predictive testing for Huntington's disease. Individuals reported they perceived they were experiencing discrimination following reporting the findings of the predictive testing in three areas: employment, insurance, and social relationships. Although 90 percent of the participants reported their test results to their employers, they all indicated they would not disclose this genetic information to subsequent employers, as a consequence of the discrimination they experienced.

Several studies have utilized the Integrated Mission System of the EEOC to determine whether employees with certain diseases report more discrimination than others and which organizations are more likely to have complaints filed against them by employees with disabilities. The implications of these studies are significant for employees' genetic information being disclosed to their employer. For example, Rumrill, Roessler, McMahon, and Fitzgerald (2005) studied multiple sclerosis (MS)[5] and workplace discrimination. They reported that individuals with MS were significantly more likely than those without MS to allege discrimination related to their terms or conditions of employment, constructive discharge, demotion, and reasonable accommodations (see Paludi, DeSouza, & Dodd, chapter 2 in this volume).

Van Wieren, Reid, and McMahon (2008) reviewed the EEOC employment discrimination reports of employees with autism spectrum disorders (ASDs),[6] including industry designation, location, and size of companies against whom employees filed complaints. Van Wieren et al. (2008) further compared employees with ASDs and employees with other kinds of sensory, physical, and neurological impairments. Their research indicated that employees with ASDs were more likely to file complaints of discrimination against retail industry employers than did employees with other impairments. In addition, the research found that individuals with ASDs were more likely to file discrimination complaints when they were younger, male, and of Native American or Alaskan Native ethnicity.

McMahon, West, Mansouri, and Belongia (2005) compared EEOC complaint charges of employees with diabetes with employees with other types of physical, neurological, and sensory impairments. McMahan et al. (2005) found that employees with diabetes were more likely than other complainants to encounter workplace discrimination involving job retention issues, that is, discipline, discharge, constructive discipline, and suspension. Employees with diabetes were less likely to encounter discrimination at the hiring stage or in seeking reasonable accommodations for their disabilities. McMahan et al. (2005) also reported that employees with diabetes were more likely to experience workplace discrimination if they were also older, ethnic minorities, or working for small businesses, especially in the southern United States.

West, Dye, and McMahon (2006) reviewed allegations of workplace discrimination filed by job applicants and employees with epilepsy. Their research found that 75 percent of discriminatory behavior toward individuals with epilepsy were the result of postselection issues, for example, discipline, hostile work environments, promotion, and termination.

These studies, in addition to research by Roessler, Neath, McMahon, and Rumrill (2007), provide compelling evidence that employees with disabilities who have a genetic link experience workplace discrimination in hiring, promotion, retention, discipline, and discharge. As Roessler et al. (2007) noted, "because employment is a significant predictor of the quality of life of people with disabilities, discrimination in the workplace that interferes with successful job acquisition or retention is a serious matter" (p. 139). Furthermore, employees with disabilities who are also members of other protected classes encounter dual discrimination (Randolph, 2005).

"GENISM"

Genetic testing has found that certain genetic markers are more common in certain races and ethnic groups than in others (Bowman, 2000; Fergus & Simonsen, 2000; Markel, 2004; Spice, 2002). For example, Ashkenazi Jewish women are more likely to have the BRCA-1 mutation that suggests a predisposition to breast cancer. In addition, the gene for sickle cell anemia is more common in African Americans. African American men are also more likely to carry a genetic mutation that, when in combination with the human herpesvirus-8, heighten's their risk of prostate cancer. Furthermore, individuals of both Ashkenazi Jewish and French Canadian ancestry have the greatest chance of being carriers of Tay Sachs disease.[7]

Wang and Sue (2005) and Ellis (2007) cautioned employers about the interface of genetic discrimination and ethnicity, sex, and other protected classes. According to Ellis, "the reasons of individual screenings could haplessly be used to make general assumptions about entire ethnic or gender groups" (p. 282), what Annas (2001a) referred to as "genism." Annas (2001a) also noted that genism is similar to racism and sexism in that it represents a collective stigma—that is, the application of a negative trait to a group or individual (Shields et al., 2005)—against an individual because of his or her genotype. According to Annas (2001b),

> Preventing genism from taking over where racism left off by substituting molecular differences for skin color differences will not be easy. . . . No matter how great the potential of population genomics to show our inter-connections, if it begins by describing our differences it will inevitably produce scientific wedges to hammer into the social cracks that already divide us. (p. 2)

Thus, focusing on differences may encourage employers to exaggerate differences they do find. One major problem with this perspective is that genes are treated as the explanation rather than as the starting point for scientific investigation. In addition, the tendency is to use research data about genetic-related diseases to formulate human resource policies that would be harmful to ethnic women and men and individuals of color (Deitch et al., 2003). Shields et al. (2005) noted that using race variables in genetic research highlights a methodological problem:

> Biological factors in disease etiology and health outcomes are often over-emphasized relative to social and environmental determinants underlying health disparities. When genetic research results are framed in racial terms, they often have the effect of inscribing racial categories with biological meaning, thereby obscuring cultural, social, and environmental factors also affecting health and behavior. (p. 92)

IMPACT OF GENETIC INFORMATION DISCRIMINATION ON EMPLOYEES

The impact of workplace discrimination on individuals can be applied to the impact of genism as well. Research on workplace discrimination (for example, race discrimination, sexual harassment) has a documented impact on several areas of functioning, including emotional and psychological, physiological or health related, career and work, social, and self-perception (Berdahl & Moore, 2006; Bergman, Palmieri, Drasgow, & Omerod, 2007; Buchanan & Fitzgerald, 2008; Cortina & Wasti, 2005; Danksy & Kilpatrick, 1997; also see Stacey & Lundberg-Love, chapter 11 in volume 2). Victims experience severe distress associated with workplace discrimination. The symptoms become exacerbated when the person is in continued contact with the perpetrator and when he or she is being retaliated against for complaining about discrimination to his or her employer. Furthermore, employees who have "multiple minority status"—that is, race, sex, genetic information (see Nelson & Probst, 2004; Randolph, 2005)—will have more negative outcomes than employees with one minority status (see Settles, Buchanan, & Yap, chapter 7 in volume 1).

Examples of emotional and psychological effects of workplace discrimination include, but are not limited to, guilt, denial, withdrawal from social settings, shame, depression, fear, anger, anxiety, phobias, isolation, fear of crime, helplessness, frustration, shock, and decreased self-esteem.

The following are reported physical and health-related effects of workplace discrimination: headaches, tiredness, respiratory problems, substance abuse, sleep disturbances, eating disorders, lethargy, gastrointestinal disorders, dermatological reactions, and inability to concentrate.

In addition, empirical research has indicated that victims of workplace discrimination experience an impact on their career goals as well as their ability to perform their job in the way they were accustomed. This impact includes, but is not limited to, the following: changes in work habits, absenteeism, and changes in career goals.

The impact of workplace discrimination on social and interpersonal relationships includes the following: withdrawal, fear of new people, lack of trust, changes in social network patterns, and relationship difficulties.

FEAR OF GENETIC INFORMATION DISCRIMINATION: IMPLICATIONS FOR HEALTH CARE UTILIZATION

Nedelcu et al. (2004) reported that concerns about discrimination because of genetic information influences individuals' access to health care. In their study, 13 percent of the 271 physicians and nurses surveyed indicated that because of genetic discrimination they would not encourage genetic testing, even when employees and job applicants had a family history of cancer. When individuals refuse testing, physicians lose the benefit of obtaining complete medical histories and therefore better diagnose and treat the disease.

Financial burden on individuals is great when they chose to pay for genetic testing themselves so their employer will not be put on notice about the results of this testing (to avoid workplace discrimination). Furthermore, individuals who do not undergo genetic testing may face significant medical expenses when they are receiving medical treatment at a later stage of their disease. Such financial burden leads to personal financial bankruptcy, a growing problem in the United States (Himmelstein, Warren, Thorne, & Woolhandler, 2005).

In addition, individuals who fear genetic testing prevent others from knowing their genetic profile. As the National Partnership for Women and Families (2004) stated, "If people with rare genetic markers are afraid to come forward, their stories cannot be heard. But by sharing what they have experienced and learned, they can raise awareness, campaign for funding and research, and help others to understand confusing symptoms and diagnoses, thereby improving public health outcomes" (p. 13).

Smedley and Smedley (2005) further noted that ethnic and racial minorities experience disparities in access to health care and actual care. For example, Latinos and African Americans receive lower quality health care across several diseases, including cancer, diabetes, HIV/AIDS, and cardiovascular disease. In addition, African Americans are more likely than whites to receive less desirable medical treatment, for example, amputations. Disparities also exist in the receipt of appropriate diagnostic testing. As Smedley and Smedley (2005) concluded:

> As long as governments fail to assess racial and ethnic inequality, racialized science will likely attempt to find explanations for racial hegemony in the biology and genetics of the "racial" group rather than in the social attitudes and institutions that perpetuate the idea of race. (p. 24)

PREVENTING AND DEALING WITH GENETIC INFORMATION DISCRIMINATION

Shinaman, Bain, and Shoulson (2003) summarized a symposium of biomedical researchers, legal experts, policy makers, clinicians, insurance company representatives, and community advocates that addressed the potential assault of genetic information on individuals' privacy. They reported that "individuals with genetic conditions harbor significant fears about discrimination" (p. 589). With GINA now in effect, employers must take the following steps to ensure compliance with Title II as well as ease individuals' concerns and fears about the use of results of genetic testing:

1. Update their nondiscrimination policy and investigatory procedures to include prohibition of discrimination and harassment based on genetic information and retaliation for being a party to a complaint. Volume 2 of this book set presents a sample Nondiscrimination Policy (see appendix 2).

2. State their commitment to a discriminatory- and retaliatory-free work environment.

3. Publicize the policy and procedures in the employee handbook on the company's intranet and post them in the human resources office.

4. Facilitate training programs on genetic information discrimination in general and their policy and procedures specifically to managers and employees. Include recommendations for how to respond to inadvertent disclosures of genetic information.

5. Provide new employee orientation programs that include training on genetic information discrimination.

6. Ensure remedies for violation of the policy are clear and commensurate with the level of discrimination and harassment and that they are not discriminatory against individuals who are members of other protected categories.

7. Facilitate training programs on GINA and applicable state laws and the company policy and procedures to investigators of complaints of equal employment opportunity.

8. Train all interviewers regarding legal and illegal questions to ask pertaining to genetic information and how to maintain confidentiality once informed about an employee's family medical history or the employee's medical history.

9. Ensure physicians working for the company in providing postoffer, preemployment medical examinations do not ask questions about family medical history.

10. Ensure separate medical files are maintained from employees' personnel files and that lawfully acquired genetic information is kept independent of other records, for example, performance appraisals, application, amd disciplinary records.

11. Post the updated "Equal Employment Opportunity Is the Law" poster (available from the U.S. Department of Labor, 2009; see www.dol.gov).

12. Review employment records to ensure that they are current with modifications from GINA.

13. Ensure written and informed consent for each request, collection, or disclosure of genetic information.

14. Sanction violators of the organization's policy and procedures related to genetic information discrimination.

15. Ensure equal employment opportunity is not denied to a job applicant or employee because of association with an individual with a disease.

16. Partner with an Employees Assistance Program that may provide support for employees involved in a complaint procedure.

17. Ensure that all employment forms, for example, leaves of absence, work- and non-work-related injuries do not request genetic information.

18. Withhold genetic information about employees in response to a subpoena, unless this subpoena specifically requests this information.

19. Foster an atmosphere of prevention by sensitizing individuals to the topic of genetic information discrimination.

Recommendations offered by contributors to this volume may be adapted for genetic information discrimination, for example, human resource audits, strength-weakness-opportunities-threats (SWOT) analyses, design and evaluation of training programs, components of effective policy statements and procedures, and investigation of complaints.

Table 4.1
Sample Organizations Concerned with Genetic Information Discrimination

The following organizations may be consulted for information about specific diseases and genetic information discrimination in particular.

American Medical Association
    www.ama-assn.org
American Osteopathic Association
    www.oseopathic.org
American Psychiatric Association
    www.psych.org
American Psychological Association
    www.apa.org
American Society for Human Genetics
    www.ashg.org
Biotechnology Industry Organization
    www.bio.org
B'nai B'rith International
    www.bnaibrith.org
Juvenile Diabetes Research Foundation
    www.jdrf.org
National Breast Cancer Coalition
    www.stopbreastcancer.org
National Organizations of Rare Disorders
    www.rarediseases.org
National Workrights Institute
    www.workrights.org
Society for Women's Health Research
    www.womenshealthresearch.org

CONCLUSION

The idea of systemic differentiations based on the genotype of a job applicant or employee rather than their individual merits was made popular in the movie, *Gattaca*. In this movie, wealthy persons selected the genetic makeup of their children; and predictions of mental and physical performance were computed from genetics collected from hair, fingernail, skin, and eyelash samples. Diseases and life expectancy were all calculated via genetic testing. Each individual's health insurance purchasing, job interviews, career development, and romantic involvements were calculated according to the perceived quality of that individual's DNA. One character in the movie, Vincent Freeman, described his life in this world:

> My father was right. It didn't matter how much I lied on my resume. My real resume was in my cells. Why should anybody invest all that money to train me when there were a thousand other applicants with a far cleaner profile? Of course, it's illegal to discriminate, genoism it's called. But no one takes the law seriously. If you refuse to disclose, they can always take a sample from a door handle or a handshake, even the saliva on your application form. If in doubt, a legal drug test can just as easily become an illegal peek at your future in the company.

According to the movie, "we now have discrimination down to a science." Geppert and Roberts (2005) concluded that

> In the wake of the Human Genome Project, the pace of genetic discovery has quickened. New genetic tests and other molecular technology have had immediate and wide relevance to American and European workers. These tests have the potential to provide improved workplace safety and protect workers' health, but they also carry the risk of genetic discrimination including loss of employment, promotion, insurance and health care. Ethical safeguards are necessary if the benefits are to outweigh the adverse consequences of genetics in the workplace. (p. 518)

Krumm (2002) noted that the consequences of genetic testing include a decrease of safety in the workplace, the creation of a genetic underclass, the violation of individual privacy rights, and the use of genetic discrimination as a pretext for other forms of discrimination" (p. 492). The passage of GINA can assist employers in affirming the principle central to GINA and all employment discrimination laws: Job applicants and employees have the right to be judged according to their ability to perform the essential job functions, not on their managers' and co-workers' stereotypes and prejudice.

NOTES

1. Fragile X syndrome is caused by a mutation in the FMRI gene. It is characterized by mental retardation. Physical features in males include a large head with long face, prominent chin and forehead, and loose joints. In addition, language and motor delays are present.

2. Huntington's disease is a neurodegenerative genetic disease affecting muscle coordination and cognitive functions. Its symptoms are most noticeable between the ages of 35 and 44 years.

3. Gaucher's disease is a genetic disease in which a lipid accumulates in certain organs and cells.

4. Sickle cell anemia is caused by a mutation in the hemoglobin gene; it is a lifelong blood disorder.

5. Multiple Sclerosis (MS) is an autoimmune disease in which the body's defenses mistakenly attack normal tissues. Some researchers believe there is a genetic link because MS runs in families.

6. Autism Spectrum Disorders (ADSs) include the following developmental disabilities: autism, Asperger syndrome, and pervasive developmental disorder not otherwise specified. These abnormalities affect communication and social interactions. Genes are considered a risk factor in developing these disorders.

7. Tay Sachs disease is caused by a genetic defect and is quite rare. It results in severe deterioration of mental and physical abilities.

REFERENCES

Adya, M. (2005). Genetic information use in hiring decisions: Psycho-legal possibilities arising from the Human Genome Project. *Dissertation Abstracts International, 65B*, 4334.

Annas, G. (2001a). Reforming informed consent to genetic research, *Journal of the American Medical Association, 286,* 2326–2328.

Annas, G. (2001b, September). *Genism, racism and the prospect of genetic genocide.* Paper presented to the World Conference on Racism. Durban, South Africa.

Berdahl, J. L., & Moore, C. (2006). Workplace Harassment: Double Jeopardy for Minority Women. *Journal of Applied Psychology, 91,* 426–436.

Bergman, M. E., Palmieri, P. A., Drasgow, F., & Ormerod, A. J. (2007). Racial and ethnic harassment and discrimination: In the eye of the beholder? *Journal of Occupational Health Psychology, 12,* 144–160.

Bertram, L., Blacker, D., Mullin, K., Keeney, D., Jones, J., Basu, S., et al. (2000). Evidence for genetic linkage of Alzheimer's Disease to chromosome 10 q. *Science, 290,* 2302–2303.

Bowman, J. (2000). Technical, genetic, and ethical issues in screening and testing of African Americans for hemochromatosis. *Genetic Testing, 4,* 229–231.

Buchanan, N. T., & Fitzgerald, L. F. (2008). The effects of racial and sexual harassment on work and the psychological well-being of African American women. *Journal of Occupational Health Psychology, 13*(2), 137–151.

Cortina, L., & Wasti, S. (2005). Profiles in coping: Responses to sexual harassment across persons, organizations, and cultures. *Journal of Applied Psychology, 90,* 182–192.

Council for Responsible Genetics. (2009). *Genetic discrimination: Position paper.* Retrieved November 28, 2009, from http://www.councilforresponsible genetics.org/pageDocuments/2RSW5M2HJ2.pdf.

Dansky, B., & Kilpatrick, D. (1997). Effects of sexual harassment. In W. O'Donohue (Ed.), *Sexual harassment: Theory, research and practice.* Boston, MA: Allyn & Bacon.

Deitch, E., Barsky, A., Butz, R., Chan, S., Brief, A., & Bradley, J. (2003). Subtle yet significant: The existence and impact of everyday racial discrimination in the workplace. *Human Relations, 56,* 1299–1324.

DiLuigi, K. (2000, October). Help for the overworked wrist. *Occupational Hazards,* 99–101.

Dinwiddie, S., Hoop, J., & Gershon, E. (2004). Ethical issues in the use of genetic information. *International Review of Psychiatry, 16,* 320–328.

Ellis, K. (2007). Genetic determinism and discrimination: A call to re-orient prevailing human rights discourse to better comport with the public implications of individual genetic testing. *The Journal of Law, Medicine and Ethics, 35,* 282–294.

Equal Employment Opportunity Commission. (2009a). *Genetic information discrimination.* Retrieved November 22, 2009, from http://www.eeoc.org.

Equal Employment Opportunity Commission. (2009b). *The Genetic Information Nondiscrimination Act of 2008.* Retrieved November 20, 2009, from http://www.eeoc.gov/laws/statutes/gina.cfm.

Feinberg, M. (2000). *Racism: Why we dislike, stereotype, and hate other groups and what to do about it.* Washington, DC: American Psychological Association.

Fergus, K., & Simonsen, J. (2000). *Breast and ovarian cancer in the Ashkenazi Jewish population.* Retrieved November 25, 2009, from http://www.genetichealth.com.

Geppert, C., & Roberts, L. (2005). Ethical issues in the use of genetic information in the workplace: A review of recent developments. *Current Opinion in Psychiatry, 18,* 518–524.

Hereditary Neuropathy Pressure Palsies. (2009). Retrieved November 28, 2009, from http://www.hnpp.org.

Himmelstein, D., Warren, E., Thorne, D., & Woolhandler, S. (2005). *MarketWatch: Illness and injury as contributors to bankruptcy.* Retrieved November 28, 2009, from http://content.healthaffairs.org/cgi/content/full/hlthaff.w5.63/DCI.

Hodge, J. (2004). Ethical issues concerning genetic testing and screening in public health. *American Journal of Medical Genetics, 125,* 66–70.

Human Genome Project Information. (2009). *Genetics privacy and legislation.* Retrieved November 28, 2009, from http://www.ornl.org/sci/techresources/Human_Genome/elsi/legislat.shtml.

Katz, P. A. (2003). Racist or tolerant multiculturalists? How do they begin? *American Psychologist, 58*(11), 897–909.

Krumm, J. (2002). Genetic discrimination: Why Congress must ban genetic testing in the workplace. *Journal of Legal Medicine, 23,* 491–521.

Malpas, P. (2008). Is genetic information relevantly different from other kinds of non-genetic information in the life insurance context? *Journal of Medical Ethics, 34,* 548–551.

Markel, H. (2004). *Scientific advances and social risks: Historical perspectives of genetic screening programs for sickle cell disease, Tay-Sachs disease, neural tube.* Retrieved November 24, 2009, from http://www.genome.gov.

McMahon, B., West, S., Mansouri, M., & Belongia, L. (2005). Workplace discrimination and diabetes: The EEOC Americans with Disabilities Act research project. *Work: Journal of Prevention, Assessment and Rehabilitation, 25,* 9–18.

Morren, M., Rijken, M., Baanders, A., & Bensing, J. (2007). Perceived genetic knowledge, attitudes towards genetic testing, and the relationship between these among patients with a chronic disease. *Patient Education and Counseling, 65,* 197–204.

National Partnership for Women and Families. (2004). *Faces of genetic discrimination: How genetic discrimination affects real people.* Retrieved November 27, 2009, from http://www.Nationalpartnership.org.

National Workrights Institute. (2009). *Genetic discrimination in the workplace fact sheet.* Retrieved November 28, 2009, from http://www.workrights.org/issue_genetic/gd_fact_sheet.html.

Nedelcu, R., Blazer, K., Schwerin, B., Gambot, P., Mantha, P., Uman, G., & Weitzel, J. (2004). Genetic discrimination: The clinician perspective. *Clinical Genetics, 66,* 311–317.

Nelson, N., & Probst, T. (2004). Multiple minority individuals: Multiplying the risk of workplace harassment and discrimination. In J. L. Chin (Ed.), *The psychology of prejudice and discrimination: Vol. 2. Ethnicity and multiracial identity* (pp. 193–217). Westport, CT: Praeger.

Ossa, D. (2004). Genetic screening, health care and the insurance industry: Should genetic information be made available to insurers? *The European Journal of Health Economics, 5,* 116–121.

Penziner, E., Williams, J., Erwin, C., Bombard, Y., Wallis, A., Beglinger, L., et al. (2007). Perceptions of discrimination among persons who have undergone predictive testing for Huntington's disease. *American Journal of Medical Genetics, 147,* 320–325.

Randolph, D. (2005). The meaning of workplace discrimination for women with disabilities. *Work: Journal of Prevention, Assessment and Rehabilitation, 24,* 369–380.

Roberts, L., Geppert, C., Warner, T., Hammond, K., Rogers, M., & Roberts, B. (2005). Perspectives on use and protection of genetic information in work settings: Results of a preliminary study. *Social Sciences and Medicine, 60,* 1855–1858.

Roessler, R., Neath, J., McMahon, B., & Rumrill, P. (2007). Workplace discrimination outcomes and their predictive factors for adults with multiple sclerosis. *Rehabilitation Counseling Bulletin, 50,* 139–152.

Rumrill, P., Roessler, R., McMahon, B., & Fitzgerald, S. (2005). Multiple sclerosis and workplace discrimination: The national EEOC ADA research project. *Journal of Vocational Rehabilitation, 23,* 179–187.

Shields, A., Fortun, M., Hammonds, E., King, P., Lerman, C., Rapp, R., & Sullivan, P. (2005). The use of race variables in genetic studies of complex traits and the goal of reducing health disparities. *American Psychologist, 60,* 77–103.

Shinaman, A., Bain, L., & Shoulson, I. (2003). Preempting genetic discrimination and assaults on privacy: Report of a symposium. *American Journal of Medical Genetics, 120,* 589–593.

Smedley, A., & Smedley, B. (2005). Race as biology is fiction, racism as a social problem is real. *American Psychologist, 60,* 16–26.

Sobel, S., & Cowan, D. (2000). The impact of genetic testing for Huntington's Disease on the family system. *American Journal of Medical Genetics, 90,* 49–59.

Spice, B. (2002). *Genetics and race: Researchers explore why rates of diseases vary from one population to another.* Retrieved November 28, 2009, from http://www.post-gazette.com/healthscience/20020507hgene0507p.3asp.

U.S. Department of Labor. (2009). *Family and medical leave act.* Retrieved November 20, 2009, from http://www.dol.gov/whd/fmla/index.htm.

Van Wieren, T., Reid, C., & McMahon, B. (2008). Workplace discrimination and autism spectrum disorders: The National EEOC Americans with Disabilities Act research project. *Work: Journal of Prevention, Assessment and Rehabilitation, 31,* 299–308.

Wang, V., & Sue, S. (2005). In the eye of the storm: Race and genomics in research and practice. *American Psychologist, 60,* 37–45.

West, M., Dye, A., & McMahon, B. (2006). Epilepsy and workplace discrimination: Population characteristics and trends. *Epilepsy and Behavior, 9,* 101–105.

Wikipedia. (2009). *Genetic information nondiscrimination act.* Retrieved November 20, 2009, from http://en.wikipedia.org/widi/Genetic_Information_Nondiscrimination_Act.

5

National Origin Discrimination

Darlene C. DeFour and Michele A. Paludi

The lyrics to "America" by Neil Diamond express the dream of immigrants to the United States: freedom, a place to work to save money, an ability to care for their families, and inventions that would guarantee their life being made easier. U.S. immigration history is typically viewed in four epochs: colonial period, mid-19th century, turn of the 20th century, and post-1965 (Archdeacon, 1984; Daniels, 2005; Portes & Rumbaut, 2006). Each epoch included distinct ethnic groups entering the United States. For example, the mid-19th century brought people from northern Europe. The early 20th century saw an influx of immigrants from Southern and Eastern Europe. Post-1965, immigrants were mostly from Latin America and Asia. In 2008, 1,046,539 individuals were naturalized as U.S. citizens. Most of these immigrants were from India, Mexico, and the Philippines (Daniels, 2005). During each period, thousands of people from other cultural groups also entered the United States. Their entry changed the ethnic landscape in the country. For example, this is the first time in history that all segments of the African Diaspora are living in one place (the United States) at the same time (Schomburg Center for Research, 2007). This trend is expected to continue (DeCenzo & Robbins, 2007; Portes & Rumbaut, 2006).

In the 18th and 19th centuries, the term "melting pot" was introduced to illustrate the joining together of many ethnicities, nationalities, races, and cultures in the United States. According to Wikipedia (2009), "melting pot" was "a metaphor for the idealized process of immigration and colonization by which different nationalities, cultures and races . . . were to blend into a new, virtuous community, and it was connected to utopian visions of the emergence of an American 'new man' " (p. 1). And, DeCenzo and Robbins (2007) noted that "organizations took a 'melting-pot' approach to personnel diversity, assuming that people who were different would somehow automatically want to assimilate" (p. 11).

To this end, organizations have facilitated diversity management programs that expected immigrants to adapt their values to fit the values of the workplace in the United States (Ivancevich & Gilbert, 2000). However, this approach equated *differences* in values and culture with *deficiencies*.

Thus, the "virtuous community" or "melting-pot" approach has not been realized (Goto, Gee, & Takeuchi, 2002; Nguyen, 1993). As Nguyen (1993) noted, "immigrants to the United States have been a source of national pride, but also the object of national prejudice" (p. 1). In fact, changes in U.S. immigration policies across the years have determined how welcome immigrants are at any point in time (Deaux, 2006). In addition, in March 2009, the EEOC (2009b) published its charge statistics for the previous year. In the fiscal year 2009, EEOC received 11,134 charges of national origin discrimination. They reported that 9,644 charges were resolved. In addition, monetary benefits for charging parties, excluding those obtained through litigation, totaled $25.7 million. Examples of complaints of national origin discrimination include the following:

> In August, 2009, the United States Equal Employment Opportunity Commission (EEOC) filed an employment discrimination case against the Sahara Hotel in Las Vegas, Nevada. The EEOC claimed that both supervisors and employees at the hotel created a hostile work environment for a kitchen worker who is Egyptian. The EEOC alleged that this employee was repeatedly told to "go back to Egypt."
>
> In *EEOC v. Prudential Insurance Company*, the EEOC alleged that Prudential discriminated against Haitian employees because of their national origin. According to the complaint, Prudential imposed a language policy prohibiting employees from speaking Creole in the workplace. No employees who spoke French, Russian, Italian, Greek, Lebanese, or Spanish were reprimanded.
>
> In 2003, nine Mexican illegal immigrants who served as janitors at Wal-Marts in New Jersey sued this company for failing to pay them

overtime, withholding taxes, and making workers' compensation contributions. In addition, these individuals alleged that Wal-Mart paid them lower wages and provided them with fewer benefits than other employees as a consequence of their national origin. They alleged that they worked seven days a week for at least 56 hours per week and were not paid for overtime.

Since the September 11, 2001, terrorist attacks on the United States, discrimination and harassment of Muslims has increased (Ball & Haque, 2003; Baqi-Aziz, 2001; EEOC, 2009a; Lee, 2003; Livengood & Stodolska, 2004). As Livengood and Stodolska (2004) noted:

> Since all 19 hijackers were identified as Muslims, anger of many Americans turned against members of this ethno-religious group. Muslims in the Middle East, Afghanistan, as well as American Muslims, many of whom resided in this country for generations, became the object of resentment and often outright hate. Public anger was directed not only against Arabs and/or Muslims, but also against anyone who could remotely be associated with people from the Middle East including Indians, Pakistanis, and people from South East Asia. (pp. 183–184)

This anger was exhibited in workplaces within the United States as well. As of December 2001, the EEOC received 166 complaints of workplace discrimination related to these attacks. For example, the Oak Room in the Plaza Hotel in New York City had complaints from Muslim employees against their supervisors alleging they were referred to as "terrorists" and "dumb Muslims." They claimed that they were physically assaulted and blamed for the September 11 attacks. In addition, the employees alleged their work hours were shortened.

In 2009, Merrill Lynch paid $1.55 million and instituted employee training to settle a lawsuit filed by the EEOC. The complainant, an Iranian Muslim and a quantitative analyst, was allegedly fired because of his national origin while Merrill Lynch retained and promoted a less-qualified employee.

Samant (2009) noted that since the terrorist attacks, much of the workplace discrimination case law dealt with an interrelationship among national origin, race, and religion (see chapters by Settles, Buchanan, & Yap and by Paludi, Ellens, & Paludi in this volume). For example, in *EEOC v. General Cable Corp.*, it was alleged that this company discriminated against two employees who were originally from Ghana, on the basis of their national origin and race. The employees claimed that their

Latino supervisor threatened and charged them with undeserved discipline and tried to deny their authorized overtime work. The employees complained to their employer about this treatment, and they were subsequently terminated for "sleeping on the job." Other employees in similar situations who were not from Ghana were given written or verbal warnings.

This chapter discusses the law and social science research regarding national origin discrimination. In addition, human resource management recommendations for preventing and dealing with national origin discrimination will be offered.

LEGAL DEFINITION OF NATIONAL ORIGIN DISCRIMINATION

National Origin was included in Title VII's list of protected classes to ensure that employers did not base their employment decisions (for example, hiring, firing, promotions, bonuses) on preconceived ideas about applicants for jobs or employees based on their country of origin. According to the EEOC (2009a),

> National origin discrimination means treating someone less favorably because she or he comes from a particular place, because of his or her ethnicity or accent, or because it is believed that he or she has a particular ethnic background. National origin discrimination also means treating someone less favorably at work because of marriage or other association with someone of a particular nationality.

As the EEOC (2002a, p. 3) stated,

> [W]hether an individual's ancestry is Mexican, Ukrainian, Filipino, Arab, American Indian, or any other nationality, he or she is entitled to the same employment opportunities as anyone else.

Thus, employment discrimination against a national origin group refers to discrimination that results from an applicant's or employee's ethnicity; physical, cultural, or linguistic traits; and perceptions about an individual being a member of a national group (for example, because of speech or appearance).

National origin discrimination also includes harassment of employees. According to the EEOC,

> Harassing conduct, such as ethnic epithets or other offensive conduct toward an individual's nationality, violates Title VII when the conduct

unreasonably interferes with the affected individual's work performance or creates an intimidating, hostile, or offensive work environment for the affected individual.

Furthermore, national origin discrimination includes the following:

- Accent discrimination
- Required English fluency
- English-only rules

Thus, unless the accent, fluency requirement, or English-only rule interferes with job performance, these violations are covered under Title VII. Furthermore, although Title VII does not specifically prohibit discrimination based on citizenship, it does prohibit using an applicant's or employee's citizenship as a pretext for discrimination because of the individual's national origin. Title VII states that national origin discrimination of employees is extended to all employees whether born in the United States or abroad.

Title VII prohibits discrimination against citizens of the United States by U.S. employers operating companies overseas and by a foreign employer that is controlled by a U.S. employer. Foreign employers operating businesses in the United states also are covered by Title VII.

Finally, Title VII prohibits retaliation against an applicant or employee because they have opposed unlawful national origin discrimination or participated in the complaint process as a complainant, accused, or witness.

In 2002, the EEOC (2002b) issued a guidance, "Questions and Answers about the Workplace Rights of Muslims, Arabs, South Asians, and Sikhs Under the Equal Employment Opportunity Laws." This guidance was developed as a consequence of charges of national origin discrimination the EEOC received following the September 11, 2001, attacks. According to the EEOC, "many of the charges have been filed by individuals who are or are perceived to be Muslim, Arab, South Asian, or Sikh. These charges most commonly allege harassment and discharge."

In the following section, we address empirical research that links stereotypes about national origins to workplace discrimination. Work in this area is fraught with conceptual ambiguity. A review of this literature revealed that researchers used the terms "race" and "ethnicity" interchangeably. In addition, nationality is sometimes conflated with ethnicity. These two may not always overlap (Deaux, 2001). This conflation is not unique to national origin research. This problem exists across various areas of research psychology (Cokley, 2007; Helms & Talleyrand, 1997; Phinney & Og, 2007).

FROM STEREOTYPES TO PREJUDICE TO DISCRIMINATION: TREATMENT OF ETHNIC MINORITIES IN THE WORKPLACE

> Prejudice is a burden that confuses the past, threatens the future and renders the present inaccessible.
>
> —Maya Angelou

As discussed by Paludi, Ellens, and Paludi in chapter 8 in this volume, stereotypes refer to individuals' thoughts and cognitions that do not correspond with reality (Feinberg, 2000; Fiske, 1993; Hilton & von Hippel, 1996). Stereotypes are organized mental frameworks that help us process information. One important aspect of this process is the formation of categories (Katz, 2003). These categories or "schemas" allow us not to have to take each new situation as a new one; we can incorporate the situation into our existing schemas.

Stereotypes occur in the workplace when employees are classified by others as having something in common because they are members of a particular group or category of people (such as Muslims, Italian Americans, Irish Americans, or Arabs). Stereotypes have the following components (Fiske, 1993):

a. Groups that are targeted for stereotypes are easily identified and relatively powerless.

b. There is little agreement between the composite picture of the group and the actual characteristics of that group.

c. This misperception is difficult to modify even though individuals who hold stereotypes have interacted with individuals of the group who disconfirm the stereotypes.

d. This misperception is the product of a bias in individuals' information-processing mechanisms.

National origin stereotyping is a process that describes individuals' structured set of beliefs about the personal attributes of individuals of various national origins (Durik et al., 2006; Fiske & Lee, 2008; Tomkiewicz, Brenner, & Adeyemi-Bello, 1998; van der Slik & Konig, 2006). Stereotypic cognitions have an emotional component: prejudice as well as behavioral components to individuals' cognitions, that is, discrimination and harassment (Tomiewicz et al., 1998). Thus, an individual's statements and nonverbal gestures toward individuals of various national origins provide insight into that individual's cognition about each ethnic group (Blair, Ma, & Lenton, 2001; Greenwald & Banaji, 1995).

Characteristics such as skin color, English fluency, and accents are salient features that individuals use to categorize an individual (Fiske, 1998). Consequently, individuals activate stereotypical traits about these characteristics (Wigboldus, Dijksterhuis, & Knippenberg, 2003). Thus, knowing or assuming an individual is an ethnic minority, an individual's stereotypes may cause them to think "unintelligent," "not dedicated," or "not possessing leadership quality." As Kite, Deaux, and Haines (2008) concluded: "Stereotypes are not simply labels, but are assumptions about traits and behaviors that people in the labeled categories are thought to possess" (p. 206).

Reskin (2000) and Fiske (1998) noted that social cognition theory may explain how ethnic minority and, by extension, immigrant applicants and employees face discrimination. This theory posits that we unconsciously classify people into one of two groups: in-group or out-group. Following the assignment of people to one of these groups, individuals exaggerate the differences between groups and reduce within-group differences. In addition, the categorization of people into the in-group and out-group is accompanied by stereotyping. Individuals attribute the behavior of those who conform to their stereotypes to inherent traits. When the behavior contradicts the stereotype, however, individuals attribute the behavior to situational explanations.

Furthermore, stereotypes concerning members of out-groups are stronger than those of in-group members. As is true with religious stereotyping (see Paludi, Ellens, & Paludi, chapter 7 in this volume), "people are more willing to ignore individuating information about members of out-groups, lumping them all into a single disliked category" (Judd, cited in DeAngelis, 2001, p. 3). Focusing on differences among national origins ignores in-group variability. The overemphasis on differences provides confirmation of the stereotype that national origins are "opposite" and that one's own cultural values are normative and other national origins are a deviation from the norm

Thus, stereotypes can have negative effects. They can cause us to make "mental mistakes." The categorization process causes people to emphasize differences between groups and similarities within groups. Thus, men are seen as radically different from women, African Americans are seen as different from white Americans, and immigrants are seen as different from nonimmigrants.

Discrimination based on ethnic stereotyping (and the interface of race and ethnic stereotyping) is normative for many employees in workplaces in the United States (Lankau & Chung, 2009; Yip, Gee, & Takeuchi, 2008). For example, Lee and Fiske (2006) and Chattalas, Kramer, and Takada (2008) reported that immigrants are depicted as untrustworthy and incompetent. Joinson (2000) noted that employers equate poor English-speaking and writing skills with lower intelligence and less education, thus not capable of performing the requisite job functions. This was also illustrated in research by Markley (2000). She asked 56 individuals who hire for corporations to listen to speakers from U.S. regions reading an identical passage. These individuals were asked to judge the speakers on characteristics typical in human resource management. In addition, they were asked to identify the speakers' regions and selected jobs for each of the speakers. Markley (2000) reported that these hiring managers assigned negative judgments to speakers of accents they correctly identified. Those speakers who did not have an accent were judged as intelligent, cultured, and competent and were recommended for prestigious jobs. Markley found that when the hiring managers could not identify the origin of the speaker's accent, they rated that person more highly than when they could identify the accent.

As another example of discrimination in hiring, Bertrand and Mullainathan (2002) sent fictitious resumes in response to help-wanted advertisements in the *Boston Globe* and *Chicago Tribune*. Approximately 5,000 resumes were sent in for positions in clerical services, administrative support, sales, and customer service. Bertrand and Mullainathan randomly assigned the resumes either a "white sounding name" (Emily, Brendan) or an "African American sounding name" (Lakisha, Jamal). Results indicated that applicants with white-sounding names were 50 percent more likely to be asked for an interview than applicants with African American sounding names. In addition, the discriminatory evaluation occurred across all occupations. This research is further addressed by Settles, Buchanan, and Yap in chapter 7 in this volume.

Tomkiewicz et al. (1998) reported that compared with white employees, African Americans commonly are found in lower management positions and therefore are paid lower wages. Similar results have been recorded with Latinos and Latinas (Browne & Askew, 2006). In addition, Latinas and Latinos who were born in the United States earn higher wages than those born in other countries. Mexican Americans who speak with an accent, however, have been shown to earn less than those who do not (Davila, Bohara, & Saenz, 1993). Forret (2006) and Gentry, Weber, and Sadri (2007) noted that ethnic minority men and women are excluded from informal social networks at work, are not selected to be mentored by senior administrators, and are kept uninformed about organizational politics.

Furthermore, stereotyping associated with career aspirations and leadership potential inhibit white employers from promoting African Americans to senior ranks. Jones (1986) found that individuals treat more favorably others who have the same skin color as themselves. Tomkiewicz et al. (1998) noted that when asked to describe a "manager," middle managers think "white." Thus, because white administrators are the primary decision makers with respect to promotions into higher levels of management, African Americans may be experiencing the expression of these administrators' stereotypes.

In addition, Browne and Askew (2006) noted similar effects of ethnic stereotyping with Latinas. Their work indicated that, because of the segregation of occupations by ethnicity, race, and sex, many jobs become ethnic-, sex-, and race-typed. Consequently, employers assign a particular type of employee with an occupation and rely on stereotypes based on protected classes. According to Browne and Askew:

> Latinos are considered to be hard workers, particularly in comparison to African Americans. These stereotypes may open doors to low-wage jobs, but they do not necessarily produce opportunities for mobility . . . studies indicate that in some workplaces, native-born Latinas are assumed to be immigrants and are therefore passed over for jobs. (p. 244)

As Ostroff and Atwater (2003) concluded, "individuals prefer to associate with and identify with 'winners' . . . the winners are those with status, power and higher salaries" (p. 727).

In some instances, the immigrant group may have better stereotypes applied to them than the native-born group. Researchers have found the following when comparing stereotypes applied to African Americans with stereotypes applied to African Caribbean immigrants.

1. Stereotypes about black Americans are more negative than stereotypes about black immigrants.
2. The content of the black immigrant and black American stereotypes is distinctly different: more broad and more negative.

3. The content of stereotypes showed a tendency for higher consensus for negative than positive traits about black Americans, and the reverse for black immigrants. (Thomas-Tormala, 2004)

African Caribbean immigrants are stereotyped as being "hardworking," whereas African Americans are stereotyped as being "lazy." As a result of these differences in stereotypes, employers might prefer to higher African Caribbean immigrants (Waters, 1999).

Other forms of workplace bias may be hidden. Women of color reported unique blocks to advancement in corporations—that is, "style bias." Style bias is "discrimination tied to characteristics such as hairstyles, tenor of speech, gestures, accents, and wardrobe" (Harris, 2006, p. 26). Individuals are stereotyped as "incompetent" or not fitting the prototype for a leader based on characteristics that are not a part of the position. Immigrants may experience this same bias.

Dovidio and Gaertner (2000) reported that new forms of bias may influence hiring decisions:

> According to the aversive-racism perspective, many people who explicitly support egalitarian principles and believe themselves to be non prejudiced also unconsciously harbor negative feelings about blacks and other historically disadvantage groups. Aversive racists thus experience ambivalence between their egalitarian beliefs and their negative thoughts about blacks. (p. 315)

This bias is more subtle. It manifests only in specific contexts. According to Dovidio (2001),

> [T]hey will not discriminate directly and openly in ways that can be attributed to racism; however, because of their negative feelings they will discriminate, often unintentionally, when their behavior can be justified on the basis of some factors other than race (e.g., questionable qualifications for a position). (p. 835)

Thus, discrimination will occur in situations in which the person can maintain their self-image as nonracist and attribute their prejudicial decisions to other factors. This form of discrimination is resistant to standard interventions (Gaertner & Dovidio, 2005), a concern to which we will return later in the chapter.

The research cited above may partially account for patterns of immigrant participation in the North American workforce. Esses, Dietz, and Bhardwaj (2006) point out that many immigrants are underemployed or unemployed. They maintain that their education backgrounds and other skills are "discounted" by employers. Employers rationalize their decisions by thinking that the potential employee "does not fit the qualifications for the job" or that "they are foreign-trained" (Esses et al., 2006).

Furthermore, ethnic minority individuals, especially women, must deal with microaggressions, incivility, and harassment (Bruce, 2006; Nadal, in press). All of these realities for ethnic minority women and men prohibit career advancement and thus affect wages, social security benefits, health insurance coverage, and saving for education for children and themselves.

In addition, ethnic minority individuals have been reported to experience stress, anxiety, depression, phobic anxiety, hostility, and interpersonal sensitivity as a consequence of their discriminatory treatment (Dion, Dion, & Pak, 1992; Finch, Kolody, & Vega, 2000; Portes & Rumbaut, 2006). Recently, Pascoe and Smart-Richman (2009) reported that perceived discrimination produces heightened stress responses. In addition, discrimination is related to individuals engaging in unhealthy behaviors while avoiding healthy ones. Having a racially or ethnically hostile work environment affects not only the targets of this treatment, but also the morale of the entire organization (Shin & Kleiner, 2001).

ORGANIZATIONAL RESPONSES TO NATIONAL ORIGIN DISCRIMINATION

> This is no simple reform. It really is a revolution. Sex and race because they are easy and visible differences have been the primary ways of organizing human beings into superior and inferior groups and into the cheap labour in which this system still depends. We are talking about a society in which there will be no roles other than those chosen or those earned. We are really talking about humanism.
>
> —Gloria Steinem

Human Resource Audits

In keeping with the recommendations from the human resource management literature (Dessler, 2009; Smith & Mazin, 2004), companies should use an audit checklist to review their anti–national origin discrimination management program. This following audit is adapted from Paludi and Barickman's (1998) recommendations for managing sexual harassment in the workplace. Audits provide information for administrators about how national origin discrimination is operating in their organization. As

Greenberg-Pophal (2008) stated, a human resource audit is "an analysis by which an organization measures where it currently stands and determines what it has to accomplish to improve its human resource function" (in Dessler, 2009; p. 412). Audit questions cover all aspects of the four major functions of human resource management: recruitment and selection, training and development, motivation (performance appraisals, compensation), and maintenance (health and safety, communications, labor relations, discipline) (DeCenzo & Robbins, 2007). Sample audit questions for national origin discrimination include the following:

1. Does the company have a policy statement for dealing with national origin discrimination and harassment?
2. Does the policy prohibit discrimination and harassment from peers and by managers?
3. Is the policy statement well publicized? Is it circulated periodically among all members of the company? Is it available on the company's Web site?
4. How do employees learn to whom they should report complaints of national origin discrimination?
5. Are remedies clear and commensurate with the level of national origin discrimination or harassment?
6. Does the company have procedures to inform new employees about national origin discrimination and harassment?
7. Does the company facilitate regular training programs on national origin discrimination and harassment?
8. What services are available at the company to employees who have experienced national origin discrimination and harassment?
9. Does the workplace foster an atmosphere of prevention by sensitizing individuals to the topic of national origin discrimination and harassment?
10. Does the company state laws with respect to national origin discrimination and harassment as well as federal law?
11. Does the company ensure that security requirements are applied to all job applicants and employees without regard to national origin?
12. Does the company ensure that its dress code policy does not discriminate against employees' national origin?
13. Does the company train its managers and supervisors so they understand their role as "agents" of the company with respect to employees informing them of their perceived national origin discrimination and harassment?
14. Does the company have investigators of discrimination or harassment complaints that speak languages common to its employees?

15. Are the company's policies, procedures, and training program resources available in languages in addition to English?

16. Does the company's Employees Assistance Program have counselors who speak languages common to its workforce?

17. Does the company ensure that corrective action is applied evenly throughout the organization when employees violate the organization's national origin policy?

18. What metrics does the company use to measure the success of its national origin discrimination management program?

The employer must learn from the audit the reason(s) for the disconnect between the company's policies and its practices with respect to national origin discrimination. Subsequently, the employer must correct the problems uncovered in the audit.

Cultural Climate Surveys

The company should conduct organizational cultural climate surveys with employees to determine their perceptions about the effectiveness of the company's national origin discrimination management program (Cooper, Cartwright, & Earley, 2001; Driskill & Brenton, 2005). These climate surveys typically measure organizational values and practices, organizational effectiveness, organizational leadership, communication, and performance management. Climate surveys profile the alignment between the organization's stated mission with respect to national origin discrimination and behaviors of management and employees, effectiveness of training programs, policies, investigations, and corrective action.

SWOT Analysis

To evaluate the strengths, weaknesses, opportunities, and threats involved in developing or improving a national origin discrimination management program, companies should conduct a SWOT analysis (Williamson, Cooke, Jenkins, & Moreton, 2003). This analysis provides information that is useful in matching the organization's resources and capabilities to the competitive environment in which it operates. The SWOT analysis filters the information to identify major issues for management to address. It classifies internal aspects of the organization as strengths or weaknesses and the external situational factors as opportunities or threats.

Using this analysis, the organization can leverage its strengths associated with its national origin discrimination management program (for example, enforcement of policy statement prohibiting national origin discrimination), correct its weaknesses in its program (for example, lack of an annual training program for managers and employees), capitalize on opportunities (for example, assistance from consulting firm), and deter devastating threats to the program's success (for example, failure to have confidential procedures to file a complaint of national origin discrimination).

A completed SWOT analysis may be used for goal setting, strategy formulation, and implementation. This analysis is best conducted with many stakeholders, including the organization president, human resource director, employees, strategic partners, vendors, clients, and consultants (Williamson et al., 2003).

Barrier Analysis

A barrier analysis may be used when an employment issue—for example, policy, procedure, training program, hiring practice, or performance evaluation—limits opportunities for members of a national origin or race or other protected category (Dineen & Bartlett, 2002). Through this analysis, an investigation of the triggers found in the employment issue are identified and resolved. Triggers include a disparity or trend that suggests a need for an inquiry into an employment issue, for example, the lack of promotions for ethnic minority employees or a high separation rate of employees who are ethnic minorities. Barriers may be found in all functions of human resource management, including recruitment, hiring, promotions, training, incentive programs, disciplinary actions, and separation from the company.

Barriers may be institutional, for example, the company may recruit only from within the organization; attitudinal, for example, managers believe that ethnic minority employees are not as committed to their job as are white employees; or physical, for example, training materials and employee handbooks are not available in languages in addition to English, Braille, and so on. A barrier analysis features six tasks:

1. Review practices, policies, and procedures. Documents include handbooks, directives, staffing charts, hiring records, and promotion records.
2. Analyze the source material.
3. Identify triggers from workplace statistics, complaints data, culture climate surveys, and reports by outside organizations.

4. Determine the root cause of the triggers.
5. If the root cause is a barrier, develop an action plan to remove the barrier.
6. Monitor the action plan periodically.

Success may be defined as a drop in the number of complaints of discrimination, favorable responses in exit interviews, increased productivity, and improved employee morale and engagement. A discussion of the application of barrier analysis to discrimination against Asian American and Pacific Islander employees may be found in report by the EEOC (2009c).

In addition, employers should consult the *Diversity Management Toolkit* offered by the Society for Human Resource Management (2005) for additional suggestions for dealing with managing national origin discrimination as well as diversity management in general (for example, focus groups, affirmative action metrics, management and employee evaluations, and training and education evaluations).

Reasonable Care

In keeping with the Supreme Court ruling in *Faragher v. Boca Raton* (1998), following the audit analysis, cultural climate survey, SWOT analysis, and/or barrier analysis, employers should exercise "reasonable care" to ensure a discriminatory-free and retaliatory-free work environment for employees because of their national origin. This "reasonable care," at a minimum, includes the following:

1. Establish and disseminate an effective anti–national origin discrimination and harassment policy.
2. Establish and disseminate effective investigative procedures.
3. Facilitate training in national origin discrimination and harassment in general and in the organization's policy and procedures specifically.

Thus, employers should enforce a policy and procedures that prohibit national origin discrimination and harassment. The policy and procedures should provide the following information:

1. Clear explanation of legal and behavioral examples of national origin discrimination and harassment.
2. Clear description of the complaint process that offers easily accessible avenues of complaints.

3. Assurance that employees' confidentiality will be maintained to the extent possible.
4. Assurance that parties to the complaint will be protected from retaliation.
5. Assurance that the investigation will be prompt, thorough, and impartial.
6. Assurance of immediate and appropriate corrective action when national origin discrimination or harassment occurs.

For detailed recommendations on developing and enforcing each of these aspects of reasonable care, see the chapter by Paludi, DeSouza, & Dodd in this volume. In addition, employers should establish a national origin discrimination and harassment training program that includes resource material in languages in addition to English.

These recommendations follow guidelines offered by the EEOC (2002b, p. 13), which state the following:

Generally, an employer will be liable for unlawful harassment by a supervisor *unless* it can show the following:

- The employer exercised reasonable care to prevent and correct promptly any harassing behavior, *and*
- The employee unreasonably failed to take advantage of any preventive or corrective opportunities provided by the employer or to avoid harm otherwise.

An employer is liable for unlawful national origin harassment by co-workers or non-employees if the employer knew or should have known about the harassment and failed to take immediate and appropriate corrective action.

Additional Affirmative Responses

Furthermore, employers should take the following recommended affirmative steps to ensure proper national origin discrimination and harassment management:

1. Use a variety of recruitment and selection techniques that are not biased toward applicants whose first language is English.
2. Encourage word-of-mouth recruitment through the organization's current employees to replicate the composition of the existing workforce. Use a variety of recruitment resources that are targeted at diverse applicant pools.

3. Establish effective, objective criteria for evaluating job candidates.

4. Establish criteria for evaluating employees' performance that are reliable, valid, and free from bias.

5. Use several interviewers to reduce the impact of discrimination and bias by any single interviewer.

6. Utilize the McDonnell-Douglas Test and the Four-Fifths Rule to determine whether discrimination against national groups is occurring in hiring (EEOC, 2009b; *McDonnell-Douglas Corp. v. Green*, 1973).

7. Learn what employees from different national origins expect from managers, performance appraisals, decision making, implementing change, and building working relationships (Nilsen, Kowske, & Anthony, 2006).

8. Train managers to be aware of stereotyping and hidden biases that may operate in all human resource functions.

9. Measure the organization's return on investment, that is, the net benefit of the national origin discrimination management program divided by the initiative costs (Gates, 2004; Hubbard, 2004; Jayne & Dipboye, 2004).

10. Include training for employees assistance program counselors for working with employees of different national origins, utilizing culturally sensitive counseling (Ali, Liu, & Humedian, 2004; Ball & Haque, 2003; Comas-Diaz, in press; Finch et al., 2000).

11. Train managers and Employees Assistance Program counselors about discrimination against ethnic minorities and how discrimination creates job stress, job pressure, and lack of organizational support (Rodriguez, 2003; Fernandez, Mutran, Reitzes, & Sudha,1998).

12. Offer family-friendly policies, including telecommuting and job sharing for ethnic minority individuals who need to balance family, including an extended family, with their job (Paludi & Neidermeyer, 2007).

Additional recommendations to reach these goals may be found in this volume in chapter 7 on race discrimination and chapter 8 on religious discrimination. Organizations should avoid the "melting-pot" approach to diversity management and instead foster a "multicultural society" approach to diversity management (Ivancevich & Gilbert, 2000) in which employees retain their cultural values and learn to work with each other and value all differences. As President Jimmy Carter is quoted as saying: "We have become not a melting pot but a beautiful mosaic. Different people, different beliefs, different yearnings, different hopes, different dreams."

REFERENCES

Ali, S., Liu, W., & Humedian, M. (2004). Islam 101: Understanding the religion and therapy implications. *Professional Psychology: Research and Practice, 35,* 635–642.

Archdeacon, T. (1984). *Becoming American: An ethnic history.* New York: Free Press.

Ball, C., & Haque, A. (2003). Diversity in religious practice: Implications of Islamic values in the public workplace. *Public Personnel Management, 32,* 315–330.

Baqi-Aziz, M. (2001). Where does she think she is? *American Journal of Nursing, 101,* 11.

Bertrand, M., & Mullainathan, S. (2002). *Are Emily and Brendan more employable than Lakisha and Jamal? A field experiment on labor market discrimination.* Retrieved September 21, 2009, from http://gsb.uchicago.edu/pdf/bertrand.pdf.

Blair, I. V., Ma, J. E., & Lenton, A. P. (2001). Imagining stereotypes away: The moderation of automatic stereotypes through mental imagery. *Journal of Personality and Social Psychology, 81,* 828–841.

Browne, I., & Askew, R. (2006). Latinas at work: Issues of gender, ethnicity and class. In M. Karsten (Ed.), *Gender, race and ethnicity in the workplace: Vol. 1. Management, gender and ethnicity in the United States* (pp. 223–251). Westport, CT: Praeger.

Bruce, T. (2006). Racial and ethnic harassment in the workplace In M. Karsten (Ed.), *Gender, race and ethnicity in the workplace: Vol. 2. Legal, psychological and power issues affecting women and minorities in business* (pp. 26–49). Westport, CT: Praeger.

Chattalas, M., Kramer, T., & Takada, H. (2008). The impact of national stereotypes on the country of origin effect: A conceptual framework. *International Marketing Review, 25,* 54–74.

Cokley, K. (2007). Critical issues in the measurement of ethnic and racial Identity: A referendum on the state of the field. *Journal of Counseling Psychology, 52,* 224–239.

Comas-Diaz, L. (in press). Ethnocultural psychotherapy: Women of color's resilience and liberation. In M. Paludi (Ed.), *Feminism and women's rights worldwide.* Westport, CT: Praeger.

Cooper, C., Cartwright, S., & Earley, C. (2001). *The international handbook of organizational culture and climate.* New York: Wiley.

Daniels, R. (2005). *Coming to America* (2nd ed.). New York: Harper.

Davila, A., Bohara, A. K., Saenz, R. (1993). Accent penalties and the earnings of Mexican Americans. *Social Science Quarterly, 74,* 902–916.

DeAngelis, T. (2001). Understanding and preventing hate crimes. *Monitor on Psychology, 32,* 1–7.

Deaux, K. (2001). Social identity. In J. Worell (Ed.), *Encyclopedia of women and gender* (pp.1059–1067). San Diego, CA: Academic Press.

Deaux, K. (2006). *To be an immigrant.* New York: Russell Sage.

DeCenzo, D., & Robbins, S. (2007). *Fundamentals of human resource management.* New York: Wiley.

Dessler, G. (2009). *Fundamentals of human resource management.* Upper Saddle River, NJ: Prentice Hall.

Dineen, M., & Bartlett, R. (2002). *Six steps to root cause analysis.* Oxford: Consequence.

Dion, K., Dion, K., & Pak, A. (1992). Personality based hardiness as a buffer for discrimination-related stress in members of Toronto's Chinese community. *Canadian Journal of Behavioural Science, 24,* 517–536.

Dovidio, J. F. (2001). On the nature of contemporary prejudice: The third wave. *Journal of Social Issues, 57* (4), 829–849.

Dovidio, J. F., & Gaertner, S. L. (2000). Aversive racism and selection decisions. *Psychological Science, 11* (4), 315–319.

Driskill, G., & Benton, A. (2005). *Organizational culture in action: A cultural analysis workbook.* New York: Sage.

Durik, A., Hyde, J., Marks, A., Roy, A., Anaya, D., & Schultz, G. (2006). Ethnicity and gender stereotypes of emotion. *Sex Roles, 54,* 429–445.

Equal Employment Opportunity Commission. (2002a). *Section 13: National origin discrimination.* Retrieved September 17, 2009, from http://www.eeoc.gov/policy/docs/national-origin.html.

Equal Employment Opportunity Commission. (2002b). *Questions and answers about employer responsibilities concerning the employment of Muslims, Arabs, South Asians and Sikhs under the equal employment opportunity laws.* Retrieved September 17, 2009, from http//www.eeoc.gov/facts/backlash-employer.html.

Equal Employment Opportunity Commission. (2009a). *National origin discrimination.* Retrieved September 18, 2009, from: http://www.eeoc.gov/origin/index.html.

Equal Employment Opportunity Commission. (2009b). *Enforcement statistics and litigation.* Retrieved September 17, 2009, from http://www.eeoc.gov/stats/enforcement.html.

Equal Employment Opportunity Commission. (2009c). *Asian American and Pacific Islander work group report to the chair of the Equal Employment Opportunity Commission.* Retrieved September 21, 2009, from: http://www.eeoc.gov/federalreport/aapi.html.

Esses V. M., Dietz, J., & Bhardwaj A. (2006). The role of prejudice in the discounting of immigrant skills. In R. Mahalingam (Ed.), *Cultural psychology of immigrants* (pp. 113–130). Mahwah, NJ: Lawrence Erlbaum Associates.

Faragher v. City of Boca Raton, 524 U.S.C. 725 (1998).

Feinberg, M. (2000). *Racism: Why we dislike, stereotype, and hate other groups and what to do about it.* Washington, DC: American Psychological Association.

Fernandez, M., Mutran, E., Reitzes, D., & Sudha, S. (1998). Ethnicity, gender and depressive symptoms in older workers. *The Gerontologist, 38,* 71–79.

Finch, B., Kolody, B., & Vega, W. (2000). Perceived discrimination and depression among Mexican-origin adults in California. *Journal of Health and Social Behavior, 41,* 295–313.

Fiske, S. (1993). Controlling other people: The impact of power on stereotyping. *American Psychologist, 48,* 621–628.

Fiske, S. (1998). Stereotyping, prejudice and discrimination. In D. Gilbert, S. Fiske & G. Lindzey (Eds.), *The handbook of social psychology: Vol. 2* (4th ed., pp. 357–411). Boston, MA: McGraw-Hill.

Fiske, S., & Lee, T. (2008). Stereotypes and prejudice create workplace discrimination. In A. Brief (Ed.), *Diversity at work* (pp. 13–52). New York: Cambridge University Press.

Forret, M. (2006). Impact of social networks on the advancement of women and racial/ethnic minority groups. In M. Karsten (Ed.), *Gender, race and ethnicity in the workplace: Vol. 3. Organizational practices and individual strategies for women and minorities* (pp. 149–166). Westport, CT: Praeger.

Gaertner, S. L., & Dovidio, J. F. (2005). Understanding and addressing contemporary racism: From aversive racism to the common ingroup identity model. *Journal of Social Issues, 61* (3), 615–639.

Gates, S. (2004). *Measuring more than efficiency: The new role of human capital metrics.* Retrieved September 20, 2009, from http://www.conference board.org.

Gentry, W., Weber, T., & Sadri, G. (2007). Examining career-related mentoring and managerial performance across cultures: A multilevel analysis. *Journal of Vocational Behavior, 72,* 241–253.

Goto, S., Gee, G., & Takeuchi, D. (2002). Strangers still? The experience of discrimination among Chinese Americans. *Journal of Community Psychology, 30,* 211–224.

Greenwald, A., & Banaji, M. (1995). Implicit social cognition: Attitudes, self-esteem and stereotypes. *Psychological Review, 102,* 4–27.

Harris, W. (2006, March). Hidden bias. *Black Enterprise, 62.*

Helms, J., & Talleyrand, R. M. (1997). Race is not ethnicity. *American Psychologist, 52,* 1246–1247.

Hilton, J., & von Hippel, W. (1996). Stereotypes. *Annual Review of Psychology, 47,* 237–271.

Hubbard, E. (2004). *The diversity scorecard: Evaluating the impact of diversity on organizational performance.* Burlington, MA: Elsevier Butterworth.

Ivancevich, J., & Gilbert, J. (2000). Diversity management: Time for a new approach. *Public Personnel Management, 29,* 75–92.

Jayne, M., & Dipboye, R. (2004). Leveraging diversity to improve business performance: Research findings and recommendations for organizations. *Human Resource Management, 43* (4), 409–424.

Joinson, C. (2000). Strength in numbers. *HR Magazine.* Retrieved September 21, 2009, from http://www.shrm.org/hrmagazine/2000index/1100/1100cov.asp.

Jones, E. (1986). Black manager: The dream deferred. *Harvard Business Review, 64,* 84–93, 95.

Katz, P. A. (2003). Racist or tolerant multiculturalists? How do they begin? *American Psychologist, 58* (11), 897–909.

Kite, M., Deaux, K., & Haines, E. (2008). Gender stereotypes. In F. Denmark & M. Paludi (Eds.), *Psychology of women: A handbook of issues and theories* (pp. 205–236). Westport, CT: Praeger.

Lankau, M., & Chung, B. (2009). A comparison of American and international prototypes of successful managers. *Journal of Leadership Studies, 3,* 7–18.

Lee, T., & Fiske, S. (2006). Not an outgroup, not yet an ingroup: Immigrants in the Stereotype Content Model. *International Journal of Intercultural Relations, 6,* 751–768.

Lee, R. (2003). Workplace discrimination against Muslims, Arabs and others since September 11, 2001. *Journal of Individual Employment Rights, 10,* 273–297.

Livengood, J., & Stodolska, M. (2004). The effects of discrimination and constraints negotiation on leisure behavior of American Muslims in the post-September 11 America. *Journal of Leisure Research, 36,* 183–208.

Markley, E. D. (2000). *Regional accent discrimination in hiring decisions: A language attitude study.* Retrieved September 21, 2009, from http://digital.library.unt.edu/data/etd/2000_2/open/meta-dc-2623.tkl.

McDonnell-Douglas Corp. v. Green, 411 U.S.C. 792 (1973), 80.

Nadal, K. (in press). Gender microaggressions: Implications for mental health. In M. Paludi (Ed.), *Feminism and women's rights worldwide.* Westport, CT: Praeger.

Nguyen, B. (1993). Accent discrimination and the test of spoken English: A call for an objective assessment of the comprehensibility of nonnative speakers. *California Law Review, 81,* 1325.

Nilsen, D., Kowske, B., & Anthony, K. (2006). Culture differences influence expectations of managers. In L. Johnson (Ed.), *HR Magazine guide to managing people* (pp. 40–43). Alexandria, VA: Society for Human Resource Management.

Ostroff, C., & Atwater, L. (2003). Does whom you work with matter? Effects of referent group gender and age composition on managers' compensation. *Journal of Applied Psychology, 88,* 725–740.

Paludi, M., & Barickman, R. (1998). *Sexual harassment, work, and education: A resource manual for prevention.* Albany: State University of New York Press.

Paludi, M., & Neidermeyer, P. (Eds.). (2007). *Work, life and family imbalance: How to level the playing field.* Westport, CT: Praeger.

Pascoe, E., & Smart-Richman, L. (2009). Perceived discrimination and health: A meta-analytic review. *Psychological Bulletin, 135,* 531–554.

Phinney, J., & Org, A. D. (2007). Conceptualization and measurement of ethnic identity: Current status and future directions. *Journal of Counseling Psychology, 54,* 271–281.

Portes, A., & Rumbaut, R. (2006). *Immigrant America: A portrait* (3rd ed.). Berkeley: University of California Press.

Reskin, B. (2000). The proximate causes of employment discrimination. *Contemporary Sociology, 29,* 319–328.

Rodriguez, M. (2003). Job stress and perceptions among Hispanic professionals of prejudice and discrimination in the workplace. *Dissertation Abstracts International Section A: Humanities and Social Sciences, 63* (7-A), 2711.

Samant, A. (2009). Race, religion, and national origin in post- 9/11 employment discrimination cases. *The Practical Litigator, 20,* 45–47.

Schomburg Center for Research on Black Culture. (2007). In motion: The African American Migration Experience. Retrieved April 17, 2009, from http://www.inmotionaame.org/home.cfm.

Shin, S., & Kleiner, R. H. (2001). The psychological effects of working in a racially hostile environment. *International Journal of Sociology and Social Policies, 21,* 59–64.

Smith, S., & Mazin, R. (2004). *The HR answer book.* New York: AMACOM.

Society for Human Resource Management. (2005). Retrieved September 20, 2009, from http://www.shrm.org.

Thomas-Tormala, T. (2004, September). *Black Americans and Black immigrants: The effect of ethnicity on perceptions of race, prejudice and individual success.* Presentation to Hunter College, City University of New York.

Tomkiewicz, J., Brenner, O., & Adeyemi-Bello, T. (1998). The impact of perceptions and stereotypes on the managerial mobility of African Americans. *The Journal of Social Psychology, 138,* 88–92.

van der Slik, F., & Konig, R. (2006). Orthodox, humanitarian and science-inspired belief in relation to prejudice against Jews, Muslims and ethnic minorities: The content of one's belief does matter. *International Journal for the Psychology of Religion, 16,* 113–126.

Waters, M. C. (1999). West Indians and African Americans at work: Structural differences and cultural stereotypes. In F. D. Bean & S. Bell-Rose (eds.), *Immigration and opportunity: Race, ethnicity, and employment in the United States* (pp. 194–227). New York: Russell Sage.

Wigboldus, D. H. J., Dijksterhuis, A., & van Knippenberg, A. (2003). When stereotypes get in the way: Stereotypes obstruct stereotype-inconsistent trait inferences. *Journal of Personality and Social Psychology, 84*, 470–484.

Wikipedia. (2009). *Melting pot*. Retrieved September 17, 2009, from http://en.wikipedia.org/wiki/Melting_pot.

Williamson, D., Cooke, P., Jenkins, W., & Moreton, K. (2003). *Strategic management and business analysis.* Burlington, MA: Butterworth-Heinemann.

Yip, T., Gee, G., & Takeuchi, D. (2008). Racial discrimination and psychological distress: The impact of ethnic identity and age among immigrant and United States-born Asian adults. *Developmental Psychology, 44,* 787–800.

6

Pregnancy Discrimination

Joan C. Chrisler and Ingrid Johnston-Robledo

Consider the following scenarios:

- A woman notices that people speak more slowly and loudly to her when she is pregnant than they did before. She wonders whether they think pregnancy affects women's hearing and cognition.
- A blue-collar worker who is four months pregnant is told by her employer that she has to go on disability because her doctor warned her not to lift anything over 10 pounds. She can still perform every other aspect of her job, and she can do other things for the company as well, but her boss has decided that it is "too complicated" to make accommodations for her.
- A middle manager told by the higher-ups to lay off workers in his unit chooses the pregnant woman and the woman on maternity leave (Alderman, 2009).
- A pregnant teacher overhears students making crude comments about her condition. They joke about what they might see if she went into labor in the classroom.
- A postpartum woman is embarrassed by the horrified expressions on her audience's faces when her breast milk leaks while she is giving a presentation (Moore, 2007).
- A high school principal refuses a teacher's request to have her babysitter bring her infant to school briefly each day so that she can breastfeed the baby

during her lunch break. The principal points to a school rule that prohibits "teachers from bringing their children to work for any reason" (Petersen & Boller, 2003, p. 384).

- A dean asks a newly hired assistant professor how she expects to make her way along the tenure track with "two children in tow."
- Female office workers complain about their manager's habit of calling meetings just before 5 P.M., even though he knows they need to leave promptly to pick up their children before the daycare centers close.
- A man says that he cannot make a meeting because of a child-related activity, and his co-workers think, "What a good father he is!" A woman says she cannot make a meeting because of a child-related activity, and her co-workers think, "She doesn't seem to care about her job."

The anecdotes above are all contemporary, and they are not particularly unusual. A few were published in recent articles, but the others were experienced or witnessed by us or someone we know. It might seem reasonable to expect that the high number of women in the workforce, and the high number of women pursuing higher education to prepare for a career, would mean that Americans are accustomed to interacting with pregnant co-workers and have fully integrated mothers into the workplace. That is not the case, however, even at some workplaces that proudly label themselves as "family friendly." In fact, Ridgeway and Correll (2004) believe that, in the 21st century, the motherhood role evokes more discriminatory biases than women's gender alone does. In this chapter, we review legal attempts to protect female workers' rights, consider reasons why the law alone can not solve pregnant women's and mothers' job problems, discuss the impact of pregnancy-related discrimination on women's well-being and career progress, and suggest ways that individuals, organizations, and public policy makers can ameliorate the situation.

HOW THE LAW DOES AND DOES NOT PROTECT WOMEN

Before the passage of Title VII of the Civil Rights Act of 1964 women in the workforce had little protection. Employers could choose not to hire women, could fire at will female workers who became pregnant, and could deny insurance coverage for pregnancy-related conditions (National Partnership for Women and Families, n.d.). Employers might choose not to hire women for many reasons, but among them were concerns that single women would get married and that married women would get pregnant and then "retire." Title VII prohibits discrimination based on race, color, religion, sex, and national origin; all labor unions, employment agencies, government agencies (local, state, and federal), and employers with at least 15 employees must abide by it. The U.S. Equal Employment Opportunity Commission (EEOC; www.eeoc.gov) enforces this law. EEOC guidelines warn employers that they may not ask job candidates direct questions about family status (for example, "Are you married?" "Are you pregnant?" "Do you have children?" "Do you plan to have children?" "If you became pregnant, would you continue to work?" "If you took a maternity leave, would you come back to the job?"), nor can they ask indirect questions designed to elicit that information (for example, "Is this your maiden name?" "Do you prefer to be called Miss, Mrs., or Ms.?" "Are babysitters easy to find in your neighborhood?"). Title VII prohibits discrimination not only in hiring, but also in all terms and conditions of employment, including wages, promotion, medical benefits, and retirement plans. This legislation was an important step in achieving women's rights.

Soon after the EEOC was formed in 1965, it began to receive inquiries about whether sex discrimination includes pregnancy- and childbirth-related employment decisions (Fuentes, 2008). The Commission determined that employers could not refuse to hire a pregnant job candidate, or terminate the employment of a pregnant worker, who was qualified and able to do the work. The Commission recommended that employers provide a leave of absence for pregnancy-related complications or childbirth and recovery, unless the job is one that cannot be left vacant or filled by a temporary employee. In such a case, in which an employer must replace the pregnant employee, she should receive "preferential consideration" for position openings at a later date (Fuentes, 2008). The U.S. Supreme Court rejected the Commission's guidelines in the 1976 case of *General Electric Company v. Gilbert*. The Court ruled that employers were not required to include pregnancy in their benefits for temporary disabilities, sickness, and accidents (Fuentes, 2008). Women reacted to that decision with anger and disappointment, and women's rights groups immediately began to lobby Congress to pass legislation that would guarantee pregnant women's rights in the workplace. Their efforts led to the enactment of the Pregnancy Discrimination Act (PDA) in 1978.

The PDA is an amendment to Title VII, which makes clear that it is unlawful to discriminate against women "on the basis of pregnancy, childbirth, or related medical conditions" and states that pregnant women "must be treated in the same manner as other applicants or employees with similar abilities or limitations" (EEOC, n.d.). Provisions of the PDA guarantee that employers "hold open a job for a pregnancy-related absence for the same length of time jobs are held open for employees on sick or disability leave," "cover expenses for pregnancy-related conditions on the same basis as costs for other medical conditions," and treat pregnant employees on leave "the same as other temporarily disabled employees for accrual and crediting of seniority, vacation calculation, pay increases, and temporary disability benefits" (EEOC, n.d.). Furthermore, the PDA makes clear that such benefits must apply equally to pregnant women regardless of their marital status (EEOC, n.d.). The PDA was an important step forward for women, but employers continue to find ways around it. For example, firings of pregnant women or women on maternity leave are not illegal if the company is downsizing or if the employer determines that a temporary worker cannot adequately fill the position (Alderman, 2009). In May 2009, the U.S. Supreme Court ruled in the case of *AT&T Corp. v. Hulteen* that the employer could pay women lower retirement benefits than their male co-workers of equivalent seniority because pregnancy leaves the women took before the PDA need not be credited toward pension benefits (Lassow, 2009). The National Partnership for Women and Families (n.d.) recently reported a 39 percent increase in pregnancy-related complaints to the EEOC between 1992 and 2003.

The next major legal advance was the Family and Medical Leave Act (FMLA) of 1993, which was designed to standardize the amount of leave time (up to 12 workweeks during any 12-month period), to extend benefits to family needs beyond pregnancy and childbirth, and to allow men to access the benefits. The law requires employers with 50 or more employees to grant leave to employees who worked at least 1,250 hours in the previous year:

> [F]or the birth and care of the newborn child of the employee; for placement with the employee of a son or daughter for adoption or foster care; to care for an immediate family member (spouse, child, or parent) with a serious health condition; or to take a medical leave when the employee is unable to work because of a serious health condition. (U.S. Department of Labor, n.d.)

The FMLA states that employees must be allowed to return to work in the same or a similar position at the end of their leave. Although the FMLA has been a help to many families, it is not the answer to all working women's problems. It applies only to businesses and agencies with 50 or more employees, so people who work for small businesses are not covered. The leaves are unpaid, which means that many people could not afford to make use of them even if they were available. Furthermore, although the act was designed to apply to men as well as women, far fewer men than women actually request these leaves, and some men have reported that their employers' told them that the FMLA only applies to women (Hall, 2008). Data from the 2000 U.S. Department of Labor report indicate that employees face a number of barriers to use of the FMLA (Casta, 2008). Most employees took time off through the FMLA to address their own serious illnesses; only 26 percent of surveyed employees used FMLA benefits to care for a new baby or to heal from maternity disabilities. Sixty-two percent of those covered by the FMLA were unclear as to how the act applied to them, and 78 percent of workers who needed leave for family reasons cited limited finances as their reason for not taking the leave.

The purpose of the FMLA is to require employers to provide leaves; it says nothing about accommodations in the workplace for mothers of infants once they return to their jobs. For example, many women who return to work after childbirth face barriers in their attempts to maintain their breastmilk supply. No federal law requires employers to provide accommodations to lactating employees, and thus women's rights activists have had to lobby state legislatures to enact the necessary legal protections. According to the National Conference of State Legislatures (www.ncsl.org), 24 states, as well as the District of Columbia and Puerto Rico, have laws that protect breastfeeding mothers in the workplace, although some laws (for example, Montana) only apply to government employees (Mattingly & Brauner, 2008), and the laws vary in what they require employers to provide. The Breastfeeding Promotion Act, which was introduced recently in the U.S. Congress as an amendment to Title VII, was designed to protect breastfeeding women from being discriminated against or fired. It also would require businesses with 50 or more employees to provide breastfeeding women with private spaces and unpaid time to express breast milk. This federal law would encourage employers to acknowledge that many employees breastfeed, that breastfeeding is a valued activity, and that breastfeeding women must be accommodated such that their work requirements and breastfeeding goals are not incompatible. Whether it will make provisions to all women regardless of job title and socioeconomic status is unclear.

According to the U.S. Bureau of Labor Statistics, nearly 70 percent of women with children under age 18, and nearly 55 percent of women with children under age 1, were in the workforce in 2005 (Cohany & Sok, 2007). More women than ever before are staying in the workforce while they are pregnant, and they are working longer into their pregnancies than would have been acceptable a generation ago (National Partnership for Women and Families, n.d.). Thus, it should not be surprising that pregnancy-related complaints continue to come to the EEOC. Examples of PDA cases include charges of hiring discrimination against pregnant employees (for example, Walmart, Dillard's), refusal to promote a pregnant employee (for example, Bean Lumber Company), and termination of employment of pregnant employees (for example, The Gap). One of the most egregious complaints was filed in 2001 against the Washington, D.C. Metropolitan Police, Fire, and Emergency Medical Services, which had required female job candidates to take a pregnancy test as a condition of employment. Several women said that they had been told to seek abortions if they wanted the job (National Partnership for Women and Families, n.d.). Recent law suits include *Martinez v. NBC Inc.* in which a producer asserted that, although her boss gave her permission to pump breastmilk three times per day, there was no appropriate place for her to do so; *Bond v. Sterling Inc. and Kay Jewelers*, in which a woman who returned to work one month after giving birth was told that she had to attend a management seminar out of state but that she could not bring her nursing infant with her; and *Fejes v. Gilpin Ventures Inc.*, in which a breastfeeding mother was unable to negotiate an appropriate schedule with the casino where she was employed as a blackjack dealer (Petersen & Boller, 2003).

Despite the enactment of the important laws discussed above, pregnant women and mothers continue to face workplace discrimination. Some workplaces are not covered by the laws, some laws have exceptions that can be used against women, and some employers are ignorant about the provisions of the laws; however, these reasons cannot explain all of the legal cases and EEOC complaints, much less the personal comments mentioned at the beginning of this chapter. Therefore, we turn to a discussion of prejudice (that is, people's attitudes toward pregnant women and mothers, and their ideas about what is appropriate for pregnant women and mothers to do) and institutional discrimination (that is, traditions, workplace design) and how they affect women in the workforce.

SOCIAL COGNITION ABOUT PREGNANCY AND MOTHERHOOD

Social cognition is a popular area of research in social psychology. It refers to people's beliefs, attitudes, and patterns of thought, which affect their interpersonal behavior and decision making. Sometimes people are aware of their attitudes and beliefs, and can report them if prompted. Often, however, people's social cognition occurs below the level of conscious awareness, and they react in ways they cannot easily explain but that "feel right" to them. Stereotypes, expectations, roles, and biases are all aspects of social cognition.

Social psychologists have determined that women have more than one generic stereotype. For example, stereotype content can vary by age, race, ethnicity, and sexual orientation (Kite, 2001). It also can vary by social role. Studies (Deaux, Winston, Crowley, & Lewis, 1985; Eckes, 2002; Sux & Eckes, 1991) of subtypes of women tend to indicate at least three different groupings: housewives (and women in traditional work roles, for example, secretary), sexy women (sometimes referred to as bimbos or vamps), and nontraditional women (for example, career women, professionals, feminists). The content of these different stereotypes of women vary in a number of ways, but the most important dimensions seem to be warmth (a central component of likability) and competence. Participants in social cognition research have rated housewives as warmer and more likable than career women (Eckes, 2002) and have rated working mothers as warmer, but less competent, than working fathers and workers (both men and women) without children (Cuddy, Fiske, & Glick, 2004).

In a series of studies, Cuddy et al. (2007) have shown that the warmth and competence dimensions can be used to identify four types of groups that elicit different behavioral tendencies from other people: admired groups (warm and competent), hated groups (cold and incompetent), envied groups (cold and competent), and pitied groups (warm and incompetent). Keep in mind that these dimensions are based on people's perceptions of groups as a whole; they are not based on evaluations of individual members of the groups. They may, however, be applied to individuals in settings (for example, job interviews) in which judgments are made based on relatively little opportunity to observe the individuals in question. Does stereotype content affect the treatment of pregnant women? Yes. In a naturalistic field study (Hebl, King, Glick, Singletary, & Kazama, 2007) conducted in the United States, research assistants visited retail stores of various types with a tape recorder. One posed as either a customer or a job applicant, and the other observed and rated the interactions with sales clerks. In one-half of the visits, the customer/applicant wore a pregnancy prosthesis. The store employees often were more hostile (for example, abrupt, rude, short) to the pregnant than to the nonpregnant job applicant, and they often were more benevolent (for example, overly friendly, helpful, physically touching) to the pregnant than the nonpregnant customer. In a recent study (Masser, Grass, & Nesic, 2007) conducted with Australian undergraduates, participants read and rated an application for a job. Each application had a photograph attached; one-half of the participants saw a photograph of a pregnant woman. Participants rated the pregnant job applicant as warmer than the nonpregnant applicant, but they were less likely to recommend that the pregnant woman be hired.

People occupy more than one social role, and these roles can "spill over" and affect how people are perceived in other roles. Gender role spillover is particularly potent, and it has been shown to affect perceptions and expectations of women in the workplace (Nieva & Gutek, 1981). For example, people often nominate female co-workers for feminine tasks such as taking minutes in meetings, hosting a party to celebrate someone's retirement, making coffee in the morning, or bringing food to a meeting. Women who accept these spillover responsibilities may be liked by their co-workers, but they also are seen as having a lower status in the workgroup (Glick & Fiske, 2007). Once pregnancy is visible it is a powerful signal of femininity, and it can make women's gendered roles even more salient to co-workers (Glick & Fiske, 2007). For example, people may believe that pregnant women are delicate, require careful tending, and should be treated gently. This may explain why the store employees in the study described above (Hebel et al., 2007) were so much more helpful to the pregnant customer. In the workplace, pregnant women may be more likely to be helped by co-workers, whether or not they need help, and more likely to be treated in patronizing ways (for example, patted on the arm, called "dear" or "hon"; Glick & Fiske, 2007). If the pregnant woman in question has a high-status position (for example, professional, manager), the patronizing treatment takes away from others' assessments of her competence. Whereas once she might have been perceived as more competent than warm, now she is perceived as more warm than competent (Cuddy et al., 2004), which can hurt her career progress.

People's beliefs about pregnant women play an important role in how they are treated in the workplace. In a recent study (Marvan, Islas, Vela,

Chrisler, & Warren, 2008), college students from Mexico and the United States were asked to list at least five words that came to mind when they read the phrase "a pregnant woman is." Only words mentioned by 50 percent of the sample were used in the analysis. The students listed 32 positive words (for example, generous, beautiful), 27 neutral words (for example, fertile, nonvirgin), and 26 negative words (for example, sad, irritable), which suggests that college students have ambivalent attitudes toward pregnant women. Would people want to hire, or work closely with, a sad and irritable co-worker, even if she is also generous and beautiful? In an early field study of social cognition and pregnancy, Taylor and Langer (1977) showed that strangers stood farther away from a pregnant than a nonpregnant woman. The researchers interpreted that behavior as an indication that pregnancy is a stigmatized condition, but participants also might have stood apart from the pregnant woman to avoid jostling her, thereby showing a benevolent, protective concern for her well-being. In a follow-up study, Taylor and Langer's participants interacted with a pregnant or nonpregnant research assistant, who behaved in either a passive or assertive manner, and then rated her on a series of dimensions. The nonpregnant woman was better liked when she behaved assertively, whereas the pregnant woman was liked more when she behaved passively, especially by women. This suggests the presence of gender-role spillover; people prefer a pregnant woman who acts in a feminine way.

Attitudes can affect people's willingness to work alongside pregnant women or with pregnant classmates. For example, a British survey of office and industrial workers (Pattison, Gross, & Cast, 1997) indicated that women were more positive than men were about the possibility of working with a pregnant woman. Negative attitudes toward pregnant women were connected to a belief that pregnant women are physically limited (for example, invalids, temporarily disabled), which means that co-workers would have to do more than their share of the group's work and adopt a protective stance toward the pregnant woman. In a survey of graduate students at a Canadian university (Cairns & Hatt, 1995) about their experiences of harassment and discrimination, 22 percent of the female students indicated that they had experienced discrimination based on their marital status or because they were pregnant. That survey was not designed to show exactly how the discrimination occurred, but participants reported that their overall experiences of harassment and discrimination came from all categories of people on campus: faculty, support staff, peers, and undergraduate students.

Studies also show that pregnancy can be a source of bias in job interviews and performance appraisals on the job, and this bias is especially likely to come from men (Halpert, Wilson, & Hickman, 1993). A survey (Halpert et al., 1993) of undergraduate students in the United States showed that men were significantly more likely than women to report negative beliefs about pregnant women's "emotionality, irrationality, and physical limitations" (p. 652); they also were more likely than women to believe that mothers should be at home rather than in the workplace and that business owners should not have to provide accommodations for pregnant women. In a follow-up study (Halpert et al., 1993) with a different sample of undergraduates, participants watched a videotape of the same woman (either pregnant or nonpregnant) doing several aspects of a job that involved customer service and then rated her performance on the tasks. Men rated the woman lower than women did in both conditions, but men's ratings were especially low when the woman was pregnant. In a more recent study (Bragger, Kutcher, & Firth, 2002), U.S. college students watched a videotape of a woman being interviewed for a job. The woman was either pregnant or not, she was interviewed for either a teaching position or a sales position, and the interviewer either followed a structured set of questions or engaged in a more free-flowing, unstructured conversation with the applicant. Students rated the pregnant candidate lower for both jobs; however, their bias against her was lower when they watched the structured interview. The researchers suggested that requiring interviewers and performance raters to use specific, rather than global, criteria as the basis for judgments could lessen bias of all types.

The stereotypes about and biases against pregnant women do not disappear once the baby is born. Gender-role spillover also affects mothers in the workplace, as do people's beliefs, attitudes, and expectations of mothers. For example, many people believe that mothers should not work outside the home, especially when their children are young (for example, Bridges & Orza, 1993; Crosby, Williams, & Biernat, 2004). Despite the increasing number of women in the workforce, women still do, and are expected to do, more childcare and housework than men do (Coltrane & Shih, in press), and even people who say that they support gender equality continue to believe that constantly available mothers are necessary for good child development (Crosby et al., 2004). In a study (Bridges & Orza, 1993) of U.S. college students' attitudes toward working mothers, participants had more negative attitudes toward a woman who went back to work after a maternity leave than they did toward mothers who interrupted their employment for several years or toward mothers who quit working entirely. They believed that children whose mothers worked during the preschool years would experience more negative psychological and developmental outcomes than would children of the other mothers.

Researchers have documented "shifting standards" against which parents are judged, that is, mothers are compared to other mothers (and people's "standard" for how mothers should behave) and fathers are compared to other fathers (and people's expectations about how fathers typically behave). It is interesting to consider that, although there has been much discussion over many decades about the effects of "working mothers" on children and society more broadly, the phrase "working fathers" is rarely used (Rhode & Williams, 2007). This suggests that there is only one standard for fathers, but at least two for mothers. In one study of attitudes toward parents (Bridges, Etaugh, & Barnes-Farrell, 2002), U.S. college students read a description about either a father or a mother; one-half of the participants read a description of an employed parent, and the others read about a parent who stayed at home full time to care for the children. The participants rated the target person on several traits and estimated the frequency with which the person carried out certain parenting behaviors (for example, playing with the child, caring for a sick child, soothing an upset child). The participants expected more parenting behaviors from the mother than from the father, regardless of whether the parent was employed. Furthermore, they rated the employed mother as less communal and as a less effective parent than the employed father; the parents who stayed at home were rated similarly on these traits. In another study (Deutsch & Saxon, 1998), the researchers interviewed parents about other people's positive and negative comments about their work and parenting status. Mothers said that they were often criticized for being too involved in their work and not involved enough in their family life, whereas fathers reported being criticized for being too involved in their family life and not involved enough in their work. Fathers who tried to be equal parents reported frequent praise for their involvement in their children's lives, whereas mothers said people often praised them for their ability to combine work and children. Criticism seems to derive from gender-role spillover, and praise seems to follow people's surprise that others do things that they are not expected to do well.

Many people believe that it is impossible for women to combine work and family successfully because the roles of "good mother" and "career woman" are fundamentally at odds. They are at odds because they fall into different stereotype groupings, as noted above, and because both roles are thought to require that individuals "give their all." A good mother should be available constantly to her children, and a career woman should be available constantly to her employer (Hall, 2008). A good father is not expected to be constantly available to his children, so this is another example of the shifting standards to which workers, and job candidates, are held. In another recent study (Fuegen, Biernat, Haines, & Deaux, 2004), U.S. college students read the file of a job applicant who was either female or male and either single without children or married with two children. The participants then rated the applicant on a series of traits. Nonparents were judged by participants to be more agentic and committed to their work than parents were, but an interaction occurred between gender and parental status. Fathers were held to more lenient standards than were mothers and men without children when participants rated the applicant on performance and time commitment and when they made a recommendation for hiring. Stereotypes of the ideal worker as masculine and the good parent as feminine are ubiquitous, and they can influence raters in such a way that motherhood seems to be more detrimental than fatherhood to a potential (or actual) worker's job performance (Ridgeway & Correll, 2004).

Researchers have documented that people's beliefs about and attitudes toward mothers in the workplace influence hiring, promotion, and salary decisions. In one study (Cuddy et al., 2004), U.S. college students read and rated a description of a business consultant with a masters of business administration degree and two "filler" descriptions that were intended as distractions and not included in the analysis. The consultant was either a woman or a man, either a parent or not. Participants rated the consultant on various traits and answered questions about how likely they would be to request the consultant's services, recommend the consultant for a promotion, and recommend that the company pay for additional training and education for the consultant. Results showed that the participants were less likely to hire, promote, or train mothers than fathers. In a similar study (Correll, Benard, & Paik, 2007), U.S. college students read applicant files for a managerial job; the applications each participant read were of the same gender and equally qualified, but one was a parent and the other was not. Participants rated the mother lower than the nonmother on a number of measures, including competence, and they recommended a lower salary for the mother. Men were not discriminated against by parental status. Correll et al. (2007) conducted a field study in which they sent applications from a same-sex pair (one parent, one not) in response to advertisements in a newspaper in the northeastern United States to monitor whether employers were more likely to be interested in candidates based on gender or parental status. Results indicate that mothers were discriminated against, but fathers were not.

INSTITUTIONAL DISCRIMINATION

Distinctions between interpersonal and institutional discrimination are difficult to make, as individuals with biases design and run institutions. For example, a manager or department chair with biases against employees with caregiving responsibilities may not be aware of or support work-family policies or may even discourage women from taking advantage of such programs (for example, stopping the tenure clock). As we mentioned above, pregnant women and mothers can experience systemic, gendered discrimination in the workplace through many different means (for example, hiring, firing, denial of promotion, denial of requests for job flexibility, creating deficiencies in performance to justify family-related dismissals; see www.worklifelaw.org).

Williams (2000) argued that mothers face a "maternal wall" that blocks their full labor force participation even before they hit the glass ceiling that limits women's upward mobility at higher levels of job status and prestige. The maternal wall is confronted when female employees become pregnant, have children, and make use of family-friendly policies, such as flexible work hours (Williams & Segal, 2003). Williams (2008) noted that the "maternal wall at work stems from the clash between the norm of the ideal, or valued, worker and the schema of the good mother" (p. 257). In many ways, the workplace is designed with the assumption that workers do not have children or that those who do also have a stay-at-home spouse. The ideal worker is available to work long hours and maintain a set schedule that can include early morning and late evening commitments. The ideal worker is available for a solid 40 years of continuous work without interruptions for childbearing.

These norms reflect and contribute to both institutional discrimination (that is, structural incompatibilities between employment and parenting, such as inconsistency between work and school hours) and interpersonal discrimination (that is, the assumption that being a good mother and a good worker are mutually exclusive). Given these ideal-worker norms and the resultant structure of many workplaces, mothers in the workforce face many different institutional barriers to fulfillment and success (Hall, 2008). The lack of access to safe, high-quality, and affordable childcare is a major structural barrier to mothers' employment, particularly for single women. An examination of the 10 occupations with the lowest wages in the United States revealed that 57 percent of the women in those occupations do not have any paid sick days (Institute for Women's Policy Research, 2007). Employees who need to attend regular prenatal medical appointments, care for sick children, or heal from maternity-related medical complications may risk being penalized or dismissed from their jobs as a result. Employers also may have mandatory overtime policies that are prohibitive for employees with young children.

Women who wish to breastfeed when they return to work face additional obstacles. The difficulty of maintaining a milk supply while adhering to work and schedule constraints may explain why many women do not breastfeed beyond the immediate postpartum period. In times of economic downturn, women may be even more challenged to maintain a breastfeeding relationship if they are unable to take adequate maternity leave after the birth of their babies. When they do return to work, many women find that there is no private, sanitary place for them to use a breast pump, that their employers will not allow a babysitter to bring the infant to the workplace for feeding, and that their breaks are too short to accommodate pumping or feeding (Petersen & Boller, 2003). Lower income women in the workplace face additional barriers to breastfeeding upon return to work, such as limited ability to unpaid leave, lack of funds to purchase a $300 breast pump, lack of access to storage facilities, and less flexibility and privacy at work. Kantor (2006) argued that breastfeeding women's rights in the workplace vary a great deal depending on their social class. For example, she cited Starbucks as a corporation that provides executives with special "Lactation Rooms" where they can express breast milk in comfortable chairs with free breast pumps and can access the Internet or listen to music as they do so. The women who work at the counter in Starbucks' stores, on the other hand, must express breast milk in the bathroom.

Lack of attention to postpartum women's needs in the United States is no doubt due in part to Americans' ambivalence about breastfeeding. Although most people know that breastfeeding is good for infants, the erotization and objectification of women's breasts in popular culture confuses the issue and leads many to feel embarrassed even to discuss breastfeeding (Forbes, Adams-Curtis, Hamm, & White, 2003; Johnston-Robledo, Wares, Fricker, & Pask, 2007). Some people think that breastfeeding in the workplace (even when done in private) is somehow indecent, and others object to what they see as pandering to the needs of "special interests."

In academe, female faculty face unique challenges to childbearing; the most obvious is the alignment of the tenure-track years with the prime reproductive years. If we assume no major breaks from undergraduate education to graduate school to tenure, a woman is likely to be at least 36 years old (Halpern, 2008) if she waits until after tenure to begin a family, older than most people's perceived ideal age to begin childbearing. The structure of the tenure-clock in academe can be construed as institutional discrimination against women, as it was designed at a time when there were few women (and no mothers) on faculties, and little has been done since then to make it more accommodating. Flexible hours and greater autonomy might facilitate work-family integration for female faculty. However, some authors (Townsley & Broadfoot, 2008) have argued that such flexibility contributes to a temporal and spatial boundary problem wherein the demands of work and family are in direct conflict for attention. Scholarly productivity, depending on the discipline, requires many long hours in the laboratory, field, or office; travel to archives or conferences; and a constant stream of published work, all of which may be difficult to achieve while raising young children. Assumptions that faculty have stay-at-home spouses can lead to expectations that one can simply work around the clock or attend faculty or committee meetings scheduled outside of daycare or school hours. Similar problems arise for women in other professional and managerial positions when their work role spills over into family time. The introduction of communication technologies (for example, e-mail, beepers, cell phones, blackberries) has ramped up the expectation that high-level employees are in constant touch with colleagues and clients.

CONSEQUENCES OF DISCRIMINATION

Women often face a significant financial penalty when they combine employment with motherhood. This wage penalty, known as the "family wage gap," "mommy gap," or "motherhood penalty," is a complex phenomenon, and its many potential causes are difficult to disentangle. Economists and sociologists estimate that motherhood partially, and increasingly, explains the wage gap between women and men (Williams, 2008); the gender wage gap is shrinking, whereas the mommy gap is widening (Waldfogel, 1998). Mothers earn, on average, 60 percent of the salary of women who are not mothers (Anderson, Binder, & Krause, 2002). Budig and England (2001) estimated the motherhood penalty as approximately 7 percent per child. This pay gap increases over time and with each additional child (Avellar & Smock, 2003). The penalty is significantly larger among women with a high school degree than among women who do not finish high school and women with a college degree (Anderson, Binder, & Krause, 2003); these women might suffer financially the most, not because they put less effort into their work, but because they are more likely to be in lower-level positions that are constrained by a rigid schedule that is incompatible with mothering. Budig and England (2001) concluded that only one-third of the motherhood penalty is explained by the fact that mothers have lower levels of seniority and job experience as a result of part-time work or breaks in employment. They speculated that the remaining variance may be explained by differences in productivity or as a result of discrimination, both of which can be difficult to measure. Estimates calculated over time indicate that women will earn only 38 percent of what men earn during their prime earning years (Rose & Hartmann, 2004). Crittenden (2001) referred to this lifetime loss as a "mommy tax," and she cited research that shows that, for a college-educated woman, the loss can be as high as $1 million. Crittenden argued that the ultimate mommy tax might be the avoidance of wanted childbearing due to finances or work constraints.

In their survey of University of California system faculty who were mothers and fathers, Mason and Goulden (2004) found that 38 percent of the women reported that they had fewer children than they wanted. In another study, based on their review of a database of 160,000 doctoral recipients, Mason and Goulden (2002) found that only 30 percent of women working at research-intensive universities became mothers and that mothers were twice as likely as fathers to work in part-time or non-tenure-track full-time positions. The most striking finding from that data set was that men who had children within five years of their doctorate (most likely while on the tenure track) were 38 percent more likely than women who had children during the same time to achieve tenure. Women who had children early in their careers were 24 percent less likely than women with later or no children to achieve tenure. This pattern held across disciplines and institutions. Dickson (2008) studied the consequences of family-responsibilities discrimination (FRD) among almost 500 people ages 21 to 40 who were full-time employees and part-time university students in the United States. She found that perceptions of FRD among employees were strongly associated with lower organizational attachment and job satisfaction, lower use of benefits, and higher job turnover.

How are employees treated when they do make use of family-friendly policies? Unfortunately, these policies may exacerbate the problems that they are designed to solve. Mason and Goulden (2004) found that 51 percent of the eligible mothers in their sample of University of California faculty did not take advantage of teaching-relief policies because they were afraid of the negative repercussions for their careers. Mason (2009) argued that the tenure track, as currently conceptualized and experienced, may be a trap for mothers (and some fathers) and that a more flexible tenure-track system would remove some of the barriers to equity for female faculty. However, others are concerned that women's careers may be stalled or derailed by policies, such as stopping the tenure track, particularly if female faculty are evaluated by members of tenure and promotion committees who are socially conservative and/or did not need to use such provisions themselves (June, 2009). Additional barriers to the use of family-friendly policies include stigma and resentment among colleagues (Hegtvedt, Clay-Warner, & Ferrigno, 2002).

To sidestep many of the negative consequences of both institutional and interpersonal discrimination against employed mothers, women may engage in bias-avoidance behaviors. Bias-avoidance strategies, which researchers thus far have explored primarily among faculty, are behaviors that allow employees to avoid caregiving bias that might interfere with career success (Drago, Colbeck, Hollenshead, & Sullivan, 2008). These strategies include productive forms, such as minimizing childrearing or being strategic about the timing of births, as well as unproductive forms, such as lying about one's reason for missing a meeting or for missing children's events to avoid the appearance of being insufficiently committed to work or family. Work-family policies could eliminate these kinds of survival tactics, which ultimately undermine gender equity. In a study of the complex relationship between faculty members' bias-avoidance strategies and the availability of work-family policies in 507 universities, Drago et al. (2008) found that official policies do little to eliminate bias-avoidance behaviors. The researchers argued that, in addition to family-friendly policies, other aspects of academia, such as deans' and department chairs' beliefs and perceptions, must change to accommodate faculty parents. Dickson (2008) came to a similar conclusion based on her study of employees' perceptions of FRD. Family-supportive benefits (for example, flexible work schedules) did not predict lower levels of perceived discrimination as strongly as did employees' beliefs that they had family-supportive supervisors. Employees who work for organizations perceived as supportive of family-friendly policies also have been shown to express less resentment toward colleagues who take advantage of such policies (Hegtvedt et al., 2002). These findings have important implications for the training of supervisors in ways to assist mothers in their attempts to learn about and utilize work-family policies and how to create an organizational culture that does not penalize women who make use of such policies.

STRATEGIES FOR FACILITATING SUCCESSFUL WORK-FAMILY INTEGRATION

Unlike in many other industrial nations around the world, U.S. workplaces have not kept pace with the needs of employees and their families in the 21st century. The traditional model of primary breadwinner and stay-at-home-parent is, and always has been, a relative rarity. Yet, as we have discussed, the structure of the workplace is best suited for this limited arrangement. As a result, many employees, primarily women, are faced with difficult and constrained choices about how best to balance work and family. Even the metaphor of work-family balance is problematic, as it suggests that women should strive for ways to manage tasks, on an individual basis, in two incompatible domains. Much of the work-family research is dominated by a conflict model: The researchers examine negative outcomes and assume that women have a finite amount of resources with which to manage multiple roles (Parasuraman & Greenhaus, 2002). It might make more sense to conceptualize work-family "balance" as work-family "integration" or "facilitation" (Wayne, Grzywacz, Carlson, & Kacmar, 2007), whereby a combination of individual and societal solutions make work and family life more compatible, fulfilling, and productive.

Mothers work for many different reasons. Whether women work out of necessity, desire, or both, researchers have demonstrated many positive effects of employment (Gottfried & Gottfried, 2008). It is critical to individual mothers, their families, the labor market, and society more broadly that workplaces and the government respond to the varied needs of the majority of women who combine parenting and other family responsibilities with employment outside the home. In this section, we offer suggestions for work-family integration that would benefit mothers, as well as fathers and other individuals with family caregiving responsibilities, across the socioeconomic spectrum.

In a study (Gornick, Meyers, & Ross, 1998) of the public policies relevant to family responsibilities (for example, paid leave, tax relief for childcare, guaranteed access to childcare) in 14 industrial countries, a strong, consistent relationship existed between the presence of such policies and mothers' employment patterns. Women at work in countries with widespread support for work-family integration (for example, Finland, France, Sweden) reported less employment disruption than did women at work in countries without such support (for example, Australia, the United Kingdom, the United States).

Williams and Cooper (2004) generated a list of ways to address through public policy the myriad conflicts faced by mothers and other caregivers in the labor force. Five of these suggestions concern schedules, because the limited amount of flexibility in work hours that most employees have makes it difficult to manage both a family and paid employment. According to a report from the Workplace Flexibility 2010 Initiative (Georgetown University Law Center, n.d.), flexibility should apply to the scheduling of hours, the number of hours, and the location of work. Based on data from many different sources, the authors of that report noted that only 38.8 percent of workers have a formal flexible work schedule (that is, flextime) and that 37 percent of employees who work part time would prefer to work full time. Given that Americans work more hours per week than people do in most other industrial countries (Gornick & Meyers, 2003), several scholars (Williams & Cooper, 2004) have made the case for a full-time schedule to be defined as a 35-hour workweek. The authors of the Workplace Flexibility 2010 Initiative report concluded that employees with flexible work schedules report being more satisfied with and committed to their jobs than do other employees. Flexibility also may reduce unplanned absenteeism, tardiness, and employee turnover as well as assist in the recruitment of valuable employees. Glass and Riley (1998) found that 300 pregnant employees identified flexible work hours as one of the three most important resources they needed to manage their job and family demands.

Some may assume that cutting one's hours down to part time is one of the most obvious solutions to work-family integration. Many women, however, cannot afford to work part time, might lose valuable benefits such as unemployment or heath insurance, may not want to work part time, or may hold positions that cannot realistically be done part time. Autonomy and control over one's work schedule and career pace may be the most important resources for employees with family caregiving responsibilities (Glass & Finley, 2002). Those who can and do choose to work part time would benefit greatly from policies that would protect them from discrimination and afford them benefits such as health insurance (Williams & Cooper, 2004).

With respect to various forms of paid leave, findings from a study of working conditions for families in 173 countries show that the United States lags far behind many other nations (Heymann, Earle, & Hayes, 2007). For example, 97 percent of the countries studied offer paid leave to new mothers, and the modal number of weeks is 12 to 16. The only nations other than the United States that do not provide paid maternity leave were Lesotho, Liberia, Papua New Guinea, and Swaziland. Canada provides paid maternity leave as part of its employment insurance program, and the amount of paid leave was recently doubled to a total of 50 weeks (Baker & Milligan, 2008). Baker and Milligan (2008) concluded that this reform allowed the number of women who reached the six-month goal of breastfeeding to increase by 40 percent. They suggested that this extension of paid leave can affect maternal and child health and bonding, as well as women's labor market outcomes. According to a review of the 100 most family-friendly employers, only 52 percent provided women with six weeks or less of paid maternity leave (Institute for Women's Policy Research, 2007). Several U.S. states (California, New Jersey, and Rhode Island) have instated temporary disability insurance programs to provide employees with income to cover leave following short-term disability, which encompasses pregnancy and childbirth (Institute for Women's Policy Research, 2007). Paid sick leave is available in 145 of the countries studied by Heymann et al. (2007); 98 countries offer 31 or more days. According to a report from the Institute for Women's Policy Research (2007), 53 percent of mothers in the workforce are unable to take time off to care for children who are sick, and those who can typically are not paid for those days. Paid sick leave should allow employees to take time off, without penalty, to manage their own illness, to attend medical appointments, and to care for the health needs of family members. Williams and Cooper (2004) proposed that the FMLA be extended to workplaces with fewer than 50 employees, that the leave be paid, and that employers be required to offer one week of paid sick leave. President Barack Obama listed all three of those initiatives as part of his plan to support working families (www.barackobama.com/issues/family/). It is unclear, however, whether the U.S. federal government will be able to act on the initiatives, given the current economy.

Clearly, access to safe, affordable childcare is central to work-family integration, especially for single mothers. Subsidies for childcare, increased funding for after-school care, and a universal preschool program would be of great assistance in facilitating work-family integration (Williams & Cooper, 2004).

Another important suggestion to aid mothers in the workplace is support for breastfeeding. According to the report by Heymann et al. (2007), 107 countries have legislation to protect breastfeeding women in the workplace, and 73 of them offer paid breaks. Although some U.S. states have similar legislation, women in many states are not yet afforded these protections. The Centers for Disease Control and Prevention (Shealy, Li, Benton-Davis, & Grummer-Strawn, 2005) has published a guide to breastfeeding interventions that includes a substantial section on ways to support breastfeeding women in the workplace. Examples of resources include the following: private space for expressing milk, flexible scheduling, extended maternity leave, childcare, lactation consultants, and access to high-quality breast pumps. Listed in the document are examples of various breastfeeding- support programs designed to eliminate barriers to breastfeeding for women in the workforce. A noteworthy example is *The Business Case for Breastfeeding*, a national workplace initiative, launched by the Maternal and Child Health Bureau of the U.S. Health Resources and Services Administration. The case presents research findings to convince employers that supporting breastfeeding employees is good for business (for example, more satisfied employees, higher retention rates, lower sick time rates, lower health insurance costs), and it provides basic guidelines about the best ways to support lactating employees (www.womenshealth.gov). The U.S. Breastfeeding Committee (www.usbreastfeeding.org), a national nonprofit organization, is another valuable resource for companies interested in accommodating lactating employees. Their Web site includes information about various programs, reports, and legislation available to assist employees and employers with breastfeeding-support issues in the workplace.

Clearly, public policy is important, but questions remain regarding some policies' effectiveness and accessibility. Glass and Finley (2002) conducted an extensive literature review of 29 studies of the effectiveness of three family-responsive policies: flextime, parental leave, and childcare. They argued that findings from this body of work are inconclusive because of numerous methodological flaws. However, these policies were associated with multiple positive business (for example, productivity, absenteeism, job satisfaction) and personal outcomes (for example, work-family conflict, psychological well-being). Glass and Finley (2002) noted the need for high-quality, theory-based research that examines the needs of a wide range of families and multiple stakeholders and includes a cost-benefit analysis of family-responsive policies. Another important area for future research concerns barriers to implementing (Scheibl & Dex, 1998) and utilizing family-friendly programs, such as employees' reluctance as a result of concerns regarding their image and status in the workplace (Veiga, Baldridge, & Eddleston, 2004).

Mothers in academe have unique needs with respect to work-family integration. Halpern (2008) recommended policies to achieve flexibility in academic schedules, such as stopping the tenure clock, part-time options, and expanded leave programs. She also suggested an institutional commitment to childcare that includes infants. The Center for the Education of Women (CEW) at the University of Michigan conducted a national survey of 545 colleges and universities to compare the existence of family-friendly policies in 2007 with earlier data from 2002. Findings indicate that the number of institutions with such policies had increased over the five-year period. For example, more institutions now offer tenure clock extension policies and reduced duties. At many of the institutions surveyed, these programs were available to fathers, as well as to non-tenure-track faculty. However, 10 percent of the institutions still had no formal leave policies for childbearing faculty, and thus they may be out of compliance with the PDA.

Interpersonal biases against academic mothers (and sometimes fathers) can affect the way faculty are treated and evaluated, which may provide grounds for FRD lawsuits (Williams, Alon, & Bornstein, 2006). For example, department chairs may be unaware of programs and policies designed to accommodate faculty parents or may actively discourage faculty from using FMLA leave. Penalizing faculty for using FMLA leave, through negative reviews or denial of tenure or promotion, is also illegal. See Smith and Waltman (2006) for an extensive guide to family-friendly policies for colleges and universities.

Williams and Calvert (2006) noted that one way to eliminate bias against mothers in the workplace is for employers' attorneys to consider ways to prevent a FRD lawsuit. They suggested that employers implement prevention programs to train supervisors to recognize biased perceptions of, and avoid making assumptions about, employees with caregiving responsibilities. They also encouraged employers' attorneys to review existing personnel policies to ensure that mothers and other caregivers are not being discriminated against (for example, attendance, leave, and pay policies).

Given that scholars (Dickson, 2008; Drago et al., 2008; Hegtvedt et al., 2002) have concluded that the presence of supportive supervisors may be as important as family-friendly policies, the need for change at the interpersonal level is dire. Human resources personnel could conduct workshops to help supervisors examine their beliefs, stereotypes, biases, and resultant treatment of mothers in the workplace. All managers, supervisors, department chairs, and other leaders should be fully aware of family-responsive policies and other resources that are available to employees in their workplace, and they should make it clear that the resources are there to be used. Good policies that clearly are supported by top officials eventually will filter down and change organizational culture for the better.

REFERENCES

Alderman, L. (2009, March 28). When the stork carries a pink slip. *New York Times*, p. B6.

Anderson, D. J., Binder, M., & Krause, K. (2002). The motherhood wage penalty: Which mothers pay it and why? *American Economic Review, 92*, 354–358.

Anderson, D. J., Binder, M., & Krause, K. (2003). The motherhood wage penalty revisited: Experience, heterogeneity, work effort, and work schedule flexibility. *Industrial and Labor Relations Review, 56*, 273–294.

Avellar, S., & Smock, P. J. (2003). Has the price of motherhood declined over time? A cross-cohort comparison of the motherhood wage penalty. *Journal of Marriage and the Family, 65*, 597–607.

Baker, M., & Milligan, K. (2008). Maternal employment, breastfeeding, and health: Evidence from maternity leave mandates. *Journal of Health Economics, 27*, 871–887.

Bragger, J. D., Kutcher, E., Morgan, J., & Firth, P. (2002). The effects of the structured interview on reducing biases against pregnant job applicants. *Sex Roles, 46*, 215–226.

Bridges, J. S., Etaugh, C., & Barnes-Farrell, J. (2002). Trait judgments of stay-at-home and employed parents: A function of social role and/or shifting standards? *Psychology of Women Quarterly, 26*, 140–150.

Bridges, J. S., & Orza, A. M. (1993). Effects of maternal employment-child rearing pattern on college students' perceptions of a mother and her child. *Psychology of Women Quarterly, 17*, 103–117.

Budig, M. J., & England, P. (2001). The wage penalty for motherhood. *American Sociological Review, 66*, 204–225.

Cairns, K. V., & Hatt, D. G. (1995). Discrimination and sexual harassment in a graduate student sample. *Canadian Journal of Human Sexuality, 4*, 168–176.

Casta, N. (2008). *Highlights of the 2000 U.S. Department of Labor Report— Balancing the needs of families and employers: Family and medical leave surveys*. National Partnership for Women & Families. Retrieved June 14, 2009, from http://www.nationalpartnership.org.

Center for the Education of Women, University of Michigan. (2007). *Family-friendly policies in higher education: A five-year report.* Retrieved July 1, 2009, from http://www.cew.umich.edu.

Cohany, S. R., & Sok, E. (2007, February). Trends in labor force participation of married mothers of infants. *Monthly Labor Review,* pp. 9–16.

Coltrane, S., & Shih, K. Y. (in press). Gender and the division of labor. In J. C. Chrisler & D. R. McCreary (Eds.), *Handbook of gender research in psychology II: Gender research in social and applied psychology.* New York: Springer.

Correll, S. J., Benard, S., & Paik, I. (2007). Getting a job: Is there a motherhood penalty? *American Journal of Sociology, 112,* 1297–1338.

Crittenden, A. (2001). *The price of motherhood: Why the most important job is still the least valued.* New York: Metropolitan Books.

Crosby, F. J., Williams, J. C., & Biernat, M. (2004). The maternal wall. *Journal of Social Issues, 60,* 675–682.

Cuddy, A. J. C., Fiske, S. T., & Glick, P. (2004). When professionals become mothers, warmth doesn't cut the ice. *Journal of Social Issues, 60,* 701–718.

Cuddy, A. J. C., Fiske, S. T., & Glick, P. (2007). The BIAS map: Behaviors from intergroup affect and stereotypes. *Journal of Personality and Social Psychology, 92,* 631–648.

Deaux, K., Winston, W., Crowley, M., & Lewis, L. L. (1985). Level of categorization and content of gender stereotypes. *Social Cognition, 3,* 145–167.

Deutsch, F. M., & Saxon, S. E. (1998). The double standard of praise and criticism for mothers and fathers. *Psychology of Women Quarterly, 22,* 665–683.

Dickson, C. E. (2008). Antecedents and consequences of perceived family responsibilities discrimination in the workplace. *Psychologist-Manager Journal, 11,* 113–140.

Drago, R., Colbeck, C., Hollenshead, C., & Sullivan, B. (2008). Work-family policies and the avoidance of bias against caregiving. In A. Marcus-Newhall, D. F. Halpern, & S. J. Tan (Eds.), *The changing realities of work and family* (pp. 43–66). Malden, MA: Blackwell.

Eckes, T. (2002). Paternalistic and envious gender stereotypes: Testing predictions from the stereotype content model. *Sex Roles, 47,* 99–114.

Equal Employment Opportunity Commission. (n.d.). *Pregnancy discrimination.* Retrieved June 14, 2009, from http://www.eeoc.gov/types/pregnancy.html.

Forbes, G. B., Adams-Curtis, L. E., Hamm, M. R., & White, K. B. (2003). Perceptions of the woman who breastfeeds: The role of erotophobia, sexism, and attitudinal variables. *Sex Roles, 49,* 379–388.

Fuegen, K., Biernat, M., Haines, E., & Deaux, K. (2004). Mothers and fathers in the workplace: How gender and parental status influence judgments of job-related competence. *Journal of Social Issues, 60,* 737–754.

Fuentes, S. P. (2008, November). Remarks at the Yale University School of Law symposium to commemorate the 30th anniversary of the Pregnancy Discrimination Act. New Haven, CT.

Georgetown University Law Center. (n.d.). *Flexible work arrangements: The fact sheet* (Workplace Flexibility 2010 Report). Retrieved July 1, 2009, from http://www.workplaceflexibility2010.org.

Glass, J., & Finley, A. (2002). Coverage and effectiveness of family-responsive workplace policies. *Human Resource Management Review, 12*, 313–337.

Glass, J., & Riley, L. (1998). Family responsive policies and employee retention following childbirth. *Social Forces, 76,* 1401–1435.

Glick, P., & Fiske, S. Y. (2007). Sex discrimination: The psychological approach. In F. J. Crosby, M. S. Stockdale, & S. A. Ropp (Eds.), *Sex discrimination in the workplace* (pp. 155–187). Malden, MA: Blackwell.

Gornick, J. C., & Meyers, M. K. (2003). *Families that work: Policies for reconciling parenthood and employment.* New York: Russell Sage Foundation.

Gornick, J. C., Meyers, M. K., & Ross, K. E. (1998). Public policies and the employment of mothers: A cross-national study. *Social Science Quarterly, 79*, 35–54.

Gottfried, A. E., & Gottfried, A. W. (2008). The upside of maternal and dual-earner employment: A focus on positive family adaptations, home environments, and child development in the Fullerton longitudinal study. In A. Marcus-Newhall, D. F. Halpern, & S. J. Tan (Eds.), *The changing realities of work and family* (pp. 25–42). Malden, MA: Blackwell.

Hall, D. M. (2008). Feminist perspectives on the personal and political aspects of mothering. In J. C. Chrisler, C. Golden, & P. D. Rozee (Eds.), *Lectures on the psychology of women* (4th ed., pp. 58–79). Boston, MA: McGraw-Hill.

Halpern, D. F. (2008). Nurturing careers in psychology: Combining work and family. *Educational Psychology Review, 20*, 57–64.

Halpert, J. A., Wilson, M. L., & Hickman, J. L. (1993). Pregnancy as a source of bias in performance appraisals. *Journal of Organizational Behavior, 14*, 649–663.

Hebl, M. R., King, E. B., Glick, P., Singletary, S. L., & Kazama, S. (2007). Hostile and benevolent reactions toward pregnant women: Complementary interpersonal punishments and rewards that maintain traditional roles. *Journal of Applied Psychology, 92*, 1499–1511.

Hegtvedt, K. A., Clay-Warner, J., & Ferrigno, E. D. (2002). Reactions to injustice: Factors affecting workers' resentment toward family-friendly policies. *Social Psychology Quarterly, 65*, 386–400.

Heymann, J., Earle, A., & Hayes, J. (2007). *The work, family, and equity index: How does the United States measure up?* Institute for Health and Social Policy. Retrieved July 1, 2009, from http://www.iwpr.org/rnr/archives/feb 07.htm#2.

Institute for Women's Policy Research. (2007, August). *Maternity leave in the United States*. Retrieved July 8, 2009, from http://www.iwpr.org.

Johnston-Robledo, I., Wares, S., Fricker, J., & Pasek, L. (2007). Indecent exposure: Self-objectification and young women's attitudes toward breastfeeding. *Sex Roles, 56*, 429–437.

June, A. W. (2009, April 22). Family-friendly policies may not help as much as they should, conference speaker says. *Chronicle of Higher Education*. Retrieved June 28, 2009, from http://chronicle.com/jobs/blogs/onhiring/1011/family-friendly-policies-may-not-help-as-much-as-they-should-conference-speaker-says.

Kantor, J. (2006, September 1). On the job, nursing mothers find a 2-class system. *New York Times*. Retrieved June 23, 2009, from http://www.nytimes.com.

Kite, M. E. (2001). Changing times, changing gender roles: Who do we want women and men to be? In R. K. Unger (Ed.), *Handbook of the psychology of women and gender* (pp. 215–227). New York: Wiley.

Lassow, D. (2009). *The court doesn't get it*. Washington, DC: National Women's Law Center. Retrieved June 30, 2009, from http://www.womenstake.org/2009/05/the-court-doesnt-get-it.html.

Marvan, M. L., Islas, M., Vela, L., Chrisler, J. C., & Warren, E. A. (2008). Stereotypes of women in different stages of their reproductive life: Data from Mexico and the United States. *Health Care for Women International, 29*, 673–687.

Mason, M. A. (2009, April 22). Is tenure a trap for women? *Chronicle of Higher Education*. Retrieved June 28, 2009, from http://chronicle.com/jobs/news/2009/04/2009042201c.htm.

Mason, M. A., & Goulden, M. (2002, November/December). Do babies matter? The effect of family formation on the lifelong careers of academic men and women. *Academe*. Retrieved June 28, 2009, from http://www.aaup.org/ publications/Academe/2002/02nd/02ndmas.htm.

Mason, M. A., & Goulden, M. (2004, November/December). Do babies matter? Closing the baby gap. *Academe*. Retrieved June 28, 2009, from http:// www.aaup.org/publications/Academe/2004/04nd/04ndmaso.htm.

Masser, B., Grass, K., & Nesic, M. (2007). We like you, but we don't want you: The impact of pregnancy in the workplace. *Sex Roles, 57*, 703–712.

Mattingly, M. L., & Brauner, L. M. (2008). *Indiana joins the list of states providing legal protections to nursing mothers at the workplace*. Retrieved June 30, 2009, from http://www.jdsupra.com/post/documentViewer.aspx?fid=879eae0b-4dd8-27a-a08f-3fdea638931.

Moore, L. J. (2007). Incongruent bodies: Teaching while leaking. *Feminist Teacher, 17*, 95–106.

National Conference of State Legislators. *Breastfeeding laws*. Retrieved June 20, 2009, from http://www.ncsl.org/IssuesResearch/Health/Breastfeeding Laws/tabid/14389/Default.asx.

National Partnership for Women and Families. (n.d.). *The Pregnancy Discrimination Act 25 years later: Pregnancy discrimination persists.* Retrieved June 30, 2009, from http://www.nationalpartnership.org.

Nieva, V. F., & Gutek, B. A. (1981). *Women and work: A psychological perspective.* New York: Praeger.

Parasuraman, S., & Greenhaus, J. H. (2002). Toward reducing some critical gaps in work-family research. *Human Resource Management Review, 12,* 299–312.

Pattison, H. M., Gross, H., & Cast, C. (1997). Pregnancy and employment: The perceptions and beliefs of fellow workers. *Journal of Reproductive and Infant Psychology, 15,* 303–312.

Petersen, D. J., & Boller, H. R. (2003). A legal analysis of breast-feeding accommodation requirements in the workplace. *Public Personnel Management, 32,* 383–395.

Rhode, D. L., & Williams, J. C. (2007). Legal perspectives on employment discrimination. In F. J. Crosby, M. S. Stockdale, & S. A. Ropp (Eds.), *Sex discrimination in the workplace* (pp. 235–270). Malden, MA: Blackwell.

Ridgeway, C. L., & Correll, S. J. (2004). Motherhood as a status characteristic. *Journal of Social Issues, 60,* 683–700.

Rose, S. J., & Hartmann, H. I. (2004). *Still a man's labor market: The long-term earnings gap* (Institute for Women's Policy Research Paper No. C355). Washington, DC: Institute for Women's Policy Research.

Scheibl, F., & Dex, S. (1998). Should we have more family-friendly policies? *European Management Journal, 16,* 586–599.

Shealy, K. R., Li, R., Benton-Davis, S., & Grummer-Strawn, L. M. (2005). *The CDC guide to breastfeeding interventions.* Centers for Disease Control and Prevention. Retrieved July 1, 2009, from http://www.cdc.gov/breastfeeding.

Smith, G. C., & Waltman, J. A. (2006). *Designing and implementing family-friendly policies in higher education.* Center for the Education of Women, University of Michigan. Retrieved July 1, 2009, from http://www.cew.umich.edu.

Sux, B., & Eckes, T. (1991). A closer look at the complex structure of gender stereotypes. *Sex Roles, 24,* 57–71.

Taylor, S. E., & Langer, E. J. (1977). Pregnancy: A social stigma? *Sex Roles, 3,* 27–35.

Townsley, N. C., & Broadfoot, K. J. (2008). Care, career, and academe: Heeding the calls of a new professoriate. *Women's Studies in Communication, 31,* 133–142.

U.S. Department of Labor. (n.d.). *Family and medical leave act.* Retrieved June 30, 2009, from http://www.dol.gov/esa/whd/fmla.

Veiga, J. F., Baldridge, D. C., & Eddleston, K. A. (2004). Toward understanding employee reluctance to participate in family-friendly programs. *Human Resource Management Review, 14,* 337–351.

Waldfogel, J. (1998). Understanding the "family gap" in pay for women with children. *Journal of Economic Perspectives, 12,* 137–156.

Wayne, J. H., Grzywacz, J. G., Carlson, D. S., & Kacmar, K. M. (2007). Work-family facilitation: A theoretical explanation and model of primary antecedents and consequences. *Human Resource Management Review, 17*, 63–76.

Williams, J. (2000). *Unbending gender.* Oxford: Oxford University Press.

Williams, J., & Segal, N. (2003). Beyond the maternal wall: Relief for family caregivers who are discriminated against on the job. *Harvard Women's Law Journal, 26*, 77–162.

Williams, J. C. (2008). What psychologists need to know about family responsibilities discrimination. In A. Marcus-Newhall, D. F. Halpern, & S. J. Tan (Eds.), *The changing realities of work and family* (pp. 255–276). Malden, MA: Blackwell.

Williams, J. C., Alon, T., & Bornstein, S. (2006). Beyond the 'chilly climate': Eliminating bias against women and fathers in academe. *Thought and Action, 22*, 79–96.

Williams, J. C., & Calvert, C. T. (2006). Family responsibilities discrimination: What plaintiffs' attorneys, management attorneys, and employees need to know. *Women Lawyers Journal, 91*, 24–28.

Williams, J. C., & Cooper, H. C. (2004). The public policy of motherhood. *Journal of Social Issues, 60*, 849–865.

7

Race/Color Discrimination

Isis H. Settles, NiCole T. Buchanan, and Stevie C. Y. Yap

INTRODUCTION

Title VII of the Civil Rights Act (1964, 1991) declared that employers must maintain a workplace free of discrimination based on sex, race, color, religion, or national origin. As a result, organizations have attempted to reduce racial discrimination, of which racial harassment is a subtype. Nevertheless, racial discrimination and harassment remain pervasive throughout the workplace, with 40 percent to 76 percent of ethnic minority employees experiencing at least one unwanted race-based behavior within a 12- to 24-month period (Harrell, 2000; Schneider, Hitlan, & Radhakrishnan, 2000). Racial discrimination has serious consequences, including negatively affecting psychological, physical, and work outcomes (Barnes et al., 2008; Darity, 2003; Forman, 2003; Sellers, Caldwell, Schmeelk-Cone, & Zimmerman, 2003). In this chapter, we will provide an overview of racial discrimination in the workplace as it is defined legally in the United States, discuss individual and organizational factors that increase the likelihood that racial discrimination will occur, and review the costs of racial discrimination to targeted individuals and the organizations within which they work.

LEGAL DEFINITIONS OF RACIAL DISCRIMINATION

Protection against workplace racial discrimination was formalized with the passage of Title VII of the Civil Rights Act (1964, 1991), which prohibited workplaces with at least 15 employees from using sex, race, color, religion, or national origin when making employment decisions. Title VII also created the Equal Employment Opportunity Commission (EEOC) to investigate claims of discrimination. As a part of the ban against racial discrimination, Title VII specifies several race-related factors that cannot be used in employment decisions. Namely, employers may not deny individuals equal employment opportunities as a result of their perceived or actual racial group membership, race-related features (for example, hair texture or skin color), relationships with members of a particular race (for example, marriage), or the employer's beliefs about individuals in certain racial groups. Although enacted to protect racial and ethnic minorities (and other protected groups), these guidelines extend to people of all races.

Title VII also prohibits discriminatory employment practices. First, employers may not discriminate in the recruitment, hiring, promotion, and retention of employees. This protection requires the employer to use the same job requirements for all individuals and to ensure that these requirements do not exclude individuals in a particular racial group. Yet, research shows that discriminatory practices persist in these domains and manifest in a variety of ways. For example, Bertrand and Mullainathan (2004) found that in the initial review of resumes, applicants were already at a disadvantage if their names suggested they were black. The researchers sent resumes with similar qualifications in response to 1,300 employment advertisements. They changed only the name of the applicant (using a name perceived as white, such as Greg Baker, or a name perceived as black, such as Jamal James) and found that applicants with white-sounding names were 50 percent more likely to receive a callback than applicants with black-sounding names. When they manipulated the quality of the resumes, higher quality white applicants were 30 percent more likely to receive a callback than lower quality white applicants, whereas black applicants with higher quality resumes only received an 8 percent boost over lower-quality black applicants. Thus, this study clearly demonstrates that racial discrimination may occur at the hiring stage, and potentially the recruitment stage, before individuals have an opportunity to demonstrate their potential.

Racial discrimination is evident in promotion practices as well, such as performance evaluations. An analysis by Stauffer and Buckley (2005) showed that white supervisors gave white workers substantially higher performance ratings than black workers, compared with black supervisors rating the same workers. Interestingly, they also found that black supervisors demonstrated smaller, but similar biases in favor of white workers. Overall, the results of this body of research suggest that racial bias and discrimination exists in the supervisor ratings of black employees, although the source of this bias is unclear. Additionally, in a three-year period early in their careers, black workers with similar credentials were dismissed from their jobs 33 percent more frequently than white workers (Wilson, 2005). To the extent that evaluations of worker performance and retention decisions are influenced by factors unrelated to actual performance, the organization is negatively affected in several ways. Employees that are not performing as well as they might be able to appear to be given an artificial lift, while the better performance of others is being overlooked. Over time, this may affect promotion decisions (promoting less qualified employees as a result of overly positive evaluations) and retention, as underappreciated employees are more likely to leave the organization.

Second, Title VII prohibits employers from discriminating in compensation, benefits or the conditions of employment (for example, the type of work assignments made). Although disparities in wages have decreased over time, they remain significant. Averaging across all working adults, white men earn one-third more than black men and twice as much as black women (Kim, 2007). After controlling for factors thought to influence earnings (for example, age, education, part-time status, children, marital status, and so on), up to a 30 percent wage disparity exists across racial groups (Bishaw & Semega, 2008; Kim, 2007). Additionally, these disparities may be exacerbated over an individual's lifetime. Maume (2004) analyzed a longitudinal panel sample and found that black workers earned significantly less than white workers, controlling for a number of individual and job related variables. Furthermore, the size of this wage gap was greater for older cohorts of workers compared with younger ones, and as individuals aged, the wage gap increased for all cohorts. The increase in wage disparity within cohorts reflects differences in starting wages among ethnic groups (which are exacerbated over time because raises are often a percentage of one's base salary) as well as persistent employer discrimination in future compensation and promotion practices over individuals' careers (Maume, 2004). Such discrimination may be responsible for up to a 15 percent loss in earnings within a 10-year period (Darity, Guilkey, & Winfrey, 1996; Gottschalk, 1997; Rodgers & Spriggs, 1996).

Third, Title VII prohibits employers from segregating employees who belong to a particular racial group or classifying the type of work employees can do because of their race. For example, physically or geographically isolating Asian employees from other employees or customers, or prohibiting Asian employees from holding certain positions would constitute Title VII violations. Four theories can be used to explain why racial segregation occurs in the workplace: (1) ethnic minorities have skill deficits compared with white employees, (2) racial groups prefer to be segregated or choose occupations that are similar to other members of their ethnic group, (3) economic and organizational structures result in race segregation (unintentionally), and (4) individuals who make employment and placement decisions engage in race-based stereotyping. Kaufman (2002) compared the four explanations for employment racial segregation and determined that racial stereotyping by employers best explained racial segregation across almost 2,000 labor sectors.

Fourth, Title VII prohibits employers from retaliating against individuals who complain about their own discrimination or that of another employee. Retaliation includes a number of adverse actions, including not hiring someone or terminating an employee who makes a claim of discrimination. Giving employees negative performance evaluations, negative job references, or denying them promotion are other examples of prohibited retaliatory tactics.

Finally, employers may not engage in other activities that threaten or harm individuals because they have made a claim of discrimination. Despite the prohibition of retaliation under Title VII, the EEOC received more than 33,000 claims of retaliation discrimination in the 2009 fiscal year alone. Retaliation claims have significant costs to employers, including a more negative workplace climate and decreased employee morale, and the potential for financial penalties as a result of declines in business or court awards to plaintiffs (Solano & Kleiner, 2003).

Individuals are protected against discriminatory acts in the above areas regardless of whether or not the acts were intended to cause them harm. Thus, Title VII distinguishes between two broad types of racial discrimination. *Disparate treatment* occurs when individuals are deliberately treated differently because of their race. Examples include offering ethnic minorities lower starting salaries, posing different interview questions to white and ethnic minority applicants, or refusing to hire applicants of color. *Disparate impact,* also referred to as adverse impact, occurs when facially neutral workplace practices have an unnecessary and negative effect on members of a protected class (for example, people of color), thereby limiting the opportunities of that group. Race-related examples of disparate impact can include a wide array of activities, including recruitment and hiring practices (such as only advertising open positions in predominantly white communities) or unnecessary requirements for one's appearance (for example, requiring men have short hair, which might eliminate qualified Native American applicants—many of whom do not cut their hair for cultural and spiritual reasons; French, 2003).

Racial harassment and the creation of a hostile work environment were included as forms of racial *discrimination* following the 1972 ruling in *Rogers v. EEOC*, which established that a hostile work environment in violation of Title VII was created for a Latina employee when her employer discriminated against Latino/a customers (Chew & Kelly, 2006). Racial harassment refers to race-based differential treatment that creates a pervasive hostile environment for targets; that is, unwanted race-based behaviors become sufficiently pervasive that the general workplace milieu becomes hostile or negatively affects one's job performance (Harrick & Sullivan, 1995). Racial harassment commonly is expressed verbally (for example, racial slurs, ethnic jokes, and derogatory race-based comments) or via exclusion (for example, not informing ethnic minority co-workers of work-related activities or social events; Schneider, Hitlan, & Radhakrishnan, 2000).

PSYCHOLOGICAL DEFINITIONS OF RACIAL DISCRIMINATION

Researchers (Kanter, 1977; Reskin, McBrier, & Kmec, 1999; Smith, 2002) have suggested that majority group members, particularly those who hold positions of power and authority, are personally motivated to maintain their positions of privilege. A primary means of doing so involves the exclusion of individuals from different racial or gender groups, and providing opportunities only to individuals who share their demographic characteristics. Thus, racial groups experience differential privilege as a result of racial discrimination, which benefits one group to the detriment of another. The benefits that are afforded to the privileged group (for example, higher salaries, more opportunities for training and promotions) necessarily limit the job-related benefits for the discriminated against group. Majority group members may engage in racial discrimination because of conscious animus toward racial minorities, or because feelings of trust and shared understanding are greater when similarities are greater among group members. Similarly, individuals may act in discriminatory ways as a result of institutional or organizational pressures.

Although people most readily recognize blatant and malicious acts of race discrimination, differential treatment need not be intentional to be harmful or to qualify as discriminatory practice under the law. Although not specifically addressed under Title VII, racial microaggressions—subtle verbal, behavioral, or environmental insults that target people of color—are frequently part of modern racial harassment (Deitch et al., 2003; Sue et al., 2007). Racial microaggressions are akin to a "death by a thousand cuts," meaning individual incidents are rarely clear acts of aggression or maliciousness. Instead, individuals are inundated with many small, nearly imperceptible injuries whose cumulative effects can be devastating (Bryant-Davis, 2007; Bryant-Davis & Ocampo, 2005). These "small" acts of discrimination easily can be explained away when viewed in isolation. As a result, racial discrimination in its subtle form is often readily visible only after many incidents have occurred across several employees.

Modern racial discrimination also may occur through unconscious processes related to prejudice and stereotyping. Recent research suggests that prejudice and stereotypes can occur unconsciously and outside people's awareness (for example, Greenwald, Banaji, Rudman, Farnham, Nosek, & Mellott, 2002). Prejudice reflects bias—negative evaluations and feelings—toward others who are members of a particular group, such as a minority racial group (Allport, 1954). A stereotype is a belief about the nature and characteristics of a group (Hilton & von Hippel, 1996), for example, that Asians are smart or blacks are lazy. Past research has indicated that discrimination—negative behaviors enacted toward members of a particular group—typically stem from prejudiced attitudes and stereotypes (Dovidio, Kawakami, & Gaertner, 2002). Furthermore, because majority group individuals often hold rigid stereotypes about minority group members, differences between groups often are exaggerated, similarities are minimized, and differences among outgroup members often are masked (Smith, 2002). Thus, opportunities are limited for individuals to change their negative prejudices and stereotypes (Hilton & von Hippel, 1996). When unchecked, such stereotypes, bias, and prejudice, conscious or unconscious, may result in employment discrimination (Fiske & Lee, 2008).

FREQUENCY OF RACIAL DISCRIMINATION

Despite laws prohibiting employer bias based on race and other characteristics, racial discrimination remains a problem for the workplace. In

2008, the EEOC received nearly 34,000 new complaints of race-based discrimination (EEOC, 2009), which is thought to reflect only a small proportion of discriminatory incidents that occur as discrimination is often unreported. Discrimination and harassment often are directed at individuals because of their membership in particular groups and reflect power and status differentials within the organization and within society more generally. Thus, it is not surprising that ethnic minorities report significantly higher rates of racial discrimination and harassment than whites (Berdahl & Moore, 2006; Bergman, Palmieri, Drasgow, & Ormerod, 2007; Buchanan, Bergman, Bruce, Woods, & Lichty, 2009; Schneider et al., 2000), with 40 percent to 76 percent of ethnic minority employees reporting at least one unwanted race-based experience at work within a 12- to 24-month period (Harrell, 2000; Schneider et al., 2000). Similarly, negative race-based behaviors are common among college students. Estimates of racial harassment suggest that 98 percent of ethnic minority students experience at least one unwanted race-based event every year (Landrine & Klonoff, 1996) and up to 66 percent report one such experience within a two-week period (Swim, Hyers, Cohen, Fitzgerald, & Bylsma, 2003).

Other demographic variables can influence the likelihood of experiencing racial discrimination and harassment. Specifically, gender appears to moderate the frequency and severity of racial discrimination and harassment. Swim et al. (2003) found that higher rates of racial harassment were reported by college women than by college men. Another study of college students found that this pattern held for black men and women in college, but among Asian and multiracial students, men reported higher rates than women (Buchanan et al., 2009). Among working adults, studies of racial discrimination and harassment usually find higher rates among men as compared with women (for example, Sigelman & Welch, 1991; Krieger et al., 2006; Utsey, Payne, Jackson, & Jones, 2002) and that men are targeted more frequently for direct and violent racial harassment (for example, being called a racial epithet, being physically assaulted due to race; Feagin, Vera, & Imani, 1996). The inconsistency of the results regarding racial harassment and gender are striking and point to the need for further research on the intersections of race and gender in harassment and discrimination (Berdahl & Moore, 2006; Buchanan & Ormerod, 2002). Similarly, age and social class, being younger or being of a lower social class, are associated with higher rates of workplace harassment (McLaughlin, Uggen, & Blackstone, 2008).

Finally, organizational factors, such as the type of workplace and racial composition, appear to influence rates of harassment. In fact, many argue that, although rarely studied, organizational factors have a greater effect than individual factors in determining the frequency and severity of discrimination (for example, Tilly, 1998; Reskin, 2000). Those organizational processes that have the greatest likelihood of reducing discrimination are those that reduce individuals' likelihood of (1) categorizing people as in-group versus out-group members, (2) acting on biased automatic cognitive processes, and (3) allowing the stereotypic beliefs of others to influence their decisions, particularly in hiring and promotion (Petersen & Saporta, 2004; Reskin, 2000; Vallas, 2003). These might be accomplished by formalizing decision-making processes in recruitment, retention, evaluation, and promotion (Reskin, 2000); increasing accountability and oversite of these processes and procedures (Kalev, Dobbin, & Kelly, 2006); and utilizing race-based hiring and promotion policies to increase workplace diversity (for example, affirmative action programs; Holzer & Neumark, 2000).

INDIVIDUAL FACTORS RELATED TO WHO PERPETRATES DISCRIMINATION

We described some of the demographic factors, such as gender and social class, that affect the likelihood that an individual will experience racial discrimination. Other important factors influence whether an individual will perpetrate racial discrimination against others. Some individuals hold more bias toward minority racial groups than others. Not surprisingly, those individuals are more likely to engage in racial discrimination. For example, in an experimental test, Ziegert and Hanges (2005) found that when given justification for discrimination by an authority, individuals with higher levels of unconscious racism rated black participants more negatively compared with those low in unconscious racism. Furthermore, research by Norton, Sommers, Vandello, and Darley (2006) demonstrated that individuals often provide nonracial justifications for race-related selection decisions, and that this is especially true for individuals high on racial prejudice.

Social dominance theory has been offered to explain group-based prejudice and discrimination (Sidanius & Pratto, 1999). This theory suggests that some individuals may have more of a social dominance orientation, which is an individual's tendency to support group-based hierarchies, including the support of higher status groups and their domination of lower status groups (Sidanius & Pratto, 1999). Thus, individuals high on social dominance orientation are thought to have a set of beliefs or values that justify inequality between groups. Parkins, Fishbein, and Ritchey (2006) found that undergraduate students who were higher on self-rated social dominance orientation reported a greater likelihood to discriminate. Similarly, in an experimental selection study, Umphress, Simmons, Boswell, and del Carmen Triana (2008) found that undergraduate students who were higher in social dominance orientation were significantly less likely to say they would choose a more qualified black male candidate over less qualified white male candidates. When participants were explicitly directed to make their decision based on job qualifications, this bias was lessened, but remained significant. Aquino, Stewart, and Reed (2005) found that undergraduate students who had a higher social dominance orientation assigned more negative performance expectation ratings for a hypothetical black candidate compared with those who had a lower social dominance orientation. Furthermore, this effect was significantly greater when individuals believed that the black candidate had benefited from affirmative action. Thus, prejudice and the tendency to support inequality appear to be significant factors in predicting who will engage in racial discrimination.

ORGANIZATIONAL AND SOCIETAL FACTORS RELATED TO WHEN DISCRIMINATION OCCURS

When examining employment discrimination, focusing solely on individuals as sources of discrimination obscures the roles and responsibilities organizations have in stemming racial discrimination (Bielby, 2008). Discrimination and harassment reflect power dynamics and differences in formal and informal status among those involved. As a result, organizational status can influence the frequency of experiencing discrimination and harassment. High organizational status is protective across a variety of negative workplace behaviors, such as incivility and harassment (Cortina, Magley, Williams, & Langhout, 2001). Conversely, low organizational status increases the likelihood that one will be more frequently targeted, especially in male-dominated organizations (for example, Buchanan et al., 2009; Gruber, 2003).

Whereas most organizations understand the need to address actions and policies that are clearly discriminatory, they often neglect more ambiguous ways in which practices can result in sizable disparities across groups. For example, racial discrimination may occur inadvertently under the guise of the "last-hired, first-fired" principle. In many occupational sectors and at higher organizational levels, minority workers are likely to have been integrated into the workplace relatively recently. Thus, they are likely to be more recently hired and have less seniority than white workers (Cummings, 1987; Sims, 1993). Organizations also can perpetuate racial discrimination by relying on informal networking and mentoring. For example, informal social gatherings among colleagues may regularly fail to include ethnic minority employees, resulting in these employees having fewer informal resources (such as information and access to influential people at work). Similarly, reliance on informal mentoring networks, may result in racial differences in the frequency, depth, and quality of mentoring provided (Bielby, 2008; Constantine, Smith, Redington, & Owens, 2008).

Organizational climate refers to an individual's perception of the organization and its policies, practices, and procedures (Kickul & Liao-Troth, 2003; Seibert, Silver, & Randolph, 2004). Although such perceptions may not always be accurate representations, they remain important because they shape individuals' behavior at work and their feelings about the organization more globally (Seibert et al., 2004). More recently, researchers have focused on aspects of the organizational climate that are of particular relevance to racial discrimination. For example, Peterson (2002) found that employees were less likely to engage in racial or sexual harassment if they perceived their work organization as placing importance on complying with legal and professional standards and showing concern for employees' well-being.

Most relevant to racial discrimination is an organization's diversity climate, or the extent to which an organization advocates for fair policies and socially integrates underrepresented employees (McKay, Avery, & Morris, 2008). McKay et al. (2008) found that black and Hispanic employees who perceived the organization as having a positive diversity climate reported higher sales performance levels than those who perceived the climate as having a less positive diversity climate. Furthermore, another study found that, although black employees reported more absences than white employees, this difference was greater when the organization was perceived as not valuing diversity (Avery, McKay, Wilson, & Tonidandel, 2007).

Finally, negative economic conditions within the broader society exacerbate racial discrimination. During times of economic recession, racial minority workers experience significantly more disruptions in their employment compared with white workers (Applied Research Center,

2009; Cummings, 1987; Sims, 1993), regardless of their gender or the occupational sector within which they work (Cummings, 1987). Moreover, patterns of disproportionate minority layoffs occur not only during times of broad recession, but also when particular industries are in decline (Sims, 1993). Furthermore, minorities are less likely than whites to recover economically after a recession. In fact, the income inequities between minority-headed and white-headed families widens, especially among low-income minority families (Applied Research Center, 2009; Michel, 1991). These trends are linked directly to racial discrimination in the labor market.

INDIVIDUAL AND ORGANIZATIONAL OUTCOMES OF RACIAL DISCRIMINATION

Research has shown that race-related discrimination and harassment experienced in the workplace can come from various sources, including supervisors and superiors, co-workers and colleagues, patients and clients, and in the policies and practices of the organization itself (that is, "systemic" racial discrimination). Indeed, discrimination and harassment from various sources have been linked to negative outcomes for both the individual employee and the organization as a whole (for example, Ensher, Grant-Vallone, & Donaldson, 2001; Shields & Price, 2000).

Racial discrimination has been associated with detriment to a variety of psychological and physical health outcomes. Discriminatory experiences have been associated with increased distress, traumatic stress (for example, Branscombe, Schmitt, & Harvey, 1999; Broman, Mavaddat, & Hsu, 2000; Forman, 2003; Kessler, Mickelson, & Williams, 1999), anxiety, depression and obsessive-compulsive disorder (Kessler et al., 1999; Klonoff, Landrine, & Ullman, 1999), lower self-esteem (Jasinskaja-Lahti & Liebkind, 2001; Wong, Eccles, & Sameroff, 2003), decreased life satisfaction (Liebkind & Jasinskaja, 2000), and lower perceived self-competence and psychological resiliency (Wong et al., 2003). Among college students and adolescents, racial discrimination is associated with decreased motivation to achieve goals and increased emotional discomfort, anger, and behavioral problems (Sellers et al., 2003; Swim et al., 2003; Wong et al., 2003). Regarding physical health, racial discrimination has been associated with increased mortality rates and elevated incidences of several chronic health conditions, such as high blood pressure, heart disease, cancer, and diabetes (Barnes et al., 2008; Guyll,

Matthews, & Bromberger, 2001; Harrell, 2000; Williams, Neighbors, & Jackson, 2003).

Research has shown that perceived workplace racial discrimination also is associated with negative work outcomes for targeted individuals. These harmful outcomes include generalized job stress, supervisor and co-worker dissatisfaction, increased perceived organizational tolerance of harassment (Buchanan & Fitzgerald, 2008; Mays, Coleman, & Jackson, 1996), intentions to quit, and job withdrawal (Pavalko, Mossakowski, & Hamilton, 2003; Schneider et al., 2000). Furthermore, racial discrimination is associated with limited career advancement and lower development of workplace skills, less effective work relationships with colleagues and supervisors, increased work tension, and decreased job satisfaction, initiative, and organizational commitment (that is, increased likelihood of changing jobs; Mays et al., 1996; Sanchez & Brock, 1996).

Although it is clear that racial discrimination is associated with many negative psychological, physical health, and work outcomes, relatively little research has addressed outcomes related specifically to racial harassment in the workplace (for recent exceptions, see Buchanan et al., 2009; Buchanan & Fitzgerald, 2008; Schneider et al., 2000). Those studies that do exist demonstrate that, within the workplace, the racial harassment has significant detrimental effects on psychological well-being and work outcomes. Namely, racial harassment is associated with increased posttraumatic stress (Buchanan et al., 2009; Buchanan & Fitzgerald, 2008; Pavalko et al., 2003), depression, general clinical symptomology, life satisfaction (Buchanan et al., 2009), decreased health satisfaction, and an increased number of poor health conditions (Buchanan et al., 2009; Darity, 2003; Mays et al., 1996; Pavalko et al., 2003).

Racial discrimination and harassment also have negative consequences for the organization. Ensher et al. (2001) found that when employees perceive the organization and its policies to be discriminatory, or perceive that they have personally experienced discrimination from supervisors or co-workers, their job satisfaction, organizational commitment, and citizenship behavior in the workplace is negatively affected. In turn, these experiences and changes in organizational commitment increase the employee's intentions to leave the organization (Podsakoff, Whiting, Podsakoff, & Blume, 2009; Shields & Price, 2002). Replacing employees requires resources be spent on a plethora of clear costs (for example, acquiring and training a new employee, lost productivity, and so on) as well as concealed costs (productivity lost by the co-workers of and the person training the new employee, processing the paperwork generated by a new hire, and so on). These costs can range from 50 to 200 percent of the individual's annual salary (Bliss, 2001; Faia, Lechthaler, & Merkl, 2009) and are independent of litigation and efforts to repair or maintain the company's reputation if charges of discrimination are levied.

SUMMARY AND CONCLUSIONS

Despite Title VII of the Civil Rights Act (1964, 1991)—which mandated that organizations eliminate workplace discrimination based on an employee's sex, race, color, religion, or national origin—racial discrimination and harassment persists with significant costs to targets, co-workers, and the organization as a whole. The ability to reduce discrimination and manage diversity in the workplace can be an asset to an organization. Organizations that effectively integrate and support workplace diversity experience many positive benefits, including improved employee retention and productivity, and increased ability to recruit the best employees (Loden & Rosenor, 1991). Indeed, being able to effectively manage diversity and reduce workplace discrimination is an important organizational concern given its effect on employee attitudes and beliefs (for example, job satisfaction), which in turn has a substantial impact on employee behavior (Barak, Cherin, & Berkman, 1998).

Despite advances in research and organizational policy regarding discrimination and harassment, gaps remain. To date, much of the research on racial harassment and discrimination is about the experiences of black versus white employees. However, an increasingly diverse workforce requires attention to the ways in which discrimination is directed toward other ethnic minority groups. It also may be necessary to conceptualize discrimination based on religion as potential racial discrimination. For example, discrimination against Muslims in the United States often reflects racism against those perceived to be Arab American. In fact, in the 14 months following the World Trade Center terrorist attacks on September 11, 2001, Arab American men and women, regardless of their religion, brought 705 charges of employment discrimination to the EEOC (EEOC, 2002).

Organizations can take a number of steps to minimize the likelihood that racial discrimination will occur. Most important, organizations need clear policies that prohibit discrimination on the basis of race, and they need consistent procedures for investigating the complaint and reprimanding offenders. Included in the policies should be examples of behavior that meet the legal or psychological definitions of racial discrimination. Organizations must develop policies and training programs that address multiple forms of discrimination and harassment. Individuals who embody multiple marginalized identities, such as ethnic minority women, are likely to experience harassment that simultaneously targets these multiple identities (for example, racialized sexual harassment; Buchanan & Ormerod, 2002) and may be perceived differently by targets based on these identities (Settles, Pratt-Hyatt, & Buchanan, 2008). Yet, organizational policies and training rarely address these intersecting forms of harassment and discrimination. Racial discrimination and harassment are related to other forms of workplace mistreatment, such as sexual harassment and general incivility, and as such, many have argued that these should not be examined in isolation (Buchanan & Fitzgerald, 2008; DeSouza, 2008). In fact, organizations rife with one form of discrimination or harassment are likely to have other forms proliferating as well (Cortina, Fitzgerald, & Drasgow, 2002). Buchanan and Fitzgerald (2008) found that experiencing both sexual and racial harassment significantly increased individuals' criticism of the organization's leadership and perception of the organization as tolerant of harassment, both of which increase the likelihood of the target seeking legal redress. Thus, by actively working to reduce racial discrimination, organizations can reduce liability while simultaneously increasing employee morale, productivity, and company profits.

Furthermore, organizational policies must prohibit racial microaggressions and other subtle and unintentional forms of discrimination. Racial microaggressions (subtle mistreatment and exclusion) often are discounted because they are ambiguous and perpetrators can argue that they are unintentional. Nevertheless, such experiences can have a significant detrimental effect (decreased morale and productivity, increased employee turnover) resulting in significant losses for an organization and putting them at risk for litigation. This form of discrimination may be most difficult to eliminate because of its subtle nature; yet its negative effects make it an important form of mistreatment that organizations must begin to address. Research suggests that seemingly neutral organizational policies can have a disparate impact on ethnic groups. Organizations must examine the outcomes of such policies on different ethnic groups. For example, if informal mentoring results in ethnic minorities receiving little or no mentoring, whereas white employees receive strong mentoring through this process, white employees will receive incremental benefits at the expense of ethnic minority employees. If this is the case, it may be beneficial to assign mentors, train them for this role to work with employees from different racial and ethnic backgrounds, and then set standards, expectations, and evaluation procedures to ensure that all employees are being given equal access to the information and benefits a mentor can provide.

Another important organizational concern is to develop objective and accurate criteria for selection, promotion, and performance evaluation. These areas can be rife with unconscious bias that result in differential hiring requirements, disparities in performance evaluations and compensation, and biased promotion decisions. Reducing the incidence and impact of unconscious bias in each of these domains is important not only from an ethical and moral standpoint, but also because of the benefits for the organization. Thus, understanding the degree to which these processes are affected by subjective biases, such as racial bias, is an important concern for social scientists and organizational leaders alike. In addition to antidiscrimination policies and improved evaluation criteria, employers should enact a process through which employees can easily make complaints of racial discrimination. Included in the complaint process must be assurances of employee confidentiality, prompt and comprehensive examination of the complaint, and appropriate remediation of any discriminatory behavior.

Although the responsibility for the elimination of racial discrimination should be placed on employers and perpetrators of discrimination, doing so is a process that will take some time. In the meantime, minority individuals can engage a number of coping strategies to reduce the negative impact of their mistreatment at work. A number of researchers have found that racial group identification (that is, attaching importance to one's racial group and having a sense of connection to racial group members; Sellers, Rowley, Chavous, Shelton, & Smith, 1997) is a protective coping strategy against racial discrimination (Jones, Cross Jr., & DeFour, 2007; Sellers et al., 2003). Racial identification may allow individuals to develop social support networks with other individuals who have had similar negative experiences (Settles, Jellison, & Pratt-Hyatt, 2009). Such social support may allow mistreated individuals to feel less alone when subjected to discriminatory experiences (Bourguignon, Seron, Yzerbyt, & Herman, 2006), enable individuals to focus on positive aspects of the group in the face of prejudice (Sellers & Shelton, 2003), and ensure that the individual benefits from other group members who can provide a wider range of mechanisms to cope with discrimination (Sellers et al., 2003).

In this chapter we have described the legal prohibitions against workplace racial discrimination, which have reduced some of the more explicit forms of unequal racial treatment. We also have noted, however, literature finding that racial discrimination remains a significant problem with significant costs for individuals, organizations, and society. Given that modern racial discrimination in the workplace is becoming more subtle, the field will need to develop new approaches to thinking about the legislation and litigation of discrimination based on such ambiguous, yet harmful, actions toward racial minorities. Finally, given the unconscious nature that racial discrimination may sometimes have, more attention will need to focus on ways to effectively reduce prejudice and change negative stereotypes.

REFERENCES

Allport, G. (1954). *The nature of prejudice*. Reading, MA: Addison Wesley.

Applied Research Center. (2009). Race and recession: How inequity rigged the economy and how to change the rules. Retrieved August 1, 2009, from http://arc.org/downloads/2009_race_recession_0909.pdf.

Aquino, K., Stewart, M. M., & Reed, A. (2005). How social dominance orientation and job status influence perceptions of African American affirmative action beneficiaries. *Personnel Psychology, 58*, 703–744.

Avery, D., McKay, P., Wilson, D., & Tonidandel, S. (2007). Unequal attendance: The relationships between race, organizational diversity cues, and absenteeism. *Personnel Psychology, 60*, 875–902.

Barak, M. E. M., Cherin, D. A., & Berkman, S. (1998). Organizational and personal dimensions in diversity climate: Ethnic and gender differences in employee perceptions. *Journal of Applied Behavioral Science, 34*, 82–104.

Barnes, L. L., Mendes de Leon, C. F., Lewis, T. T., Bienias, J. L., Wilson, R. S., & Evans, D. A. (2008). Perceived discrimination and mortality in a population-based study of older adults. *American Journal of Public Health, 98*, 1241–1247.

Berdahl, J. L., & Moore, C. (2006). Workplace harassment: Double jeopardy for minority women. *Journal of Applied Psychology, 91*, 426–436.

Bergman, M. E., Palmieri, P. A., Drasgow, F., & Ormerod, A. J. (2007). Racial and ethnic harassment and discrimination: In the eye of the beholder? *Journal of Occupational Health Psychology, 12*, 144–160.

Bertrand, M., & Mullainathan, S. (2004). Are Emily and Greg more employable than Lakisha and Jamal? A field experiment on labor market discrimination. *The American Economic Review, 94*(4), 991–1013.

Bielby, W. T. (2008). Promoting racial diversity at work: Challenges and solutions. In A. P. Brief (Ed.), *Diversity at work: Cambridge companions to management* (pp. 53–86). New York: Cambridge University Press.

Bishaw, A., & Semega, J. (2008). *U.S. Census Bureau, American Community Survey Reports, ACS-09, Income, Earnings, and Poverty Data From the 2007 American Community Survey.* Washington, DC: U.S. Government Printing Office.

Bliss, W. G. (2001). The business cost and impact of employee turnover. Retrieved August, 8, 2009, from http://www.blissassociates.com/html/articles/employee_turnover01.html.

Bourguignon, D., Seron, E., Yzerbyt, V., & Herman, G. (2006). Perceived group and personal discrimination: Differential effects on personal self-esteem. *European Journal of Social Psychology, 36,* 773–789.

Branscombe, N., Schmitt, M., & Harvey, R. (1999). Perceiving pervasive discrimination among African Americans: Implications for group identification and well-being. *Journal of Personality and Social Psychology, 77,* 135–149.

Broman, C. L., Mavaddat, R., & Hsu, S. (2000). The experience and consequences of perceived racial discrimination: A study of African Americans. *Journal of Black Psychology, 26,* 165–180.

Bryant-Davis, T. (2007). Healing requires recognition: The case for race-based traumatic stress. *The Counseling Psychologist, 35,* 135–143.

Bryant-Davis, T., & Ocampo, C. (2005). An exploration of racist-incident trauma. *The Counseling Psychologist, 33,* 479–500.

Buchanan, N. T. (2005). The nexus of race and gender domination: The racialized sexual harassment of African American women. In P. Morgan, & J. Gruber (Eds.), *In the company of men: Re-discovering the links between sexual harassment and male domination* (pp. 294–320). Boston, MA: Northeastern University Press.

Buchanan, N. T., Bergman, M. E., Bruce, T. A., Woods, K. C., & Lichty, L. F. (2009). Unique and joint effects of sexual and racial harassment on college students' well-being. *Basic and Applied Social Psychology, 31,* 267–285.

Buchanan, N. T., & Fitzgerald, L. F. (2008). The effects of racial and sexual harassment on work and the psychological well-being of African American women. *Journal of Occupational Health Psychology, 13*(2), 137–151.

Buchanan, N. T., & Ormerod, A. J. (2002). Racialized sexual harassment in the lives of African American Women. *Women & Therapy, 25,* 107–124.

Buchanan, N. T., Settles, I. H., & Woods, K. C. (2008). Comparing sexual harassment subtypes for Black and White women: Double jeopardy, the Jezebel, and the cult of true womanhood. *Psychology of Women Quarterly, 32,* 347–361.

Chew, P. K., & Kelley, R. E., (2006). Unwrapping racial harassment law. *Berkley Journal of Employment and Labor Law, 27,* 49–110. Retrieved September 20, 2009, from http://ssrn.com/abstract=1273737.

Civil Rights Act of 1964, Pub. L. No. 88-352, Title VII, § 701, 78 Stat. 253 (codified as amended by 42 U.S.C. §§ 2000e et seq.) (2000).

Constantine, M. G., Smith, L., Redington, R. M., & Owens, D. (2008). Racial microaggressions against black counseling and counseling psychology faculty: A central challenge in the multicultural counseling movement. *Journal of Counseling and Development. Special Issue: Multicultural Counseling, 86,* 348–355.

Cortina, L. M., Fitzgerald, L. F., & Drasgow, F. (2002). Contextualizing Latina experiences of sexual harassment: Preliminary tests of a structural model. *Basic and Applied Social Psychology, 24,* 295–311.

Cortina, L. M., Magley, V. J., Williams, J. H., & Langhout, R. D. (2001). Incivility in the workplace: Incidence and impact. *Journal of Occupational Health Psychology, 6,* 64–80.

Cummings, S. (1987). Vulnerability to the effects of recession: Minority and female workers. *Social Forces, 65,* 834–857.

Darity, W. A. (2003). Employment discrimination, segregation, and health. *American Journal of Public Health, 93,* 226–231.

Darity, W., Guilkey, D., & Winfrey, W. (1996). Explaining differences in economic performance among racial and ethnic groups in the USA: The data examined. *American Journal of Economics and Sociology, 55,* 411–426.

Deitch, E., Barsky, A., Butz, R. M., Chan, S., Brief, A. P., & Bradley, J. C. (2003). Subtle yet significant: The existence and impact of everyday racial discrimination in the workplace. *Human Relations, 56,* 1299–1324.

DeSouza, E. (2008). Workplace incivility, sexual harassment and racial microaggression: The interface of three literatures. In M. Paludi (Ed.), *The psychology of women at work: Challenges and solutions for our female workforce: Vol. 2. Obstacles and the identity juggle* (pp. 65–84). Westport, CT: Praeger.

Dovidio. J. F., Kawakami, K., & Gaertner, S. L. (2002). Implicit and explicit prejudice and interracial interaction. *Journal of Personality and Social Psychology, 82,* 62–68.

Ensher, E. A., Grant-Vallone, E. J., & Donaldson, S. I. (2001). Effects of perceived discrimination on job satisfaction, organizational commitment, organizational citizenship behavior and grievances. *Human Resource Development Quarterly, 12,* 53–72.

Equal Employment Opportunity Commission. (2002). *Muslim/Arab employment discrimination charges since 9/11.* Retrieved August 15, 2009, from http://www.eeoc.gov/origin/z-stats.html.

Equal Employment Opportunity Commission. (2009). *EEOC charge statistics.* Retrieved July 9, 2009, from http://www.eeoc.gov/stats/race.html.

Faia, E., Lechthaler, W., Merkl, C. (2009). *Labor turnover costs, workers' heterogeneity, and optimal monetary policy* (Institute for the Study of Labor, Discussion paper #4322). Retrieved August 8, 2009, from http://ftp.iza.org/dp4322.pdf.

Feagin, J. R., Vera, H., & Imani, N. (1996). *The agony of education: Black students at white colleges and universities.* New York: Routledge.

Fiske, S. T., & Lee, T. L. (2008). Stereotypes and prejudice create workplace discrimination. In A. P. Brief (Ed.), *Diversity at work: Cambridge companions to management* (pp. 13–52). New York: Cambridge University Press.

Forman, T. A. (2003). The social psychological costs of racial segmentation in the workplace: A study of African Americans' well-being. *Journal of Health and Social Behavior, 44,* 332–352.

French, L. A. (2003). *Native American justice.* Lanham, MD: Rowman & Littlefield Publishers, Inc.

Gottschalk, P. (1997). Inequality, income growth and mobility: The basic facts. *Journal of Economic Perspectives, 11,* 21–40.

Greenwald, A. G., Banaji, M. R., Rudman, L. A., Farnham, S. D., Nosek, B. A., & Mellott, D. S. (2002). A unified theory of implicit attitudes, stereotypes, self-esteem, and self-concept. *Psychological Bulletin, 109,* 3–25.

Gruber, J. E. (2003). Sexual harassment in the public sector. In M. Paludi & C. Paludi (Eds.), *Academic and workplace sexual harassment: A handbook of cultural, social science, management, and legal perspectives* (pp. 49–75). Westport, CT: Praeger Publishers/Greenwood Publishing Group, Inc.

Guyll, M., Matthews, K. A., & Bromberger, J. T. (2001). Discrimination and unfair treatment: Relationship to cardiovascular reactivity among African American and European American women. *Health Psychology, 20*(5), 315–325.

Harrell, S. P. (2000). A multidimensional conceptualization of racism-related stress: Implications for the well-being of people of color. *American Journal of Orthopsychiatry, 70,* 42–57.

Harrick, E. J., & Sullivan, G. M. (1995). Racial harassment: Case characteristics and employer responsibilities. *Employee Responsibilities and Rights Journal, 8,* 81–95.

Hilton, J. L., & von Hippel, W. (1996). Stereotypes. *Annual Review of Psychology, 47,* 237–271.

Holzer, H. J., & Neumark D. (2000). What does affirmative action do? *Industrial and Labor Relations Review, 53,* 240–271.

Jasinskaja-Lahti, I., & Liebkind, K. (2001). Perceived discrimination and psychological adjustment among Russian-speaking immigrant adolescents in Finland. *International Journal of Psychology, 36,* 174–185.

Jones, H. L., Cross, W. E., Jr., & DeFour, D. C. (2007). Race-related stress, racial identity attitudes, and mental health among Black women. *Journal of Black Psychology, 33,* 208–231.

Kalev, A., Dobbin, F., & Kelly, E. (2006). Best practices or best guesses? Diversity management and the remediation of inequality. *American Sociological Review, 71,* 589–917.

Kanter, R. M. (1977). *Men and women of the corporation.* New York: Basic Books.

Kaufman, R. L. (2002). Assessing alternative perspectives on race and sex employment segregation. *American Sociological Review, 67,* 547–572.

Kessler, R. C., Mickelson, K. D., & Williams, D. R. (1999). The prevalence, distribution, and mental health correlates of perceived discrimination in the United States. *Journal of Health and Social Behavior, 40*, 208–230.

Kickul, J., & Liao-Troth, M. A. (2003). The meaning behind the message: Climate perceptions and the psychological contract. *Mid-American Journal of Business, 18*(2), 23–32.

Kim, M. (2007). *Race and economic opportunity in the twenty-first century.* London: Routledge.

Klonoff, E. A., Landrine, H., & Ullman, J. B. (1999). Racial discrimination and psychiatric symptoms among Blacks. *Cultural Diversity and Ethnic Minority Psychology, 5*, 329–339.

Krieger, N., Waterman, P. D., Hartman, C., Bates, L. M., Stoddard, A., Quinn, M. M., et al. (2006). Social hazards on the job: Workplace abuse, sexual harassment and racial discrimination: A study of Black, Latino, and White low-income women and men workers in the United States. *International Journal of Health Services, 36*, 51–85.

Landrine, H., & Klonoff, E. A. (1996). The schedule of racist events: A measure of racial discrimination and a study of its negative physical and mental health consequences. *Journal of Black Psychology, 22*, 144–168.

Liebkind, K., & Jasinskaja, I. (2000). The influence of experiences of discrimination on psychological stress: A comparison of seven immigrant groups. *Journal of Community and Applied Social Psychology, 10*, 1–16.

Loden, M., & Rosener, J. B. (1991). *Workforce America! Managing employee diversity as a vital resource.* Burr Ridge, IL: Irwin.

Maume, D. (2004). Wage discrimination over the life course: A comparison of explanations. *Social Problems, 51*, 505–527.

Mays, V. M., Coleman, L. M., & Jackson, J. S. (1996). Perceived race-based discrimination, employment status, and job stress in a national sample of black women: Implications for health outcomes. *Journal of Occupational Health Psychology, 1*, 319–329.

McKay, P., Avery, D., & Morris, M. (2008). Mean racial-ethnic differences in employee sales performance: The moderating role of diversity climate. *Personnel Psychology, 61*, 349–374.

McLaughlin, H., Uggen, C., & Blackstone, A. (2008). Social class and workplace harassment during the transition to adulthood. *Social Class and Transitions to Adulthood. New Directions for Child and Adolescent Development, 119*, 85–98.

Michel, R. C. (1991). Economic growth and income equality since the 1982 recession. *Journal of Policy Analysis and Management, 10*, 181–203.

Norton, M. I., Sommers, S. R., Vandello, J. A., & Darley, J. M. (2006). Mixed motives and racial bias: The impact of legitimate and illegitimate criteria on decision making. *Psychology, Public Policy, and Law, 12*, 36–55.

Parkins, I. S., Fishbein, H. D., & Ritchey, P. N. (2006). The influence of personality on workplace bullying and discrimination. *Journal of Applied Social Psychology, 36,* 2554–2577.

Pavalko, E. K., Mossakowski, K. N., & Hamilton, V. J. (2003). Does perceived discrimination affect health? Longitudinal relationships between work discrimination and women's physical and emotional health. *Journal of Health and Social Behavior, 43,* 18–23.

Petersen T, & Saporta I. (2004). The opportunity structure for discrimination. *American Journal of Sociology, 109,* 852–901.

Peterson, D. K. (2002). Deviant workplace behavior and the organization's ethical climate. *Journal of Business and Psychology, 17,* 47–61.

Podsakoff, N. P., Whiting, S. W., Podsakoff, P. M., & Blume, B. D. (2009). Individual- and organizational-level consequences of organizational citizenship behaviors: A meta-analysis. *Journal of Applied Psychology, 94,* 122–141.

Reskin, B. F. (2000). The proximate causes of employment discrimination. *Contemporary Sociology, 29,* 319–328.

Reskin, B. F., McBrier, D. B., & Kmec, J. A. (1999). The determinants and consequences of workplace sex and race composition. *Annual Review of Sociology, 25,* 335–361.

Rodgers, W., & Spriggs, W. (1996). What does AFQT really measure: Race, wages, schooling and the AFQT score. *The Review of Black Political Economy, 24,* 13–46.

Rogers v. EEOC, 454 F.2d 234 (5th Cir. 1971). *Cert. denied,* 406 U.S. 957 (1972).

Sanchez, J. I., & Brock, P. (1996). Outcomes of perceived discrimination among Hispanic employees: Is diversity management a luxury or a necessity? *Academy of Management Journal, 39,* 704–719.

Schneider, K. T., Hitlan, R. T., & Radhakrishnan, P. (2000). An examination of the nature and correlates of ethnic harassment experiences in multiple contexts. *Journal of Applied Psychology, 85,* 3–12.

Seibert, S. E., Silver, S. R., & Randolph, W. A. (2004). Taking empowerment to the next level: A multiple-level model of empowerment, performance, and satisfaction. *Academy of Management Journal, 47,* 332–349.

Sellers, R. M., Caldwell, C. H., Schmeelk-Cone, K. H., & Zimmerman, M. A. (2003). Racial identity, racial discrimination, perceived stress, and psychological distress among African American young adults. *Journal of Health and Social Behavior, 44,* 302–317.

Sellers, R. M., Rowley, S. A. J., Chavous, T. M., Shelton, J. N., & Smith, M. A. (1997). Multidimensional inventory of black identity: A preliminary investigation of reliability and construct validity. *Journal of Personality and Social Psychology, 73,* 1–11.

Sellers, R. M., & Shelton, J. N. (2003). The role of racial identity in perceived racial discrimination. *Journal of Personality and Social Psychology, 84,* 1079–1092.

Settles, I. H., Pratt-Hyatt, J. S., & Buchanan, N. T. (2008). Through the lens of race: Black and White women's perceptions of their gender. *Psychology of Women Quarterly, 32*, 454–468.

Shields, M. A., & Price, S. W. (2002). Racial harassment, job satisfaction and intentions to quit: Evidence from the British nursing profession. *Economica, 69*, 295–326.

Sidanius, J., & Pratto, F. (1999). *Social dominance: An intergroup theory of social hierarchy and oppression.* New York: Cambridge University Press.

Sigelman, L., & Welch, S. (1991). *Black Americans' views of racial inequality: The dream deferred.* New York: Cambridge University Press.

Simons, T., Friedman, R., Liu, L. A., & McLean Parks, J. (2007). Racial differences in sensitivity to behavioral integrity: Attitudinal consequences, in-group effects, and "trickle down" among Black and non-Black employees. *Journal of Applied Psychology, 92*, 650–665.

Sims, C. (1993). Last hired, first fired? Minorities retreat in defense. *Science, 262*, 1125–1126.

Smith, R. A. (2002). Race, gender, and authority in the workplace: Theory and research. *Annual Review of Sociology, 28*, 509–542.

Solano, F., & Kleiner, B. H. (2003). Understanding and preventing workplace retaliation. *Management Research News, 26*(2–4), 206–211.

Stauffer, J. M., & Buckley, M. R. (2005). The existence and nature of racial bias in supervisory ratings. *Journal of Applied Psychology, 90*, 586–591.

Sue, D. W., Capodilupo, C. M., Torino, G. C., Bucceri, J. M., Holder, A. M. B., Nadal, K. L., & Esquilin, M. (2007). Racial micro-aggressions in everyday life. *American Psychologist, 62*, 271–286.

Swim, J. K., Hyers, L. L., Cohen, L. L., Fitzgerald, D. C., & Bylsma, W. H. (2003). African American college student's experiences with everyday racism: Characteristics of and responses to these incidents. *Journal of Black Psychology, 29*, 38–67.

Tilly C. (1998). *Durable inequality.* Berkeley: University of California Press.

Umphress, E., Simmons, A., Boswell, W., & Triana, M. (2008). Managing discrimination in selection: The influence of directives from an authority and social dominance orientation. *Journal of Applied Psychology, 93*, 982–993.

Utsey, S. O., Giesbrecht, N., Hook, J., & Stanard, P. M. (2008). Cultural, socio-familial, and psychological resources that inhibit psychological distress in African Americans exposed to stressful life events and race-related stress. *Journal of Counseling Psychology, 55*, 49–62.

Utsey, S. O., Payne, Y. A., Jackson, E. S., & Jones, A. M. (2002). Race-related stress, quality of life indicators, and life satisfaction among elderly African Americans. *Cultural Diversity and Ethnic Minority Psychology, 8*, 224–233.

Vallas, S. P. (2003). Rediscovering the color line within work organizations: The 'knitting' of racial groups revisited. *Work and Occupations, 30*, 379–400.

Williams, D. R., Neighbors, H. W., & Jackson, J. S. (2003). Racial/ethnic discrimination and health: Findings from community studies. *American Journal of Public Health, 93*, 200–208.

Wilson, G. (2005). Race and job dismissal: African American/White differences in their sources during the early work career. *American Behavioral Scientist, 48*, 1182–1199.

Wong, C. A., Eccles, J. S., & Sameroff, A. (2003). The influence of ethnic discrimination and ethnic identification on African American adolescents' school and socioemotional adjustment. *Journal of Personality, 71*, 1197–1232.

Ziegert, J. C. & Hanges, P. J. (2005). Employment discrimination: The role of implicit attitudes, motivation, and a climate for racial bias. *Journal of Applied Psychology, 90*, 553–562.

8

Religious Discrimination

Michele A. Paludi, J. Harold Ellens, and Carmen A. Paludi, Jr.

> We have just enough religion to make us hate, but not enough to make us love one another.
> —Jonathan Swift, essay "Thoughts on various subjects"

> Let us let our own children know that we will stand against the forces of fear. When there is talk of hatred, let us stand up and talk against it. When there is talk of violence, let us stand up and talk against it.
> —President William Jefferson Clinton

INTRODUCTION

In the United States, approximately 8 out of 10 adults report that they belong to one of various forms of Christianity, approximately 5 percent to other faiths, and one in six are not affiliated with any particular religion (Pew Forum on Religion and Public Life, 2009). In addition, 63 percent of Americans report that they are members of a synagogue or church; 43 percent report that they participate in religious services either once a week or almost every week (Gallup, 2006). Eck (2001), Ball and Haque (2003), and Mathias (2008) noted that the United States is among the most religiously diverse countries in the world, and its citizens belong to more than 2,000 faiths and denominations. Ellens (2007) describes individual humans as needing to fill their souls and satisfy their spirits by understanding the meaning of God, the meaning of relationships, and the meaning of intimacy.

Mathias (2008) suggested:

[M]any Americans regard their religion as a very public matter. For the devout, religion provides the overarching framework that orients them in the world and provides them with motivation and direction for living. (p. 112)

Nasr (1993) illustrated this view with respect to Islam:

In the Islamic perspective, religion is not seen as a part of life or a special kind of activity along with art, thought, commerce, social discourse, politics and the like. (p. 439)

Rather, it is the matrix and worldview within which these and all other human activities, efforts, creations, and thoughts take place or should take place (see also Ellens, 2004g). Henry Ford has been quoted as saying, "Why is it that I always get the whole person when all I really want is a pair of hands?" (see Pollard, 1996). An individual's religion accompanies them to the workplace, just as does their race, national origin, disability, sex, and age. Moreover, in many cases, religious beliefs and practices are questioned, ridiculed, denied, or treated in an offensive way. The Institute for Corporate Productivity (2008) reported that one-third of 278 employers surveyed indicated that they had seen religious conflict between co-workers in their organizations, but they were not certain of how to handle such religious differences and conflicts.

The Equal Employment Opportunity Commission (EEOC) has reported a rapid increase in complaints of religious discrimination by employees in a variety of American workplaces, especially since the terrorist attacks of September 11, 2001. For example, as of December 6, 2001, the EEOC had received 166 formal complaints of workplace discrimination related to the September 11 attacks (also see Ball & Haque, 2003). In 2008, 3,386 cases of religious discrimination against employers were filed with the EEOC, an increase of approximately 1,500 complaints since 1997. In addition, the EEOC recovered $7.6 million for complainants in 2008, not including monetary benefits obtained through litigation. This is more than triple the annual monetary benefits recovered based on religious discrimination claims from 1997. In 2008, the

EEOC issued new guidelines recommending courses for action for dealing with religious discrimination and harassment.

Examples of cases of religious discrimination in the past few years include the following:

- In 2002, in *Bernstein v. Sephora, Div. of DFS Group*, statements by an administrator who was involved in personnel decisions for the organization (even though not the ultimate deciding manager) was found to constitute direct proof of discrimination. Statements were directed at an employee including antipathy toward Jewish individuals and made in proximity to a promotion decision of this employee. Comments included: "We must work together to get rid of that JAP bitch" and "She and her princess ways have to go."

- *Riback v. Las Vegas Metropolitan Police Department, et al.* Police detective Steve Riback has worked for the Las Vegas Metropolitan Police Department for 10 years. He wears, as required by his religious beliefs, a beard and a yarmulke or alternative head covering. In 2006, his deputy chief ordered him to shave his beard. This police department had a no-beards policy but waived it for employees with medical conditions. Furthermore, police officers were allowed to wear the "International Fellowship of Christian Officers" pin on their uniforms. Officer Riback alerted his superiors that his beard and wearing a head covering were not inconsistent with the department's existing procedures nor did they create an undue hardship (to be defined later in this chapter) for the department. Subsequently, the department changed its policy and banned all group- identifying pins and the wearing of any hats while indoors. A federal judge ruled that the police department's no-beard policy violated the First Amendment Right of religious freedom.

- Kimberlie Webb was a police officer in Philadelphia, Pennsylvania, who was disciplined by her supervisors for wearing a khimar while on police duty. She requested permission to wear her headscarf because of religious necessity. She wore her headscarf covering her hair, forehead, sides of her head, neck, shoulder, and chest but left her face visible. She wanted to tuck the lower portion of the scarf inside of her police uniform. Her request was denied since the policy of the department prohibited on-duty police officers from wearing religious symbols. When she refused to take off the headscarf, she was not permitted to work. When she complied with the uniform requirements, she was able to return to police duty. She brought this issue to the attention of the police commissioner, also a Muslim, who suspended her for two weeks. Ms. Webb lost her appeal of this case, which she initially brought in 2008 in the spring of 2009. The appeals court indicated that a law enforcement agent should be a religiously neutral official.

- Connie Rehm, in Savanah, Missouri, sued Rolling Hills Consolidated Library because of religious discrimination. In September 2006, a federal jury ruled in her favor and reinstated her to her job. Rehm was fired from the library because she refused to work on Sundays. She stated: "What price is my religious freedom? What is it worth? It's not a matter of displaying the Ten Commandments. It's being able to live the Ten Commandments, and that's what my employer was asking me not to do."

- In 2004 in *Tyson v. Methodist Health Group, Inc.*, the employer's motion for summary judgment was denied because a jury could reasonably infer a discriminatory motive from comments made to a Muslim woman from her supervisor, including referring to Muslims as "you guys," and informing the employee that people did not like Muslims and expressed his surprise to this employee when she returned to work after getting married because he believed that married Muslim women did not work.

In this chapter, we define religious discrimination and religious harassment and discuss employers' legal responsibilities for preventing and dealing with religious discrimination and harassment. In addition, we discuss social science research on prejudice and discrimination of employees because of their religious beliefs and practices. We provide recommendations for employers for preventing and responding to religious discrimination in workplaces, including exercising "reasonable care," and an antireligious discrimination policy investigatory procedures and training programs to inform all members of the workplace community about their rights and responsibilities with respect to religious discrimination. As Romanow and Karakowsky (2007) have noted, "For some employees, achieving a balance between religion and work is of fundamental importance to personal well-being" (p. 25). In keeping with this perspective, we offer a human resource toolkit to assist employees and employers with this type of workplace discrimination (Downey, 2008; Kelly, 2008) and enable them to set an atmosphere of respect for the workplace community.

TITLE VII AND RELIGIOUS DISCRIMINATION

Title VII of the 1964 Civil Rights Act prohibits employers from discriminating against individuals because of their religion in recruitment, hiring, firing, compensation, transfer, leave, layoff, testing, use of company facilities, training, and other terms and conditions of employment. Title VII covers employers with 15 or more employees and also applies to state and local governments, federal government, labor organizations, and employment agencies. Title VII makes illegal any type of harassment on the basis of an employee's religion. Furthermore, Title VII prohibits retaliation against an employee for filing a charge of religious discrimination or participating in an investigation of religious discrimination and taking actions that oppose discriminatory practices in the organization. Exceptions from coverage by Title VII's religion provisions include the following: religious organizations, clergy members, and religious education institutions.

Title VII has defined *religion* as "all aspects of religious observance and practice as well as belief." According to the EEOC's Guidelines (2009b), however, *religion* is defined as "moral or ethical beliefs as to what is right or wrong which are sincerely held with the strength of traditional religious views."

The EEOC (2009b) also states that—

[A]n employer may not refuse to hire individuals of a certain religion, may not impose stricter promotion requirements for persons of a certain religion, and may not impose more or different work requirements on an employee because of that employee's religious beliefs or practices.

The EEOC (2009b) provides the following examples of religious discrimination in the workplace:

Not hiring an otherwise qualified applicant because he is a self-described evangelical Christian; a Jewish supervisor denying a promotion to a qualified non-Jewish employee because the supervisor wishes to give a preference based on religion to a fellow Jewish employee; or, terminating an employee because he told the employer that he recently converted to the Baha'i faith.

Title VII defines "religion" to include the following:

[N]ot only traditional organized religions such as Christianity, Judaism, Islam, Hinduism, and Buddhism, but also religious beliefs that are new, uncommon, not part of a formal church or sect, only subscribed to by a small number of people, or that seem illogical or unreasonable to others. (EEOC, 2009b)

In addition, Title VII defines religious practices to include praying, wearing religious clothing or symbols, displaying religious objects, attending worship services, observing dietary rules, and refraining from activities.

REASONABLE ACCOMMODATIONS

According to the EEOC, employers must reasonably accommodate employees "sincerely held religious practices unless doing so would impose an undue hardship on the employer." Employers' responsibilities to accommodate employees' religious beliefs is governed by the 1977

U.S. Supreme Court decision in *TWA v. Hardison* (Prenkert & Magid, 2006). The Supreme Court ruled that an employer has the legal duty to accommodate its employees' exercise of religious practices in the workplace so long as the accommodation requested does not create more than a *de minimis* cost to the employer.

In 1986, in *Ansonia Board of Education v. Philbrook,* the Supreme Court ruled that an employer can meet its duty to accommodate employees' religious practices by offering any reasonable accommodation, not just the one identified by the employee. The only restriction is that the accommodation must not disadvantage the employee's work opportunities for advancement, benefits, and so on (also see Prenkert & Magid, 2006).

Examples of reasonable accommodations include providing employees time off for religious observances, a place to pray, flexible job schedules, job reassignments, and exemptions from dress code and grooming requirement policies. Under Title VII "undue hardship" is generally an accommodation that would cost the employer more than a minimal sum, impairs safety practices, conflicts with other laws or workplace policies, or infringes on co-workers' job benefits.

The Institute for Corporate Productivity (2008) found that 61 percent of the 278 employers surveyed reported they had provided an accommodation to an employee based on the employee's religious beliefs, but only 12 percent of the employers indicated they had a policy that identified what constituted a "religious belief." Two-thirds of the employers surveyed indicated they had no written policy prohibiting religious discrimination and harassment of employees. Furthermore, 29 percent of the employers stated that they train managers on how to avoid religious bias in their decision making.

Smith (2004)'s critique of religious accommodation claims provided the following conclusion:

> The safeguards provided for employee religious practices have been so restricted by court decisions that an employee who requests a religious accommodation must rely more on an employer's generosity and good-will than on statutory protection. In case after case, employers have chosen to deny employees' requests for accommodation by citing some trivial difficulty, perhaps even a "potential" hardship, as undue; in other words, requiring more than a *de minimus* cost. (p. 64)

And, as Downey (2008) recommended,

> As a general rule, employers need to consider reasonable requests for accommodation as long as a true undue hardship is not created. Much like

the Americans with Disabilities Act, employers probably will not be required to hire additional employees just to cover for another employee who needs an accommodation based on religious needs. Employers also will not be required to give employees unrestricted leave time. (p. 87)

RELIGIOUS HARASSMENT IN THE WORKPLACE

According to Title VII, religious harassment in the workplace occurs when employees are subjected to the following:

> Required or coerced to abandon, alter, or adopt a religious practice as a consequence of employment or subjected to unwelcome statements or conduct that is based on religion and is so severe or pervasive that the individual being harassed reasonably finds the work environment to be hostile or abusive, and there is a basis for holding the employer liable. (EEOC, 2009b)

Similar to sexual harassment, there are types of religious harassment: *quid pro quo* and hostile environment harassment. *Quid pro quo* harassment is defined as when an individual with organizational power (for example, a manager) makes decisions that affect an employee's job on the basis of whether the employee complies with their demands. Thus, if a manager puts pressure on an employee to change their religious practices to keep their job or some job related benefit, it is *quid pro quo* religious harassment. If an employee is harassed by an individual with organizational power or a co-worker as a result of their religious preference or practice, an actionable hostile environment may result, if the harassment unreasonably interferes with the employee's ability to get the work done and is perceived by the employer to be intimidating, offensive, and hostile, as it would be perceived by a reasonable woman or man.

Employers are liable for religious harassment if the conduct results in a tangible employment action. The employer must prove that it exercised reasonable care (EEOC, 2009a, 2009c; Smith & Mazin, 2004) to prevent and promptly deal with harassing behavior, and the employee unreasonably failed to take advantage of the employers' prevention efforts (that is, procedures for filing an internal complaint). In addition, an employer is liable for religious harassment by co-workers in cases in which the employer "knew or should have known about the harassment, and failed to take prompt and appropriate corrective action" (EEOC, 2009b).

SUMMARY OF LEGAL ISSUES

There are four types of workplace discrimination because of religion:

1. Harassment of an employee as a result of their religious beliefs.
2. Failure to accommodate an employee's religious beliefs and practices in cases in which it would not be an undue hardship to do so.
3. Disparate treatment of an employee because of their religious beliefs and practices.
4. Retaliation against an employee for coming forth with a complaint of religious discrimination or for participating in an investigation of a complaint of religious discrimination.

TOWARD AN UNDERSTANDING OF RELIGIOUS DISCRIMINATION IN THE WORKPLACE

Stereotypes and Prejudice

The American Psychological Association (APA, 2007) issued a resolution on religious, religion-based, or religion-derived prejudice. According to the APA,

> Prejudice based on or derived from religion has been used to justify discrimination, prejudice and human rights violations against those holding different religious beliefs, those who profess no religious beliefs, individuals of various ethnicities, women, those who are not exclusively heterosexual, and other individuals and groups depending on perceived theological justification or imperative. . . . The APA condemns prejudice and discrimination against individuals or groups based on their religious or spiritual beliefs, practices, adherence, or background.

Negative attitudes and feelings about people of different religions, like race, develop as a consequence of cognitive, motivational, and sociocultural processes (Ellens, 2004d, 2004h). The cognitive aspect refers to placing individuals in categories that activate stereotypes. The motivational aspect refers to the need for individual power, status, and control. Finally, the sociocultural aspect refers to viewing derogatory religious or racist attitudes and behavior as normal.

Stereotypes refer to individuals' thoughts and cognitions that typically do not correspond with reality (Feinberg, 2000; Fiske, 1993; Hilton & von Hippel, 1996). Stereotypes occur when individuals are classified by others as having something in common because they are members of a particular group or category of people (for example, Muslims, Roman Catholics, Jews). Psychological research has identified that stereotypes have the following characteristics (Fiske, 1993):

- Groups that are targeted for stereotypes are easily identified and relatively powerless.
- There is little agreement between the composite picture of the group and the actual characteristics of that group.
- This misperception is difficult to modify even though individuals who hold stereotypes have interacted with individuals of the group who disconfirm the stereotypes.
- This misperception is the product of a bias in individuals' information-processing mechanisms.

Religious stereotyping is a psychological process that describes individuals' structured set of beliefs about the personal attributes of individuals of various religions (Ellens, 2004b, 2004d, 2004h). Psychologists have identified an emotional component to stereotypic cognitions: prejudice as well as behavioral components to individuals' cognitions, that is, discrimination and harassment (Allport, 2000; Batson & Stocks, 2005; Herek, 1987; Hunsberger & Jackson, 2005; Kawakami, Spears, & Dovidio, 2002; Maass, Castelli, & Acuri, 2000). Thus, individuals' statements and nonverbal gestures toward individuals of various religious beliefs and practices provide insight into their structured set of beliefs about each religion.

Out-group Homogeneity Bias

Related to stereotyping is the "outgroup homogeneity bias" (Judd, Park, Yzerbyt, Gordijn, & Muller, 2005). This is a process by which individuals view groups in which they are not a part (for example, a religion different from their own) as more homogeneous than their own group (for example, their own religion). Thus, stereotypes concerning members of out-groups are stronger than those of in-group members. According to Judd (cited in DeAngelis, 2001), "people are more willing to ignore individuating information about members of outgroups, lumping them all into a single disliked category" (p. 3). In actuality, focusing on differences among religions or other protected categories ignores in-group variability. The overemphasis on differences provides confirmation of the stereotype that religions are "opposite" and that one's own religious beliefs are normative and other religions are a deviation from the norm (Ellens, 2004a, 2006).

ORGANIZATIONAL CONTEXTS THAT ELICIT DISCRIMINATION

The organizational context affects whether discriminatory behaviors and harassment will be expressed (Ellens, 2004i). According to psychological research, religious stereotyping, similar to other forms of stereotyping (for example, due to sex, race, age, disability) in the workplace is likely to be elicited (that is, discriminatory statements and behavior occurs) under the following conditions (Fiske & Stevens, 1993): (1) rarity (for example, one or a few members of a particular religion present in a particular occupation), (2) priming (that is, religiously explicit comments present in the workplace), (3) participation in the behavior by supervisors, and (4) inadequate and ineffective policies to prohibit the verbal and nonverbal expression of religious stereotypes.

Religious Hate Crimes

Social scientists have devoted considerable research to studying hate crimes, including religious hate crimes (Boeckmann & Turpin-Petrosino, 2002; DeAngelis, 2001; Steinberg, 2004; Volpe & Strobl, 2005). A hate crime is generally defined as a crime that in whole or part is motivated by the offender's bias toward the victim's status. Hate crimes are intended to hurt and intimidate individuals because they are perceived to be different with respect to their religion, race, color, national origin, sexual orientation, gender, or disability (Ellens, 2004f).

Legislation list specific crimes that are identifiable as a hate crime, including murder, manslaughter, robbery, aggravated assault, burglary, motor vehicle theft, arson, forced and nonforced sex offenses, intimidation, destruction, damage or vandalism of property, and other crimes involving injury to any person or property in which the victim is intentionally selected because of the actual or perceived religion, race, sex, sexual orientation, ethnicity, or disability of the victim.

Bias-Motivated Incidents

When the behavior does not fall into one of the listed criminal categories identified above, hate offenses are referred to as bias-motivated incidents. These incidents may include cases of verbal slurs, etc. and be precursors to more serious hate crimes.

Incidence of Hate Crimes   The Department of Justice (2004) reported that victims of religious hate crimes made up 16.7 percent of the victims of incidents of hate crimes involving a single incident. Of these religious hate crimes, 67.8 percent were victims of anti-Jewish bias and 12.7 percent were victims of anti-Islamic bias. In addition, The Council on American-Islamic Relations reported a sharp increase of hate bias complaints by Muslims in the years following the September 11, 2001, terrorist attacks and the subsequent wars in Iraq and Afghanistan. The FBI National Uniform Crime Reporting Program also reported that, after the September 11 attacks, Muslim Americans became the second-highest group to report faith-based hate crimes in 2001. The highest group was Jewish Americans.

Sheridan's (2006) research also documented the heightened irrational fears about Muslims and Arabs after September 11, 2001, contributing to discrimination and hate crimes.

Rippy and Newman (2006) noted the following:

> Arabs and Muslims in the United States find themselves in the precarious situation of belonging, through either ethnic or religious ties, to a group that has staged an attack on American soil. This unique situation has not been faced by any ethnic group in this nation since the Japanese attack on Pearl Harbor on December 7, 1941. (p. 6)

These realities prompted the EEOC (2009d) to issue a separate guidance, following the September 11, 2001, terrorist attacks, about increased efforts to prevent religious discrimination in the workplace stemming from hate crimes and bias-motivated incidents.

IMPACT OF RELIGIOUS DISCRIMINATION, HARASSMENT, AND HATE CRIMES ON EMPLOYEES

Several empirical studies have documented the high cost of workplace discrimination and harassment, including religious discrimination (Bierman, 2006; Endler, Parker, Bagby, & Cox, 1991; Katz, Joiner, & Kwon, 2002; Miville, Rohrbacker, & Kim, 2005). Since most experiences of religious discrimination and harassment (similar to other forms of discrimination) are not isolated events but rather a series of escalating behaviors, victims experience many reactions to the behaviors as they intensify over time. The outcomes of the victimization process can be examined from the following perspectives: emotional or psychological, physiological or health-related, career and work, social effects, and self-perception.

Not all victims of religious discrimination and harassment experience all of the listed symptoms. Most victims experience severe distress associated with discrimination and harassment. The symptoms become exacerbated when in continued contact with the perpetrator, when the harassment is done in front of co-workers, and when it is retaliation against a victim's complaining about harassment or discrimination to an employer. Harassment occurring at one point sometimes affects job and psychological variables two years later, suggesting that the negative consequences of harassment are enduring and often compounded by further discrimination and harassment.

Examples of emotional and psychological effects of religious discrimination and harassment include, but are not limited to, guilt, denial, withdrawal from social settings, shame, depression, fear, anger, anxiety, phobias, isolation, fear of crime, helplessness, frustration, shock, and decreased self-esteem. The following are reported physical and health-related effects of religious harassment: headaches, tiredness, respiratory problems, substance abuse, sleep disturbances, eating disorders, lethargy, gastrointestinal disorders, dermatological reactions, and inability to concentrate. In addition, victims of religious harassment and discrimination experience an affect on their career goals as well as their ability to perform their job in the way they were accustomed. This impact includes, but is not limited to, changes in work habits, absenteeism, and changes in career goals.

The affect of religious harassment on social and interpersonal relationships has included the following: withdrawal, fear of new people, lack of trust, changes in social network patterns, and relationship difficulties.

Similar results have been noted with respect to victims of hate crimes (Craig-Henderson & Sloan, 2006; DeAngelis, 2001; Kessler, Mickelson, & Williams, 1999; Rippy & Newman, 2006). Staub (quoted in DeAngelis, 2001) noted: "When people are victimized as individuals or as a group, it creates a diminished sense of self, a view that the world is a more dangerous place" (p. 1). Rippy and Newman (2006) reported that perceived discrimination among Muslim Americans is associated with their being increasingly vigilant, mistrusting, and suspicious of others. They also found that Muslim Americans who perceived themselves to be religiously discriminated against had subclinical paranoid ideation.

ROLE OF EMPLOYEES ASSISTANCE PROGRAMS

Employees Assistance Programs (EAPs) can help employees deal with non-work-related issues that interfere with their ability to perform their job (Smith & Mazin, 2004). EAPs provide short-term counseling on the telephone or in-person as well as refer employees for help in the community. An EAP can be utilized to assist employees in dealing with the symptomatology of religious harassment and discrimination reviewed in this chapter. Recommendations for EAPs include the following: (1) helping employees to develop a sense of trust and safety in their current environment, (2) understanding employees' insecurity about their future in the organization, (3) countering any sense of guilt about having caused the discrimination or harassment and not being able to prevent the discrimination, and (4) increasing employees' self-esteem and self-confidence in seeking redress or problem solving.

EAPs can play an important role in training supervisors to recognize changes in employees' behavior, as a consequence of religious discrimination and harassment, and to know how to refer them to the EAP in a confidential manner (DeCenzo & Robbins, 2007; Smith & Mazin, 2004).

It is important to note, however, that employees view counseling in general and the EAP interventions differently. Racial minority individuals underutilize mental health services because of a sense of stigma attached to seeking support for problems (Brinson & Kottler, 1995; Comas-Diaz & Jacobsen, 1991; Dixon & Wright, 2009; Landrine, 1995; Marmion & Faulkner, 2006; Ramirez, 1991). For example, Amer (cited in Winerman, 2006) noted that Muslim and Arab employees are reluctant to seek counseling because of cultural barriers to disclosing to strangers. Amer noted that Muslim and Arab Americans are at increased risk for depression, anxiety, and other mental health problems due to the stress of trying to acculturate to mainstream America.

Ali (cited in Winerman, 2006) further noted that Muslim women must deal with additional stressors because their traditional attire makes their religion identifiable. Ali noted that employees should hire more Muslim women to increase their visibility as well as acceptance in the workplace. Ali also recommended that employers develop and post acceptance policies regarding head coverings. Ghumman and Jackson (2010) noted that Muslim women who wear hijabis have lower expectations of receiving a job offer than Muslim women who do not wear this headscarf.

IMPACT OF RELIGIOUS DISCRIMINATION AND HARASSMENT ON WORKPLACES

Religious discrimination and harassment affects the primary employed individual, as well as family, co-workers, clients, vendors, and customers. Religious discrimination, similar to all forms of discrimination, thus contributes to stress for all in the workplace. This stress consequently results in lost productivity, decreased morale, increased absenteeism, and increased employee turnover. Religious discrimination has a sweeping effect on work performance and potentially on workplace conflict and violence. The employee may need to pursue mental health care for several years after the initial discrimination and harassment. Thus, the estimated costs of religious discrimination in the workplace are underestimated significantly in the official statistics given for any specific year.

ORGANIZATIONS' USE OF REASONABLE CARE

"Reasonable care," adapted from rulings in *Burlington Industries, Inc. v. Ellerth* (1998) and *Faragher v. City of Boca Raton* (1998), includes the following, at a minimum:

- Establish and enforce an effective policy
- Establish and enforce effective investigative procedures
- Facilitate training in prevention of religious discrimination and harassment in general, and the organization's policy and procedures specifically

These cases focused on sexual harassment, however, the EEOC (1999) has maintained that these basic standards apply to "all types of prohibited harassment." In describing this "reasonable care" perspective to religious discrimination, we integrate management theory, case law, and social science research to effectively enforce policies and procedures in an atmosphere of trust that encourages individuals to come forth with their experiences of religious discrimination and harassment.

We discuss the following prevention strategies to assist organizations in preventing and dealing with religious discrimination: (1) primary, (2) secondary, and (3) tertiary. Primary prevention strategies include the development and enforcement of policies, investigatory procedures and training programs on religious discrimination, and an organizational policy prohibiting this form of discrimination. Secondary prevention strategies include facilitating individualized training with employees who are at high risk for being victims of religious discrimination. Finally, tertiary prevention includes working with victims of religious discrimination and harassment, and providing counseling services for them. Each of these strategies is addressed in the following sections and is based on recommendations made by the EEOC (2009a) psychologists, human resource management scholars, and labor and employment attorneys (for example, Downey, 2008; Pearce, Kuhn, & DiLullo, 2005; Prenkert & Magid, 2006; Schramm, 2009; Winerman, 2006).

PRIMARY PREVENTION STRATEGIES

Policies and Procedures

Policies that establish a zero-tolerance for religious discrimination and harassment in the workplace require more than a general statement against the behavior (Downey, 2008; EEOC, 2009a). They require the efforts and support of management at all levels and continual training of all employees, as well as procedures that encourage employees to disclose their discrimination and harassment to the organization.

Components of Policies and Procedures   Downey (2008), the EEOC, and Society for Human Resource Management (2009a) recommend an explicit policy statement and investigatory procedures for assisting victims of religious discrimination and harassment. According to the EEOC (2009a),

> Employers should have a well-publicized and consistently applied anti-harassment policy that: (1) covers religious harassment; (2) clearly explains what is prohibited; (3) describes procedures for bringing harassment to management's attention; and (4) contains an assurance that complainants will be protected against retaliation. The procedures should include a complaint mechanism that includes multiple avenues for complaint; prompt, thorough, and impartial investigations; and prompt and appropriate corrective action.

Downey (2008) and Pearce et al. (2005) further advised that employers should make it clear in their policy statements that discrimination and harassment based on religion are illegal, just as are harassment based on other protected categories, that is, sex, race, national origin, and sexual harassment. For a discussion of components of effective policy statements, see Paludi and Paludi (2003).

An important consideration for the policy is whether it sets a tone of appropriate seriousness and concern for employees' rights. Thus, the policy needs to specify the types of behaviors that are prohibited in the workplace and the potential consequences of these behaviors, should they occur.

Empirical research has indicated that employees will feel more encouraged to discuss their experiences with discrimination and harassment when they understand what the process entails (Paludi & Paludi, 2003). Thus, employees must be given accurate and adequate information about disclosing their victimization, written in understandable language and terms. Failure to provide such information makes the policy statement inhibitive. We also recommend including a comparable policy statement on hate crimes and bias-motivated incidents.

Training Programs

According to Downey (2008),

> Merely having established policies will not be enough. . . . Employers need to train their managers about acceptable and unacceptable conduct involving religious beliefs. Religious, social and political controversies are less likely to erupt in a workplace where a company's anti-discrimination, anti-harassment, religious accommodation, and dispute-resolution policies are all communicated clearly, early and often. (p. 86)

Ball and Haque (2003) and Paludi and Paludi (2003) recommended that human resource specialists facilitate training programs for managers and employees in two sections: (1) information on religious discrimination awareness, for example, definitions, incidence frequency, and impact on victims and the workplace; and (2) information on the organization's policy and procedures, so that managers know their rights and responsibilities with respect to assisting employees who are victims of religious discrimination and harassment.

Their recommendations for training programs on sexual harassment may be implemented with religious discrimination as well. They identified the following components of effective training programs for managers:

- Ways to encourage employees to report problems
- Skills in behaving compassionately and supportively to employees who disclose religious discrimination or harassment
- Skills in handling crises

Similar recommendations have been identified by Karp and Sammour (2000) and Chavez and Weisinger (2008) in their training on "managing for diversity," which emphasizes cognitive, attitudinal, and behavioral change.

In addition, Paludi and Paludi (2003) recommended including a unit in the training programs for managers that deals with stereotypes, what Grothues and Marmion (2006) refer to as "dismantling the myths." This should include dismantling the myth that lurks behind the inclination to blame employees for their victimization, and the myth that religious discrimination is a rare occurrence. Resources for this aspect of training may be found in Oskamp (2000), Inman (2001), and Aboud and Levy (1999).

Paludi and Paludi (2003) recommend that the same components of the training program for managers be provided for employees as well. Emphasis should be placed on ensuring that the employer will take each victim seriously and will provide assistance to the victimized employee. The training program for employees should include a discussion on ways that they can assist co-workers who are victims of religious discrimination or other forms of discrimination and harassment. Employee and manager training must include methods for being alerted to changes in any person's behavior. In addition, training should be provided on how to respond to a co-worker who confides in other employees. This training should include development of the abilities of listening without judging, recognizing the difficulty it took for an individual to discuss the topic in the first place, and being an advocate for victimized employees by referring them to human resources, to a manager, or to the EAP. Religious discrimination and harassment training should be part of all new employee orientations. Training must include sections on hate crimes and bias-motivated incidents. We refer the reader to the chapter by Paludi, Paludi, Strauss, Coen, Fuda, Gerber, & Adams in this volume for a discussion of training programs, including conducting needs assessments and post-training evaluations (DeCenzo & Robbins, 2007; Dessler, 2009).

ADDITIONAL HUMAN RESOURCE RESPONSIBILITIES

Educational materials may be developed for distribution and posting throughout the workplace, including posters with tear-off tabs containing hotline phone numbers. In addition, the EAP can offer the following services in primary prevention of religious harassment and discrimination as well as other equal employment opportunity violations:

- Short-term counseling for managers and employees
- Referrals for counseling outside of the workplace
- Managers' training for dealing with employee victims without diagnosing the employee

- Referrals for legal counseling
- Referrals for financial counseling
- Human resource programs to monitor the employee victims to protect their safety

We invite the reader to consult Ball and Haque (2003), Jackson (1992), and Karp and Sammour (2000) for additional recommendations for human resource professionals.

SECONDARY AND TERTIARY PREVENTION

Relying on the symptomatology of victims of religious discrimination and harassment reviewed in this chapter, managers should receive the following list of symptoms of discrimination during training programs:

- Unexplained tardiness and absences
- Unplanned use of leave time
- Lack of concentration
- A tendency to remain isolated from co-workers or reluctance to participate in social events
- Discomfort when communicating with others

In addition, we recommend EAP personnel and human resource personnel reach out to Arab and Muslim employees, because these employees may be reluctant to seek counseling because of cultural barriers to discussing personal issues outside of the family.

Adams (2006) reported that approximately two-thirds of Muslim employees report being uncomfortable at work. This represents the highest rate of workplace problems because of religion on any religions surveyed, including Hindus, Jews, and Buddhists. Adams (2006, p. 49) offered recommendations for accommodating Muslim employees. For example, in dealing with Muslims' daily prayer obligations, managers can—

- Offer "floating" breaks that any worker can use for any reason, including prayer
- Require employees to use leave time for daily prayer or weekly services
- Require workers to make up time taken for prayer
- Provide separate rooms that anyone can use for any reason, including prayer

As another example, Adams (2006) suggested that during Ramadan, a month-long observance of prayer and discipline, employees may adjust their meal breaks as needed because Muslims must fast until sunset. Digh (1998) provides additional recommendations for employers for accommodating religious holidays.

CONCLUSION

This chapter described the key psychological and spiritual sources of human conflict and violence, and applied the difficulties of this human proclivity to the tensions of workplaces. The chapter offered elaborate and empirically documented recommendations for assisting people who are responsible for the quality of workplaces. Our recommendations provide concrete and operational guides for implementing effective interventions in religious discrimination and harassment, as well as for interventions in other types of bias or prejudice in workplaces. We borrow from the Higher Education Center's (Langford, 2006, p. 5) suggestions for campus violence in that workplace interventions for religious discrimination and harassment must meet the following criteria:

- Prevention focused
- Comprehensive
- Planned and evaluated
- Strategic and targeted, using results from a risk assessment of the vulnerability of the workplace
- Research based
- Multicomponent focused
- Coordinated and synergistic, ensuring all prevention and response efforts complement and reinforce each other
- Multisectoral and collaborative
- Supported by infrastructure and institutional commitment

For these recommendations for primary, secondary, and tertiary prevention strategies to be successful, senior leadership of the organization must support and initiate the approach. Without this commitment, the prevention strategies will not be effectively implemented, contributing to employees believing the organization is not committed to the issue of religious discrimination. Employees will, in this way, be silenced regarding their experiences. Furthermore, the approach to dealing with religious and other forms of discrimination must be based on a multidisciplinary team approach, including human resources, EAP, security, managers, law enforcement, attorneys, and employees (Pearce et al., 2005; Spelber & Kleiner, 2000). Unions may offer assistance by supporting the company's policy, facilitating training for new stewards and delegates, and ensuring all employees have received the company's policy and have been trained on issues of religious discrimination in general and the company's policy and procedures specifically.

We recommend that organizations should conduct a human resource audit to determine whether the prevention strategies are working effectively (Smith & Mazin, 2004), including conducting anonymous climate surveys to inquire about employees' perceptions of the company's commitment to preventing and dealing with religious discrimination. Such an audit could uncover disconnects between the workplaces policies, procedures, and practices, on the one hand, and what the organization wants to achieve in terms of meeting the needs of victims of religious discrimination, on the other. Results from the audit and climate survey should be used to better understand the reasons for employees' perceptions and to correct policies, procedures, and training. This approach will ensure that employees feel safe disclosing the discrimination and harassment situations or experiences. Recommendations can be prioritized based on the risk level assigned to each item: high (requires immediate attention), medium (requires action in a short timeframe), and low (suggestions to make the policies and practices more efficient). From this risk matrix, a plan can be developed to address the most pressing issues first (Crouhy, Galai, & Mark, 2005).

The law advocates for tolerance, understanding, and respect in dealing with people of different faiths and belief systems. Downey (2008) concluded the following:

> An employer has an affirmative duty to treat all employees with respect and dignity, regardless of whatever religion or other protected class they belong to. That employer should benefit from creating an atmosphere in which everyone feels valued and part of the same team. (p. 88)

Ending religious discrimination and hate crimes is a human rights issue and, therefore, it is the responsibility of all members of a workplace community. We share Carol Bellamy's sentiment: "Each of us can practice rights ourselves, treating each other without discrimination, respecting each other's dignity and rights."

REFERENCES

Aboud, F., & Levy, S. (1999). Reducing racial prejudice, discrimination and stereotyping: Translating research into programs. *Journal of Social Issues, 55,* 621–625.

Adams, M. (2006). Showing good faith toward Muslim employees. In Society for Human Resource Management (Ed.), *HR Magazine guide to managing people* (pp. 48–50). Alexandria, VA: Society for Human Resource Management.

Allport, G. (2000). The nature of prejudice. In C. Stangor (Ed.), *Stereotypes and prejudice: Essential readings* (pp. 20–48). New York: Psychology Press.

American Psychological Association (2007). *American Psychological Association resolution on religious, religion-based and/or religion-derived prejudice.* Retrieved July 9, 2009, from http://www.apa.org.

Ansonia Board of Education v. Philbrook, 479 U.S. 60 (1986).

Ball, C., & Haque, A. (2003). Diversity in religious practice: Implications of Islamic values in the public workplace. *Public Personnel Management, 32,* 315–330.

Batson, C., & Stocks, C. (2005). Religion and prejudice. In J. Davidio, P. Glick, & L. Rudman (Eds.), *On the nature of prejudice: Fifty years after Allport* (pp. 413–427). Malden, MA: Blackwell.

Bernstein v. Sephora, Div. of DFS Group, 182 F. Supp.2d 1214 (S.D. Fla. 2002).

Bierman, A. (2006). Does religion buffer the effects of discrimination on mental health? Differing effects by race. *Journal for the Scientific Study of Religion, 25,* 551–565.

Boeckmann, R., & Turpin-Petrosino, C. (2002). Understanding the harm of hate crime. *Journal of Social Issues, 58,* 207–225.

Brinson, J., & Kottler, J. (1995). Minorities' underutilization of counseling centers' mental health services: A case for outré consultation. *Journal of Mental Health Counseling, 17,* 371–385.

Burlington Industries, Inc., v. Ellerth, 524 U.S. 742 (1998).

Chavez, C., & Weisinger, J. (2008). Beyond diversity training: A social infusion for cultural inclusion. *Human Resource Management, 47,* 331–350.

Comas-Diaz, L., & Jacobsen, F. (1991). Ethnocultural transference and countertransference in the therapeutic dyad. *American Journal of Orthopsychiatry, 61,* 392–402.

Craig-Henderson, K., & Sloan, L. (2006). After the hate: Helping psychologists help victims of racist hate crime. *Clinical Psychology: Science and Practice, 10,* 481–490.

Crouhy, M., Galai, D., & Mark, R. (2005). *The essentials of risk management.* New York: McGraw-Hill.

DeAngelis, T. (2001). Understanding and preventing hate crimes. *Monitor on Psychology, 32,* 1–7.

DeCenzo, D., & Robbins, S. (2007). *Fundamentals of human resource management.* New York: Wiley.

Dessler, G. (2009). *Fundamentals of human resource management.* Upper Saddle River, NJ: Prentice Hall.

Digh, P. (1998). Religion in the workplace: Make a good-faith effort to accommodate. *HR Magazine, 43,* 85–91.

Dixon, C., & Wright, T. (2009). Cultural diversity issues in employee assistance programs. In W. Hutchison, W. Emener, & M. Richard (Eds.), *Employee assistance programs: Wellness/enhancement programming* (pp. 294–303). Springfield, IL: Charles C. Thomas.

Downey, M. (2008). Keeping the faith. *HR Magazine, 53,* 85–88.

Eck, D. (2001). *A new religious America: How a "Christian country" has become the most religiously diverse nation.* San Francisco, CA: Harper.

Ellens, J. H. (2004a). Introduction: The destructive power of religion. In J. H. Ellens (Ed.), *The destructive power of religion, violence in Judaism, Christianity, and Islam* (pp. 1–10). Westport, CT: Praeger.

Ellens, J. H. (2004b). Religious metaphors can Kill. In J. H. Ellens (Ed.), *The destructive power of religion, violence in Judaism, Christianity, and Islam* (pp. 255–274). Westport, CT: Praeger.

Ellens, J. H. (2004c). Introduction: The interface of religion, psychology, and violence. In J. H. Ellens (Ed.), *The destructive power of religion, violence in Judaism, Christianity, and Islam* (pp. 1–10). Westport, CT: Praeger.

Ellens, J. H. (2004d). The dynamics of prejudice. In J. H. Ellens (Ed.), *The destructive power of religion, violence in Judaism, Christianity, and Islam* (pp. 85–98). Westport, CT: Praeger.

Ellens, J. H. (2004e). Introduction: Toxic Texts. In J. H. Ellens (Ed.), *The destructive power of religion, violence in Judaism, Christianity, and Islam* (pp. 1–14). Westport, CT: Praeger.

Ellens, J. H. (2004f). The violent Jesus. In J. H. Ellens (Ed.), *The destructive power of religion, violence in Judaism, Christianity, and Islam* (pp. 15–38). Westport, CT: Praeger.

Ellens, J. H. (2004g). Jihad in the Qur'an, then and now. In J. H. Ellens (Ed.), *The destructive power of religion, violence in Judaism, Christianity, and Islam* (pp. 39–52). Westport, CT: Praeger.

Ellens, J. H. (2004h). Introduction: Spirals of violence. In J. H. Ellens (Ed.), *The destructive power of religion, violence in Judaism, Christianity, and Islam* (pp. 1–18). Westport, CT: Praeger.

Ellens, J. H. (2004i). Fundamentalism, orthodoxy, and violence. In J. H. Ellens (Ed.), *The destructive power of religion, violence in Judaism, Christianity, and Islam* (pp. 119–142). Westport, CT: Praeger.

Ellens, J. H. (2006). Fundamentalism, violence, and war. In M. Fitzduff, & C. E. Stout (Eds.), *The psychology of resolving global conflicts: From war to peace* (pp. 109–136). Westport, CT: Praeger.

Ellens, J. H. (2007). *Understanding religious experience.* Westport, CT: Praeger.

Endler, N., Parker, J., Bagby, R., & Cox, B. (1991). Multidimensionality of state and trait anxiety: Factor structure of the Endler Multidimensional Anxiety Scales. *Journal of Personality and Social Psychology, 60,* 919–926.

Equal Employment Opportunity Commission. (1999). *Enforcement guidance: Vicarious employer liability for unlawful harassment by supervisors.* Washington, DC: EEOC.

Equal Employment Opportunity Commission. (2009a). *Best practices for eradicating religious discrimination in the workplace.* Retrieved July 8, 2009, from http://www.eeoc/gov/policy/dics/best_practices_religion.html.

Equal Employment Opportunity Commission. (2009b). *Questions and answers: Religious discrimination in the workplace.* Retrieved July 8, 2009, from http//www.eeoc.gov/policy/docs/qanda_religion.html.

Equal Employment Opportunity Commission. (2009c). *Religious discrimination.* Retrieved July 8, 2009, from http://www.eeoc.gov/types/religion.html.

Equal Employment Opportunity Commission. (2009d). *Questions and answers about employer responsibilities concerning the employment of Muslims, Arabs, South Asians and Sikhs.* Retrieved July 8, 2009, from http//www.eeoc.gov/facts/backlash-employer.html.

Faragher v. City of Boca Raton, 524 U.S. 725 (1998).

Feinberg, M. (2000). *Racism: Why we dislike, stereotype, and hate other groups and what to do about it.* Washington, DC: American Psychological Association.

Fiske, S. (1993). Controlling other people: The impact of power on stereotyping. *American Psychologist, 48,* 621–628.

Fiske, S., & Stevens, L. (1993). What's so special about sex? Gender stereotyping and discrimination. In S. Oskamp, & M. Costanzo (Eds.), *Gender issues in contemporary society* (pp. 173–196) Newbury Park, CA: Sage.

Gallup Poll. (2006). *Religion.* Retrieved August 1, 2009, from http://www.galluppoll.com.

Ghumman, S., & Jackson, L. (2010). The downside of religious attire: The Muslim headscarf and expectations of obtaining employment. *Journal of Organizational Behavior, 31,* 4–23.

Grothues, C., & Marmion, S. (2006). Dismantling the myths about intimate violence against women. In P. Lundberg-Love, & S. Marmion (Eds.), *Intimate violence against women* (pp. 9–14). Westport, CT: Praeger.

Herek, G. (1987). Religious orientation and prejudice: A comparison of racial and sexual attitudes. *Personality and Social Psychology Bulletin, 13,* 33–44.

Hilton, J., & von Hippel, W. (1996). Stereotypes. *Annual Review of Psychology, 47*, 237–271.

Hunsberger, B., & Jackson, L. (2005). Religion, meaning and prejudice. *Journal of Social Issues, 61*, 807–826.

Inman, M. (2001). Do you see what I see? Similarities and differences in victims' and observers' perceptions of discrimination. *Social Cognition, 19*, 521–546.

Institute for Corporate Productivity. (2008, April). *Taking the pulse: Religious discrimination.* Retrieved June 12, 2009, from http://www.i4cp.com.

Jackson, S. (1992). *Diversity in the workplace: Human resources initiatives.* New York: Guilford Press.

Judd, C., Park, B., Yzerbyt, V., Gordijn, E., & Muller, D. (2005). Attributions of intergroup bias and outgroup homogeneity to ingroup and outgroup others. *European Journal of Social Psychology, 35*, 677–704.

Karp, H., & Sammour, H. (2000). Workforce diversity: Choices in diversity training programs and dealing with resistance to diversity. *College Student Journal, 34*, 451–458.

Katz, J., Joiner, T., & Kwon, P. (2002). Membership on a devalued social group and emotional well-being: Developing a model of personal self-esteem, collective self-esteem and group socialization, *Sex Roles, 47*, 419–431.

Kawakami, K., Spears, R., & Dovidio, J. (2002). Disinhibition of stereotyping: Context, prejudice, and target characteristics. *European Journal of Social Psychology, 32*, 517–530.

Kelly, E. (2008). Accommodating religious expression in the workplace. *Employee Responsibilities and Rights Journal, 20*, 45–56.

Kessler, R., Mickelson, K., & Williams, D. (1999). The prevalence, distribution and mental health correlates of perceived discrimination in the United States. *Journal of Health and Social Behavior, 40*, 208–230.

Landrine, H. (Ed.). (1995). *Bringing cultural diversity to feminist psychology.* Washington, DC: American Psychological Association.

Langford, L. (2006). *Preventing violence and promoting safety in higher education settings: Overview of a comprehensive approach.* Newton, MA: Higher Education Center for Alcohol and Other Drug Abuse and Violence Prevention.

Maass, A., Castelli, L., & Acuri, L. (2000). Measuring prejudice: Implicit versus explicit techniques. In D. Capozza, & R. Brown (Eds.), *Social identity process: Trends in theory and research* (pp. 96–116). London: Sage.

Marmion, S., & Faulkner, D. (2006). Effects of class and culture on intimate partner violence. In P. Lundberg-Love, & S. Marmion (Eds.), *Intimate violence against women* (pp. 131–143). Westport, CT: Praeger.

Mathias, M. (2008). Religion and women at work. In M. Paludi (Ed.)., *The psychology of women at work* (pp. 109–141). Westport, CT: Praeger.

Miville, M., Rohrbacker, J., & Kim, A. (2005). From prejudice and discrimination to awareness and acceptance. In J. L. Chin (Ed.), *The psychology of prejudice and discrimination: Disability, religion, physique and other traits* (pp. 207–232). Westport, CT: Praeger.

Nasr, S. (1993). Islam. In A. Sharma (Ed.), *Our religions* (pp. 425–532). San Francisco, CA: Harper.

Oskamp, S. (2000). Multiple paths to reducing prejudice and discrimination. In S. Oskamp (Ed.), *Reducing prejudice and discrimination* (pp. 1–19). Mahwah, NJ: Lawrence Erlbaum Associates.

Paludi, C., & Paludi, M. (2003). Developing and enforcing effective policies, procedures, and training programs for educational institutions and businesses. In M. Paludi, & C. Paludi (Eds.), *Academic and workplace sexual harassment: A handbook of cultural, social science, management, and legal perspectives* (pp. 176–198). Westport, CT: Praeger.

Pearce, J., Kuhn, D., & DiLullo, S. (2005). U.S. employers' legal responsibilities for preventing religious discrimination. *Managerial Law, 47,* 208–222.

Pew Forum on Religion and Public Life. (2009). Retrieved July 10, 2009, from http://religions.pewforum.org/reports.

Pollard, C. (1996). *The soul of the firm.* Grand Rapids, MI: Harper Business.

Prenkert, J., & Magid, J. (2006). A Hobson's choice model for religious accommodation. *American Business Law Journal, 43,* 467–514.

Ramirez, M. (1991). *Psychotherapy and counseling with minorities: A cognitive approach to individual and cultural differences.* New York: Pergamon.

Rehm v. Rolling Hills Consolidated Library, U.S. Dist. Ct. (W.D. Mo.) 2007, 04-6088-CV-SJ-JTM.

Riback v. Las Vegas Metropolitan Police Department, et al., 2008 WL 3211279 (CD.Nev., Aug. 6, 2008).

Rippy, A., & Newman, E. (2006). Perceived religious discrimination and its relationship to anxiety and paranoia among Muslim Americans. *Journal of Muslim Mental Health, 1,* 5–20.

Romanow, M., & Karakowsky, L. (2007). HR needs to be proactive about religious accommodation. *Canadian HR Reporter, 20,* 25.

Schramm, J. (2009). Human resources gets religion. *HR Magazine, 54,* 96.

Sheridan, L. (2006). Islamophobia pre and post September 11th, 2001. *Journal of Interpersonal Violence, 21,* 317–336.

Smith, D. (2004). Workplace religious freedom: What is an employer's duty to accommodate? A review of recent cases. *The ALSP Journal of Employment and Labor Law, 10,* 49–65.

Smith, S., & Mazin, R. (2004). *The HR answer book.* New York: AMACOM.

Society for Human Resource Management. (2009). Retrieved May 25, 2009, from http://www.shrm.org.

Spelber, S., & Kleiner, B. (2000). Discrimination against employees who exercise their First Amendment rights: A US perspective. *International Journal of Sociology and Social Policy, 20,* 103–110.

Steinberg, R. (2004). *The psychology of hate.* Washington, DC: American Psychological Association.

Tyson v. Methodist Health Group, Inc., 2004 WL 1629538 (S.D. Ind. June 17, 2004).

TWA v. Hardison, 432 U.S. 63 (1977).

Volpe, M., & Strobl, S. (2005). Restorative justice responses to post September 11 hate crimes: Potential and challenges. *Conflict Resolution Quarterly, 22,* 527–535.

Webb v. City of Philadelphia, No. 05-5283 (2007).

Weiss, J. (2005). Working with victims of hate crimes. In G. Greif, & P. Ephross (Eds.), *Group work with populations at risk* (pp. 197–211). New York: Oxford University Press.

Winerman, L. (2006). *Reaching out to Muslim and Arab Americans.* APA Monitor on Psychology. Retrieved June 12, 2009, from http://www.apa.org/monitor/oct06/reaching.html.

9

Retaliation

Diane E. Sammons

While there has been continued emphasis on educating and training practitioners, students, managers and employees on understanding the necessary elements of a discrimination claim based upon physical characteristics such as race, sex, gender, and national origin, one of the most serious, yet often misunderstood, threats to employer liability in employment remains workplace retaliation. The number of these claims as reported to the Equal Employment Opportunity Commission (EEOC) has nearly doubled in the past ten years.[1] As will be described herein, the probable reason for this growth is twofold: (1) employers and others do not fully comprehend the law that a retaliation claim can exist apart from a discrimination claim; and (2) the burden of proof required to substantiate a retaliation claim is far easier to establish than that for a discrimination claim.

As will be shown, retaliation claims are not dependent upon the success of an underlying discrimination claim and can be filed by co-workers who merely participated in an investigation as well as one who actively opposed discriminatory treatment in their workplace. Remarkably, a prospective employer can be held liable for not hiring a candidate after they learn of discrimination complaints brought by that candidate at a former job. The EEOC and the Supreme Court have clarified and emphasized the lessened degree of burden of proof necessary for complainants for establishing a *prima facie* case of retaliation aimed at achieving the far-reaching goal of the statutory law: to protect employees who are asserting discrimination claims regardless of the merits of the claim itself.

WHAT ARE RETALIATION CLAIMS?

The EEOC protects individuals "filing a charge, testifying, assisting or participating in . . . an investigation, proceeding or hearing" or "opposing a practice made unlawful" under the discrimination statutes.[2] The protective reach of the EEOC extends to multiple federal employment statutes: Title VII of the Civil Rights Act of 1964,[3] the Americans with Disabilities Act,[4] the Age Discrimination in Employment Act,[5] and the Equal Pay Act.[6]

The EEOC views its commitment to a broad interpretation of the retaliation statutes as a critical mechanism to stamp out discrimination.[7] Indeed, while some federal circuit courts in the past have taken a narrower view on standards for claims of retaliation, the Supreme Court has weighed in to support the EEOC's commitment to broadly interpret the law in order to vigorously protect those complaining of retaliatory conduct.[8]

ELEMENTS OF A RETALIATION CLAIM

The key elements for establishing a retaliation claim are fairly consistent across courts, statutes, and the EEOC guidelines: (1) participation in a covered proceeding or opposition to discrimination; (2) an adverse employment action; and (3) a causal connection between the protected activity and the adverse action.[9]

The lethal potential of retaliation claim is that it need not be accompanied by a claim of discriminatory treatment based upon race, religion, sex, national origin, age, or disability.[10] Thus, a charging party who alleges violation under the ADA need not have a disability nor be included in a protected age group in order to allege retaliation for protesting discrimination against persons with disability or in the protected age group.[11] Finally, those who accompany their discrimination claim with a retaliation claim need not be successful nor even reasonable in their underlying discrimination claim to succeed with their retaliation claim.[12]

PARTICIPATION CLAUSE

The participation prong of anti-retaliation makes it unlawful to discriminate against any "individual because s/he has made a charge, testified, assisted, or participated in any manner in an investigation, proceeding, hearing, or litigation under Title VII, the ADEA, the EPA or the ADA."[13] It protects those alleging employment discrimination under statutes enforced by the EEOC, under EEOC proceedings, in state administrative or court proceedings, as well as, in federal court proceedings, and to those who testify or participate in those proceedings.[14] Likewise, not only is retaliation prohibited against the individual who testified, assisted, or participated, it is also prohibited against someone "so closely related to or associated with the person exercising his or her statutory rights that it would discourage or prevent the person from pursuing those rights."[15] For instance, if the husband of an employee is subjected to retaliation for the claim filed by his wife; both have a claim for retaliation.[16] The law protects an individual from retaliation, even when the participation itself occurred when the charging party was employed by a different entity. Thus, a subsequent employer could be responsible when it does not hire or retaliates against a potential or current employee who had participated or brought a charge against a former employer.[17]

OPPOSITION CLAUSE

It is unlawful to discriminate against an "individual because s/he has opposed any practice made unlawful under the employment discriminations statutes, protecting both explicit and implicit communications to the employer that its activity constitutes a form of employment discrimination."[18] Thus, telling a co-worker, manager, attorney, or reporter of one's intent to bring a complaint, or merely complaining to a co-worker about alleged employment discrimination constitutes opposition.[19] Likewise, nonverbal communication, such as participation in picketing, or engaging in a production slow-down can constitute opposition.[20] The complaint need not use magic words, such as "employment discrimination," but can constitute opposition when one makes broad or ambiguous complaints of unfair treatment.[21] Even an employee who does not initiate an investigation, but merely answers a question during an investigation of another has been deemed protected.[22]

Additionally, the refusal to obey an order because of a reasonable belief that it is discriminatory constitutes protected opposition. An employee who works at an employment agency and refuses to follow his manager's instruction to not refer any African-American applicants to a client has opposed an unlawful practice.[23] A correction officer's refusal to cooperate with the practice of allowing white but not black inmates to shower after work shifts constituted protected opposition.[24]

Not every protest against discrimination is protected. An individual's protest is tested against a reasonableness standard. The courts and the EEOC engage in a weighing process, balancing the public's interest in enforcement of discrimination laws versus the right of the employer to a stable work environment. The following examples of actions are not protected: copying and photocopying confidential documents relating to an alleged ADEA discrimination claim and showing them to co-workers,[25] bypassing the chain of command to bring a complaint,[26] badgering a witness to give a statement of support,[27] or expecting amnesty from appropriate discipline or discharge for neglect of job duties or poor performance.[28]

ADVERSE EMPLOYMENT ACTION

The EEOC and the courts have grappled with the level or severity of retaliation that will provide a basis for a legal challenge, as not every adverse act taken against an employee will rise to a level to support a claim. The Supreme Court has adopted the view that to sustain a claim, a "reasonable employee would have found the challenged action materially adverse," meaning the action might have "dissuaded a reasonable worker from making or supporting a charge of discrimination."[29] By requiring "material adversity" the court seeks to differentiate between "trivial" harms that reflect the ordinary tribulations of a workplace and material harms.[30] However, the Supreme Court provides flexibility by framing the standard in general terms, because the significance of any particular act of retaliation will depend on the circumstances and "context matters."[31] Thus, while a schedule change in an employee's work schedule may make little difference to many workers, it may make a significant difference to a young mother with school age children.[32] Likewise, a supervisor's refusal to invite an employee to lunch would normally be trivial, but to retaliate by excluding an employee from a weekly training lunch that contributes to professional development might prevent a reasonable employee from complaining about discrimination.[33] However, where an employee's job duties were changed to a different product specialty; where she had to take on the responsibilities of a co-worker on disability leave and was also forced to process certain papers, the Second Circuit Court concluded that this did not constitute adverse action where other males were asked to perform the tasks and they did not harm the employee's career advancement.[34]

The EEOC guidelines seek to keep the minimal standard to judge an adverse action very low, believing that the severity goes to the level of damage, and not to the existence of the harm itself.[35] Thus, while the most obvious forms of harm consist of denial of promotions, refusals to hire, denial of job benefits, demotions, suspensions, and discharges, other harms can include threats, reprimands, negative evaluations, harassment, and increased surveillance.[36] While the Supreme Court has adopted a bit of a higher standard in this area than the EEOC guidelines by requiring "materiality," the Supreme Court elevates the value and importance of the EEOC manuals in that they "reflect 'a body of experience and informed judgment to which courts and litigants may properly resort for guidance.'"[37]

CAUSALITY

The last necessary element of a retaliation claim is proof that the respondent took the adverse action because of the individual's involvement in a protected activity. This does not necessarily require a statement by the respondent admitting to the motive for the alleged retaliatory act, but can be inferred from circumstantial evidence. The most common inference of retaliatory conduct is where the adverse action occurred shortly after the protected activity, and where the person taking the action had knowledge of the complainant's protected activity before taking action.[38] Even when the action occurred as many as 18 months after the filing of an EEOC complaint, the court found that there was an inference of causation where the plaintiff manager mentioned the EEOC charge at least twice a week during the interim and termination of the employee occurred two months after the EEOC dismissed the charge.[39] However, a D.C. Circuit Court recently found that an African-American female employee's alleged fear of retaliation did not excuse a delay of five to six months before reporting harassment, despite confiding in a friend who was also a manager regarding the incident shortly after its occurrence.[40]

DAMAGES

A party against whom retaliation has occurred has a number of remedies. One is temporary injunctive relief pending a final resolution,[41] meaning the court or EEOC can, among other possibilities, order the temporary reinstatement of the employee or demand an end to harassing treatment. Compensatory or punitive damages are also available for retaliation claims under the EPA, ADEA, Title VII, and the ADA. Punitive damages are allowed when proof exists that the practice was undertaken "with malice or with reckless indifference to the federally protected rights of an aggrieved individual."[42]

CONCLUSION

While employers and potential complainants may spend tremendous resources and time in analyzing, training, and defending against discrimination claims based upon physical characteristics such as gender, race, age, disability, or national origin, few practitioners or lay people understand that making a claim of retaliation is far easier to prove and more difficult to defend. Moreover, both the EEOC and the Supreme Court have chosen to stringently enforce retaliation provisions, broadly construing and interpreting the necessary standard so as to favor the complainant and enforce the overall goal of the retaliation statutes: to maintain unfettered access to the remedial purposes of the discrimination statutes.

Following are key points for employers to prevent claims of retaliation:

- Assign a well-trained, fair, and sympathetic manager to hear all discrimination complaints. Post appropriate signs throughout the workplace identifying this person.
- Promptly investigate complaints of discrimination and in the process advise all parties that they are not to discuss claims with others or engage in any acts that might be in any way perceived as retaliation against complainants. Give specific examples of retaliatory actions: transfers, demotions, negative work evaluations, social isolation, hostile comments, changing work responsibilities to those less favorable than before the complaint.
- Secure the name of an experienced employment lawyer to confer with regarding proper steps for handling complaint.
- Take prompt and effective disciplinary action against an offender if the complaint has validity.
- Regularly monitor the work environment after a valid complaint has been made.
- Ensure that all personnel receive periodic training on employment discrimination, sexual harassment, and retaliation.
- Keep accurate and timely records of training, investigations, and all actions taken by management.

NOTES

1. The number of claims filed with the EEOC in 1998 was 19,114, while in 2008, the number rose to 32,690. See http://www.eeoc.gov/stats/charges.html.

2. *EEOC Compliance Manual*, § 8–1(A) (1998) *EEOC 1998 Compliance Manual*.

3. Section 704(a) of Title VII, 42 U.S.C. § 2000(e) –3(a).

4. Section 503(a) of the ADA, 42 U.S.C. § 12203(a) and (b).

5. Section 4(d) of the ADEA, 29 U.S.C. § 623(d).

6. Section 15(a)(3) of the Fair Labor Standards Act (FLSA), 29 U.S.C. § 215(a)(3): The anti-retaliation provision of the Fair Labor Standards Act does not contain a specific "opposition" clause. However, courts have recognized that the statute prohibits retaliation based on opposition to allegedly unlawful practices. *EEOC 1998 Compliance Manual*, § 8–II (B)(1) n.12. See EEOC v. Romeo Community Sch., 976 2d. 985, 989–90 (6th Cir. 1992); EEOC v. White & Son Enterprises, 881 F.2d 1006, 1011 (11th Cir. 1989); Cf. Crowley v. Pace Suburban Bus Div., 938 F.2d 797, 798, n.3 (7th Cir. 1991): Section 215(a)(3) of FSLA has been construed broadly to include retaliation by the employer for an employee's assertion of protected rights. Brock v. Richardson, 812 F.2d 121, 124 (3d Cir. 1987): Courts have the "animating spirit" to apply to activities not explicitly covered by the language and, thus, applying it to protect employees protesting FSLA violations. Love v. RE/MAX of America Inc., 738 F.2d 383, 387 (10th Cir. 1984): The Act applies to unofficial assertions of rights through complaints at work. Contra, Lambert v. Genesee Hospital, 10 F.3d 46, 55 (2d Cir 1993), *cert. denied*, 511 U.S. 1052 (1994), cited in *EEOC 1998 Compliance Manual* at n.12. The circuit courts have split, however, as to whether retaliation under FSLA requires a written complaint or whether more informal actions to oppose discrimination will suffice: See Kasten v. Saint-Gorbain Performance Plastics Corp. 570 F.3d 834, 840, n.3 (7th Cir. 2009): written complaint necessary; Bartis v. John Bommarito Oldsmobile Cadillac Inc., 626 F. Supp 994, 999–1000 (E.D. Mo. 2009): informal complaint to supervisor insufficient under FSLA, also acknowledging the First, Third, Sixth, Seventh, Ninth, Tenth and Eleventh Circuits have all held informal workplace complaints are protected, while the Second and First Circuits have held they are not.

7. *Id.* "Voluntary compliance with and effective enforcement of anti-discrimination statutes depend in large part on the initiative of individuals to oppose employment practices that they reasonably believe to be unlawful, and to file charges of discrimination. If retaliation for such activities were permitted to go unremedied, it would have a chilling effect upon the willingness of individuals to speak out against employment discrimination or to participate in the EEOC's administrative process or other employment discrimination proceedings."

8. Burlington Northern & Santa Fe Railway Co. v. White, 548 U.S. 53, 54–55 (2006). Anti-retaliation provision seeks to prevent employer interference with "unfettered access" to Title VII's remedial mechanisms by prohibiting employer actions that are likely to deter discrimination victims from complaining to the EEOC, the courts, and employers. See also Gomez-Perez v. Potter, __U.S.___, 128 S.Ct. 1931, 170 L.Ed.2d 887 (2008): Claim of retaliation may be brought under federal sector provision of ADEA despite sovereign immunity defense; CBOS West Inc. v. Humphries, __U.S.___, 128, S.Ct. 1951, 170 L.Ed.2d 864 (2008): Section 1981 encompasses retaliation claims.

9. Goldsmith v. Bagby Elevator Co, Inc, 513 F.3d 1261 (11th Cir. 2008) citing Burlington Northern & Santa Fe v. White; *EEOC 1998 Compliance Manual*, § 8–II (A).

10. *EEOC 1998 Compliance Manual*, § 8 (I)(B).

11. Krouse v. American Sterilizer, 126 F.3d 494 (3d Cir. 1997): Complainant was not disabled, but brought claim under ADA; Anderson v. Phillips Petroleum, 722 F. Supp. 668, 671–72 (D. Kan. 1984): Complainant was not discriminated against, but filed claim on behalf of union members who claimed discrimination.

12. See Wyatt v. Boston, 35, F3d 13, 15 (1st Cir. 1994).

13. *EEOC 1998 Compliance Manual*, § 8–II(C)(1).

14. *Id.*

15. *Id.* § 8–II(c)(3).

16. Murphy v. Cadillac Rubber & Practice, Inc. 946 F. Supp. 1108, 1118 (W.D.N.Y 1996): Plaintiffs stated a claim for retaliation when he suffered adverse employment action based upon his wife's initiation of a complaint; EEOC v. Ohio Edison Co., 7 F.3d 541 (6th Cir. 1993): Claim stated for retaliation where relative suffered from other relative's claim; Thursman v. Robershaw Control Co., 869 F. Supp. 934, 941 (N.D. Ga. 1994): Close relative engaged in protected activity supports one element of *prima facie* case. Gonzalez v. N.Y. State Dept. of Corr. Svcs. Fishkill Corr. Facility, 122 F. Supp. 2d 335, 346–47 (N.D.N.Y. 2000); EEOC v. Nalbandian Sales, Inc., 36 F. Supp. 2d 1206, 1213 (E.D. Cal. 1998); Mondia v. ARCO Chem. Co., 618, F. Supp. 1248, 1250 (W.D. Pa. 1985): All concur with Gonzalez v. NY State Dept, of Corr. Svcs. Cf, Holt v. JTM Indus. 89 F. 3d 1224 (5th Cir. 1996), *cert. denied*, 520 U.S. 1229 (1997): No retaliation where plaintiff was put on paid leave when wife filed age discrimination claim; Eisensohn v. St. Tammany Parish Sheriff's Office, 530 F.3d 368, 374 (5th Cir 2008): Refusal to allow third-party spouse claim where third party did not participate in co-worker's complaint. Fogelman v. Mercy Hosp., Inc. 283 F.3d 561, 568, 569 (3d Cir. 2002): Neither the ADA nor ADEA permits third-party retaliation claims; Smith v. Riceland Foods, 151 F3d 813, 819 (8th Cir. 1998): Third party claims unsupported by plain language of Title VII; Thompson v. N. Am. Stainless L.P., 567 F.3d 804 (6th Cir. 2009): Title VII does not protect employee's spouse from retaliation.

17. *EEOC Compliance Manual*, § 8–II(c)(4) and n.28, citing Christopher v. Strouder Memorial Hosp., 936 F.2d 870, 873–74 (6th Cir. 1991): Continual references to applicant's prior discrimination action created inference that company's refusal to hire was indeed retaliatory.

18. *EEOC Compliance Manual*, § 8–II (B)(1).

19. *Id.* § 8–II (B)(2).

20. *Id.*

21. *Id.*

22. Crawford v. Metropolitan Govt. of Nashville, ____U.S.____, 129 S.Ct. 846, 172 L.Ed. 2d 650 (2009).

23. *Id.*

24. *Id.* Citing n.14; Moyo v. Gomez, 40 F.3d 982 (9th Cir. 1994), *cert. denied*, 513 U.S. 1081 (1995). But see Rossell v. County Banks, 2006 WL 777074,*3 (D.Del. March 27, 2006): Plaintiff-employee's claim dismissed where she alleged her termination was in retaliation for having allowed two African-American customers' checks to clear, which was later revealed to be fraudulent. Court refused to extend Title VII protection to employees protecting customers. McMenemy v. City of Rochester, 241 F.3d 279 (2d Cir. 2001): In accord, refusing firefighter's claim of retaliation where he had previously conducted an investigation for firefighters union regarding harassment complaint brought against another firefighter in union. Lamb-Bowman v. Delaware State University, 152 F. Supp 2d 553, 561, n.17 (D.Del. 2001): Woman coach unsuccessful in claiming retaliation where her contract was not renewed after complaints that men's athletic department received superior treatment than women's department. Court concluded she was not protected when seeking to protect nonemployee students.

25. *Id.* (3)(a) citing O'Day v. McDonnell Douglas Helicopter Co., 79 F.3d 756 (9th Cir. 1996).

26. *Id.* Citing Rollins v. Florida Dept. of Law Enforcement, 868 F.2d 397 (11th Cir. 1989).

27. *Id.* Citing Jackson v. St. Joseph State Hospital, 840 F.2d 1387 (8th Cir.), *cert. denied*, 488 U.S. 892 (1988).

28. *Id.* Citing Coutu v. Martin County Board of Comm'rs., 47 F.3d 1068, 1074 (11th Cir. 1995).

29. Burlington Northern & Santa Fe Railway Co. v. White, 548 U.S. 53, 68 (2006), citing Rochon v. Gonzales, 438 F.3d 1211, 1219 (DC Cir. 2006), quoting Washington v. Illinois Dept. of Revenue, 420 F.3d 658, 662 (7th Cir. 2005).

30. *Id.* "An employee's decision to report discriminatory behavior cannot immunize the employee from those petty sleights or minor annoyances that often take place at the workplace and that all employees experience."

31. *Id.* 68.

32. *Id.* Citing Washington v. Illinois Dept. of Revenue, supra at 662: Finding flex-time schedule critical to employee with disabled child.

33. *Id*. Citing *EEOC 1998 Manual*, § 8.

34. Byrne v. Telesector Resources Group Inc., 2009 WL 2019951, *3 (2d Cir. July 14, 2009).

35. *1998 EEOC Manual*, § 8(D)(3): "Regardless of the degree or quality of harm to the particular complainant, retaliation harms the public interest by deterring the harm. . . . As the Ninth Circuit has stated, the degree of harm suffered by the individual goes to the issue of damages not liability".

36. *Id.*

37. Federal Express Corp. v. Holowecki, 552 U.S. ___, 128 S.Ct. 1147, 1156 (2008) quoting Bragdon v. Abbott, 524 U.S. 624 (1998).

38. *1998 EEOC Compliance Manual*, § 8 (E)(2).

39. Shirley v. Chrysler First, Inc., 970 F.2d 39 (5th Cir. 1992).

40. Taylor v. Solio, 2009 WL 2014144, *4 (DC Cir. July 10, 2009); also see Thomas v. CVS/Pharmacy, 2009 WL 1956256, *3 (11th Cir. July 9, 2009): Three and a half month delay between the filing of the EEOC charge and a failure to promote was insufficient to sustain retaliation; Clark County School Dist. v. Breeden, 532 U.S. 268 (2001): A three month delay, by itself, does not allow a reasonable inference of retaliation.

41. *1998 EEOC Compliance Manual*, § 8–III (A): Section 706(f)(2) allows the EEOC to seek temporary injunctive relief. Section 107 of the ADA incorporates the same provision. While the ADEA and EPA do not authorize a court to give interim relief pending resolution of an EEOC charge, the EEOC can seek such review as part of a lawsuit for permanent relief pursuant to Rule 65 of the Federal Rules of Civil Procedure.

42. *1998 EEOC Compliance Manual*, § 8–III (B)(1) and (2) citing Kim v. Nash Finch Co., 123 F.3d 1046 (8th Cir. 1997).

REFERENCES

ADA, 42 U.S.C. § 12203(a) and (b), Section 503(a).

ADEA, 29 U.S.C. § 623(d), Section 4(d).

Anderson v. Phillips Petroleum, 722 F. Supp. 668, 671–72 (D. Kan. 1984).

Bartis v. John Bommarito Oldsmobile Cadillac Inc., 626 F. Supp 994, 999–1000 (E.D. Mo. 2009).

Bragdon v. Abbott, 524 U.S. 624 (1998).

Brock v. Richardson, 812 F.2d 121, 124 (3d Cir. 1987).

Burlington Northern & Santa Fe Railway Co. v. White, 548 U.S. 53, 54–55 (2006).

Byrne v. Telesector Resources Group Inc., 2009 WL 2019951, *3 (2d Cir. July 4, 2009).

CBOS West Inc. v. Humphries, ___U.S.___, 128, S.Ct. 1951, 170 L.Ed.2d 864 (2008).

Cf. Crowley v. Pace Suburban Bus Div., 938 F.2d 797, 798, n.3 (7th Cir. 1991).

Cf, Holt v. JTM Indus. 89 F. 3d 1224 (5th Cir. 1996), *cert. denied*, 520 U.S. 1229 (1997).

Christopher v. Strouder Memorial Hosp., 936 F.2d 870, 873–74 (6th Cir. 1991).

Clark County School Dist. v. Breeden, 532 U.S. 268 (2001).

Contra, Lambert v. Genesee Hospital, 10 F.3d 46, 55 (2d Cir 1993), *cert. denied*, 511 U.S. 1052 (1994).

Coutu v. Martin County Board of Comm'rs., 47 F.3d 1068, 1074 (11th Cir. 1995).

Crawford v. Metropolitan Govt. of Nashville, ____U.S.____, 129 S.Ct. 846, 172 L.Ed. 2d 650 (2009).

EEOC v. Nalbandian Sales, Inc., 36 F. Supp. 2d 1206, 1213 (E.D. Cal. 1998).

EEOC v. Ohio Edison Co., 7 F.3d 541 (6th Cir. 1993).

EEOC v. Romeo Community Sch., 976 2d. 985, 989–90 (6th Cir. 1992).

EEOC v. White & Son Enterprises, 881 F.2d 1006, 1011 (11th Cir. 1989).

Eisensohn v. St. Tammany Parish Sheriff's Office, 530 F.3d 368, 374 (5th Cir 2008).

Equal Employment Opportunity Commission. (1998). *EEOC 1998 Compliance Manual*. Washington, DC: U.S. Government Printing Office.

Fair Labor Standards Act (FLSA), 29 U.S.C. § 215(a)(3) Section 15(a)(3).

Federal Express Corp. v. Holowecki, 552 U.S. ___, 128 S.Ct. 1147, 1156 (2008).

Fogelman v. Mercy Hosp., Inc. 283 F.3d 561, 568, 569 (3d Cir. 2002).

Goldsmith v. Bagby Elevator Co, Inc, 513 F.3d 1261 (11th Cir. 2008).

Gomez-Perez v. Potter, __U.S.___, 128 S.Ct. 1931, 170 L.Ed.2d 887 (2008).

Gonzalez v. N.Y. State Dept. of Corr. Svcs. Fishkill Corr. Facility, 122 F. Supp. 2d 335, 346–47 (N.D.N.Y. 2000).

Jackson v. St. Joseph State Hospital, 840 F.2d 1387 (8th Cir.), *cert. denied*, 488 U.S. 892 (1988).

Kasten v. Saint-Gorbain Performance Plastics Corp. 570 F.3d 834, 840, n.3 (7th Cir. 2009).

Kim v. Nash Finch Co., 123 F.3d 1046 (8th Cir. 1997).

Krouse v. American Sterilizer, 126 F.3d 494 (3d Cir. 1997).

Lamb-Bowman v. Delaware State University, 152 F. Supp 2d 553, 561, n.17 (D.Del. 2001).

Love v. RE/MAX of America Inc., 738 F.2d 383, 387 (10th Cir. 1984).

McMenemy v. City of Rochester, 241 F.3d 279 (2d Cir. 2001).

Mondia v. ARCO Chem. Co., 618, F. Supp. 1248, 1250 (W.D. Pa. 1985).

Moyo v. Gomez, 40 F.3d 982 (9th Cir. 1994), *cert. denied*, 513 U.S. 1081 (1995).

Murphy v. Cadillac Rubber & Practice, Inc. 946 F. Supp. 1108, 1118 (W.D.N.Y 1996).

O'Day v. McDonnell Douglas Helicopter Co., 79 F.3d 756 (9th Cir. 1996).

Rochon v. Gonzales, 438 F.3d 1211, 1219 (DC Cir. 2006).

Rollins v. Florida Dept. of Law Enforcement, 868 F.2d 397 (11th Cir. 1989).
Rossell v. County Banks, 2006 WL 777074,*3 (D.Del. March 27, 2006).
Shirley v. Chrysler First, Inc., 970 F.2d 39 (5th Cir. 1992).
Smith v. Riceland Foods, 151 F3d 813, 819 (8th Cir. 1998).
Taylor v. Solio, 2009 WL 2014144, *4 (DC Cir. July 10, 2009).
Thomas v. CVS/Pharmacy, 2009 WL 1956256, *3 (11th Cir. July 9, 2009).
Thompson v. N. Am. Stainless L.P., 567 F.3d 804 (6th Cir. 2009).
Thursman v. Robershaw Control Co., 869 F. Supp. 934, 941 (N.D. Ga. 1994).
Title VII, 42 U.S.C. § 2000(e) –3(a) Section 704(a).
Washington v. Illinois Dept. of Revenue, 420 F.3d 658, 662 (7th Cir. 2005).
Wyatt v. Boston, 35, F3d 13, 15 (1st Cir. 1994).

10

Sex Discrimination

Florence L. Denmark, Shanna T. German, and Jessica B. Brodsky

INTRODUCTION

The workplace has long been thought of as a man's domain: Men are in charge, they carry out the crucial tasks, and they make the critical decisions. It also has been thought that women should be at home taking care of the house and the children. The emergence of working women has vastly altered the dynamics, but not without some residual resentment manifesting itself in the form of entitlement and bias, with ensuing suffering levied against women worldwide. It has lead to a substantial degree of sex discrimination in the workplace forcing the enactment of laws to restore a sense of order and values.

The relationship between sex and career choice is a complicated one. Numerous aspects may help steer an individual toward a specific job, including knowledge, aptitude, and skills. Social processes, however, also may largely affect one's decision. Many people feel that they need to choose a career or occupation based on what is stereotypically appropriate for their own sex. Additionally, stereotypes and social processes often interact with skills, delineating which skills are more common or considered better suited to be performed by a male or female due solely to their biological makeup. England, Herbert, Kilbourne, Reid, and Megdal (1994) suggest that the skills that women perform are valued less than if a man performed them. This is a result of the stigmatization that accompanies a skill that is designated "female," and therefore, its concomitant contribution to organizational goals is devalued. They further purport that skills involved in providing face-to-face service, such as nurturance, are seen as "female" because of the importance of nurturing in parenting. By examining the skills needed for specific occupations, the male-female ratio of those engaged, and the hourly wage received by both sexes, the researchers discerned that sex composition indeed affects the compensation for the entire profession. This means that women and men who work in jobs that are made up of mostly females and employ predominantly "female" skills such as nurturance, earn less than those in jobs that contain more males. Because society associates nurturance with women, pay equity discrimination may be a result of the gendered nature of skills (England et al., 1994).

For years, it has been debated that the skills women are perceived to have, such as nurturance, lead them to occupations that are typically lower paying. Similarly, the skills that men are perceived to have, such as leadership, direct them to higher paying jobs and higher managerial positions. Rudman and Glick (2008) stress how women need to disconfirm stereotypes regarding men's greater agency, initiative, and ambition to be hired for leadership positions. Even after being hired, women's contributions tend to be devalued relative to men's because women are presumed to be less competent, less influential, and less likely to have played a leadership role (Heilman & Haynes, 2005). Because of these stereotypes, identical qualifications do not mean the same thing for men and women, a concept that is explained by the feminist adage "for a woman to be good, she has to be twice as good as a man" (Rudman & Glick, 2008). It is unfair to hold women to a higher standard and place them at such a disadvantage.

Fortunately, the federal government has passed regulations against such discrimination. Under Title VII of the Civil Right Act of 1964, the Americans with Disabilities Act, and the Age Discrimination in Employment Act, it is illegal to discriminate in employment based on race, color, religion, national origin, disability, age, or sex. This includes discrimination in the following:

> [T]he hiring and firing process; compensation, assignment or classification of employees; transfer, promotion, layoff, or recall; job advertisements; recruitment; testing; use of company facilities; training and apprenticeship programs; fringe benefits; pay, retirement plans, and disability leave; or other terms and conditions of employment. (EEOC, 2004)

Sex discrimination more specifically refers to the differential treatment of an individual because of their biological sex when it negatively affects the aforementioned aspects of employment. Additionally, sexual harassment in the workplace, including practices ranging from direct requests for sexual favors to sexually uncomfortable workplace environments, affects members of either sex, but is of particular concern to many women (EEOC, 2004).

Even though sex discrimination in the workplace has long been an issue, the number of sex discrimination cases reported to the EEOC has remained virtually unchanged over the past 10 years. In 2008, the EEOC received 28,372 cases of sex discrimination; however, only 15.9 percent of those charges were filed by men (EEOC, 2009). It is obvious that women are more often the victims in this type of workplace discrimination. Besides the overarching discriminatory practices that by law, under the Civil Rights Act of 1964, are illegal, women may encounter other more subtle discriminatory practices. These include not being hired because of their sex, not being considered for promotions, being given menial jobs or jobs typically thought to be "women's work" such as answering phones, being ignored when offering suggestions or solutions, and being monitored more closely by men (Kyzer, 2008).

Sex discrimination in the workplace has resulted in disparities in men and women's pay for equal work, an overrepresentation of men in leadership positions, and a devaluation of women's skills. Differences in qualifications of men and women no longer provide a valid explanation for why men earn significantly more than women for equal work. Sex discrimination is a substantial cause for a pay gap, which is larger than ever and reflects a devaluation of work associated with women. Even when women dominate an occupation and perform at least as well as their male counterparts, their work is regarded and rewarded less (Lips, 2003). Similarly, the difference in the ranks of men and women in occupations with male-dominated upper management is overwhelming. Finally, occupational choices for women often are limited, as they are forced to prove themselves more in typically male dominated professions (Catalyst, 2009a). Throughout time, these consequences of sex discrimination have only become more pronounced, leading to changes in the laws that govern and the way society views employment.

HISTORY OF WOMEN IN THE WORKPLACE

According to the U.S. Department of Labor *Monthly Labor Review* (2009), employment of women has increased by 13.4 percent from 1998 to 2008. In 2008, 6 out of every 10 women age 16 and older were in the labor force. From March 1975 to March 2000, the employment rate of mothers who had children under the age of 18 rose from 47 to 73 percent. Women not only are working more, but also are receiving college degrees at higher rates. Compared with only 11 percent of women ages 25 to 64 who held a college degree in 1970, 35 percent were degree holders in 2007. Furthermore, economic conditions have greatly increased the need for families to have dual incomes. Egalitarian norms have vastly changed the way society thinks about women in the workplace. These developments may paint an uplifting and hopeful picture, but history reminds us that this has not always been the case.

At one time, hiring a woman was economically risky for a company because women were responsible for childrearing and domestic activities. In the 21st century, it is legally risky for a company not to hire a woman based on those same discriminatory criteria. This change has come about since the passage of Title VII of the Civil Rights Act of 1964. The Pregnancy Discrimination Act (PDA) of 1978 and President Clinton's Family and Medical Leave Act (FMLA) enacted in 1993, gave further rights to women with children (U.S. Department of Labor, 2009). These laws ensure that women have the ability to take care of their responsibilities at the office as well as at the home.

While women have made large strides, even with the help of legal actions, gender inequities in the workplace persist. Men are still favored as candidates for more prestigious jobs and also earn higher wages than females in the same positions (Denmark, Rabinowitz, & Sechzer, 2005). Even though the Equal Pay Act was adopted in 1963 requiring that men and women be given equal pay for equal jobs in the same place of work (EEOC, 2009), women still are compensated only approximately 80 percent of a man's salary (Bureau of Labor Statistics, 2009). This is an increase from the 1980 U.S. Census numbers that showed a sex gap in pay such that women earned only 61 percent of what men earned (England et al., 1994). The latter percentage is of all employed men and women, not only those who are working equal jobs. The occupation with the highest weekly earnings in 2007 was professional and technical services for both women and men. Women earned $794 per week, whereas men grossed $1,250 per week (Bureau of Labor Statistics, 2007). Therefore, this suggests that women tend to be employed in lower paying jobs, whether it is by choice or by way of discriminatory practices.

The picture becomes bleaker when broken down by race. In general, race discrimination in the workplace is perceived to be more prevalent among African American and Latino employees than their Caucasian colleague (Avery, McKay, & Wilson, 2008). Therefore, the most discriminated against segment of all the population is African American and Latino working women. Earnings of Asian and Caucasian women have been substantially higher than that of their African American and Latino counterparts. Caucasian women are far more likely to be employed as managers and professionals than any other female group besides Asian American women. Service jobs, which tend to be the worst paying, are most likely to be held by African American women (Denmark et al., 2005).

In 2008, nearly half (46.5 percent) of the labor force at *Fortune* 500 companies were women, whereas only 15.7 percent were corporate officers, and a mere 3 percent were chief executive officers. In 2007, females encompassed 46.7 percent of law students, 34.1 percent of all lawyers, and only 18.7 percent of partners in firms. Moreover, equity male partners earned $87,000 more than their female counterparts (Catalyst, 2009b). A 2006 labor statistics summary indicated that women accounted for only 31 percent of the highest earners in the United States (Bureau of Labor Statistics, 2006). An unbelievable and unfortunate realization was observed in the median usual weekly earnings of full-time wage and salary workers by industry and sex. The 2007 annual averages found that men's wages were higher than women's for the same position 100 percent of the time and were never once equal (Bureau of Labor Statistics, 2007).

OCCUPATIONAL BREAKDOWN

Looking at the gender division of various occupations, it is obvious that many are disproportionate. For example, in 2008, women accounted for just 11 percent of engineers and 33 percent of lawyers but 92 percent of registered nurses and 82 percent of social workers (Bureau of Labor Statistics, 2008). This phenomenon in which specific occupations are overwhelmingly male or female has been termed occupational segregation. Occupational segregation is said to occur when some quantitative rule, such as 70 percent, is reached in terms of the percentage of gender ratio. This can occur at all levels of employment, from entry-level positions to upper management (Denmark et al., 2005).

MATHEMATICS, PHYSICAL, SOCIAL, AND OTHER SCIENCES

Women have long been the minority in male-dominated science-related fields such as engineering, computer science, and chemistry. As of

December 2008, women made up 25 percent of computer and mathematic occupations, 13 percent of architecture and engineering occupations, and 44 percent of life, physical, and social science occupations, which include psychologists and social workers, fields known to be traditionally female dominated (Bureau of Labor Statistics, 2008). As well, women in academic positions in these fields are less likely to obtain tenure (29 percent of women compared with 58 percent of men) and are less likely to achieve status as a full professor (23 percent of women compared with 50 percent of men; Ginther & Kahn, 2006).

Many researchers have suggested, however, that the underrepresentation of women in math and science is the result of women choosing other careers. This is due to the inflexibility of the field in terms of achieving a work-family balance, and the belief that women themselves have concerning success in these fields. Frome, Alfed, Eccles, and Barber (2006) investigated a cohort of women who graduated from college with aspirations of science and math careers, but who later changed their aspirations. They found that, along with the desire for a more family flexible job, the change toward a less male-dominated field was the result of the lower intrinsic value women placed on the math and sciences. Similarly, many of these fields were described as being inflexible toward women who wanted to have children, go on maternity leave, and have a work and family balance. Echoing this, Halpern et al. (2007) suggests that achieving high success in a math or science career requires more than 40 hours of work per week. Given this, many women may believe that such a career would interfere with family life. Additionally, some argue that women excel in verbal abilities, whereas men typically outperform women on visuo-spatial tasks. This verbal ability may lead women, early on, to choose careers where they can best use these skills (Halpern et al., 2007).

MEDIA AND SPORTS

Although the numbers of women pursuing degrees in sports and media careers have grown tremendously, female representation is still relatively small. Although the 2008 Bureau of Labor Statistics reports that 44 percent of those who work in entertainment, media, and sports are women, this number is highly influenced by the overwhelming numbers of men in sports careers and the lower echelon positions held by women. According to the 2008 Racial and Gender Report Card of the Associated Press Sports Editors covering more than 378 Associated Press Web sites and newspapers, 94 percent of sports editors, 90 percent of assistant sports editors, 94 percent of columnists, 91 percent of reporters, and 84 percent of copy editors and designers are male. Women in news radio are just as rare; according to the Radio-Television News Directors Association and Foundation, only 22 percent of radio news staff and directors are female.

In general, the pervasive perception is that women do not "know" enough about sports to justify a career in the field, or that they do not have anything to say on the topic that is worthwhile listening to. In a study by Staurowsky and DiManno (2002), women reported that many of the males with whom they worked, expressed disbelief and skepticism with regard to women's knowledge of sports. Women in such careers find that they have to prove themselves much more to their superiors than their male counterparts. These women feel much more pressure about making mistakes, knowing that they represent all other women looking to enter the field.

Many male bosses will compliment the capabilities of their female employees but only within the context of all female workers such as "you do a good job for a woman." Their status as women was always considered when being assessed and praised, devaluing their achievements (Staurowsky & DiManno, 2002). Similarly, many women in sports media careers would say that the division of labor is based on gender. Some are told by their superiors that they could not do certain jobs in sports because of their sex. Staurowsky and DiManno (2002) reported that many women were negotiating for assignments that their male counterparts were routinely delegated.

Network executives, through their hiring and advancement practices, have created a barrier beyond which women cannot progress. Some executives who have assigned women to their teams have had to become overzealous to convince others that their designees are capable. With regard to pay, prestige, and acceptance, women sportscasters are behind not only their male colleagues in sports but also are behind their female counterparts in news organizations. In careers dominated by masculinity, men often will allow women to break into the profession through entry-level positions and early promotional opportunities. As they try to progress, however, they are faced with greater resistance and limited promotional opportunities. Women such as Oprah Winfrey prove that becoming a highly ranked media executive is not impossible, although it is rare. Nearly all of the officers and managers of the National Association of Broadcasters, as well as executives of other broadcasting and publishing companies, are male (Bollinger & O'Neill, 2008). This male dominance creates a "good old boy" network that often makes it impossible for women to enter upper positions.

A huge disadvantage for women in sports and media careers is the lack of networking, role models, and superiors to whom they can relate and talk. All of these disadvantages are the result of the fact that so many fewer women work in the field than men. Staurowsky and DiManno's (2002) study determined that networking and establishing professional liaisons with individuals who can act as mentors were the two most important priorities when moving into sports careers. The evolution of the Association of Women in Sports Media (AWSM), organized in 1987, represents the growth that continues to occur in the numbers of women who are writing and talking sports and the increasing availability of networking and role models for women in the field. Women in sports and the media are on the rise, however the challenge remains for women to breach the wall into the higher ranks of these professionals.

EDUCATION, SOCIAL SERVICES, AND HEALTH CARE

The prevailing view of education and teaching in the United States, as well as around the world, is that it is an occupation dominated by females. Much research has pointed out that women are more inclined to become teachers, because it fits with their role as caretaker in working with younger children. Additionally, the field has discouraged many men from entering because of its apparent low status, low pay, and association with mothering (Burgess & Carter, 1992). Men who enter the profession tend to teach older children or take on the higher status positions, such as school principal or administrator (Carrington, 2002). While women account for 84 percent of preschool, elementary school, and middle school teachers, the percentage drops to 50 percent when looking at high school and postsecondary teachers (Bureau of Labor Statistics, 2008). Because teaching is considered a feminized profession, it becomes less attractive to men, which therefore is self-discriminating. Many professions are considered more masculine, yet to earn such a position for a woman is considered an achievement rather than a stigma. This is a double standard that often is seen in female-dominated occupations. Similarly, not only are males more likely to hold positions of higher authority in teaching, but also are likely to be promoted more quickly than their female counterparts (Thornton & Bricheno, 2000).

Nursing is another occupation that is dominated by women and is stigmatized to some extent for any male interested in pursing it. Career advancement in nursing appears to be largely based on adherence to a masculine work pattern, including the ability to work long hours and to have an uninterrupted work history (that is, not taking time off for pregnancy). Additionally, advancing relies on pursuing additional degrees, which becomes difficult for women who are raising a family, especially considering that most nursing positions are lower wage (Bullock & Waugh, 2004). Ninety percent of all registered nurses are female, and women make up 88 percent of all health care support occupations. This is in contrast to the fact that only 32 percent of physicians and surgeons are women, creating a hierarchy in which, once again, men are in the more authoritative positions. Interestingly enough, men who are registered nurses and physicians have higher weekly earnings than their female counterparts in both occupations. In fact, across all health care practitioner occupations, men make more money than women (Bureau of Labor Statistics, 2008).

Research suggests that men and women in medical school and beyond have different experiences. It has been found that women physicians do not feel welcome in medical school environments and are made to feel like they are not equal members of their scientific community (Shrier et al., 2007). One study even found that female family practice students reported performing and completing significantly fewer procedures than the male students (Sharp, Wang, & Lipsky, 2003). Additionally, male and female doctors are often preferred based on the gender-stereotyped qualities that a patient is looking for in their doctor. Patients have said that they preferred male doctors for their perceived technical competence, whereas others preferred female doctors for their beliefs that women express more humanistic behavior (Fennema, Meyer, & Owen, 1990).

Just as with nursing, the overrepresentation of women in the social service field has to do with their stereotypical caretaking and mothering nature. Surprisingly, in 1985 males and females were almost equally represented in psychology, with men making up 49 percent of all clinical psychologists. By 2001, however, male representation had decreased to 25 percent. Similarly, social work has grown to be considered a highly female-dominated occupation (nearly 85 percent of masters of social work graduates are female; Schilling, Moorish, & Liu, 2008). Because of the female dominance, males in this field may encounter difficulties in terms of discrimination and inclusion. They may find themselves socially isolated or having difficulty obtaining or keeping a job. Additionally, it has been questioned whether men have the empathy and communication skills necessary for a career in social services (Murphy & Monsen, 2008). Yet, although men may face discrimination against entering clinical psychology or social work, many point out that these fields struggle for recognition, status, and pay, further deterring men from entering (Schilling et al., 2008). This notion adds to the societal devaluation of women and the skills that they have as "not good enough" because they are not masculine. These fields also provide better work-life balances for women raising a family, as many women in the professions can work from home or create their own schedules if they are in private practice.

While careers in social services, such as social workers and clinical psychologists, are more flexible and common among women, academic positions in these fields are not as welcoming for women. Women in academia still have a difficult time gaining tenure and moving up the career ladder. In recent years, women have made great strides and have achieved both more non-tenure-track and part-time faculty positions. Women's pay in these positions, nevertheless, still lags behind that of their male counterparts, as remuneration is largely based on research productivity. Women have time constraints when they are managing both family and job; thus, they have less time to devote to research or achieving tenure (Halpern, 2008).

BUSINESS AND FINANCE

In the fields of business and finance, women account for 58 percent of jobs, according the 2008 Bureau of Labor Statistics. While this number may seem surprising, many departments within these two fields are overrepresented by women, such as human resources and accounting, while others, such as financial advising are male dominated. In addition, these statistics do not break down the level of the position that men and women hold. If the data were to include that information, one would see that a disproportionate number of men hold the higher paying and higher level positions (Roth, 2004). Interestingly enough, although the Bureau of Labor Statistics (2008) finds that more women hold positions in these occupations, they also found that these women make only 75 percent of what men in the same occupation take home. Breaking the numbers down further, in the occupations in which a much larger number of women are employed, men still make 25 percent more money, indicating that they are more likely to be holding the higher level positions with lower paid females working below them.

As a result of the pay gap and other discriminatory practices in business and finance, many women have decided to become entrepreneurs and open their own businesses. Women entrepreneurs may be attracted to self-employment for the flexibility it offers. According to the National Association of Women Business Owners (NAWBO), more than 10 million women run businesses across the United States, which is almost half of all small businesses. Many suggest that women open their own businesses to get away from discriminatory practices in large corporations, but Weiler and Bernasek (2001) find that women entrepreneurs face a different type of discrimination. Oftentimes, discrimination occurs in customer or product markets and supplier or factor markets, resulting in lower earnings for women than men. This includes discrimination by those who serve as a financial support system or capital for a startup, or in the preferential treatment in timing and delivery of orders. It is suggested that people providing loans, capital, or services to entrepreneurs find more comfort in male-run businesses.

With the surge in women entering business careers, it is no coincidence that the number of women receiving their masters of business administration and doctorates in business has been increasing steadily as well. In 2004–2005, women accounted for 40 percent of all new business doctorates, which is up from 26 percent just three years earlier. That stands in contrast with the percentage of men receiving the same degree over the same period, a number that declined two percentage points. Women are continuing to reach higher levels of academia in business as nearly 17 percent (113 of 668) of business school deans and 27.6 percent of faculty at business schools are women (Damast, 2009). In 1990, there were only six women who served as business school deans. While these numbers still pale in comparison to the percentage of men in the same level occupation, it is important to think about the progress that has been made.

When it comes to finance and investment banking, one must have a specific set of qualifications regardless of gender. It is a high-intensity, competitive environment that is best served by employees who are extremely high on motivation and ambition. During the early years of these careers, junior employees typically put in 80-hour weeks. Promotions come at specific intervals after "putting in the time" (Roth, 2004). Thus, the first few years in a finance position is usually a test of strength and endurance. While women and men in these jobs tend to have the same motivation, ambition, and skills, sex discrimination still occurs. The wages that men in finance receive far surpass the wages that women receive. Women get paid approximately 60.5 percent of what men get paid, a figure that is 19.5 percent below the national average. Women also are more likely to start their careers in jobs that pay less, and experience other forms of discrimination such as being left out of meetings or having their credibility undermined. Some companies even have time and travel demands that prohibit family involvement beyond breadwinning (Roth, 2004). Because of the time demand that jobs in finance and investment banking place on its employees, many women leave the field to spend more time with their families.

Not dissimilar to other fields, in studying the experiences of female corporate managers of businesses, Schuck and Liddle (2004) found that the most common experiences were that the "good old boys" network still exists, and that the work environment is still male dominated. Additionally, women felt that it was more difficult to get promoted to higher positions, and that they were seen first as a woman and second as a manager. Promisingly, the women in the study did not feel left out of conversations with their male counterparts or employees and they experienced acceptance and respect by both the men and the women whom they supervised. This increasing acceptance of women managers is confirmed by a study Duehr and Bono (2006) performed in which current gender and management stereotypes were compared with those found 30 years prior. Male managers characterized their female counterparts as less passive and submissive and more confident, ambitious, analytical, and assertive. Basically, male managers rated female managers as more leader-like than they had 15 or 30 years ago. Even though male managers' views of women have changed, males' views in general may not have changed as much. Male students were found to hold the same gender stereotypes as male managers 15 years ago and men tended to view women as possessing fewer of the characteristics of successful managers.

INTERNATIONAL GENDER GAP

Sex discrimination in the workplace is not just a product of the American system of business and commerce. The labor participation of men and women in Taiwan remained steady across an 11-year review (1990–2001). Women's participation in the workforce marginally fluctuated from 44.5 to 46.25 percent, while the swing in the percentage of working males to total male population ranged between 73.96 and 68.52 percent. Taiwanese women are "viewed as a temporary and marginal labour force. They are the last to get hired and the first to be let go"

(Bowen, 2003, p. 299). In a 20-year overview, the percentage of employed Taiwanese women consistently remained the highest in clerical positions (55 to 76 percent), followed by professional, service, production, and finally managerial (approximately 10 percent) industries. Furthermore, it is culturally acceptable to blatantly discriminate between which sex is desired for a specific job, as indicated in the classified ads (41 percent of 7,037 classifieds). Unlike the focus of most discrimination against women, this type of sex discrimination affects men as well. Additionally, as practiced in the United States, sex discrimination is found in Taiwan with regard to women's average pay. There, females receive 71.6 percent of a man's compensation, varying by industry (Bowen, 2003).

Similarly, at the turn of the millennium, women's presence in the workplace was highly visible within the 15 states of the European Union (EU). Fifty-four percent of women between the ages of 15 and 64 worked, accounting for 40 percent of those employed in each state. More than one-third of women, however, were working only part-time as opposed to a mere 6 percent of part-time male workers. A gender gap in compensation correspondingly occurs within the EU, with women making 86 percent of the comparable male wages (Haas, 2003).

Bankers, specifically those in high level positions, earn the highest average income in Turkey. There is a widely held, but misconceived, belief that Turkish women equally gain from this profession. In truth, women are disproportionately underrepresented at the managerial levels. Both male and female managers indicated positive reasons to hire men, such as having the option to disperse them to different branches and utilizing them as debt collectors. Female managers admitted to the fact that they made significantly lower wages than the men who preceded them, while accomplishing even more work. Likewise, British women in banking earn 62 to 73 percent of their male managerial or nonmanagerial co-workers, respectively. Both Turkish and British women bankers were less likely to be promoted because of their perceived lack of commitment—classified through long hours they had more difficulty fulfilling than their male counterparts because of domestic commitments (Ozbilgin & Woodward, 2004).

This international data delineates the global trend of sex discrimination in the workplace, especially against women, around the world. Although the transparency of the discrimination varies from country to country, it remains overwhelmingly abundant. This truth persists despite women making up approximately 40 percent of the workforce of these industrial countries. Foremost among these practices is the gap between the compensation afforded men and women on a global scale. Women are consistently earning 62 to 86 percent of the pay of men.

BARRIERS FOR WOMEN

The Glass Ceiling

According to a Catalyst report, as of July 2009, only 29 of the *Fortune* 1000 companies had women chief executive officers. Similarly, the Glass Ceiling Commission, which was set up by the federal government in 1991, reported that, in 1995, although women made up 57 percent of the national workforce, they held only 5 percent of senior management positions (Stead, 1996). This trend has persisted for decades, pointing to the existence of a glass ceiling for women who hope to achieve the high ranks of a career. The expression "glass ceiling" was first printed in a *Wall Street Journal* article in 1986, and has since been used as a term to acknowledge the recurring failure of women who attempt to reach as far up the corporate ladder as possible. It signifies a transparent barrier that prohibits women from achieving such ranks and obtaining equality with men ("Idea: The Glass Ceiling," 2009). While more women than men are graduating from college, and more women are earning degrees in business, they still are vastly outnumbered in upper-managerial positions.

The term "glass ceiling" has been used to describe the inequality that exists in the pay received by men and women performing the same work. Most studies report that even when women do reach the highest ranks of corporate management, they only receive approximately 80 percent of the pay given to men in those same jobs (Bureau of Labor Statistics, 2009). In 2008, median yearly earnings for full-time workers were $35,102 for women and $45,113 for men (U.S. Department of Labor, 2009). Additionally, Cotter, Hermsen, Ovadia, and Vanneman (2001) found that the disadvantages resulting from the glass-ceiling effect are larger at the top of the hierarchy than at lower levels, and these disadvantages become worse later in a person's career. At high earning levels, the gap between Caucasian men's chances of reaching higher levels of earnings and Caucasian women's chances grows larger over their careers.

Certain hypotheses are suggested for the glass ceiling, including the issue of time. Qualifications for senior management usually include a masters of business administration and 25 years of continuous work experience. However, in the 1970s, when today's senior managers were graduating, less than 5 percent of law and masters of business administration degrees were awarded to women. Those numbers have now risen to 40 percent, and therefore, it is suggested that women will reach the upper-echelon ranks of corporations. Another hypothesis is that motherhood distracts women from their career paths, and women who take time off from working or are raising children, do not have the time to complete the tasks required to reach those ranks. Finally, women do not have as many female role models to aspire to and induce the self-efficacy needed to break through the glass ceiling ("Idea: The Glass Ceiling," 2009). This issue becomes important in determining career choice for young women as well.

The Motherhood Penalty

A considerable barrier for working women is that of being a mother. In an employment discrimination situation, properly termed the "motherhood penalty," women with children are significantly discriminated against at work in a variety of ways, including hiring, promotion, and salary (Budig & England, 2001; Correll, Benard, & Paik, 2007). Budig and England (2001) delineate two ways in which employers' hiring practices discriminate against mothers. The first is a preconceptual prejudice in which employers find hiring mothers distasteful. Statistical discrimination, the second model for employers, is hiring based on education and experience, the latter of which mothers tend to lack. These discriminatory behaviors are likely consequences of how Americans stereotype families: Women are the primary caregivers, while men are the primary financial providers (Correll et al., 2007; Deutsch & Saxon, 1998). The working mother according to American culture and standards experiences conflicting demands. The "good mother . . . prioritizes meeting the needs of dependent children above all other activities, [while] the 'ideal worker' [is] unencumbered by competing demands and [is] 'always there' for his or her employer" (Correll et al., 2007, p. 1306). This ultimately leads to impossible expectations and eventual disappointment.

One way in which mothers are discriminated against in the workplace is through salary. The "mother wage," or "family," gap is the discrepancy in pay between women with children, compared with women without children. The "mother wage gap" has existed for as long as mothers have been in the workforce. Some explanations for this include the belief that mothers exert less effort in their jobs or, simply, that they have had less of an opportunity to progress in their field (Waldfogel, 1998). When analyzing 11 years of data on American women (from 1982 to 1993), Budig and England (2001) determined that a wage gap of 7 percent for the first child existed between mothers and nonmothers. Furthermore, an increased wage penalty ensued for each additional child as well as the sacrifice of a full-time position and loss of experience. When reviewing the data, the authors explain that "there is no evidence that penalties are proportionately greater for women in more demanding or high-level jobs, or 'male' jobs, or for more educated women" (p. 220). Waldfogel (1998) concluded that 30-year-old mothers, on average, earn 90 percent of nonmother's pay and 70 percent of what men make. International findings were similar, with a 20 percent family gap between 33-year-old British mothers and nonmothers.

Another inequitable behavior fostered against mothers is that of perceived competence. In a study with 122 college students providing their impressions about a management consultant, discrimination toward mothers was evident. Although both mothers and fathers were delineated as warmer individuals than nonparents, the working moms were viewed as marginally less competent than the childless workingwomen. Succinctly put, working mothers were perceived as less competent than before having had children. Working fathers were viewed as not only warmer, but equally as competent as childless men. More significantly, working mothers were discriminated against when study participants reported being less likely to hire, promote, or train them, as compared with nonmothers, fathers, and nonfathers (Cuddy, Fiske, & Glick, 2004).

Evidence has shown that the motherhood penalty begins even before the birth of her baby. "Pregnancy discrimination" occurs when expectant mothers are either fired, not hired, or receive a reduction in pay because of intending to or becoming pregnant (Discrimination.com, 2008). The pregnancy of a woman is often her most prominent feature and she likely will be stereotyped or treated differently than before having a child. In an experiment with college students for both masculine- and feminine-typed positions, pregnant candidates were discriminated against because they were considered less likely to be recommended for hire and were penalized with a lower starting salary than candidates that were not pregnant (Masser, Grass, & Nesic, 2007). The study participants, however, found pregnant women to be just as competent and warmer than nonpregnant woman. The discrepancy between the Masser et al. (2007) and Cuddy et al. (2004) findings could be the perception that women do not lose their competency until they have actually given birth.

Cuddy et al. (2007) displayed great surprise in their findings of 122 college students discriminating against mothers in the workplace:

> The participants, many of whom will be decision-makers of the future, are male and female students at an Ivy League college—men and women who, for the most part, expect to have careers and families. The women in our study most likely expect to have both careers and families and the men most likely expect to marry women who will pursue careers as well as have children. These participants are also predominantly the products of families in which their mothers worked (which is known to produce more egalitarian attitudes about gender roles). (p. 713)

In a laboratory experiment, followed by a simulated real-world study, Correll et al. (2007) discovered considerable discrimination against mothers, while men benefited from their status as fathers. One hundred and ninety-two undergraduate participants (84 male, 108 female) were asked to evaluate two equally qualified applicants (same race, same gender) differing only in parental standing (child or no child). Notably, parental status was only subtly indicated via resume (Parent-Teacher Association coordinator) and memo (mother/father to Tom and Emily). In the laboratory experiment, significant mother discrimination took the form of less competence (10 percent lower), less commitment (15 percent lower), higher and harsher standards of performance, lower starting salary recommendation by $11,000 (7.4 percent), and less promotability when equated to nonmothers. Most significant, 84 percent of childless women compared with 47 percent of women with children were recommended for hire. Incredibly, fathers were offered a significantly higher salary when judged against childless fathers, along with being viewed as more committed to their work and held to lower punctuality expectations.

As Correll et al. (2007) indicates, undergraduates "lacking workplace and hiring experience might be more likely to rely on stereotypes when making hiring decisions" (p. 1327). Therefore, their audit study attempted to seek out how the laboratory findings measure up to the behaviors of real-world employers by observing the frequency of their "applicants" to be called for an interview after receiving applications via mail. Applicants were, again, similar in qualification, race, and sex, contrasting only on parental status. Childless women were called back twice as many times as mothers and, also, more than childless fathers. Authors explain that evaluators possibly "perceive childless women as especially committed to paid work" (p. 1333). Once again, fathers were not penalized for their parental status.

"The consequences among mothers who [attain and] remain in . . . inflexible jobs are stress, fatigue, frequent absenteeism, and career interruptions that impair wage growth" (Glass, 2004, p. 370). While mothers are more often splitting their time between paid and unpaid work (that is, household responsibilities and childcare), fathers have the option to opt for either paid work or leisure time (Bittman, 1999). Bittman (1999, p. 29) succinctly encapsulates the motherhood penalty:

- interrupted labor force attachment and downward social mobility—few women recapture the career trajectory they had before childbirth;
- lower lifetime earning, and less employment security;
- increased exposure to the risk of poverty;
- increased dependency on a male "provider" and low marital bargaining power;
- restricted opportunities for public participation, since family responsibilities are organized around private homes.

PARENTAL LEAVE AND POLICIES

Women have not only been discriminated against within the workplace, but also when taking maternity leave. Not until the PDA of 1978 (U.S. Department of Labor, 2009), under the EEOC did women have the right to take leave from work to care for a new child. Maternity leave rights were permitted for all pregnant women as long as the employer had similar plans for those with disabilities. Longitudinal evidence of policies throughout a span of 30 years (1955–85) indicates that maternity leave benefits are more likely to be created in large employment firms that desire consistency (for example, finance and manufacturing), while older employers are less likely to adopt maternity leave (Kelly & Dobbin, 1999). Unfortunately, in 2007, the EEOC still accumulated 5,587 allegations of pregnancy discrimination in the United States (Discrimination. com, 2008). Family leave in the United States averages 20 weeks (five months) and is unpaid, compared with 40 weeks (10 months), 18 of which are paid, in Britain (Waldfogel, 1998).

A similar but expanded policy exists for parental leave in the European Union. Parental leave is "gender-neutral, job-protected leave from employment designed to facilitate employed parents' care of small children at home" (Haas, 2003, pg. 91). Some EU member countries, like Greece and Portugal, offer the minimum parental leave acceptable within the European Union of three months unpaid per parent, while other countries, such as Spain and France, permit an unpaid leave of up to three years with job-security (Bruning & Plantenga, 1999). Paid leave and job protection are offered in other EU countries, such as, Austria, Belgium, France, and Germany, for up to three years per child at approximately $400–$500 per month, while Luxembourg provides higher pay for a shorter period of time ($1,336 per month for six months). Although this compensation may be more in the short term, long-term leave compensation is both financially and personally more favorable (Haas, 2003).

Before 1993 and the Family and Medical Leave Act (FMLA), no national maternity-leave legislation existed in the United States (Find Us Law, 2008). This act allows and encourages both mothers and fathers to take time off of work to care for a new child (birth, adoption, or foster care) and maintain a work-family balance, as a new member enters the family. Major struggles for families regarding the FMLA are the stipulations in which it can be implemented. Although the act sanctions job protection up to 12 weeks in which employees can return to the same or similar job with equal wages, this voluntary leave is unpaid. Furthermore, the FMLA only covers employees if they have worked for at least 12 months (nonconsecutive under the same employer) tallying at least 1,250 hours, and the individual's place of employment includes 50 or more employees.

Under the FMLA terms, employers, also, confront the drawbacks of having to pay for the health insurance of the mother during her leave, as well as finding a replacement in her absence. They also, likely, face uncertainty as to whether or not their employee will even return once the maternity leave is completed. Although there may be some disadvantages for employers to offer maternity leave, research suggests that the right to a leave plan will increase the likelihood of the mothers returning to their previous jobs in the future. In fact, as reported by Waldfogel (1998), employers are likely to only pay an average of $220 per year of maternity leave. The author suggests measures taken by British employers, in which pregnant mothers voluntarily sign a contract by which they receive the maternity leave money only if they return to their position for a specified duration of time.

In a seven-year longitudinal study, following 162 employed soon-to-be mothers, Glass (2004) investigated the consequences of work-family employment policies on the mother's wage growth. The sample was followed from 1992, after all mothers had recently given birth, to 1999, and took into account all employment changes. The author examined the worker benefits, which included flexible scheduling, telecommuting (working from home), reduced weekly work hours, and childcare assistance. Additionally, there was interest in looking at whether employers who offer these policies pay less in wages. Findings indicate that mothers did not monetarily gain from the work-family policies. Specifically, mothers in managerial and professional positions, who lessened their physical time at work, whether that be working from home for months or reducing their hours, faced significantly negative consequences. These mothers, when compared with those who remained at the office, experienced an average of 27 percent decrease in wages. A likely explanation for this is the employee commitment phenomenon described in the previous section.

A further fascinating discovery was that mothers found a loophole that negatively affected work-family policies and wage loss by switching employment. Managerial and professional women especially benefited from this change, often utilizing a flexible schedule policy and minimizing their wage loss. Maximizing on the childcare assistance policy, however, had a slightly positive impact on increasing wage growth, though only for those who remained with the same employer.

According to Haas (2003), Sweden is the closest country in the European Union to achieving parental leave equality with adequate compensation. It is important to note that Swedish policy makers "want parents home during a child's first year . . . [and] fathers were encouraged to take leave to develop relationships with young children and the nurturing aspects of their personalities" (Haas, 2003, p. 106). In Denmark, government subsidies were implemented to encourage fathers to take parental leave receiving 60 percent of wages, although only 4 percent of Danish fathers partook of this opportunity. Individual parental leave in this country is not transferable to the other parent; a benefit enjoyed in other EU countries. Evidence has bolstered the belief that fathers take far less leave than mothers (Bruning & Plantenga, 1999). In 1974, Sweden mandated paid leave for both mothers and fathers. In fact, Swedish fathers are more inclined to take parental leave because otherwise they will lose a substantial amount of benefits. Fathers take two months on average, sharing the additional 450 days of paid leave (80 percent of salary) with the mother. Parental leave is provided through the employers' tax contributions. Yet even with the government's attempt to involve fathers in a work-life balance through unprecedented parental leave policies, the childrearing responsibilities have not achieved equivalent division (Haas, 2003).

Finland also has attempted to reduce the motherhood penalty through munificent parental leave and childcare policies. The majority of parents in Finland (80 percent) worked outside the home after the birth of their child, which assumes parents utilized work-family benefits. Finnish mothers received three months of full paid maternity leave under a government grant, followed by an additional 7.5 months at 80 percent salary. Fathers also were eligible for the latter benefit for up to 6.5 months, although only 5 percent availed themselves of this policy (Bittman, 1999). In fact, men take an average of 11 days parental leave compared with 263 days taken by women (Bruning & Plantenga, 1999). Finnish maternity benefits additionally include clothing, bedding, and other paraphernalia for the new baby, up to three years unpaid nursing leave with a cash benefit equivalent to municipal daycare, and approaching four years of reduced work hours. State-provided high-quality subsidized childcare was also provided under the Children's Day Care Act of 1973 (Bittman, 1999). These policies allow Finnish mothers to emotionally and financially provide for their children, while also maintaining a strong connection to the workplace.

Bruning and Plantenga (1999) delineated four models utilized among eight EU parental leave policies. These include time, sequential, parallel, and facilitation of service models. Time care primarily permits parents to take time off to care for their children without integrating childcare policies. The sequential model promotes initial full-time paid parental leave for a set period of time, then shifts to another policy, such as childcare. The parallel model takes family circumstances into account by allowing the parents to choose between time off and services provided. Finally, the facilitation of services model focuses more on assistance to provide care for the child and less on the parental leave itself. Perhaps the United States could follow or integrate several of the EU policies to increase both maternal and paternal leave policies, thereby equalizing the sharing of responsibilities and ultimately aim at decreasing the motherhood penalty.

OTHER ASPECTS WORTH CONSIDERING

Although the abundance of literature and research evidences significant acts of discrimination against women and mothers in the workplace, one noteworthy paradigm is worth considering: Perhaps women are not discriminated against in careers; perhaps they are entering fields that make it easier to have a family. Given the obvious responsibilities that women are charged with concerning chores and childrearing, this theory may not seem so foreign. Women are pulled toward "female" occupations for three reasons: "women's preferences and characteristics and/or because employers prefer to employ women in these occupations, or that occupations become 'female' because of sex stereotyping—with flexible working conditions emerging as a consequence of the fact that these are 'female' occupations" (Anker, 1997, p. 329). Furthermore, "female" occupations lend a higher flexibility for women than in other lines of work.

An alternative means to distinguish whether women are selectively choosing certain professions is analyzing college majors by gender. When examining the majors of both men and women, the most salient findings are those with the biggest gender discrepancies (National Center for Educational Statistics, 2007). According to the 2007 statistics, 69,696 females majored in psychology compared with 20,343 males. Similarly in education, 83,125 females sought their bachelors in education in contrast to 22,516 males. A common major for men is computer and information sciences and support services, strikingly exceeding women 34,342 to 7,828. Likewise, 68,230 males pursued an undergraduate major in engineering, outnumbering women (13,842) by nearly five to one.

In a final thought regarding occupational choices, consideration should acknowledge the place of role models and how they affect career development. Individuals tend to choose role models who are similar to themselves in easily identifiable ways, such as gender or race, and judge their own potential self-efficacy against that of those to whom they relate (Bandura, 1999). In a study administered to 368 college females, Quimby and DeSantis (2006) discovered that role models affected all six career types investigated (Realistic, Investigative, Artistic, Social, Enterprising, and Conventional [RIASEC]). Furthermore, role models directly affect all career choices, except investigative. This study supports the idea that young girls often aspire to do just as the women have before them. It is likely that these girls have not seen or experienced women in high positions, so therefore, they do not even know to which career to aspire. Not only is identifying with a role model critical for women who want to pursue nontraditional careers (Gilbert, 1985), but also the availability of role models may actually directly and indirectly influence the career choice that women make (Quimby & DeSantis, 2006).

EMPLOYER RESPONSES TO PREVENTING AND DEALING WITH SEX DISCRIMINATION

Title VII of the Civil Rights Act makes it illegal to discriminate against an applicant or employee because of their sex in hiring, termination, compensation, promotion, opportunities for training, or other conditions of employment. Furthermore, Title VII bans employment decisions based on managers' stereotypes about men's and women's abilities, personality characteristics, or work performance.

We recommend the following approach to ensure that the organization is taking "reasonable care" in preventing and dealing with sex discrimination: (1) conducing a human resource audit; (2) using risk management to resolve employer's practices in violation of the EEOC's guidance on sex discrimination, and (3) obtaining employees' views of the changes made to the organization with respect to preventing and dealing with sex discrimination.

Human Resource Audit

All of the employer's practices and policies must be reviewed to determine whether sex discrimination is operating in any or all functions of the employment process, that is, recruitment and selection, training and development, and performance appraisals. A human resource audit (see DeFour & Paludi, this volume) can assist employers in determining whether sex discrimination exists in their organization. The audit is a discovery tool that outlines (1) vulnerability in the workplace for sex discrimination and (2) changes that need to be made in the organization so the discriminatory practices are corrected (Smith & Mazin, 2004). An audit also ensures legal compliance with federal and state employment laws to reduce the organization's potential exposure to complaints and litigation.

With respect to sex discrimination, the audit will include the following components, representing basic functions of human resource management (DeCenzo & Robbins, 2007):

- Legal compliance
- Compensation/Salary Administration
- Employment/Recruiting
- Orientation
- Terminations

- Training and Development
- Employee Relations
- Communications
- Files/Record Maintenance/Technology
- Policies and Procedures (including employee handbook)
- Communications

We offer sample audit questions with respect to sex discrimination in the workplace (also see Paludi, D'Aiuto, & Paludi, chapter 7 in volume 2).

Legal Compliance

1. Is the human resource department following state laws with respect to sex discrimination and harassment as well as federal laws?
2. Does the employer ensure that sanctions and corrective action are applied evenly throughout the organization when employees violate the organization's sex discrimination policy?
3. Does the employer follow the EEOC's fundamentals in investigating sex discrimination and harassment complaints: promptness, confidentiality, and impartiality?

Compensation and Salary Administration

1. Does the employer ensure that we establish salaries based on skill, responsibility, effort, and working conditions?
2. Does the employer examine job grades to ensure that women and men have equal opportunity for advancement?
3. Does the employer ensure that there is no job segregation because of sex?

Employment and Recruiting

1. Does the employer ensure that all employees wanting to become a manager or supervisor follow the same procedure regardless of sex?
2. Does the employer ensure that we do not inquire as to a job applicant's sex on the application form?
3. Does the employer ensure that its recruitment practices reach the widest array of women and men applicants?
4. Does the employer ensure that we conduct interviews with uniformity by interviewers?

ORIENTATION

1. Does the company have a new-employee orientation program that includes training on sex discrimination policies and procedures?
2. Does the employer request new employees to sign and date an acknowledgment form indicating they received the employee handbook and understand the organization's policy and procedures on sex discrimination and harassment?

TERMINATIONS

1. Does the employer ensure that discipline and termination is applied evenly for violations of the equal employment opportunity policies regardless of the sex of the employee?
2. Does the employer have male and female investigators to conduct investigations of policy violations?

Training and Development

1. Does the company facilitate regular training programs on sex discrimination, including the company's policies and procedures?
2. How do employees learn to whom they should report complaints of sex discrimination and harassment?
3. Do we offer training opportunities and career development opportunities to all employees regardless of sex?
4. Does the employer have both women and men trainers who are facilitating programs for employees?
5. Does the employer have a glass ceiling with respect to women in upper management positions?
6. Does the employer address stereotypes and hidden biases about sex in our training programs?

EMPLOYEE RELATIONS

1. What services are available at the company to employees who have experienced sex discrimination and harassment?
2. Does the employer ensure that investigators of complaints of sex discrimination/harassment are sensitive to collective bargaining agreements?
3. Does the employer have in place effective mentoring and coaching programs for both women and men?

COMMUNICATIONS

1. Does the workplace foster an atmosphere of prevention by sensitizing individuals to the topic of sex discrimination and harassment?

2. Does the employer conduct anonymous culture climate surveys with employees to determine their perceptions about the effectiveness of the company's sex discrimination and harassment management program?

FILES, RECORD MAINTENANCE, AND TECHNOLOGY

1. What metrics does the employer have in place to measure the success of its sex discrimination and harassment management program?

2. Does the employer ensure that the content of the case file of an investigation of a complaint of sex discrimination and harassment contains the following?
   - Complaint
   - Response to Complaint from Accused Employee
   - Notes from Meetings with all Parties to the Investigation
   - Letters from Individuals Involved in the Investigation
   - Copies of all Standard Notification Letters to all Parties to the Investigation
   - Documents (for example, copies of e-mails, letters, cards) Supplied by Individuals in the Investigation Procedure
   - Report by Investigator to the President of the Organization
   - Signed Acknowledgment Forms Regarding Confidentiality, Retaliation, and Request for Witnesses

3. Does the employer have in its files copies of signed and dated acknowledgement forms for the following:
   - Receipt of the policy concerning sex discrimination and harassment
   - Participation in a training program dealing with sex discrimination and harassment

4. Does the employer provide a summary at the end of each fiscal year that includes the following:
   - Number of complaints of sex discrimination/harassment received
   - Number of complaints sustained
   - Number of complaints that were false
   - Number of complaints for which insufficient information was present to sustain the allegation
   - Sanctions and corrective action provided

5. Does the employer's information technology department routinely check e-mails to ensure that negative comments and jokes about employees' sex are not included?

Policies and Procedures

1. Does the employer have policy statements that deal with sex discrimination in employment and sex harassment?
2. Do the policies prohibit discrimination/harassment from peers in addition to discrimination and harassment by managers?
3. Do employees know to whom they should report complaints related to sex discrimination and harassment?
4. Are remedies clear and commensurate with the level of sex discrimination and harassment?
5. Does the employer offer flexible job arrangements for all employees, regardless of sex (for example, flex time, job sharing, desk sharing, time off/career break, telecommuting)?

Communications, Including Employee Handbook

1. Is the sex discrimination and harassment policy statement well publicized? Are they on the company's intranet? Posted in the human resources office? Included in the employee handbook?
2. Does the employer ensure that performance appraisals do not contain stereotypic references to the sex of the employee as well as ratings that are based in stereotypes and not reflections of the individual employee?

Risk Management

Following the completion of the audit, the employer must then correct the practices found to be in violation of the EEOC's guidance on sex discrimination to meet their responsibility for ensuring reasonable care (Ostroff & Atwater, 2003). Employers should use risk management to correct the problems identified in the audit: identification, assessment, and prioritization of risks (for example, lack of effective policy statement, failure to hold annual training for employees, wage inequities, glass ceiling for women). After risks are identified and prioritized, the employer can mitigate the risks, with the most serious risk being remedied initially, followed by the next serious risk, and so on (Crouhy, Galai, & Mark, 2005).

ORGANIZATIONAL CULTURE CLIMATE SURVEYS

Once the employer has instituted changes with respect to the risks identified through the human resource audit and prioritized through risk management techniques, employees can be surveyed anonymously about their perceptions of and experiences with the organization's sex discrimination management program (see DeFour & Paludi, chapter 5 in this volume; Cooper, Cartwright, & Earley, 2001; Driskill & Brenton, 2005). These climate surveys will provide employers with a metric of the alignment between the organization's stated mission with respect to sex discrimination and the actual behaviors of management via their training programs, policies, and investigatory procedures.

Please review the chapters in this volume on equal compensation discrimination (chapter 3), pregnancy discrimination (chapter 6), sexual harassment (chapter 11), and sexual orientation (chapter 12) for additional recommendations for employers in preventing and dealing with discriminatory behavior.

REFERENCES

Anker, R. (1997). Theories of occupational segregation by sex: An overview. *International Labour Review, 136,* 315–339.

Associated Press Sports Editors. (2008, June). *The 2008 Racial and Gender Report Card of the Associated Press Sports Editors.* Retrieved July 29, 2009, from http://apse.dallasnews.com/convention/2008/062808rgrc_report. html.

Avery, D. R., McKay, P. F., & Wilson, D. C. (2008). What are the odds? How demographic similarity affects the prevalence of perceived employment discrimination. *Journal of Applied Psychology, 93,* 235–249.

Bandura, A. (1999). Social cognitive theory of personality. In L. Pervin, & O. John (Eds.), *Handbook of personality* (3rd ed., pp. 192). New York: Guilford Press.

Bittman, M. (1999). Parenthood without penalty: Time use and public policy in Australia and Finland. *Feminist Economics, 5,* 27–42.

Bollinger, L., & O'Neill, C. (2008). *Women in media careers: Success despite the odds.* Lanham, MA: University Press of America.

Bowen, C. C. (2003). Sex discrimination in selection and compensation in Taiwan. *International Journal of Human Resource Management, 14,* 297–315.

Bruning, G., & Plantenga, J. (1999). Parental leave and equal opportunities: Experiences in eight European countries. *Journal of European Social Policy, 9,* 195–209.

Budig, M. J., & England, P. (2001). The wage penalty for motherhood. *American Sociological Review, 66*, 204–255.

Bullock, H. E., & Waugh, M. W. (2004). Caregiving around the clock: How women in nursing manage career and family demands. *Journal of Social Issues, 60*, 767–786.

Bureau of Labor Statistics, U.S. Department of Labor. (2006). *Current Population Survey: women still under represented.* Retrieved August 5, 2009, from http://www.bls.gov/opub/ils/pdf/opbils55.pdf.

Bureau of Labor Statistics, U.S. Department of Labor. (2007). *Current Population Survey: Median usual weekly earnings of full-time wage and salary workers by industry and sex, 2007 annual averages.* Retrieved August 5, 2009, from http://www.bls.gov/cps/wlf-table19-2008.pdf.

Bureau of Labor Statistics, U.S. Department of Labor. (2008). *Current Population Survey: Median weekly earnings of full-time wage and salary workers by detailed occupation and sex, 2008 annual averages.* Retrieved August 3, 2009, from http://www.bls.gov/cps/cpsaat39.pdf.

Bureau of Labor Statistics, U.S. Department of Labor. (2009). *Usual weekly earnings of wage and salary workers: Second quarter 2009.* Retrieved August 13, 2009, from http://stats.bls.gov/news.release/archives/kyeng_07162009.htm.

Burgess, H., & Carter, B. (1992). 'Bringing out the best in people': Teacher training and the 'real' teacher. *British Journal of Sociology of Education, 3*, 49–59.

Carrington, B. (2002). A quintessentially feminine domain? Student teachers' constructions of primary teaching as a career. *Educational Studies, 28*, 287–303.

Catalyst. (2006). *2005 Catalyst census of women corporate officers and top earners of the Fortune 500.* New York: Catalyst.

Catalyst. (2009a). *Sexual discrimination and sexual harassment.* New York: Catalyst.

Catalyst. (2009b). *Statistical overview of women in the workplace.* Retrieved August 5, 2009, from http://www.catalyst.org/publication/219/statistical-overview-of-women-in-the-workplace.

Cooper, C., Cartwright, S., & Earley, C. (2001). *The international handbook of organizational culture and climate.* New York: Wiley.

Correll, S. J., Benard, S., & Paik, I. (2007). Getting a job: Is there a motherhood penalty? *American Journal of Sociology, 112*, 1297–1338.

Cotter, D. A., Hermsen, J. M., Ovadia, S., & Vanneman, R. (2001). The glass ceiling effect. *Social Forces, 80*, 655–682.

Crouhy, M., Galai, D., & Mark, R. (2005). *The essentials of risk management.* New York: McGraw-Hill.

Cuddy, A., Fiske, S. T., & Glick, P. (2004). When professionals become mothers, warmth doesn't cut the ice. *Journal of Social Issues, 60*, 701–718.

Damast, A. (2009, February 20). Women shattering B-schools' glass ceiling. *BusinessWeek*, 1–3.

DeCenzo, D., & Robbins, S. (2007). *Fundamentals of human resource management.* New York: Wiley.

Denmark, F. L., Rabinowitz, V., & Sechzer, J. (2005). *Engendering psychology, women and gender revisited* (2nd ed.). Boston, MA: Allyn & Bacon.

Deutsch, F. M., & Saxon, S. E. (1998). Traditional ideologies, nontraditional lives. *Sex Roles, 38,* 331–362.

Discrimination.com. (2008). *Pregnancy Discrimination Act of 1978.* Retrieved August 1, 2009, from http://discrimination.com/pregnancydiscrimination. htm.

Driskill, G., & Benton, A. (2005). *Organizational culture in action: A cultural analysis workbook.* New York: Sage.

Dueher, E. E., & Bono, J. E. (2006). Men, women, and managers: Are stereotypes finally changing? *Personnel Psychology, 59,* 815–846.

England, P., Herbert, M. S., Kilbourne, B. S., Reid, L. L., & Megdal, L. M. (1994). The gendered valuation of occupations and skills: Earnings in 1980 census occupations. *Social Forces, 73,* 65–99.

Equal Opportunity Employment Commission. (2004, September 2). *Discriminatory Practices.* Retrieved August 8, 2009, from http://www.eeoc.gov/abouteeo/ overview_practices.html.

Equal Employment Opportunity Commission. (2009a, March 11). *Sexual harassment charges EEOC & FEPA's combined: FY 1997 to FY 2008.* Retrieved August 7, 2009, from http://www.eeoc.gov/stats/harass.html.

Equal Employment Opportunity Commission. (2009b, March 11). *Charge statistics FY 1997 through FY 2008.* Retrieved August 7, 2009, from http:// www.eeoc.gov/stats/charges.html.

Fennema, K., Meyer, D. L., & Owen, N. (1990). Sex of physician: Patients' preferences and stereotypes. *The Journal of Family Practice, 30,* 441–446.

Find Us Law. (2008). *Family and Medical Leave Act - FMLA - 29 U.S. Code Chapter 28.* Retrieved August 1, 2009, from http://www.finduslaw.com/ family_and_medical_leave_act_fmla_29_u_s_code_chapter_28.

Frome, P. M., Alfed, C. J., Eccles, J. S., & Barber, B. L. (2006). Why don't they want a male-dominated job? An investigation of young women who changed their occupational aspirations. *Educational Research and Evaluation, 12,* 359–372.

Gilbert, I. A. (1985). Dimensions of same-gender student-faculty role-model relationships. *Sex Roles, 12,* 111–123.

Ginther, D. K., & Kahn, S. (2006). *Does science promote women: Evidence from academia 1973–2001.* Retrieved July 27, 2009, from http://www. nber.org/papers/w12691.

Glass, J. (2004). Blessing or curse? Work-family policies and mother's wage growth over time. *Work and Occupations, 31,* 367–394.

Haas, L. (2003). Parental leave and gender equality: Lessons from the European Union. *The Review of Policy Research, 20,* 89–114.

Halpern, D. F. (2008). Nurturing careers in psychology: Combining work and family. *Educational Psychology Review, 20,* 57–64.

Halpern, D. F., Benbow, C. P., Geary, D. C., Gur, R. C., Hyde, J. S., & Gernsbacher, M. (2007). The science of sex differences in science and mathematics. *Psychological Science in the Public Interest, 8,* 1–51.

Heilman, M. E., & Haynes, M. C. (2005). No credit where credit is due: Attributional rationalization of women's success in male-female teams. *Journal of Applied Psychology, 90,* 431–441.

"Idea: The Glass Ceiling." (2009, May 5). Retrieved July 29, 2009, from http://www.economist.com/businessfinance/management/displayStory.cfm?story_id=13604240.

Kelly, E., & Dobbin, F. (1999). Civil rights law at work: Sex discrimination and the rise of maternity leave policies. *The American Journal of Sociology, 105,* 455–492.

Kyzer, C. (2008, July 4). *Handling sex discrimination in the workplace.* Retrieved July 29, 2009, from http://www.blackcollegian.com/index.php?option=com_content&view=article&id=184:chaz-kyser&catid=48:workplace-issues&Itemid=124.

Lips, H. (2003). The gender pay gap: Concrete indicator of women's progress toward equality. *Analyses of Social Issues and Public Policy, 3,* 87–109.

Masser, B., Grass, K., & Nesic, M. (2007). 'We like you, but we don't want you'—the impact of pregnancy in the workplace. *Sex Roles, 57,* 703–712.

Murphy, A., & Monsen, J. J. (2008). Gender balance amongst educational psychologists: An attempt to explain the male minority. *Educational Psychology in Practice, 24,* 29–42.

National Association of Women Business Owners. (2009, February 25). *NAWBO survey finds women business owners holding their own amid economic downturn.* Retrieved August 8, 2009, from http://nawbo.org/content_4970.cfm.

Ostroff, C., & Atwater, L. (2003). Does whom you work with matter? Effects of referent group gender and age composition on managers' compensation. *Journal of Applied Psychology, 88,* 725–740.

Ozbilgin, M. F., & Woodward, D. (2004). 'Belonging' and 'otherness': Sex equality in banking in Turkey and Britain. *Gender, Work and Organization, 11,* 668–688.

Quimby, J., & DeSantis, A. (2006). The influence of role models on women's career choices. *Career Development Quarterly, 54,* 297–306.

Radio-Television News Directors Association & Foundation. (2008). *Women and minorities in radio and television news.* Retrieved July 29, 2009, from http://www.catalystwomen.org.

Roth, L. M. (2004). Engendering inequality: Processes of sex-segregation on wall street. *Sociological Forum, 19,* 203–228.

Rudman, L. A., & Glick, P. (2008). *The social psychology of gender: How power and intimacy shape gender relations.* New York: The Guilford Press.

Schilling, R., Moorish, J. N., & Liu, G. (2008). Demographic trends in social work over a quarter-century in an increasingly female profession. *Social Work, 53,* 103–114.

Schuck, K., & Liddle, B. J. (2004). The female manager's experience: A concept map and assessment tool. *Consulting Psychology Journal, 56,* 75–87.

Shrier, D. K., Zucker, A. N., Mercurio, A. E., Landry, L. J., Rich, M., & Shrier, L. A. (2007). Generation to generation: Discrimination and harassment experiences of physician mothers and their physician daughters. *Journal of Women's Health, 16,* 883–894.

Smith, S., & Mazin, R. (2004). *The HR answer book.* New York: AMACOM.

Sharp, L. K., Wang, R., & Lipsky, M. S. (2003). Perception of competency to perform procedures and future practice intent: A national survey of family practice residents. *Academic Medicine, 78,* 926–932.

Staurowsky, E., & DiManno, J. (2002). Young women talking sports and careers: A glimpse at the next generation of women in sport media. *Women in Sport & Physical Activity Journal, 11,* 127–144.

Stead, D. (1996, January 7). Breaking the glass ceiling with the power of words. *New York Times.* Retrieved August 4, 2009, from http://www.ny times.com/books/business/9601shelf.html.

Thornton, M., & Bricheno, P. (2000). Primary school teachers' careers in England and Wales: The relationship between gender, role, position and promotion aspirations. *Pedagogy, Culture, and Society, 8,* 187–206.

U.S. Department of Education, National Center for Education Statistics. (2007). *Integrated Postsecondary Education Data System (IPEDS).* Retrieved August 5, 2009, from http://nces.ed.gov/programs/digest/d08/tables/dt08_275.asp.

U.S. Department of Labor. (2009). *Fact sheet #28: The Family and Medical Leave Act of 1993.* Washington, DC: US Wage and Hour Division.

U.S. Department of Labor, Bureau of Labor Statistics. (2009). *Monthly Labor Review.* Retrieved July 20, 2009, from http://www.dol.gov/wb/factsheets/ Qf-ESWM08_txt.htm.

Waldfogel, J. (1998). The family gap for young women in the United States and Britain: Can maternity leave make a difference? *Journal of Labor Economics, 16,* 505–545.

Weiler, S., & Bernasek, A. (2001). Dodging the glass ceiling? Networks and the new wave of women entrepreneurs. *The Social Science Journal, 38,* 85–103.

11

Sexual Harassment

Eros R. DeSouza

It is important to understand sexual harassment from a multidisciplinary perspective (that is, legal, social, psychological), because sexual harassment is a complex problem that is widespread across organizations and settings. This chapter addresses sexual harassment in the U.S. workplace. It begins by legally defining sexual harassment, including a review of important legal cases concerning sexual harassment in the workplace, with an emphasis placed on federal and Supreme Court cases. Next, it examines sexual harassment from a social-psychological perspective, including empirical studies on frequency rates, recent conceptual frameworks, as well as predictors and consequences of sexual harassment. Finally, it concludes with practical recommendations for managers and human resource personnel.

DEFINING SEXUAL HARASSMENT IN LEGAL TERMS

The U.S. Congress passed Title VII of the Civil Rights Act in 1964. This federal law prohibits discrimination based on race, color, religion, *sex* (emphasis added), or national origin, protecting members of these groups who are employed in businesses with 15 or more employees working for 20 or more weeks per year. In 1991, Congress amended the Civil Rights Act, expanding the rights of the complainant for the recovery of monetary compensation and punitive damages for psychological injury (that is, up to $300,000 for employers with more than 500 employees). In sum, sexual harassment is a type of sex discrimination—a civil rights violation.

The Equal Employment Opportunity Commission (EEOC), the federal agency that enforces Title VII, developed its rules regarding sexual harassment in 1980, which are still used in the 21st century. According to the EEOC, sexual harassment is defined as follows:

> Unwelcome sexual advances, requests for sexual favors, and other verbal or physical conduct of a sexual nature constitutes sexual harassment when (1) submission to such conduct is made either explicitly or implicitly a term or condition of an individual's employment, (2) submission to or rejection of such conduct by an individual is used as the basis for employment decisions affecting such individuals, or (3) such conduct has the purpose or effect of unreasonably interfering with an individual's work performance or creating an intimidating, hostile, or offensive work environment. (*Code of Federal Regulations*, 2000, p. 186)

Based on this definition, there are two types of sexual harassment: *quid pro quo* and hostile environment. The first two parts define *quid pro quo*, which typically involves a person in authority, like a supervisor, in which the employer is always held liable. The third part defines hostile environment, with the employer being liable if the organization knew or should have known and failed to take appropriate remedial action. These two types theoretically are important, but in reality, they are blurred because they often occur together.

According to the EEOC (2009), the current law is gender neutral—the victim of sexual harassment may be a woman or a man, and the harasser does not have to be of the opposite sex. The harasser may or may not have more power than the victim; thus, the harasser can be the victim's supervisor, an agent of the employer, a supervisor in a different area, a co-worker, or a nonemployee (for example, a customer). The victim does not have to be the person directly harassed but could be anyone affected by the offensive behavior. The victim does not have to suffer economic losses or receive tangible injury for sexual harassment to occur. The conduct, however, must be unwelcome.

During 2008, 13,867 sexual harassment charges were filed with the EEOC (2009). Of these, 84 percent were filed by women and 16 percent were filed by men. Overall, in 2008 the EEOC recovered $47.4 million in monetary benefits, not including monetary benefits obtained through sexual harassment litigation.

A recent study has analyzed claims made by women to the EEOC during 1992–2006 (Cunningham & Benavides-Espinoza, 2008). The analysis showed a sharp increase from 1992 to 1997, a leveling off during 1998–2001, and a steady decline thereafter. According to Cunningham and Benavides-Espinoza (2008), the political environment seems to influence sexual harassment claims, with a more liberal political climate during the Clinton presidency accounting for the increase of claims filed with the EEOC, and a steady decline during the more conservative political climate of the George W. Bush presidency.

As stated, the EEOC's definition of sexual harassment was developed in 1980, and since then it has remained intact. What has altered, as my colleague and I have discussed (DeSouza & Solberg, 2003), is how the courts have refined the interpretation of sexual harassment laws; that is, only Congress can pass federal laws, but agencies, such as the EEOC, can develop workplace rules and investigate complaints of sexual harassment, and all courts must interpret those laws and rules.

THE LEGAL EVOLUTION OF SEXUAL HARASSMENT

My colleague and I (DeSouza & Solberg, 2003) examined *Williams v. Saxbe* (1976) and noted that it was the first case that a federal court established the legal concept of *quid pro quo* sexual harassment, and also noted that the concept of hostile environment was recognized in *Bundy v. Jackson* (1981), with a federal court of appeals ruling that employers were liable for sexual insults and propositions regardless of whether an employee lost any job benefits as a consequence of the harassment. In *Henson v. City of Dundee* (1982) a court of appeals clarified the concept of hostile environment:

> Sexual harassment which creates a hostile or offensive environment for members of one sex is every bit the arbitrary barrier to sexual equality at the workplace that racial harassment is to racial equality. Surely, a requirement that a man or a woman run a gauntlet of sexual abuse in return for the privilege of being allowed to work and make a living can be as demeaning and disconcerting as the harshest of racial epithets. (p. 902)

In *McKinney v. Dole* (1985), a court of appeals ruled that a physically aggressive, but not sexually explicit, act could constitute sexual harassment if the physical force would not have happened but for the sex of the employee.

It was in 1986 in *Meritor Savings Bank v. Vinson* that the Supreme Court first ruled on sexual harassment as a form of sex discrimination. Its decision reinforced the concept that sexual harassment is illegal, defined *quid pro quo* sexual harassment, and more important, issued an opinion on the concept of hostile environment as a barrier to sexual equality in the workplace, and thereby prohibited by Title VII. The Supreme Court stated that a hostile work environment constitutes grounds for action if the conduct is unwelcome, based on sex, and severe or pervasive enough to interfere with the victim's employment, echoing the EEOC guidelines. Other cases would follow, further refining the concept of sexual harassment.

In *Andrews v. City of Philadelphia* (1990), a court held that hostility does not have to be tinged with sexual innuendos, ruling that aggressive inappropriate behavior targeted at women creates a hostile work environment. The court used a reasonable woman standard in its ruling. In 1991, in *Ellison v. Brady*, a federal court of appeals also endorsed a reasonable woman standard rather than a reasonable person standard, ruling that unsolicited love letters and unwanted sexual attention that might not be perceived as offensive to the average man, might be perceived by the average woman as so offensive that it creates a hostile environment.

The courts have used the reasonable woman standard inconsistently. Perry, Kulik, and Bourhis (2004) examined the impact of a reasonable woman standard on the outcomes of federal district-level cases of hostile environment sexual harassment after controlling for severity of the harassing behavior, status of the alleged harasser, consequences, witnesses, and other variables. They found that the odds of winning a case were 3.17 times more likely under a reasonable woman standard than under a reasonable person standard. Although this is a modest increase, their hypothesis was supported, suggesting that in an average hostile environment sexual harassment case the plaintiff's odds of winning increases by 26 percent under a reasonable woman standard. Interestingly, they found no effect for the judge's sex on court decisions.

A landmark case reached the Supreme Court in *Harris v. Forklift Systems* (1993). Harris testified that she was often insulted and received unwanted sexual comments while employed at Forklift Systems. The Supreme Court ruled that it was not necessary for the conduct to actually cause serious psychological harm to be considered hostile work environment. The Court attempted to create a balance between making any conduct that is simply offensive actionable and requiring the conduct to inflict substantial psychological harm, reiterating the factors that contribute to a hostile or abusive work environment that were discussed earlier in the *Meritor* (1986) case. Based on the language used in *Harris v. Forklift Systems* (1993), the Court seemingly endorsed the reasonable person standard rather than the reasonable woman standard.

In 1998, two Supreme Court cases significantly changed the standard of proof required in hostile work environment cases, clarifying responsibilities of workers and of employers. In *Faragher v. City of Boca Raton* (1998), Faragher, a college student, resigned as a lifeguard with the City of Boca Raton and then sued the city and her two immediate supervisors, alleging that they had created a sexually hostile atmosphere at work by repeatedly subjecting her and other female lifeguards to uninvited and offensive touching, by making lewd remarks, and by speaking of women in offensive terms, and that this conduct constituted discrimination under Title VII of the Civil Rights Act of 1964. The Court upheld the conclusion that the supervisors' conduct was sufficiently serious to alter conditions of employment and create an abusive working environment.

In *Burlington Industries v. Ellerth* (1998), Ellerth quit her job after 15 months as a salesperson, alleging that she had received constant sexual harassment by her supervisor, including comments that could be construed as threats of retaliation. Despite her refusals to all sexual advances, she suffered no tangible retaliation and, in fact, was promoted once. In addition, she never informed anyone in authority about her supervisor's misconduct, despite knowing that her company had a policy against sexual harassment. Again, the Supreme Court ruled for employer liability when a supervisor creates a hostile environment.

Before these cases, plaintiffs needed to show that their employer knew or should have known of the harassment and did not take appropriate corrective action (Lindemann & Kadue, 1999); however, such strict conditions in hostile environment cases involving a superior are no longer required after *Faragher* (1998) and *Ellerth* (1998). In addition, recall that cases based on carried-out threats are defined as *quid pro quo*, whereas conduct that interferes with an employee's work or creates an offensive climate is defined as hostile work environment. In *Faragher* (1998) and *Ellerth* (1998), the Supreme Court blurred such distinctions and focused instead on whether the alleged perpetrator had authority over the victim, with the Court stating in *Ellerth*:

> An employer is subject to vicarious liability to a victimized employee for an actionable hostile environment created by a supervisor with

immediate (or successively higher) authority over the employee. When no tangible employment action is taken, a defending employer may raise an affirmative defense to liability or damages, subject to proof by a preponderance of the evidence. The defense comprises two necessary elements: (a) that the employer exercised reasonable care to prevent and correct promptly any sexually harassing behavior, and (b) that the plaintiff employee unreasonably failed to take advantage of any preventive or corrective opportunities provided by the employer or to avoid harm otherwise (p. 765). Thus, if the harassing behavior involves a person of authority (for example, a manager or supervisor), the employer is held liable for tolerating a hostile environment, unless the employer can establish both elements of the affirmative defense established by the Supreme Court. These cases encourage employers to take responsibility in preventing and dealing with sexual harassment in the workplace promptly and justly.

SAME-SEX SEXUAL HARASSMENT

When Congress passed the sex component of Title VII of the Civil Rights Act in 1964, it meant to address the problems faced by women being sexually harassed by men in the workplace. It did not have in mind the issue of same-sex sexual harassment. Although Title VII is, on its face, gender neutral, before the Supreme Court ruled on *Oncale v. Sundowner Offshore Services* (1998) many courts were unwilling to protect men from being sexually harassed by other men. The first case on same-sex sexual harassment to reach a federal court of appeals was *Garcia v. Elf Atochem North America* (1994), in which a male employee accused his male supervisor of unwanted sexual advances. The federal court of appeals dismissed the hostile environment claim, ruling that if a man is being sexually harassed by his male supervisor, it is not in violation of Title VII.

Another court of appeals reached the same conclusion in *McWilliams v. Fairfax County Board of Supervisors* (1996). Although McWilliams was ridiculed by his co-workers about his sexual behavior, humiliated with insulting remarks, and physically assaulted in a sexual way, the court ruled against him, stating that sexual harassment cannot exist where "both the alleged harassers and the victim are heterosexuals of the same sex" (p. 1195). It concluded that a ruling in favor of the victim would broaden the interpretation of Title VII beyond what Congress intended. It, however, mentioned that establishing the homosexuality or bisexuality of the supervisor is relevant in same-sex sexual harassment cases with sexual overtones. The court did not mention anything about establishing the heterosexuality in different-sex cases, in which heterosexuality is presumed.

The question of whether the sexual orientation of the person of authority over the victim is a determining factor in same-sex sexual harassment cases was answered affirmatively by a federal court of appeal in *Wrightson v. Pizza Hut of America* (1996). The court ruled in favor of the victim, a 16-year-old heterosexual male employee of Pizza Hut, who alleged that he was the victim of several sexual advances by his openly gay supervisor and by five openly gay co-workers. The court concluded that this case differed from *McWilliams* (1996), which involved sexual harassment between heterosexual men, because Wrightson's perpetrators were homosexual. In addition, this court based its decision on the EEOC Compliance Manual (1987), which states the following:

> The victim does not have to be of the opposite sex of the harasser. . . . [T]he crucial inquiry is whether the harasser treats a member of or members of one sex differently from members of the other sex. The victim and the harasser may be of the same sex where, for instance, the sexual harassment is based on the victim's sex (not on the victim's sexual preference) and the harasser does not treat employees of the opposite sex the same way. (Section 615.2(b)(3))

The appeals court stated that the *Wrightson's* (1996) case "presented a cognizable claim not only that he was sexually harassed by his homosexual supervisor and coworkers, but also that he would not have been harassed but for the fact that he is male" (p. 143).

The *Oncale* case refers to Joseph Oncale, who worked for Sundowner on an offshore oil platform from August to November 1991. He alleged that he had been subjected to humiliating, sex-related acts by his supervisors and co-workers. He complained to supervisory personnel, but his employer took no action to remedy the situation. He quit his job because he was afraid that his co-workers would rape him and then he sued Sundowner. In 1996, the appellate court ruled against Oncale on the basis of the *Garcia v. Elf Atochem North America* (1994) decision, which concluded that sexual harassment between two men is not a violation of Title VII. In 1998, the case reached the Supreme Court.

In a unanimous decision, the Supreme Court reversed the decision by the court of appeals and ruled in favor of Oncale (1998), settling once and for all that Title VII applies to same-sex sexual harassment. The Court stated that same-sex sexual harassment is illegal in every jurisdiction, regardless of whether the discrimination was motivated by sexual desire or by same-sex hostility. The Court cited as an example a discriminatory situation in which a female victim is humiliated by another woman who is hostile to women in the workplace. This is the position in which Oncale found himself. He was sexually harassed because of his sex, although the harassers were heterosexual men who were not motivated by sexual desire.

Although same-sex sexual harassment is actionable since the 1998 Oncale decision, federal claims of discrimination based on sexual orientation is not. In other words, if the victim is homosexual and there is no evidence of sexual desire or same-sex hostility by the perpetrator, then the Title VII (1964) definition does not apply in federal courts. This is exactly the conclusion that was reached in *Bibby v. Coca Cola Bottling Company* (2001). Bibby, a gay man, claimed that he was subjected to same-sex sexual harassment. The federal court of appeals dismissed his case because there was no evidence that the harassment was based on sexual desire or on same-sex hostility. Sexual minorities (for example, lesbians, gay men, bisexuals, and transsexuals) who are victims of sexual harassment often sue based on sex stereotyping in the workplace, which has long affected women.

In *Price Waterhouse v. Hopkins* (1989), the Supreme Court ruled that sex stereotyping played a key role in evaluating Hopkins' candidacy for partnership at the male-dominated accounting firm of Price Waterhouse. Her employers admitted that she was qualified to be considered for partnership and probably would have become a partner, but for her acting "too masculine." They told her to "walk more femininely, talk more femininely, dress more femininely, wear make-up, have her hair styled, and wear jewelry" (p. 235). Thus, Hopkins was discriminated against because she failed to conform to traditional sex role stereotypes, in which women are expected to be communal by showing, but not limited to, the following: warmth, nurturance, kindness, and understanding. Men, however, are expected to show agency by behaving, but not limited to, in the following manner: competitively, independently, and self-confidently (Glick & Fiske, 2007; Kite, Deaux, & Haines, 2008). Women who show masculine traits in the workplace often are evaluated negatively and punished (Rudman & Glick, 2001). According to Steinberg, True, and Russo (2008):

Gender stereotyping has long been linked to distinct employment issues for women, who must deal with evaluation bias, greater pressure on their performance, exclusion from certain jobs and promotional opportunities, differential supervision, overprotection, unprofessional sexual remarks, incivility and harassment, unequal employment rewards, and gender segregation between and within occupations. (p. 657)

Until recently, federal and state courts typically did not hold that sex discrimination toward transsexuals was protected under Title VII (1964). However, largely based on the case of *Price Waterhouse v. Hopkins* (1989), recent rulings have challenged such a view; that is, transsexuals, by definition, challenge stereotypes about their particular birth sex. For example, in *Smith v. City of Salem* (2004), Smith, a transitioning preoperative male-to-female transsexual who was biologically and by birth a male, was diagnosed with gender identity disorder and began to express a more feminine appearance in the Salem Fire Department where he worked as lieutenant. Smith's co-workers began to ridicule him, telling him that his appearance and mannerisms were not "masculine enough." The appeals court ruled that Smith's gender-related expressions failed to conform to his employers' stereotypes of how men should look and behave—that is Smith was perceived as insufficiently masculine at work, given his biological sex as a male. The court said:

Sex stereotyping based on a person's gender nonconforming behavior is impermissible discrimination, irrespective of the cause of that behavior; a label, such as transsexual, is not fatal to a sex discrimination claim where the victim has suffered discrimination because of his or her gender nonconformity. (p. 11)

Another federal court of appeals reached the same conclusion in *Barnes v. City of Cincinnati* (2005). Barnes was a preoperative male-to-female transsexual police officer who was promoted to sergeant after passing a promotional exam, but he was demoted afterward due to his nonconformity to traditional sex role stereotypes (that is, all other male sergeants acted and looked masculine, whereas Barnes had a feminine demeanor). The appeals court ruled in favor of Barnes based on the earlier case of *Smith v. City of Salem* (2004).

As recently as 2008, the same argument was evidenced in *Schroer v. Billington* (2008). As a male, Schoer applied for a terrorism-related policy analyst position with the Library of Congress. He was offered the job because he was the best candidate. After disclosing his transsexuality and informing his supervisor of his intention to undergo transgender surgery, the offer was withdrawn the next day. The supervisor showed sex stereotyping, as evidenced by her statement that when she would see Schoer dressed as a woman, the supervisor would only see a man in women's clothing. The federal court of appeals' position was in favor of Schroer, stating that discrimination against transsexuals is actionable due to sex stereotyping.

According to York, Tyler, Tyler, and Gugel (2008), increased awareness to the ever-changing face of discrimination in the workplace is needed. That is, sex stereotyping affects both women and men who fail to conform to traditional sex role norms. Moreover, these cases suggest that, on the one hand, federal courts increasingly are willing to apply the rationale to sex discrimination claims based on sex stereotyping of transsexual individuals. On the other hand, the courts usually distinguish gender identity or expression from sexual orientation, which, as stated earlier, is not protected by federal sex discrimination laws. Notably, the courts have been influenced by testimonials given by researchers, who provide valuable information in sexual harassment cases.

SEXUAL HARASSMENT FROM A SOCIAL-PSYCHOLOGICAL PERSPECTIVE

This section presents findings from past empirical studies. It includes a discussion of the frequency rates of sexual harassment in the workplace. In the following studies, sexual harassment was defined by asking respondents whether they had experienced a list of unwanted sexually harassing behaviors. These surveys assessed the psychological rather than the legal aspect of sexual harassment. From a psychological viewpoint, sexual harassment refers to "unwanted sex-related behavior at work that is appraised by the recipient as offensive, exceeding her [or his] resources, or threatening her [or his] well-being" (Fitzgerald, Swan, & Magley, 1997, p. 15). According to Gutek and Done (2001), the psychological definition of sexual harassment allows researchers to understand gender roles, power dynamics, and coping skills "without focusing on whether particular behavior would rise to the level of actionable conduct in a court of law" (p. 370).

In May 1980, Congress requested that a survey be conducted to ascertain the frequency of sexual harassment in the federal workplace (U.S. Merit Systems Protection Board, 1981). A representative national sample reported on their sexually harassing experiences (that is, uninvited sexual teasing, jokes, remarks, or questions; uninvited sexually suggestive looks or gestures; uninvited and deliberate touching, leaning over, cornering, or pinching; uninvited letters, phone calls, or materials of a sexual nature; uninvited pressure for dates; and uninvited pressure for sexual favors) at work during the past two years prior to the survey. The federal workforce was surveyed in 1987 (U.S. Merit Systems Protection Board, 1988) and again in 1994 (U.S. Merit Systems Protection Board, 1995). The findings indicated that 42 percent to 44 percent of women and 14 percent to 19 percent of men reported having experienced at least one sexually harassing behavior at work during the past two years (U.S. Merit Systems Protection Board, 1981, 1988, 1995).

Data from the Department of Defense (DoD) support the above gender differences in frequency rates of sexual harassment experiences among active-duty members in the Army, Navy, Marine Corps, Air Force, and Coast Guard. The first survey on sexual harassment in the U.S. Armed Forces was in 1988, using a list of 10 unwanted sexual behaviors modeled after the U.S. Merit Systems Protection Board behavioral survey. The results revealed that 64 percent of the women and 17 percent of the men reported at least one sexually harassing experience at work during the past year (Martindale, 1991).

In 1995, the DoD surveyed the sexual harassment of active military personnel, but this time using an adapted version of Fitzgerald et al.'s (1988) Sexual Experiences Questionnaire (SEQ). The SEQ-DoD consists of 25 unwanted sexually harassing behaviors. The findings showed that 76 percent of the women and 37 percent of the men reported having experienced sexual harassment at least once during the past year (Bastian, Lancaster, & Reyst, 1996).

In 2002, the DoD assessed sexual harassment of active military personnel using the 19-item SEQ-DoD. Compared with the 1995 survey, the findings showed a significant drop for both women and men. The gender difference pattern, however, remained the same, with more women (45 percent) than men (23 percent) reporting having experienced some form of sexual harassment during the past year before the survey (Lipari & Lancaster, 2003).

The above studies from civilian and military personnel samples, as well as information provided by the EEOC (2009), show that women are much more likely than men to experience sexual harassment. The social-psychological literature also has shown a consistent pattern of gender differences in perceptions of sexual harassment, with women perceiving a broader range of behaviors as sexual harassment than men do (see the meta-analytic reviews conducted by Blumental, 1998, and

Rotundo, Nguyen, & Sackett, 2001; meta analysis is a statistical procedure that summarizes effect sizes across many different studies). In addition, studies have shown that men perceive sexually harassing experiences as less severe, less offensive, less improper, less troublesome, and less intimidating than women do (for example, Berdahl, Magley, & Waldo, 1996; Berdahl & Moore, 2006; Cochran, Frazier, & Olson, 1997; Hurt, Maver, & Hoffman, 1999; LaRocca & Kromrey, 1999). Studies also have found that men are less likely than women to judge sociosexual behavior involving same-sex individuals as constituting sexual harassment (DeSouza & Solberg, 2004; DeSouza, Solberg, & Elder, 2007).

The findings from these studies have important implications for legal scholars and managers by supporting the notion that the courts should use the reasonable woman standard rather than the reasonable person standard. In addition, it seems that women tend to side with the victim in same-sex sexual harassment cases, which would be relevant for attorneys to know when selecting jury members (DeSouza et al., 2007). Moreover, the more men learn about how upsetting, bothersome, and threatening sexually harassing behaviors are to women, the more likely men's understanding of sexual harassment may resemble women's understanding (Kovera, McAuliff, & Herbert, 1999), thus preventing future harassing behaviors from emerging in the workplace.

Although the overall prevalence of sexual harassment is much greater among women than among men, studies on civilian employees (U.S. Merit Systems Protection Board, 1981, 1995) and military personnel (Bastian et al., 1996; DuBois, Knapp, Faley, & Kustis, 1998; Lipari & Lancaster, 2003; Stockdale, Visio, & Batra, 1999) revealed that men were more likely than women to experience same-sex sexual harassment. In addition, men were much more likely to be bothered, insulted, troubled, humiliated, and distressed by it than by different-sex sexual harassment (Stockdale et al., 1999). Researchers concluded that men are harmed by same-sex sexual harassment because such experiences threaten their masculinity (Berdahl et al., 1996; DuBois, et al., 1998; Stockdale et al., 1999). In addition, male perpetrators use sexual harassment as a weapon against other men who violate stereotypical gender norms of how men should act.

By definition, homosexuality and transsexuality challenge traditional gender norms, and sexual harassment is a tool to punish gender role violators. For example, in 2000, the DoD conducted a study in military settings with respect to the homosexual conduct policy of "Don't ask, don't tell" that has been in effect since 1993. Based on 71,550 completed surveys, the findings showed that 80 percent of respondents reported having heard offensive speech, derogatory names, jokes, or remarks about homosexuals during the past year before the survey; 37 percent of respondents reported that they had witnessed or experienced a harassing event or behavior based on perceived homosexuality of the victim (Office of the Inspector General, 2000).

Moradi (2006) examined harassment based on perceived homosexuality among 200 active military personnel and 196 college students (civilians) during the past year before the survey. In both groups, men were likely to be both perpetrators (73 percent military and 78 percent civilian) and victims (64 percent military and 78 percent civilian) of harassment based on perceived homosexuality. Civilians reported significantly higher levels of offensive speech and gestures about perceived homosexuals than did military participants. Compared with civilians, more military participants reported that a superior (for example, immediate supervisor and/or unit commander) perpetrated and witnessed the harassment.

Concerning the sexual harassment of men, Berdahl et al. (1996) identified a new set of behaviors that men perceived as harassing—for example, "punishments for deviating from the masculine gender role" (p. 542)—that previously were not identified as such in studies that assessed the sexual harassment of women. These behaviors were integrated into a new measure called the Sexual Harassment of Men (SHOM; Waldo, Berdahl, & Fitzgerald, 1998).

Waldo et al. (1998) examined the frequency of male sexual harassment using the SHOM among three diverse samples of men (420 men from western agribusiness food processing plants, 378 men from a large public utility company in the northwest, and 209 male faculty and staff from a large midwestern university). The findings showed that 47 percent to 50 percent of men reported having experienced a sexually harassing behavior at least once during the past two years. In each sample, men were more likely to report male perpetrators (40 percent to 53 percent) than female perpetrators (30 percent to 32 percent).

RECENT CONCEPTUAL FRAMEWORKS TO UNDERSTANDING SEXUAL HARASSMENT

Legal scholars and social scientists suggest that men who depart from traditional masculine gender roles (for example, men perceived to be gay or effeminate) are likely to be sexually harassed by heterosexual men to reinforce patriarchal values (Foote & Goodman-Delahunty,

1999; Franke, 1997; Stockdale et al., 1999; Waldo et al., 1998). According to Franke (1997), sexual harassment is a means of enforcing traditional gender roles of what men and women should be, punishing women who are not feminine enough and men who are not masculine enough. The reason that sexual harassment constitutes sex discrimination is "not the fact that the conduct is sexual, but that the sexual conduct is being used to enforce or perpetuate gender norms and stereotypes" (Franke, 1997, p. 745).

A similar framework has been proposed by Berdahl's (2007a) sex-based harassment theory, in which sexual harassment is motivated by a need to restore an individual's social status whenever it is threatened (for example, putting a woman working in a male-dominated field "in her place" by sexually harassing her). Berdahl (2007b) conducted three studies to test her theory. The findings showed that "uppity" women (that is, those with masculine personality traits like assertiveness, aggressiveness, and independence; the same qualities evidenced by *Price Waterhouse v. Hopkins,* 1989) were the most likely to be sexually harassed in their social and working lives. She found that women who worked in more traditionally masculine jobs experienced more sexual harassment than women in female-dominated jobs; such a finding echoes other studies, which found that women experienced more sexual harassment in male-dominated occupations than in female-dominated ones (for example, Gutek & Cohen, 1987; O'Connell & Korabik, 2000). According to Gutek and Cohen (1987), women in "nontraditional jobs" are visible role "deviants" who are perceived and treated differently. Lastly, Berdahl (2007b) found that women with masculine personalities who worked in male-dominated jobs experienced sexual harassment the most. Berdahl concluded that sexual harassment seems to be motivated by sexist hostility toward those who violate gender-role norms rather than by sexual desire.

The previous studies reviewed in this chapter indicate that women typically are targets of sexual harassment and men generally are perpetrators. Maass and Cadinu (2006) reviewed evidence from their experiments using "the computer harassment paradigm" (p. 112), which simulates sexual harassment by leading male participants to believe that they are virtually interacting with a female participant and by measuring the frequency and offensiveness of pornographic material sent to the (fictitious) female participant. The findings from various experimental studies suggest that the motive for sexual harassment is social identity threats, which is congruent with Berdahl's (2007a) sex-based harassment theory.

Maass and Cadinu (2006) reported that men were much more likely to sexually harass feminist women than traditional women, presumably because the latter were not a threat to men's social identity, whereas the former challenged their masculinity and dominant position in society. Moreover, male participants exposed to feminists, in comparison to those without such exposure, reported greater intentions to engage in sexual coercion with other women in hypothetical hiring situations. Maass and Cadinu reported individual differences among men exposed to feminists. That is, those most likely to engage in sexual harassment are men with sexist attitudes, those who identify with their gender (for example, hypermasculine men), those with a propensity for sexual coercion, and those with a social dominance orientation.

Research has shown that organizational climate perceptions (for example, how tolerant employers are toward sexual harassment, including lack of policies and procedures for dealing with sexual harassment and perceived risk for reporting sexual harassment) and job-gender context (for example, the sex ratio of the workgroup, including whether the job is traditionally male dominated or female dominated) are the best predictors of frequency of sexual harassment (Berdahl, 2007b; Fitzgerald, Swan, & Fischer, 1995; Fitzgerald, Drasgow, Hulin, Gelfand, & Magley, 1997). In a meta-analytic review of 41 empirical studies, with a total sample size of almost 70,000 employees, Willness, Steel, and Lee (2007) examined these organizational predictors of sexual harassment. The findings showed that organizational climate had the strongest effect, followed by job-gender context. These findings confirmed Fitzgerald, Drasgrow, et al.'s model (1995, 1997), indicating that organizational climate is a fundamental predictor of sexual harassment. Although weaker, the findings also indicated substantial support that having fewer women in the work group or working in male-dominated jobs (that is, job gender context) are risk factors for the incidence of sexual harassment.

Workplace incivility, sexual harassment, and ethnic harassment have not been integrated sufficiently into empirical studies (DeSouza, 2008). Workplace incivility is associated with sexual and ethnic harassment. Workplace incivility refers to low-level, ambiguous deviant behavior that violates norms of mutual respect (Andersson & Pearson, 1999). Ethnic harassment refers to behavior that has an ethnic component and is perceived as threatening to racial and ethnic minority members (Schneider, Hitlan, & Radhakrishnan, 2000). A recent study with faculty members from a public university found that workplace incivility predicted sexual harassment for men and women; however, workplace incivility only predicted ethnic harassment for men (DeSouza, in press). The relationship between workplace incivility and sexual harassment is in keeping with findings from Lim and Cortina's (2005) studies with two different samples of female workers employed in a large public sector organization. Lim and Cortina also found that these women's well-being declined with the addition of each type of mistreatment, with women who experienced incivility and sexual harassment having the worst job-related and psychological outcomes.

The recent study did not find gender differences for workplace incivility, sexual harassment, or ethnic harassment (DeSouza, in press). The lack of gender differences for workplace incivility is congruent with findings reported by Pearson et al. (2000; Pearson, Andersson, & Porath, 2005; Pearson, Andersson, & Wegner, 2001). Other researchers, however, found significant gender differences, with women experiencing more workplace incivility during the previous five years than their male counterparts (Cortina et al., 2002; Cortina, Magley, Williams, & Langhout, 2001). Conversely, my recent study (Desouza, in press), did find negative consequences for workplace incivility, sexual harassment, and ethnic harassment, with faculty members, regardless of their gender. Those who experienced these behaviors at least once during the past two years reported worse job-related outcomes than faculty members who never experienced such behaviors.

Willness et al.'s (2007) meta-analytic study also examined three types of consequences of sexual harassment experiences: job-related, psychological, and health-related consequences. The findings revealed that sexually harassing experiences had negative consequences in all three of these domains. That is, sexual harassment was linked to lower job satisfaction (especially dissatisfaction with co-workers and supervisors), decreased organizational commitment, work withdrawal (for example, missing work, neglecting tasks), job withdrawal (for example, turnover intent), decreased productivity, ill mental health (including symptoms of post-traumatic stress disorder and lower life satisfaction), and ill physical health.

One does not have to experience sexual harassment directly to suffer its ill effects. Indirect exposure to sexual harassment (for example, watching, hearing, or knowing about individuals who have been harassed) is called ambient sexual harassment (ASH) by Glomb et al. (1997), who defined it as "the frequency of sexually harassing behaviors perpetrated against others in a woman's work group" (p. 314). Glomb et al. (1997) examined predictors and consequences of ASH using samples of female employees from a large public utility company and a food-processing company. ASH was measured based on the mean SEQ score for all female employees in a work team, without the focal individual's score. The findings showed that ASH has similar predictors and consequences as directly experiencing sexual harassment. That is, the best predictor of ASH is organizational tolerance of sexual harassment. Moreover, the consequences of ASH parallel those of directly experiencing sexual harassment, even after controlling for general job stress and direct exposure to sexual harassment. Women exposed to ASH reported lower job satisfaction and greater psychological distress.

Miner-Rubino and Cortina (2004) found that male and female public-sector employees who worked in a climate of hostility toward women, but were not directly targeted by such hostility (akin to ASH), experienced a significant decline in their occupational and physical well-being, especially in male-dominated environments, even after controlling for general stress, occupational position, racial minority status, and age. These findings suggest that all employees (that is, not just women) suffer from working in a climate hostile to women. In another study with male and female employees from a public university, Miner-Rubino and Cortina (2007) found that observing hostility toward women and perceiving the organizational climate as tolerant of sexual harassment predicted lower psychological well-being and job satisfaction for all employees.

Another study with male and female employees from a food services organization further showed that even after controlling for general stress, racial diversity, team size, and gender ratio, ASH had negative consequences on team processes (for example, relationship and task conflict), including the financial performance of teams (Raver & Gelfand, 2005). These studies have important legal implications (for example, they provide further evidence of the harm that hostile environment causes victims and bystanders), as well as implications for management (for example, ASH is an organizational problem that affects the bottom line).

CONCLUSIONS AND RECOMMENDATIONS

From a legal perspective, organizations need to defend against charges of sexual harassment by being able to show an affirmative defense (*Burlington Industries v. Ellerth*, 1998; *Faragher v. City of Boca Raton*, 1998). Furthermore, research from the social sciences that was reviewed in this chapter highlights the importance of the organization climate.

That is, it is paramount that organizations show that they are fostering a climate that clearly conveys the message to everyone that sexual harassment will not be allowed. This typically is done by disseminating and enforcing a zero-tolerance policy that deters potential harassers and encourages reporting of sexual harassment incidents when they occur.

Moreover, researchers (for example, Berdahl, 2007b; Glick & Fiske, 2007; Gutek & Cohen, 1987; O'Connell & Korabik, 2000) have indicated that sex segregation of jobs create skewed gender ratios that contribute to the occurrence of sexual harassment and that higher power differentials between men and women and gender stereotyping foster sexual harassment. Thus, human resource departments should assess women's roles, status, and position in the organization, as well as examine all employees' satisfaction with the current sexual harassment policy and their experiences with direct and ambient sexual harassment (Bell, Quick, & Cycyota, 2002), as well as incivility. In addition, human resource departments periodically should evaluate how well their procedures to investigate occurrences of sexual harassment have been implemented as well as the effectiveness of their education and training prevention programs.

Education and training should include information of how gender stereotypes contribute to sexual harassment and updates on legislation concerning sexual harassment, including the harassment of sexual minorities. For example, although no federal law currently protect sexual minorities from workplace discrimination in the private sector (see chapter 12 on sexual orientation by Barron & Hebl, this volume, for a review of how legislation may affect behavior and attitudes toward protecting sexual minorities in the workplace), on June 17, 2009, President Obama signed an executive order specifically prohibiting discrimination based on sexual orientation in the federal government (Meckler, 2009). In addition, Crary (2009) argues that Congress faces increasing pressure to pass the Employment Non-Discrimination Act (ENDA), which would prohibit discrimination in the workplace (except the military, religious organizations, and businesses with fewer than 15 employees) based on sexual orientation and transsexuality.

REFERENCES

Andersson, L. M., & Pearson, C. M. (1999). Tit for tat? The spiraling effect of incivility in the workplace. *Academy of Management Review, 24,* 452–471.
Andrews v. City of Philadelphia, 895 F.2d 1469, 1481 (3rd Cir. 1990).

Barnes v. City of Cincinnati, 401 F.3d 729 (6th Cir 2005).

Bastian, L. D., Lancaster, A. R., & Reyst, H. E. (1996). *Department of Defense 1995 Sexual Harassment Survey*. Arlington, VA: Defense Manpower Data Center.

Bell, M. P., Quick, J. C., & Cycyota, C. (2002). Assessment and prevention of sexual harassment of employees: An applied guide to creating healthy organizations. *International Journal of Selection and Assessment, 10*,160–167.

Berdahl, J. L. (2007a). Harassment-based on sex: Protecting social status in the context of gender hierarchy. *Academy of Management Review, 32*, 641–658.

Berdahl, J. L. (2007b). The sexual harassment of uppity women. *Journal of Applied Psychology, 92*, 425–437.

Berdahl, J. L., Magley, V. J., & Waldo, C. R. (1996). The sexual harassment of men? Exploring the concept with theory and data. *Psychology of Women Quarterly, 20*, 527–547.

Berdahl, J. L., & Moore, C. (2006). Workplace harassment: Double jeopardy for minority women. *Journal of Applied Psychology, 91*, 426–436.

Bibby v. Philadelphia Coca Cola Bottling Company, 260 F.3d 257 (3rd Cir. 2001).

Blumenthal, J. A. (1998). The reasonable woman standard: A meta-analytic review of gender differences in perceptions of sexual harassment. *Law and Human Behavior, 22*, 33–59.

Bundy v. Jackson, 641 F. 2d 934 (DC Cir. 1981).

Burlington Industries, Inc., v. Ellerth, 524 U.S. 742 (1998).

Civil Rights Act, 42 U.S.C.S § 2000e (1964).

Civil Rights Act, Pub. L. No. 102–166, § (1991).

Cochran, C. C., Frazier, P. A., & Olson, A. M. (1997). Predictors of responses to unwanted sexual attention. *Psychology of Women Quarterly, 21*, 207–226.

Code of Federal Regulations. Vol. 29, Section 1604.11. Washington, DC: U.S. Government Printing Office.

Cortina, L. M., Longsway, K. A., Magley, V. J., Freeman, L. V., Collinsworth, L. L., Hunter, M., & Fitzgerald, L. F. (2002). What's gender got to do with it? Incivility in the federal courts. *Law and Social Inquiry, 27*, 235–270.

Cortina, L. M., Magley, V. J., Williams, J. H., & Langhout, R. D. (2001). Incivility in the workplace: Incidence and impact. *Journal of Occupational Health Psychology, 6*, 64–80.

Crary, D. (2009, August 27). New impetus for bill banning anti-gay bias at work. *The Washington Post*. Retrieved August 28, 2009, from http://www.washingtonpost.com/wpdyn/content/article/2009/08/27/AR2009082702679.html.

Cunningham, G. B., & Benavides-Espinoza, C. (2008). A trend analysis of sexual harassment claims: 1992–2006. *Psychological Reports, 103*, 779–782.

DeSouza, E. R. (2008). Workplace incivility, sexual harassment, and racial micro-aggression: The interface of three literatures. In M. Paludi (Ed.), *The psychology of women at Work: Vol 2. Obstacles and the identity juggle* (pp. 65–84). Westport, CT: Praeger.

DeSouza, E. R. (in press). Frequency rates and correlates of contrapower harassment in higher education. *Journal of Interpersonal Violence.*

DeSouza, E., & Solberg, J. (2003). Incidence and dimensions of sexual harassment across cultures. In M. Paludi & C. A. Paludi, Jr. (Eds.), *Academic and workplace sexual harassment: A handbook of cultural, social science, management, and legal perspectives* (pp. 3–30). Westport, CT: Praeger.

DeSouza, E., & Solberg, J. (2004). Women's and men's reactions to man-to-man sexual harassment: Does the sexual orientation of the victim matter? *Sex Roles, 50,* 623–639.

DeSouza, E. R., Solberg, J., & Elder, C. (2007). A cross-cultural perspective on judgments of woman-to-woman sexual harassment: Does sexual orientation matter? *Sex Roles, 56,* 457–471.

DuBois, C. L. Z., Knapp, D. E., Faley, R. H., & Kustis, G. A. (1998). An empirical examination of same- and other-gender sexual harassment in the workplace. *Sex Roles, 9,* 731–749.

Ellison v. Brady, 924 F. 2d 872 (9th Cir. 1991).

Equal Employment Opportunity Commission. (1987). *Compliance Manual.* CCH § 615.2 (b) (3). Washington, DC: U.S. Government Printing Office.

Equal Employment Opportunity Commission. (2009, March 11). *Sexual Harassment.* Retrieved June 24, 2009, from http://www.eeoc.gov/types/sexual_harassment.html.

Faragher v. City of Boca Raton, 524 U.S. 775 (1998).

Fitzgerald, L. F., Drasgow, F., Hulin, C. L., Gelfand, M. J., & Magley, V. J. (1997). Antecedents and consequences of sexual harassment in organizations: A test of an integrated model. *Journal of Applied Psychology, 82,* 578–589.

Fitzgerald, L. F., Shullman, S., Bailey, N., Richards, M., Swecker, J., Gold, Y., et al. (1988). The incidence and dimensions of sexual harassment in academia and the workplace. *Journal of Vocational Behavior, 32,* 152– 175.

Fitzgerald, L. F., Swan, S., & Fischer, K. (1995). Why didn't she just report him? The psychological and legal implications of women's responses to sexual harassment. *Journal of Social Issues, 51,* 117–138.

Fitzgerald, L. F., Swan, S., & Magley, V. J. (1997). But was it really sexual harassment? Legal, behavioral, and psychological definitions of the workplace victimization of women. In W. O'Donohue (Ed.), *Sexual harassment: Theory, research, and treatment* (pp. 5–28). Boston, MA: Allyn & Bacon.

Foote, W. E., & Goodman-Delahunty, J. (1999). Same-sex harassment: Implications of the Oncale decision for forensic evaluation of plaintiffs. *Behavioral Sciences and the Law, 17,* 123–139.

Franke, K. M. (1997). What's wrong with sexual harassment? *Stanford Law Review, 49*, 691–772.

Garcia v. Elf Atochem North America, 28 F.3d 446 (5th Cir. 1994).

Glick, P., & Fiske, S. T. (2007). Sex discrimination: The psychological approach. In F. J. Crosby, M. S. Stockdale, & S. A. Ropp (Eds.), *Sex discrimination in the workplace* (pp. 155–187). Malden, MA: Blackwell Publishing.

Glomb, T. M., Richman, W. L., Hulin, C. L., Drasgow, F., Schneider, K. T., & Fitzgerald, L. F. (1997). Ambient sexual harassment: An integrated model of antecedents and consequences. *Organizational Behavior and Human Decision Processes, 71*, 309–328.

Gutek, B. A., & Cohen, A. G. (1987). Sex ratios, sex role spillover, and sex at work: A comparison of men's and women's experiences. *Human Relations, 40*, 97–115.

Gutek, B. A., & Done, R. S. (2001). Sexual harassment. In R. K. Unger (Ed.), *Handbook of the psychology of women and gender* (pp. 367–387). New York: Wiley.

Harris v. Forklift Systems, 510 U.S. 17 (1993).

Henson v. City of Dundee, 682 F. 2d 897, 902 (11th Cir. 1982).

Hurt, J. L., Maver, J. A., & Hoffman, D. (1999). Situational and individual influences on judgments of hostile environment sexual harassment. *Journal of Applied Social Psychology, 29*, 1395–1415.

Kite, M. E., Deaux, K., & Haines, E. L. (2008). Gender stereotypes. In F. L. Denmark & M. A. Paludi (Eds.), *Psychology of women: A handbook of issues and theories* (2nd ed., pp. 237–270). Westport, CT: Praeger.

Kovera, M. B., McAuliff, B. D., & Herbert, K. S. (1999). Reasoning about scientific evidence: Effects of juror gender and evidence quality on juror decisions in a hostile work environment case. *Journal of Applied Psychology, 84*, 362–375.

LaRocca, M. A., & Kromrey, J. D. (1999). Perception of sexual harassment in higher education: Impact of gender and attractiveness. *Sex Roles, 40*, 921–940.

Lim, S., & Cortina, L. M. (2005). Interpersonal mistreatment in the workplace: The interface and impact of general incivility and sexual harassment. *Journal of Applied Psychology, 90*, 483–496.

Lindemann, B. T., & Kadue, D. D. (1999). *Sexual harassment in employment Law: 1999 cumulative supplement*. Washington, DC: The Bureau of National Affairs, Inc.

Lipari, R. N., & Lancaster, A. R. (2003). *Armed forces 2002 sexual harassment survey*. Arlington, VA: Defense Manpower Data Center.

Maass, A., & Cadinu, M. R. (2006). Protecting a threatened identity through sexual harassment: A social identity interpretation. In R. Brown & D. Capozza, *Social identities: Motivational, emotional and cultural influences* (pp. 109–131). Hove, UK: Psychology Press.

Martindale, M. (1991). Sexual harassment in the military: 1988. *Sociological Practice Review, 2,* 200–216.

McKinney v. Dole, 765 F. 2d 1129 (DC Cir. 1985).

McWilliams v. Fairfax County Board of Supervisors. 72 F. 3d 1191 (4th Cir. 1996).

Meckler, L. (2009, June 17). Obama directive to bar bias based on sexual orientation. *The Wall Street Journal.* Retrieved July 19, 2009, from http://online .wsj.com/article/SB124526168275024051.html.

Meritor Savings Bank v. Vinson, 477 U.S. 57 (1986).

Miner-Rubino, K., & Cortina, L. M. (2004). Working in a context of hostility toward women: Implications for employees' well-being. *Journal of Occupational Health Psychology, 9,* 107–122.

Miner-Rubino, K., & Cortina, L. M. (2007). Beyond targets: Consequences of vicarious exposure to misogyny at work. *Journal of Applied Psychology, 92,* 1254–1269.

Moradi, B. (2006). Perceived sexual-orientation-based harassment in military and civilian contexts. *Military Psychology, 18,* 39–60.

O'Connell, C. E., & Korabik, K. (2000). Sexual harassment: The relationship of personal vulnerability, work context, perpetrator status, and type of harassment outcomes. *Journal of Vocational Behavior, 56,* 299–329.

Office of the Inspector General. (2000). *Military environment with respect to the homosexual conduct policy* (Report No. D-2000-101). Arlington, VA: Office of the Inspector General, Department of Defense.

Oncale v. Sundowner Offshore Services Inc., 83 F. 3d 118 (5th Cir. 1996).

Oncale v. Sundowner Offshore Services, Inc., 523 U.S. 75 (1998).

Pearson, C. M., Andersson, L. M., & Porath, C. L. (2000). Assessing and attacking workplace incivility. *Organizational Dynamics, 29,* 123–137.

Pearson, C. M., Andersson, L. M., & Porath, C. L. (2005). Workplace incivility. In S. Fox & P. E. Spector (Eds.), *Counterproductive work behavior: Investigation of actors and targets* (pp. 177–200). Washington, DC: American Psychological Association.

Pearson, C. M., Andersson, L. M., & Wegner, J. W. (2001). When workers flout convention: A study of workplace incivility. *Human Relations, 54,* 1387– 1419.

Perry, E. L., Kulik, C. T., & Bourhis, A. C. (2004). The reasonable woman standard: Effects on sexual harassment court decisions. *Law and Human Behavior, 28,* 9–27.

Price Waterhouse v. Hopkins, 490 U.S. 228 (1989).

Raver, J. L., & Gelfand, M. (2005). Beyond the individual victim: Linking sexual harassment, team processes, and team performance. *Academy of Management Journal, 48,* 387–400.

Rotundo, M., Nguyen, D. H., & Sackett, P. R. (2001). A meta-analytic review of gender differences in perceptions of sexual harassment. *Journal of Applied Psychology, 86,* 914–922.

Rudman, L. A., & Glick, P. (2001). Prescriptive gender stereotypes and backlash toward agentic women. *Journal of Social Issues, 57*, 743–762.

Schneider, K. T., Hitlan, R. T., & Radhakrishnan, P. (2000). An examination of the nature and correlates of ethnic harassment experiences in multiple contexts. *Journal of Applied Psychology, 85*, 3–12.

Schroer v. Billington, 577 F. Supp. 2d 293 (DC Cir. 2008).

Smith v. City of Salem, 369 F.3d 912; LEXIS 10611 (6th Cir. 2004).

Steinberg, J. R., True, M., & Russo, N. F. (2008). Work and family roles: Selected issues. In F. L. Denmark, & M. A. Paludi (Eds.), *Psychology of women: A handbook of issues and theories* (2nd ed., pp. 652–700). Westport, CT: Praeger.

Stockdale, M. S., Visio, M., & Batra, L. (1999). The sexual harassment of men: Evidence for a broader theory of sexual harassment and sexual discrimination. *Psychology, Public Policy, & Law, 5*, 630–664.

Title VII, 42 U.S.C.S § 2000e (1964).

U.S. Merit Systems Protection Board. (1981). *Sexual harassment in the Federal workplace: Is it a problem?* Washington, DC: U.S. Government Printing Office.

U.S. Merit Systems Protection Board. (1988). *Sexual harassment in the federal government: An update.* Washington, DC: U.S. Government Printing Office.

U.S. Merit Systems Protection Board. (1995). *Sexual harassment in the federal government: Trends, progress, continuing challenges.* Washington, DC: U.S. Government Printing Office.

Waldo, C. R., Berdahl, J. L., & Fitzgerald, L. F. (1998). Are men sexually harassed? If so by whom? *Law and Human Behavior, 22*, 59–79.

Williams v. Saxbe, 413 F. Supp. 654 (DC Cir. 1976).

Willness, C. R., Steel, P., & Lee, K. (2007). A meta-analysis of the antecedents and consequences of workplace sexual harassment. *Personnel Psychology, 60*, 127–162.

Wrightson v. Pizza Hut of America, Inc., 99 F. 3d 138 (4th Cir. 1996).

York, K. M., Tyler, C. L., Tyler, J. M., & Gugel, P. E. (2008). The ever-changing face of sex stereotyping and sex discrimination in the workplace. *Journal of Leadership & Organizational Studies, 15*, 123–134.

12

Sexual Orientation: A Protected and Unprotected Class

Laura G. Barron and Michelle Hebl

In the United States, sexual orientation is an unevenly protected class. At the national level, protection is absent; however, some, but far from all, state and local jurisdictions have a patchwork of employment anti-discrimination laws. In this chapter, we review evidence of the existence of both overt and subtle employment discrimination against gay men and lesbians in the absence of legislation. We provide a theoretical rationale for how legislation can effectively reduce discrimination, and review empirical evidence to date for the efficacy of legislation in reducing discrimination. Finally, we discuss limitations of existing research and provide directions for future research.

SEXUAL ORIENTATION: A PROTECTED AND UNPROTECTED CLASS

Because of the long-established legal doctrine of employment at will, most employers in the United States may choose whom to hire, whom to promote, and whom to fire at their own discretion, even when those decisions are unmotivated by a concern for employee merit or bottom-line profits and productivity. Although Title VII of the historic Civil Rights Act does provide national-level protection against employment discrimination on the basis of race, color, national origin, religion, and gender, national protection on the basis of sexual orientation is absent.

Despite the absence of U.S. national-level protection, to date, 20 of the 50 states have outlawed sexual orientation employment discrimination (see appendix B), and some local jurisdictions offer legal protection within 15 of the 30 states without statewide protection.

Legislative efforts have sought to extend protection to the national level in the form of the proposed Employment Non-Discrimination Act (ENDA), which would protect gay, lesbian, and bisexual individuals from employment discrimination with disparate treatment provisions similar to those found in Title VII of the Civil Rights Act. Yet civil rights for gays and lesbians remains a controversial issue, with more than 40 percent of the U.S. population still of the opinion that homosexuality should not be accepted by society. Faced with an electorate in which most direct voter referendums have opposed such legislation (Gamble, 1997; Haider-Markel, Querze, & Lindaman, 2007), even politicians who may privately support such rights may find themselves speaking against protective laws to avoid angering their constituents.

In the absence of conclusive evidence for the efficacy of such legislation, politicians have been afforded a unique face-saving opportunity. Rather than having to oppose legislation by claiming that discrimination toward gays and lesbians does not exist, or should in fact be allowed to exist, politicians simply can oppose such legislation by stating that, despite their support for the goals of the legislation, such legislation would not work. The Senate Committee testimony of Susan Collins (R-Maine), a moderate who may play a key role in whether ENDA becomes law, best illustrates this tactic (The Employment Non-Discrimination Act, 2002):

> To me, the key issue before us is how we can best promote acceptance, true acceptance, of the underlying principle that we all endorse . . . of non-discrimination. And the question for me is how best to achieve that goal. . ..
> So the question to me and the question I want to ask all of you is if we impose a Federal law which some may view as an unwanted edict . . . is that really going to promote acceptance and compliance with the underlying principle that we all want to see? (p. 13)

Hence, while the current patchwork of legal protection and nonprotection may be personally or morally loathed by advocates on both sides of the issue, this also presents a much-needed opportunity for empirical scholarship on the efficacy of sexual orientation antidiscrimination laws. State and local governments often have served as "laboratories" for evaluating new policies before their implementation at the federal level

(Inman & Rubinfield, 1997), and sexual orientation antidiscrimination policy is no exception. With the national ENDA still awaiting passage, we can draw on evidence of the efficacy of corresponding state and local laws to inform legislative debate with empirically based research estimates for the likely efficacy of pending national legislation.

Before discussing the efficacy of legislation directly, we consider conditions, or prerequisites, that must be met for sexual orientation antidiscrimination legislation to have an impact. That is, while we do not believe that legislation will have an impact on all communities in which it is adopted, we do believe that legislation may have the potential to affect positive change under certain conditions. We discuss three such prerequisites: (1) overt disclosure or more indirect cues leading to inference of one's sexual orientation, (2) sexual orientation discrimination in the absence of legislation, and (3) knowledge among employers of the existence of antidiscrimination legislation.

PREREQUISITES OF LEGAL EFFICACY

Identification of Homosexual Employees

Put simply, employers cannot discriminate on the basis of perceived group membership (for example, sexual orientation). Thus, unlike the visible stigmas of race and gender, for which antidiscrimination legislation generally has been accepted as having had a causal effect on discrimination reduction (Burstein, 1985; Donohue & Heckman, 1991; Gunderson, 1989), "gays and lesbians have had the option to hide their sexual orientation from employers and coworkers" (Klawitter and Flatt, 1998, p. 677). Indeed, the majority of gay and lesbian individuals are not "out" at work (Ragins & Cornwell, 2001).

While one "solution" to workplace discrimination might be to discourage gays from disclosing their orientation, substantial evidence shows that not disclosing one's identity is related to a number of negative outcomes, both for the individual (diminished personal well-being) and the organization (diminished cognitive processing). Furthermore, at least in some cases, the decision to disclose may be moot. Even if sexual orientation is never indicated directly, individuals often are able to accurately infer sexual orientation on the basis of cues that may not be altered easily. For instance, heterosexuals' accuracy in inferring sexual orientation on the basis on brief exposure to cues such as body shape, motion, and other nonverbal behavior has shown to be above chance levels (Ambady,

Hallahan, & Conner, 1999; Johnson, Gill, Reichman, & Tassinary, 2007; Rule, Ambady, Adams, & Macrae, 2008).

Empirical Evidence of Sexual Orientation Discrimination

When sexual orientation is known or inferred, discrimination becomes possible. Thus, it is relevant to discuss the evidence regarding the existence of employment discrimination against gay men and lesbians in the absence of legislation. If sexual orientation discrimination were not evident, antidiscrimination legislation would be both unnecessary and ineffective. We describe empirical evidence that sexual orientation discrimination in the employment sphere remains substantial.

Evidence of objective sexual orientation discrimination has been investigated using two major types of studies: (1) economic studies of wage disparities, in which wage differences that remain after controlling for numerous relevant variables are presumed to be attributable to discrimination, and (2) experimental field studies, in which interpersonal treatment is compared when individuals are equated in all respects except for the overt indication of sexual orientation. Numerous survey studies additionally document perceptions of discrimination among gay and lesbian employees, but because critics may argue that such investigations are subjective, we limit our discussion here to objective measures of discrimination. We address wage and field experimental studies in turn. When reviewing wage discrimination evidence, we address gay men and lesbians separately, reflecting the fact that these findings diverge substantially based on gender.

Evidence of Sexual Orientation Wage Discrimination

Economic studies that control for factors such as experience, education, occupation, urban area, region of residence, and marital status have approximated that gay and bisexual men earn from 11 percent to 27 percent less than their heterosexual male counterparts, with larger effects found (1) when gay and bisexual is defined as having had more male sexual partners than female partners than (2) when gay and bisexual is defined as having had at least one male sexual partner (Badgett, 1995; Berg & Lien, 2002; Clain & Leppel, 2001). In fact, raw wages of gay men tend to be lower than those of heterosexual men despite the fact that gay men (1) tend to be more highly educated (that is, nationally representative surveys find that 23.7 percent of gay men have college

degrees, compared with 17 percent of married men) and (2) live disproportionately in urban areas (for example, New York City, Los Angeles,
San Francisco) in which average wages (even within the same profession) are higher than in other parts of the country (Black, Gates, Sanders, & Taylor, 2000; Klawitter & Flatt, 1998).

Not all researchers attribute the gay-straight male wage disparity to
discrimination. Berg and Lien (2002) have suggested two alternative
possibilities that merit consideration. One possibility is that homosexual
men might have a stronger preference for leisure over income because
they are less likely than heterosexual men to have children. This seems
a plausible theory because of the substantial costs associated with raising
children, and heterosexuals may be motivated to earn more because parents
often wish to pass on money to their children. Census data indeed show
that heterosexual male partners are more than six times more likely to have
children in the household than homosexual male partners (36.2 percent versus 5.2 percent; Black et al., 2000). Empirical research shows that even
when children in the household are controlled for, heterosexual partnered
men still earn substantially more than homosexual partnered men (Klawitter
& Flatt, 1998).

Another possibility is that homosexual men may have a stronger preference for leisure over income because decisions about the labor-leisure
trade-off are made taking household income into account. That is,
because men typically earn more than women, a worker of either gender
with a male partner has a higher expected household income. Hence, to
enjoy the same standard of living (that is, total household income), a
same-sex partnered male would not need to work at as high paying a
job to enjoy the same standard of living as an opposite-sex partnered
male. Although this theory potentially could explain gender disparities
between same-sex and opposite-sex partnered men, the sexual orientation wage disparity between partnered versus single men seems to be
lower. Domestic partnership (even when unrecognized legally) seems to
attenuate, although not eliminate, wage discrimination toward gay men.
Using similar control variables as the previously mentioned economic
studies, men living with gay unmarried partners are estimated to earn 16
to 24 percent less than married men living with women and 2 to 9 percent less than unmarried men living with women (Allegretto & Arthur,
2001; Elmslie & Tebaldi, 2007; see also Klawitter & Flatt, 1998). Such
estimates are based on the 1990 U.S. Census, which for the first time
asked whether an individual's relationship to the head of household was
"unmarried partner."

Wage discrimination toward lesbian women relative to heterosexual women is less clear, and wage gaps are not always found. In fact, nationally representative surveys have found that lesbian women earn more than heterosexual women, with partnered lesbians earning more than both single and heterosexually partnered women. These effects are robust to various definitions of sexual orientation (Black et al., 2000). Even more so than gay men, lesbian women tend to be more likely than their heterosexual counterparts to be highly educated. Nationally representative data show that 25 percent of same-sex partnered women have college degrees (13.9 percent have postcollege education), while only 16 percent of married women have college degrees (6.1 percent have postcollege education). Also, like gay men, if to a somewhat lesser extent, lesbian women are more likely than their heterosexual counterparts to live in major urban areas in which average wages are higher than in other parts of the country (Black et al., 2000). Research that has controlled for covariates such as age, race, education, marital status, region, and occupation (Badgett, 1995) generally has not found evidence of either a wage advantage or wage disadvantage for lesbian women relative to heterosexual women.

Field Experiments Documenting Sexual Orientation Discrimination

It is important to distinguish between correlational wage studies, and rigorous experimental methodologies conducted in the field. Although the economic wage-based studies seem to suggest that lesbians may not be subjected to formal discrimination, substantial experimental evidence appears to show that both gay men and lesbians are targets of discrimination.

In one of the strongest paradigms to date, Weichselbaumer (2003) conducted a resume correspondence field study, in which a female applicant's curriculum vitae (CV) and other application materials were sent out to real clerical job openings in Vienna, Austria. The thorough, multiple pages of the CV listed education and experience that were counterbalanced to achieve equivalency in all aspects except for a single activity, which was manipulated to presumably identify the applicant's sexual orientation. Specifically, in one condition, the applicant listed volunteer experience with a gay rights advocacy group, while in the control (presumably nonlesbian) conditions, the applicant listed volunteer experience with alternate nonprofit organizations (a school for learning disabilities or a cultural center). Prospective employers were more than 12 percent less likely to contact the presumed lesbian applicants than the control applicants who were unaffiliated with the gay rights organization (control applicants were contacted by 49 to 61 percent of employers, whereas presumed lesbian applicants were contacted by 36 to 48 percent of employers). Resume studies matching applicants in all respects except for one activity presumably indicative of sexual orientation are scarce, but, when conducted in a realistic field setting, they are consistent in their findings. The findings of Weichselbaumer (2003) are in line with a smaller sample resume correspondence field study conducted in Toronto, Canada, before sexual orientation was added to the Ontario Human Rights Code as a prohibited ground of discrimination in 1986 (Adams, 1981). In that study, prospective law firm employers were 11 percent less likely to contact lesbian applicants than presumed nonlesbian applicants.

Despite the existence of two published studies in which sexual orientation discrimination was not found (Van Hooye & Lievens, 2003; conducted in Flanders, Belgium, before national legislation was introduced in 2003), or discrimination relative to heterosexual applicants of the same gender was found for gay men but not for lesbians (Horvath & Ryan, 2003), these findings were likely due to high demand characteristics (that is candidate profiles overtly indicated that the applicant was living with a man, woman, or alone) in hypothetical application situations (undergraduate students or human resource managers rated fictitious applicants knowing that no real job was as stake). Correspondence studies conducted in the field under realistic conditions do document formal discrimination, and confidence in the existence of employment discrimination toward both gay men and lesbians is further strengthened by rigorous experimental field studies of more subtle interpersonal discrimination.

As defined in Hebl, Foster, Mannix, and Dovidio (2002), formal discrimination refers to the most overt types of discrimination, including discrimination in hiring and promotion, access, and distribution of resources. This type of discrimination that can be tracked and exposed most directly, and, in cases in which antidiscrimination legislation does exist, can be most unambiguously proven in a court of law. In contrast, interpersonal discrimination refers to more subtle nonverbal and indirect verbal behaviors that occur during interactions with others—for instance, whether members of a given group are more likely to receive glares or scowls, or less likely to be greeted with friendliness and enthusiasm—relative to members of other groups.

Although it may seem that interpersonal discrimination is less important, substantial studies show that the consequences of interpersonal discrimination are far from trivial. From the perspective of organizations' bottom-line profits, interpersonal discrimination ought to be a source of concern because stigmatized individuals pay substantial attention, and respond, to such subtle forms of discrimination (Valian, 1998). Notably, it is the nonverbal behaviors of interaction partners—rather than direct verbal behaviors—on which stigmatized group members base their perceptions of whether bias has occurred (Dovidio, Kawakami, & Gaertner, 2002). As such, interpersonal discrimination toward stigmatized customers relates to decreases in purchases, return visits, and referrals (King, Shapiro, Hebl, Singletary, & Turner, 2006), and interpersonal discrimination toward stigmatized employees relates to decreases in organizational helping behaviors and increased intentions to leave (King, Hebl, George, & Matusik, 2006). Furthermore, evidence suggests that, within the employment interview, interpersonal discrimination from prospective employers may diminish the interview performance of stigmatized applicants. That is, even nonverbal behaviors of prospective employers affect both nonverbal and verbal behavior of applicants. When interviewees are exposed to a "warmer" interviewer (that is who smiles, makes eye contact, and leans toward the applicants), the subsequent verbal responses of interviewees are rated more positively by independent raters (blind to interviewer behavior) than applicants exposed to an interviewer who uses less positive nonverbal behavior (Liden, Martin, & Parsons, 1993). Word, Zanna, and Cooper's (1974) study in which some interviewers sat farther away from targets, had more speech dysfluencies, and conducted shorter interviews also shows applicants subject to "colder" interviewers to be rated more poorly (by independent judges). This result provides a reason to expect that interpersonal employment discrimination ultimately may translate into formal discrimination, even if the effects on the more distal hiring outcome are relatively small.

To date, only two field studies have been conducted of interpersonal employment discrimination toward gay and lesbian applicants. In these studies (Hebl et al., 2002), male and female applicants were sent to apply for retail jobs in the Houston area (where no private employment sexual orientation antidiscrimination legislation exists), with each applicant applying in some stores wearing a hat identifying them as "Gay and Proud," and in others wearing a hat identifying them as (presumably nonstigmatized) "Texan and Proud." This is a particularly rigorous methodology in that the applicants remain blind to their condition (that is they do not know which hat they are wearing at any given time) and prevents expectancies of discrimination from altering applicant behavior. Although these studies may have lacked the statistical power to detect significant formal discrimination (that is differences in the proportion of applicants invited to interview), store managers interacted with applicants who were visibly identifiable as gay or lesbian for less time and were less likely to respond to presumably gay or lesbian applicants with friendliness and positivity. No differences in the extent of interpersonal discrimination were found for gay male relative to lesbian applicants.

Similar findings regarding interpersonal discrimination toward gays and lesbians have been documented across multiple domains, including general assistance (request for phone call: Ellis & Fox, 2001; Gabriel et al., 2001; Gabriel & Banse, 2006; Gore, Tobiasen, & Kayson, 1997; Shaw, Borough, & Fink, 1994; requests for change: Gray, Russel, & Blockley, 1991; Tsang, 1994), customer service treatment in retail establishments (Walters & Curran, 1996), and hotel reservation policies (Jones, 1996). Of this research, requests for a phone call using the wrong number technique (Gaertner & Bickman, 1971) is of particular interest because it has been conducted across cultures that vary in their acceptance of gays and lesbians. In this paradigm, random digit dialing is used, and those who answer the phone are asked by a male to call his male partner or (control) female partner, or are asked by a female to call her male partner (control) or female partner. As Gabriel and Banse (2006) noted, effect sizes for sexual orientation for callers of both genders are higher in studies conducted in the United States than in Britain and Germany, which are in turn higher than in Switzerland, and this pattern of effect sizes corresponds to the level of acceptance for gays and lesbians found in national surveys (Kelly, 2001). This pattern also corresponds to the time frame in which sexual orientation antidiscrimination policies were adopted, with the first nationwide protection coming from Switzerland (in 2000), with legal protections coming later in the United Kingdom and Germany (2003 and 2006), and the United States still without nationwide protection.

Substantial wage discrimination (at least relative to members of one's own gender) seems to exist for gay men, but not lesbian women. Rigorous experimental research conducted in field settings, however, clearly shows that both gay men and lesbian women are subject to more discrimination, including hiring discrimination as well as more subtle forms of interpersonal discrimination (for example, decreased friendliness, helping) inside as well as outside of the employment sphere.

LEGAL AWARENESS

For legislation to have an impact, at a minimum, the public needs to be aware of the existence of such legislation. Yet, particularly at the state and local levels, much of the public may be unaware of the laws in their jurisdiction. To our knowledge, no study to date has documented awareness of sexual orientation antidiscrimination legislation in the United States. Yet a large-scale study of working-age people in the United Kingdom has been conducted (Meager, Tyers, Perryman, Rick, & Willison, 2002), and we suspect the same basic findings hold true in the United States as well: (1) people are not well aware of the groups that are protected from discrimination, but (2) substantial variability exists in this knowledge across different segments of the working population. First, this study found that most people were unaware of which groups were or were not protected from employment discrimination. Although British law protected individuals from discrimination on the basis of marital status, but not on the basis of age, people were below chance levels in identifying which of the two was protected. However, the Meager et al. (2002) study shows substantial variability in the knowledge of antidiscrimination legislation. Those in managerial, professional, and administrative occupations were more than twice as likely to know which groups were or were not protected from discrimination relative to those in blue-collar occupations. That said, even among those in white-collar occupations, individuals were only just above chance levels in their ability to identify which groups were or not covered by antidiscrimination law.

Hence, to a large extent, the efficacy of sexual orientation antidiscrimination laws likely will hinge on the success of public campaigns and media coverage in creating awareness of such laws among the public. In this respect, the efficacy of state and local laws may underestimate the efficacy of national laws, for which media coverage and corresponding public awareness is apt to be greater.

We now move into a theoretical discussion of why antidiscrimination legislation can be expected to reduce sexual orientation discrimination. An additional condition not discussed as a prerequisite of legal efficacy is legal enforcement. Depending on the existence of legal enforcement or not, we discuss two types of effects of legislation on behavior: instrumental and symbolic.

HOW LEGISLATION AFFECTS BEHAVIOR AND ATTITUDES

Instrumental Effects of Legislation on Behavior

Deterrence theory (for example, Becker, 1968) posits that outlawing a given behavior reduces that behavior to the extent that punishment is certain and severe as a result of rational cost-benefit analysis. Deterrence theory has received substantial empirical support, at least with regard to effects of punishment certainty (Cook, 1980). When applied to antidiscrimination laws specifically, prejudiced employers are said to discriminate less because such laws create an "expected cost" of a magnitude that equals the cost of law violation if caught (for example, attorney's fees, fines) multiplied times the probability of being caught (Landes, 1968).

If legislation only affected behavior to the extent that punishment was expected, antidiscrimination laws likely would have little effect. Fundamentally, the probability of an employer facing legal consequences for engaging in employment discrimination is quite small. In states with sexual orientation antidiscrimination laws, the likelihood of a gay or lesbian employee in those areas even filing a legal complaint is estimated at only 0.01 to 0.08 percent annually (Rubenstein, 2002). Nationally, roughly 60 percent of gays and lesbians report that they experience employment discrimination (Waldo, 1999). If the incidence of discrimination in areas with legislation was even a fraction of the national average, that still would be much lower than the likelihood of a gay or lesbian employee in those areas filing a legal complaint.

A consideration of instrumental effects alone is incomplete, however. Despite the fact that the likelihood of a gay or lesbian employee in areas with sexual orientation antidiscrimination laws filing a legal complaint is estimated at only 0.01 to 0.08 percent annually, that is no less likely than the proportion of women and minorities who file legal complaints of discrimination (Rubenstein, 2002), both groups for whom antidiscrimination legislation largely has been accepted as having had a causal impact on reducing discrimination (for blacks, see Burstein, 1985; Donohue & Heckman, 1991; for women, see Gunderson, 1989).

Symbolic Effects of Legislation on Attitudes and Behavior

Much of the effects of laws likely derive from symbolic rather than purely instrumental effects (for example, Zimring & Hawkins, 1973). The symbolic effects of legislation are such that, absent any possibility of tangible punishment, legislation may reduce a given act (discrimination) simply by designating it as illegal, criminal, or deviant. In line with this, empirical work shows that the extent to which a law is seen as morally valid correlates with the extent to which the law is obeyed (Grasmick & Green, 1980; Sarat, 1977). Thus, the force of law is not simply a fear of punishment; people fear violating the law because it authoritatively describes moral rules of conduct (Robinson & Darley,

1995). As such, antidiscrimination legislation may create a clear social norm that discrimination is societally unacceptable.

Thus, antidiscrimination legislation may deter both prejudice and discrimination toward a given group because it changes attitudes about the morality of inequality. Simply learning the stance of one's community has been shown to affect the extent of prejudice one expresses, even when attitudes are indicated privately, absent any real possibility of conflict or criticism (Stangor, Sechrist, & Jost, 2001; Wittenbrink & Henly, 1996). This effect is strong enough that even learning the opinion of a single community member (a stranger) has been shown to change one's attitudes toward out-group members (Blanchard, Lilly, & Vaughn, 1991; Blanchard, Crandall, Brigham, & Vaughn, 1994; Monteith, Deneen, & Tooman, 1996; Zitek & Hebl, 2007), and resulting attitude change has been shown to last beyond the short term (Stangor et al., 2001; Zitek & Hebl, 2007). Notably, more attitude change has been shown toward gays and other groups for which ambiguity about the social acceptability of prejudice is greater than that shown toward groups for which prejudice is more clearly socially accepted (racists) or unaccepted (blacks) (Zitek & Hebl, 2007).

Sexual orientation employment antidiscrimination laws can reduce hiring discrimination and prejudice under certain conditions: (1) when individuals with hiring authority are likely aware of such laws, and (2) when gay employees disclose their sexual orientation. In describing the theoretical rationale explaining why antidiscrimination laws may affect discrimination, although instrumental effects (that is tangible threat of lawsuit) may decrease discrimination somewhat, the threat of lawsuit likely is not so large as to account for major decreases. Rather, it is the symbolic effect of legislation, in prescribing disregard and mistreatment for an out-group (that is gays) as wrong or immoral, that creates major decreases in both prejudice and corresponding behaviors of discrimination. The mechanisms underlying legal efficacy remain theoretical, but empirical evidence is available to address the issue of whether sexual orientation antidiscrimination legislation does in fact reduce employment discrimination. We turn to this now.

THE EFFICACY OF SEXUAL ORIENTATION ANTIDISCRIMINATION LAWS

Three empirical studies, conducted in the United States, using diverse methodologies, have sought to address the efficacy of state and local sexual orientation laws (Barron, 2009; Klawitter & Flatt, 1998; Ragins

& Cornwell, 2001). Despite the opportunity that the current patchwork of state and local legal protections presents, these studies, as well as future studies that seek to determine the efficacy of antidiscrimination laws, face a challenge: The presence of less discrimination in areas with legal protection than in areas without does not necessarily imply that legislation caused the reduced discrimination. Rather, prejudice and discrimination may be greater in locales that legislate against discrimination for two reasons: (1) areas that are more accepting of gays and lesbians are simply more likely to enact antidiscrimination laws (reduced discrimination causes legislation), or (2) legislation causes a reduction in discrimination.

Given that the adoption of local gay rights ordinances has been shown to relate positively to the presence of the gay and lesbian community and negatively to the presence of conservative political and religious groups (Haeberle, 1996; Wald, Button, & Rienzo, 1996), it is a fairly safe assumption that the level of discrimination is already lower in areas that adopt gay rights laws than in areas that do not adopt such laws— even before the laws take effect. However, this does not preclude the possibility that legislation itself also has a major effect on discrimination reduction. This simply means that research on the efficacy of legislation has the difficult task of controlling for those factors that may affect both (1) the adoption of antidiscrimination legislation and (2) the extent of community discrimination at baseline.

We discuss each of the three extant studies in turn, noting limitations, and then suggest directions for future research.

Klawitter and Flatt (1998): Effects of Legislation on Wage Discrimination

Klawitter and Flatt (1998) examined the discrepancy between wages of same-sex and opposite-sex partnered individuals, and investigated whether this wage gap was lessened in areas governed by state and local antidiscrimination ordinances. As in previous research investigating the sexual orientation wage gap, they used data from the 1990 U.S. Census, which had, for the first time, allowed gay and lesbian couples to be identified by adding an "unmarried partner" category to the list of household relationships. They then compared same-sex couples' incomes to those of opposite-sex unmarried couples, and to opposite-sex married couples, within areas with and without legal protection.

The raw data do appear to support a decrease in the sexual orientation wage gap in areas with antidiscrimination policies relative to areas without, at least with regards to men. That is, gay men who live in areas lacking sexual orientation antidiscrimination laws do appear to be subject to greater wage discrimination than gay men who live in areas with such legal protection. Although overall wages were higher in areas with antidiscrimination legislation than in areas without legislation for both heterosexual and homosexual individuals, that difference was larger for gay men than for their heterosexual counterparts. Although the incomes of married men and unmarried men living with an opposite-sex partner were 0.11 standard deviations higher in areas with legislation than in areas without, the incomes of men living with a same-sex partner were 0.23 standard deviations higher in areas with legislation than in areas without. The magnitude of difference was smaller for women, which should be expected given that the wage gap for lesbian women relative to heterosexual women is not consistent (that is, as discussed, wage discrimination must exist if antidiscrimination laws are to reduce wage discrimination).

When variables that affect both (1) adoption of sexual orientation antidiscrimination laws, and (2) wages are controlled for, however, the effect of antidiscrimination laws on wage discrimination disappears. Although Klawitter and Flatt (1998) did not control for presence of the gay community or absence of religious conservatives directly, they did control for a decent proxy for the gay community (absence of children), and two other variables related to acceptance of alternative lifestyles (education and urban location). After controlling for these variables, in addition to a standard set of variables that typically affect earnings (age, race, work-related disability, English proficiency, and region), they found no effect of antidiscrimination legislation on the sexual orientation wage gap.

Differential Disclosure

We believe the most serious limitation of Klawitter and Flatt's (1998) study is how gays and lesbians were identified for inclusion in the study: an anonymous indication on Census forms. In the workplace, sexual orientation is not indicated anonymously, and public disclosure is a choice. The majority of gay and lesbian individuals are not "out" at work (for example, Griffith & Hebl, 2002; Ragins & Cornwell, 2001). Employers cannot discriminate on group membership that they do not know, and empirical findings show that employees are less likely to disclose when they have witnessed or experienced discrimination (Button, 2001; Ragins & Cornwell, 2001). Although sexual orientation may be inferred at above chance levels, the accuracy of such inferences in the absence of disclosure, and the resulting discrimination on the basis of nondisclosed sexual orientation likely is limited substantially.

Additionally, because the Census data used for this study were collected in 1989 when only two states' laws (Wisconsin and Massachusetts) prohibited private sector sexual orientation employment discrimination, most of the "protected" areas in the study were governed only by city ordinances. Legislation must be accompanied by awareness of such laws among the public (or at least among those in management who are apt to be involved in hiring and compensation decisions). National laws may be accompanied by greater public awareness than state laws among those constituents affected, because of greater national media coverage. Additionally, awareness of state laws may similarly exceed awareness of city laws among those constituents affected. Furthermore, state laws are often backed by stronger enforcement resources relative to city laws (Rubenstein, 2002). Both of these limitations (differential disclosure and the possibility of more limited legal awareness and enforcement) are better addressed in the studies that follow.

RAGINS AND CORNWELL (2001): EFFECTS OF LEGISLATION ON PERCEPTIONS OF DISCRIMINATION

Ragins and Cornwell's (2001) research surveyed gay and lesbian individuals recruited through national gay rights organizations about their perceptions of discrimination in their workplace, and found less perceived discrimination among employees who work in areas with antidiscrimination legislation than in unprotected areas. Although individuals may be inclined to conflate reports of discrimination with the absence of legal protection, the findings are methodologically strengthened by the fact that the presence of legislation was coded by researchers rather than reported by those indicating the extent of discrimination. This finding is further bolstered by complementary evidence at the organizational level: Gay and lesbian employees also perceive less discrimination when organizational sexual orientation nondiscrimination policies are in place than when they are not (Button, 2001; Griffith & Hebl, 2002; Ragins & Cornwell, 2001).

Most notably, the relationship between legislation and perceived discrimination remained even after controlling for the extent of sexual orientation disclosure, co-worker and supervisor sexual orientation, and gay-friendly organizational policies (that is, a company nondiscrimination statement, same-sex partner benefits). That is, gay and lesbian employees in areas with legal protection are more likely to disclose that they are gay, to have gay co-workers and supervisors, and to work for organizations with gay-friendly company policies relative to gay and lesbian employees in areas without legal protection. Disclosing one's sexual orientation, having gay co-workers and supervisors, and working for a company with gay-friendly policies are all related to reduced discrimination individually. The statistical evidence suggests that even if gays and lesbians in areas with and without legal protection were to disclose equally, and work in companies with proportions of gay staff and gay-friendly company policies equally, gay and lesbian employees in areas with antidiscrimination laws still would perceive less discrimination than those in areas without such laws.

Although solid, the findings are somewhat limited by the analysis of differences in perception. That is, by assessing perceptual differences rather than objective differences in workplace treatment, it is possible that individuals in areas with and without laws apply different standards in determining whether or not discrimination has occurred. Many gays and lesbians may be knowledgeable of their legal protections, and view the lack of antidiscrimination law as indicative of a greater likelihood of discrimination. That is, interpersonal slights at work are often subtle and ambiguous (that is "is my boss being rude because he found out I'm gay or because I botched a work assignment?"), and individuals may perceive discrimination more readily when they know that no legal mandate will prevent their employers from discriminating.

Additionally, the Ragins and Cornwell (2001) study did not control for two of the community variables shown to affect both community adoption of sexual orientation antidiscrimination laws (Haeberle, 1996; Wald et al., 1996) and the extent of sexual orientation prejudice in the absence of legislation (for example, Herek, 1988, 1994): political and religious conservatism. We address these limitations in recent research conducted in our own lab.

BARRON (2009): EFFECTS OF LEGISLATION ON OBJECTIVE HIRING DISCRIMINATION AND PREJUDICE

Barron (2009) objectively assessed the extent of hiring discrimination, using a between-subjects design in which human resource managers evaluated resumes of a hypothetical male applicant for a management position that were matched on all qualifications. Sexual orientation was manipulated by presenting the candidate as either (1) recipient of the university "Alumni Scholarship" and president of the "Student Activities Association" (control condition) or (2) recipient of the university "Gay and Lesbian Alumni Scholarship" and president of the "GLBT Student Activities Association" (gay condition). To increase the likelihood of awareness of the presence or absence of antidiscrimination laws in their areas, the chosen sample included human resource managers, whose occupation requires familiarity with employment legislation and typically allows for ample involvement in hiring decisions. The researcher recruited participants through local chapters of a national professional organization of human resource management, with participants roughly evenly divided between those who worked in states with and without sexual orientation employment antidiscrimination legislation (32 chapters in 28 states were represented).

Human resource managers in areas without antidiscrimination laws evaluated the applicant as less hireable when presented as gay relative to when the applicant was presented as nongay; in contrast, no hireability differences between the gay and nongay applicants were found in areas with antidiscrimination laws. Although statistical power was insufficient to detect differences in hiring discrimination after controlling for participant sexual orientation, organizational gay-friendly policies, and political and religious views, strong support emerged for the ability of legislation to reduce prejudice toward gays. Despite the fact that almost 50 percent of the variability in human resource managers' attitudes toward gays can be explained by political and religious conservatism, even after controlling for these factors, the presence of antidiscrimination legislation further decreases sexual orientation prejudice. That is, antidiscrimination legislation was substantially related to decreased prejudice toward gays, even after controlling for those factors previously shown to affect community adoption of legislation. As such, these findings suggest that employment antidiscrimination legislation goes beyond affecting the specific behaviors that are outlawed (that is, hiring discrimination) to affecting the underlying principles of acceptance and tolerance toward gays. Even privately held attitudes of prejudice toward gays—which are not, and cannot be legally enforced—appear to be affected by antidiscrimination legislation. This provides initial theoretical support for the idea that the effects of legislation are not simply instrumental effects based on the tangible threat of lawsuit, but also are symbolic, in morally prescribing disregard and mistreatment for an out-group (that is, gays) as wrong or immoral.

LIMITATIONS AND FUTURE RESEARCH DIRECTIONS

Research to date has just begun to take advantage of the current status of sexual orientation as a protected and unprotected class. Given the currently pending status of the national ENDA, researchers have a unique and timely opportunity to compare the level of discrimination in areas with and without local protections under controlled conditions, to begin to speak to the likely effectiveness of national legislation. This is particularly important given that some politicians likely will play a key role in whether ENDA becomes law (for example, moderate Republican Senator Collins) and will attempt to oppose sexual orientation antidiscrimination legislation by characterizing the likely efficacy of such legislation as dubious.

Although antidiscrimination laws corresponded to decreased attitudes of prejudice after controlling for all variables previously shown to relate to the adoption of legislation, we were not able to show this same finding with regard to discrimination. That is, the relationship between such legislation and discrimination did not reach levels of statistical significance after controlling for religious beliefs. Further research will need to revisit the issue of the effects of legislation on hiring discrimination using a larger sample, or more salient manipulation of sexual orientation (many of the participants within the Barron, 2009, study did not recall the applicant's sexual orientation when asked). Importantly, future research ought to measure public or managerial knowledge of antidiscrimination legislation directly, given the need for legal awareness if legislation is to affect employment behavior. It is probably more likely that human resource managers are aware of their current state employment legislation (Barron, 2009) than co-workers and supervisors across all occupations (Ragins & Cornwell, 2001) or than the management that was involved in compensation decisions in 1989 when few state laws covered sexual orientation discrimination (Klawitter & Flatt, 1998). No research to date has studied the effects of sexual orientation antidiscrimination legislation on employment discrimination among a sample with documented knowledge and awareness of these laws.

Beyond this, the prevalence of state and local sexual orientation laws continues to expand to new jurisdictions. We see the need for research designs that use pre- and post-test designs, such as those used in the 1960s to document the efficacy of Title VII of the Civil Rights Act in reducing employment discrimination toward southern blacks (for example, Heckman & Payner, 1989). In particular, the combination of field setting realism and experimental control afforded by correspondence testing (for example, Adams, 1981; Weichselbaumer, 2003) begs the extension of this methodology to comparisons of jurisdictions with and without sexual orientation antidiscrimination legislation. Further research on legislation efficacy ought to broaden the type of discrimination studied to include more subtle, less readily legally enforceable interpersonal discrimination as well (for example, Hebl et al., 2002).

CONCLUSION

Clearly, researchers do not have the power to experimentally manipulate the presence or absence of legislation in a given community. Research to date goes far in statistically controlling for those factors previously shown to influence whether legislation is adopted in a given community, which otherwise equalizes jurisdictions. As such, we can go a long way toward responding to Senator Collins' claims that employment sexual orientation antidiscrimination laws may not "promote true acceptance, of the underlying principle" of nondiscrimination. Research findings to date provide strong evidence that such laws do reduce true, underlying principles of prejudice in the employment sphere. Future research is needed to understand how this reduction in prejudice can translate into a reduction in discriminatory behavior.

REFERENCES

Adams, B. D. (1981). Stigma and employability: Discrimination by sex and sexual orientation in the Ontario legal profession. *Canadian Review of Sociology and Anthropology, 18,* 216–221.

Allegretto, S. A., & Arthur, M. M. (2001). An empirical analysis of homosexual/ heterosexual male earnings differentials: Unmarried and unequal? *Industrial and Labor Relations Review, 54,* 631–646.

Ambady, N., Hallahan, M., & Conner, B. (1999). Accuracy of judgments of sexual orientation from thin slices of behavior. *Journal of Personality and Social Psychology, 77,* 538–547.

Badgett, M. V. L. (1995). The wage effects of sexual orientation discrimination. *Industrial and Labor Relations Review, 48,* 726–739.

Barron, L. G. (2009). Sexual orientation employment anti-discrimination legislation and hiring discrimination and prejudice. In G. T. Solomon (Ed.), *Proceedings of the Sixty-Sixth Annual Meeting of the Academy of Management,* Atlanta, GA [CD: ISSN 1543-8643].

Becker, G. (1968). Crime and punishment: An economic approach. *Journal of Political Economy, 76,* 169–217.

Berg, N. & Lien, D. (2002). Measuring the effect of sexual orientation on income: Evidence of discrimination? *Contemporary Economic Policy, 20,* 394–414.

Black, D., Gates, G., Sanders, S., & Taylor, L. (2000). Demographics of the gay and lesbian population in the United States: Evidence from available systematic data sources. *Demography, 37,* 139–154.

Blanchard, F. A., Crandall, C. S., Brigham, J. C., & Vaughn, L. A. (1994). Condemning and condoning racism: A social context approach to interracial settings. *Journal of Applied Psychology, 79,* 993–997.

Blanchard, F. A., Lilly, T., & Vaughn, L. A. (1991). Reducing the expression of racial prejudice. *Psychological Science, 2,* 111–115.

Burstein, P. (1985). *Discrimination, jobs, and politics: The struggle for equal opportunity in the United States since the New Deal.* Chicago: University of Chicago Press.

Button, S. B. (2001). Organizational efforts to affirm sexual diversity: A cross-level examination. *Journal of Applied Psychology, 86,* 17–28.

Clain, S. H., & Leppel, K. (2001). An investigation into sexual orientation discrimination as an explanation for wage differences. *Applied Economics, 33,* 37–47.

Cook, P. (1980). Research in criminal deterrence: Laying the groundwork for the second decade. In N. Morris & M. Tonry (Eds.), *Crime and justice: Vol. 2* (pp. 211–268). Chicago: University of Chicago Press.

Donohue, J. J., III, & Heckman, J. (1991). Continuous versus episodic change: The impact of civil rights policy on the economic status of Blacks. *Journal of Economic Literature, 29,* 1603–1643.

Dovidio, J. F., Kawakami, K., & Gaertner, S. L. (2002). Implicit and explicit prejudice and interracial interaction. *Journal of Personality and Social Psychology, 82,* 62–68.

Ellis, J., & Fox, P. (2001). The effect of self-identified sexual orientation on helping behavior in a British sample: Are lesbians and gay men treated differently? *Journal of Applied Social Psychology, 31,* 1238–1247.

Elmslie, B., & Tebaldi, E. (2007). Sexual orientation and labor market discrimination. *Journal of Labor Research, 28,* 436–453.

The Employment Non-Discrimination Act Hearings before the Committee on Health, Education, Labor, and Pensions. 107th Cong., 2d. Sess., 14 (2002) (testimony of Susan Collins).

Gabriel, U., & Banse, R. (2006). Helping behavior as a subtle measure of discrimination against lesbians and gay men: German data and a comparison across countries. *Journal of Applied Social Psychology, 36,* 690–707.

Gabriel, U., Beyeler, G., Daniker, N., Fey, W., Gutweniger, K., Lienhart, M., et al. (2001). Perceived sexual orientation and helping behaviour: The wrong number technique, a Swiss replication. *Journal of Cross-Cultural Psychology, 32,* 763–769.

Gaertner, S., & Bickman, L. (1971). Effects of race on the elicitation of helping behavior: The wrong number technique. *Journal of Personality and Social Psychology, 20,* 218–222.

Gamble, B. S. (1997). Putting civil rights to a popular vote. *American Journal of Political Science, 41,* 245–269.

Gore, K., Tobiasen, M., & Kayson, W. (1997). Effects of sex of caller, implied sexual orientation of caller, and urgency on altruistic response using the wrong-number technique. *Psychological Reports, 80,* 927–930.

Grasmick, H. G., & Green, D. E. (1980). Legal punishment, social disapproval, and internalizations as inhibitors of illegal behavior. *Journal of Criminal Law and Criminology, 71,* 321–335.

Gray, C., Russell, P., & Blockley, S. (1991). The effects upon helping behaviour of wearing a pro-gay identification. *British Journal of Social Psychology, 30,* 171–178.

Griffith, K., & Hebl, M.(2002). *Acknowledgment of sexual orientation in the workplace. Rice University. Journal of Applied Psychology, 87* 1191–1199.

Gunderson, M. (1989). Male-female wage differentials and policy responses. *Journal of Economic Literature, 27,* 46–72.

Haeberle, S. (1996). Gay men and lesbians at city hall. *Social Science Quarterly, 77,* 190–197.

Haider-Markel, D. P., Querze, A., & Lindaman, K. (2007). Lose, win, or draw? A reexamination of direct democracy and minority rights. *Political Research Quarterly, 60,* 304–314.

Hebl, M., Foster, J. M., Mannix, L. M., & Dovidio, J. F. (2002). Formal and interpersonal discrimination: A field study examination of applicant bias. *Personality and Social Psychological Bulletin, 28,* 815–825.

Heckman, J., & Payner, B. (1989). Determining the impact of federal antidiscrimination policy on the economic status of blacks: A study of South Carolina. *American Economic Review, 1,* 138–177.

Herek, G. M. (1988). Heterosexuals' attitudes toward lesbians and gay men: Correlates and gender differences. *The Journal of Sex Research,* 25, 451–477.

Herek, G. M. (1994). Assessing heterosexuals' attitudes toward lesbians and gay men: A review of empirical research with the ATLG scale. In B. Greene, & G. M. Herek (Eds.) *Lesbian and gay psychology: Theory, research, and clinical applications* (pp. 206–228). Thousand Oaks, CA: Sage Publications.

Horvath, M. & Ryan, A. M. (2003). Antecedents and potential moderators of the relationship between attitudes and hiring discrimination on the basis of sexual orientation. *Sex Roles, 48,* 115–130.

Inman, R. P., & Rubinfield, D. L. (1997). Rethinking federalism. *Journal of Economic Perspectives, 11,* 43–64.

Johnson, K. L., Gill, S., Reichman, V., & Tassinary, L. G. (2007). Swagger, sway, and sexuality: Judging sexual orientation from body motion and morphology. *Journal of Personality and Social Psychology, 93,* 321–334.

Jones, D. A. (1996). Discrimination against same-sex couples in hotel reservation policies. *Journal of Homosexuality, 31,* 153–159.

Kelly, J. (2001). Attitudes toward homosexuality in 29 nations. *Australian Social Monitor, 4,* 15–22.

King, E., Hebl, M., George, J., & Matusik, S. (2006, July). *Understanding tokenism: Antecedents and consequences of psychological climate for gender inequity.* Presented at Perceptions of discrimination at work: Prevalence, correlates and consequences, a symposium at Society of Industrial Organizational Psychologists Conference. Dallas, TX.

King, E. B., Shapiro, J. L., Hebl, M., Singletary, S., & Turner, S. (2006). The stigma of obesity in customer service: A mechanism of remediation and bottom-line consequences of discrimination. *Journal of Applied Psychology, 91,* 579–593.

Klawitter, M. M., & Flatt, V. (1998). The effects of state and local antidiscrimination policies on earnings for gays and lesbians. *Journal of Policy Analysis and Management, 17,* 658–686.

Landes, W. M. (1968). The economics of fair employment laws. *Journal of Political Economy, 76,* 507–552.

Liden, R. C., Martin, C. L., & Parsons, C. K. (1993). Interviewer and applicant behaviors in employment interviews. *Academy of Management Journal, 36,* 372–386.

Meager, N., Tyers, C., Perryman, S., Rick, J., & Willison, R. (2002). Awareness, knowledge, and exercise of individual employment rights. Retrieved October 1, 2009, from http://www.dti.gov.uk/er/emar/ies.pdf.

Monteith, M. J., Deneen, N. E., & Tooman, G. D. (1996). The effect of social norm activation on the expression of opinions concerning gay men and blacks. *Basic and Applied Social Psychology, 18,* 267–288.

Ragins, B. R., & Cornwell, J. M. (2001). Pink triangles: Antecedents and consequences of perceived workplace discrimination against gay and lesbian employees. *Journal of Applied Psychology, 86,* 1244–1261.

Robinson, P. H., & Darley, J. M. (1995). *Justice, liability, and blame: Community views and the criminal law.* Boulder, CO: Westview.

Rubenstein, W. B. (2002). Do gay rights laws matter? An empirical assessment. *Southern California Law Review, 75,* 65–119.

Rule, N. O., Ambady, N., Adams, R. B., & Macrae, C. N. (2008). Accuracy and awareness in the perception and categorization of male sexual orientation. *Journal of Personality and Social Psychology, 95,* 1019–1028.

Sarat, A. (1977). Studying American legal cultures: An assessment of survey evidence. *Law and Society Review, 11,* 427–488.

Shaw, J., Borough, H., & Fink, M. (1994). Perceived sexual orientation and helping behavior by males and females: The wrong-number technique. *Journal of Psychology and Human Sexuality, 6,* 73–81.

Stangor, C., Sechrist, G. B., & Jost, J. T. (2001). Changing racial beliefs by providing consensus information. *Personality and Social Psychology Bulletin, 27,* 486–496.

Tsang, E. (1994). Investigating the effect of race and apparent lesbianism upon helping behavior. *Feminism and Psychology, 4,* 469–471.

Valian, V. (1998). *Why so slow? The advancement of women.* Cambridge, MA: M.I.T. Press.

Van Hooye, G., & Lievens, F. (2003). The effects of sexual orientation on hirability ratings: An experimental study. *Journal of Business and Psychology, 18,* 15–30.

Wald, K. D., Button, J. W., & Rienzo, B. A. (1996). The politics of gay rights in American communities: Explaining antidiscrimination ordinances and policies. *American Journal of Political Science, 40,* 1152–1178.

Waldo, C. (1999). Working in a majority context: A structural model of heterosexism as minority stress in the workplace. *Journal of Counseling Psychology, 46*(2), 218–232.

Walters, A. S., & Curran, M. (1996). "Excuse me, sir? May I help you and your boyfriend?" Salespersons' differential treatment of homosexual and straight customers. *Journal of Homosexuality, 31,* 135–152.

Weichselbaumer, D. (2003). Sexual orientation discrimination in hiring. *Labour Economics, 10,* 629–642.

Wittenbrink, B., & Henly, J. R. (1996). Creating social reality: Informational social influence and content of stereotypic beliefs. *Personality and Social Psychology Bulletin, 22,* 598–610.

Word, C. O., Zanna, M. P., & Cooper, J. (1974). The nonverbal mediation of self-fulfilling prophecies. *Journal of Experimental Social Psychology, 10,* 109–120.

Zimring, F., & Hawkins, G. (1973). *Deterrence: The legal threat in crime control.* Chicago: University of Chicago Press.

Zitek, E. M., & Hebl, M. R. (2007). The role of social norm clarity in the influenced expression of prejudice over time. *Journal of Experimental Social Psychology, 43,* 867–876.

13

Exercising "Reasonable Care": Policies, Procedures, and Training Programs

Carmen A. Paludi, Jr., Michele A. Paludi, Susan Strauss, Paul Coen, Marie Fuda, Thomas Gerber, and Benjamin Adams

> Prejudices subsist in people's imagination long after they have been destroyed by their experience.
>
> —Ernest Dimnet
>
> In overcoming prejudice, working together is even more effective than talking together.
>
> —Ralph W. Sockman

In this chapter, we offer recommendations for employers for exercising "reasonable care" in preventing and resolving cases of workplace discrimination. "Reasonable care," adapted from rulings in *Burlington Industries, Inc. v. Ellerth* (1998) and *Faragher v. City of Boca Raton* (1998) includes the following, at a minimum:

1. Establish and enforce an effective policy
2. Establish and enforce effective investigative procedures
3. Facilitate training in workplace discrimination in general and in the organization's policy and procedures specifically

In *Faragher* and *Ellerth,* the U.S. Supreme Court stated that the standard of liability is premised on the following principles: "(1) an employer is responsible for the acts of its supervisors, and (2) employers should be encouraged to prevent harassment and employees should be encouraged to avoid or limit the harm from harassment" (EEOC, 1999). A supervisor is defined as an individual who has the authority to hire, fire, promote, demote, discipline, or transfer an employee.

In *Faragher,* the Supreme Court ruled that employers are subject to vicarious liability for hostile environment sexual harassment created by a supervisor with immediate or successively higher authority over the victimized employee. When no tangible employment action is taken, an employer may raise an affirmative defense to liability or damages. This requires that the employer prove by a preponderance of the evidence that they exercised reasonable care to prevent and correct promptly any sexually harassing behavior and that the employee unreasonably failed to take advantage of any preventive or corrective opportunities provided by the employer or to avoid harm otherwise.

The *Ellerth* affirmative defense reiterated the Supreme Court's focus on the requirement that employers be involved in comprehensive programs to rid the workplace of harassment to avoid liability. The Equal Employment Opportunity Commission's (EEOC, 1999) guidance on employer liability for harassment by co-workers states that the employer is liable unless it can prove it took immediate and corrective remedial action.

These cases focused on sexual harassment. The EEOC (1999), however, has maintained that these basic standards apply to "all types of prohibited harassment." According to the EEOC (1999),

> The rule in *Ellerth* and *Faragher* regarding vicarious liability applies to harassment by supervisors based on race, color, sex (whether or not of a sexual nature), religion, national origin, protected activity, age, or disability. Thus, employers should establish anti-harassment policies and complaint procedures covering *all* forms of unlawful harassment.

We pursue an institutional level of analysis to explain the prevalence of workplace discrimination and harassment and to recognize the contexts within which discrimination and harassment are more likely to occur. We thus focus on educational, psychotherapeutic, legal, management, and sociocultural factors in preventing and resolving workplace discrimination and harassment. We also discuss the importance of social science research in helping organizations understand why discrimination still exists despite federal and state legislation, including stereotyping about protected classes. We thus integrate management theory, case law, and social science research to effectively enforce policies and procedures in an atmosphere of trust that encourages individuals to come forth with their complaints of workplace discrimination (Paludi & Paludi, 2003; Reese & Lindenberg, 1999; Tsai & Kleiner, 2001).

The chapter begins with a discussion of preventative strategies for employers. According to the EEOC (2009),

> Prevention is the best tool to eliminate . . . harassment in the workplace. Employers are encouraged to take steps necessary to prevent . . . harassment from occurring. They should clearly communicate to employees that . . . harassment will not be tolerated. They can do so by providing . . . harassment training to their employees and by establishing an effective complaint or grievance process and taking immediate and appropriate action when an employee complains.

Furthermore, according to the EEOC (1999),

> An employer's responsibility to exercise reasonable care to prevent and correct harassment is not limited to implementing an anti-harassment policy and complaint procedure. As the Supreme Court stated, "the employer has a greater opportunity to guard against misconduct by supervisors than by common workers; employers have greater opportunity and incentive to screen them, train them, and monitor their performance." (*Faragher*, 118 S. Ct. at 2291)

REASONABLE CARE AS PREVENTION

Policies and Procedures

> I know we can't abolish prejudice through laws, but we can set up guidelines for our actions by legislation.
>
> —Belva Ann Lockwood

Legally defensible policies for preventing discrimination and harassment in the workplace require more than a general statement against behavior (Hedge, & Pulakos, 2002; Levy & Paludi, 2002; Smith & Mazin, 2004). It requires the efforts and support of management at all levels and continual training of all employees (to be discussed later in this chapter) as well as investigatory procedures that encourages employees to come forward with complaints (EEOC, 1999). This aspect of reasonable care will put organizations on stronger footing in a legal action. In addition, all employees would benefit from a workplace climate of respect and cooperation.

Components of Policies and Procedures

According to the EEOC's "Enforcement Guidance: Vicarious Employer Liability for Unlawful Harassment by Supervisors" (1999),

> An anti-harassment policy and complaint procedure should contain, at a minimum, the following elements:
>
> - A clear explanation of prohibited conduct;
> - Assurance that employees who make complaints of harassment or provide information related to such complaints will be protected against retaliation;
> - A clearly described complaint process that provides accessible avenues of complaint;
> - Assurance that the employer will protect the confidentiality of harassment complaints to the extent possible;
> - A complaint process that provides a prompt, thorough, and impartial investigation; and
> - Assurance that the employer will take immediate and appropriate corrective action when it determines that harassment has occurred.

Recommendations identified by the EEOC have been translated by attorneys, human resource management specialists, and social scientists (for example, Association of the Bar of the City of New York, 1993; Connell, 1991; Gutek, 1997; Reese & Lindenberg, 1999; Smith & Mazin, 2004; Trotter & Zacur, 2004). In keeping with EEOC policy guidance, the harassment and discrimination literature has identified components of effective policy statements. These components of effective policy statements are the following (also see Paludi & Paludi, 2003):

- Statement of Purpose
- Legal Definition
- Behavioral Examples
- Statement Concerning Impact of Discrimination on Individuals and Workplace
- Statement of Individual's Responsibility in Filing Complaint

- Statement of Workplace's Responsibility in Investigating Complaint
- Statement Concerning Confidentiality of Complaint Procedures
- Statement Concerning Sanctions Available
- Statement Regarding Retaliation
- Statement of Sanctions for Retaliation
- Statement Concerning False Complaints
- Identification and Background of Individual(s) Responsible for Hearing Complaints

In addition, the harassment literature has identified components for effective complaint procedures for organizations. Empirical research has indicated that employees will feel more encouraged to file a complaint of harassment or discrimination when they understand what the process entails (Levy & Paludi, 2002). Thus, complainants must be given accurate and adequate information about the complaint procedure, written in understandable language and terms. Failure to provide such information makes the policy statement inhibitive (Trotter & Zacur, 2004).

According to Riger's (1991) research with sexual harassment of employees, when policy statements are not clearly written and communicated, women will be reluctant to label their experiences as sexual harassment and thus not report their discrimination. Furthermore, O'Connell and Korabik (2000) reported that the number of severe sexual harassment incidents will be reduced when businesses adhere to and enforce their antisexual harassment policy. Thus, simply having a policy does not isolate an employer. The policy must be disseminated to the employees; employees must be trained on its content (*Frederick v. Spring/United Management Company*, 2001).

Employers should adhere to the following recommendations (also see Paludi & Paludi, 2003):

- The policy should contain an alternative procedure for complaints if the investigator is the person alleged to have engaged in disability discrimination or harassment.
- The policy statement should be made available in languages in addition to English for individuals and their support systems for whom English is not their first language.
- The policy statement must be made available in Braille and in large type as well as be made available on audio tape.

Scheid (1999) also found that organizations are expected to comply with the Americans with Disabilities Act (ADA), but their organizational responses to applicants and employees with disabilities are more likely to be influenced by their own attitudes toward individuals with physical and mental disabilities. Employees with disabilities who work in organizations that were focused on disability management are less likely to experience disability discrimination or disability harassment.

Components of effective procedures include all of the following, at a minimum:

- Informing employees that the workplace will not ignore any complaint of discrimination and harassment;
- Informing employees that the investigator of complaints will not make determinations about the complaint based on the reputations or organizational status of the individuals involved;
- Informing employees that investigations of complaints will be completed promptly;
- Informing employees that witnesses to incidents or to changes in the parties' behavior will be interviewed;
- Informing employees that all documents presented by the complainant, alleged harasser, and witnesses will be reviewed; and
- Informing employees that the complainant and the accused will be interviewed in details.

Sanctions and Discipline   Furthermore, the EEOC (1999) has stated that a vital part of the harassment policy statement informs employees what sanctions will be imposed if they violate the policy. Discipline should be designed to end the harassment and prevent the harassment from reoccurring. Specific examples of progressive discipline should be provided in the policy statement and procedures, including verbal warning, written reprimand in the harasser's personnel file, pay increase denials, pay reduction, transfer of the harasser, demotion, or dismissal (Dessler, 2009; Smith & Mazin, 2004). Employees should be reminded that the harassment policy provides for stricter penalties for continued misbehavior.

Corrective Action   In addition to disciplining employees who have violated their organization's policy statement on discrimination and harassment, employers should provide corrective action. Discipline does not correct the behavior or performance in question. Depending on the particular situation, other measures may be effective and appropriate, for example, individualized training program in discrimination and harassment (Salisbury & Jaffe, 1996) or counseling through an Employees Assistance Program or community-based therapist (Dessler, 2009; Paludi & Paludi, 2003).

Training Programs   Ample empirical research indicates that training in workplace discrimination and harassment changes attitudes and behavior (for example, Anand & Winters, 2008; Antecol & Cobb-Clark, 2003; Blakely, Blakely, & Moorman, 1998; Dwairy, 2004; Kluge, 2008; Pendry, Driscoll, & Field, 2007; Perry, Kulik, & Schmidtke, 2006; Rynes & Rosen, 1995; York, Barclay, & Zajack, 1997). For example, research indicates that training increases knowledge acquisition and reduces the inappropriate behavior of men who had a high propensity to harass. In addition, research also indicates that sexual harassment training is associated with an increased probability, especially for men, of considering unwanted sexual gestures, remarks, touching, and pressure for dates to be a form of sexual harassment (Antecol & Cobb-Clark, 2003; Beauvais, 1985). Furthermore, men who receive such training have greater knowledge of sexual harassment and less tolerant attitudes toward sexual harassment than men who are not trained (Frisbie, 2002; Moyer & Nath, 2006).

With respect to diversity training, Ellis and Sonnenfeld (1994) surveyed 922 employees in a department in a large firm that had recently participated in diversity training. Ellis and Sonnenfeld reported that employees who received training reported themselves to be more supportive of diversity and perceived their employer to be more supportive of diversity than those who were not trained. More recently, De Meuse and Hostager (2001) reported that diversity training significantly increased knowledge about race and ethnicity.

The courts and EEOC have been clear: Employers must train employees on all types of workplace discrimination and harassment. In *Burlington Industries, Inc. v. Ellerth* (1998) and *Faragher v. City of Boca Raton* (1998), the Supreme Court advised employers to conduct, on at least an annual basis, training on sexual harassment for management and nonmanagerial and nonsupervisory employees. The Supreme Court ruled in *Kolstad v. American Dental Association* (1999) that:

> The purposes underlying Title VII are . . . advanced where employers are encouraged to adopt antidiscrimination policies and to educate their personnel on Title VII's prohibitions.

Thus, an important feature of an effective policy statement and investigatory procedure on harassment and discrimination is a training program designed to enforce the policy (Levy & Paludi, 2002; Paludi & Paludi, 2003; Smith & Mazin, 2004). The impact of the absence of effective or enforced policies through training programs includes employees not fully comprehending what behaviors do, in fact, constitute discrimination and retaliation and how the organization will deal with complaints and sanctions for violating the policy (EEOC, 1999; Wentling & Palma-Rivas, 2002). Training should encourage employees who have complaints to promptly report their complaints to the individual charged with investigating them (EEOC, 1990, 1999; Tsai & Kleiner, 2001).

Training programs include three major components: (1) needs assessment, (2) facilitating the training programs and (3) post-training evaluations (DeCenzo & Robbins, 2007; Goldstein & Ford, 2002). In this section, we discuss each of these components. We note that poorly conceptualized and poorly facilitated training programs on workplace discrimination cause more harm than good (Chavez & Weisinger, 2008; Society for Human Resource Management, 2009; Stockdale & Crosby, 2004). According to Stockdale and Crosby (2004) and Sacco and Schmitt (2005), despite the fact that employees liked participating in training on workplace discrimination, the impact of such training may not translate into sustained, positive organizational results. The approach identified in this chapter will assist organizations in measuring employee behaviors and organizational outcomes, not solely changes in employee attitudes and perceptions.

Needs Assessment Employers should address several topics in any training program on workplace discrimination and harassment (for example, legal definitions, behavioral examples, the organization's policy, and investigatory procedures). In fact, California, Connecticut, and Maine mandate training in sexual harassment and provide recommendations for training content. In keeping with the literature in human resource management (for example, Barbazette, 2006; Brown, 2002; Jones, 2000), we recommend conducting a needs assessment with employees to identify additional issues they expect to be covered in a training session.

Examples of additional topics include the following: the role of hidden biases and stereotypes (Babcock, 2006); the impact of workplace discrimination on employees' emotional and physical health, self-concept, and interpersonal relationships; the role the Employees Assistance Program plays in counseling individuals involved in a workplace discrimination complaint procedure; and the interface of homophobia and workplace discrimination. The topics typically are suggested to the trainer based on the organization's prior complaints.

Brown (2002) identified four reasons why needs assessments must be conducted before facilitating training programs: (1) to identify problem areas in the company, (2) to obtain management support, (3) to develop data for measuring the effectiveness of the training program, and (4) to determine the costs and benefits of the training program. Needs assessments may be conducted through anonymous surveys or focus groups (Lucier, 2008; Roberson, Kulik, & Pepper, 2003; Tyler, 2002). We recommend the following process (also see Levy & Paludi, 2002):

1. Ask individuals to provide answers to questions regarding discrimination in the workplace via an anonymous mail survey.
2. Facilitate two-hour focus groups with randomly selected employees (no more than 15 to 20 per session) to elicit in-depth responses. Structured interview questions for individuals who participate in the focus groups center around employees' goals for training, including their needs with regard to better understanding victims of discrimination and individuals with viewpoints different from their own.
3. Analyze responses from the previous steps using qualitative and quantitative analyses.
4. Prepare a written report that summarizes the needs assessment, including suggestions for the following:
   • How to increase awareness
   • Ways to examine attitudes
   • Alternatives to stereotyping
   • Methods of supportive action
5. Make recommendations for post-training evaluations.

The main goal of the needs assessment is to obtain information concerning the manner in which discrimination is addressed in the organizational climate of the company, including topics such as empowerment, the establishment of mutual trust and respect, methods of inclusion or exclusion, and verbal and nonverbal communication indicative of discrimination. The process of the assessment will be consistent with the goal of the training programs in which the employees will subsequently participate (Tyler, 2002). An example of a needs assessment for training content on sexual harassment may be found in Levy and Paludi (2002).

Training Program

Training on workplace discrimination must be geared toward the accomplishment of organizational goals and based on key performance indicators. Perhaps, for example, the training strategy is connected to the organization's compliance and ethics goal. Failure to demonstrate that the training is tied to the organization's mission, values, and strategic plan (goals), denies the importance of the role of training in the prevention and intervention of unlawful workplace misconduct that diminishes productivity and morale, increases absenteeism and turnover, ruins reputations, and thereby negatively effects the bottom line.

Training Goals   Goals for training programs that have been identified in the workplace discrimination literature include the following (Bell & Kravitz, 2008):

- To provide all members of the workplace with a clear understanding of their rights and responsibilities with respect to discrimination.
- To enable employees to distinguish between behavior that is discrimination and is not discrimination.
- To provide employees with information concerning the policy statements and procedures against discrimination set up by the organization.
- To discuss the emotional and physical reactions to being discriminated against.
- To encourage employees to examine their personal feelings and those of others with respect to discrimination.
- To dispel myths about discrimination and victims of discrimination.
- To explore responsible behavior in dealing with employees who engage in discrimination.
- To empower employees to take control of their behavior.
- To discuss the concept of unwelcomeness and how this is communicated verbally and nonverbally.
- To discuss the employer's central role in preventing discrimination.
- To create an environment that is free of discrimination and free of the fear of retaliation for speaking out about discrimination.

Once the goals have been established, the company's policies and procedures regarding discrimination must be revised, taking into account new case law and research from the behavioral sciences (see the section on Policy in this chapter). Because the policy statements and procedures are part of the training session content, they must be completed before the training.

Training Components   According to the EEOC (1999) guidelines, manager and supervisor training "should explain the types of conduct that violate the employer's anti-harassment policy; the seriousness of the policy; the responsibilities of supervisors and managers when they learn of alleged harassment; and the prohibition against retaliation."

The organization's chief executive officer (CEO) should introduce *each* training session, and provide the strategic rationale for why the training is occurring. The executive should stress the organization's commitment to a respectful, discriminatory-, harassment-, and retaliatory-free work environment. The CEO's attendance at each session signifies the importance of the training to the organization.

Training sessions should, ideally, include no more than 20 to 25 participants to facilitate discussion, encourage small-group exercises, and reduce the risk for those participants who are reluctant to speak up and ask questions. Key discussion topic areas for a comprehensive training program include the following:

- Explanation on how the training supports the organization's mission and values and why the training is occurring.
- Legal definitions of all types of discrimination and harassment, including quid pro quo and hostile environment, and examples of each—must be inclusive of all legally protected classes based on federal and state's laws such as sex, race, color, religion, national origin, age, disability, and sexual orientation.
- Definitions of "welcomeness," "severe or pervasive," "reasonable person/ victim/woman," "gender," and "sexual in nature" (race, disability, religion, and so on).
- Organization's policies related to discrimination and harassment, including the following: electronic communication, workplace violence, respectful conduct, affirmative action, and the discrimination and harassment policy—with an emphasis on intolerance of the misconduct.
- Organization's grievance procedure.
- List of staff and other people to whom the policy applies, including outside vendors, visitors, and clients.
- Explanation that retaliation against anyone involved in a complaint is against the law and against company policy; include examples of behavior that constitutes retaliation.

- Consequences and impact to the target of the behavior, the work unit and organization, and to the perpetrator.
- Discussion of confidentiality.
- The role and responsibility of the bystander or witness.
- Comparison of bullying with discrimination and harassment, emphasizing the relationships inherent in the behaviors of the three constructs.
- Assertive communication on how to tell the perpetrator to stop.
- Brief overview of the investigation process and why it occurs.
- Employees' right to contact the EEOC or their state's human rights department.

In addition to these topics, supervisors and managers require the following additional information:

- That supervisor or management behavior will be held to a stricter standard than nonsupervisory employees; behavior executed by an employee may not be considered unlawful, but the same behavior committed by a supervisor may be.
- The role and responsibility of supervisors and managers in preventing discrimination and harassment.
- Consensual relationships with one of their direct reports.
- The responsibility of supervisors and managers to report any discrimination and harassment of which they are aware.
- The issue of *knew or should have known.*
- Importance of monitoring the workplace environment for any signs or symptoms of potential discrimination or harassment.

At the end of the training, supervisors and managers should write down at least three tasks that they will implement, or three things they will do differently, as a result of the training. These three elements should be provided to their managers so they can be included in the supervisor's or manager's performance review. This will transfer the learning to the work environment.

Furthermore, discrimination and harassment are emotionally charged topics that are threatening and confusing to many individuals. Stereotypes about members of protected classes often remain unchallenged unless individuals participate in effective trainer-guided intervention programs, such as a training program in discrimination and harassment awareness (Bell & Kravitz, 2008; Paludi & Paludi, 2003).

Training programs on discrimination awareness involve more than a recitation of individuals' rights and responsibilities and what the law and organization policy requires. Training also requires dealing with individuals' assumptions and misconceptions about protected classes and power issues as well as the anxieties about the training itself. Thus, training sessions must devote ample time to dealing with the participants' feelings, misconceptions, and questions (Levy & Paludi,2002).

Trainees frequently want to discuss topics related to workplace discrimination following the training program with the trainer without hearing any comments from other participants. Because workplace discrimination is intimate for employees, they are unlikely to ask questions in public. Thus, the trainer should be available after the formal training program to answer questions privately.

Mandatory Training

California, Connecticut, and Maine, have mandatory sexual harassment training. The regulations of California require training on other forms of harassment, discrimination, and retaliation. Connecticut's law and Maine's law do not mandate other forms of discrimination training.

Maine mandates training for all employees in organizations with 15 or more employees. Maine provides guidance on the content of the training program. At a minimum, training must include the legal definition of sexual harassment, case law, behavioral examples, internal complaint procedures available for employees, and protection against retaliation. New supervisors must be trained within one year of assuming the supervisory position.

Connecticut has mandated that all employers, including the state and political subdivisions with 50 or more employees, as well as the company's partners for a minimum of 13 weeks during the training year, must comply with sexual harassment training. The law mandates sexual harassment training for supervisors and all employees. Employers must provide a minimum of two hours of sexual harassment training. Furthermore, the state mandates that sexual harassment training must be effective, engaging, and of high quality. Connecticut requires employees to be able to ask questions and receive feedback related to the sexual harassment training.

Connecticut has identified topics that must be covered in the sexual harassment training program. These topics include the following:

For Employees:

- Definition of sexual harassment under Connecticut law
- Types of conduct that can constitute sexual harassment

- Remedies
- Prevention strategies

For Management:

- Specific responsibilities of managerial employees
- Methods that employees must take to ensure immediate and appropriate corrective action in addressing sexual harassment complaints

In California, all employers with 50 or more employees (including full-time, part-time, and temporary employees) and contractors for each working day in any consecutive 20 week period during the current or prior training year must receive sexual harassment training. All employees are counted even if they do not live in California. California mandates biennial training in sexual harassment. California also has identified the content of this training, including the following: definitions of sexual harassment, statutory provisions and case law, behavioral examples of sexual harassment, remedies, strategies for prevention, confidentiality of the complaint procedures, resources on how to report sexual harassment, employer obligation to investigate, and policy information. Employers must provide at least a two-hour training program. If e-learning is used, the course must take at least two hours to complete. Newly hired supervisors must be trained within six months of assuming the supervisory position. In addition, employers are required to keep records of training for a minimum of two years.

Sexual harassment training for employees is not mandated in California, but periodic training of all employees is advisable under both federal and state law.

Ecological Approach to Training

Paludi and Paludi (2003) offered an "ecological approach" for conducting training programs organizations. It stresses that workplace discrimination training be provided in a sequence that ensures optimum assistance for all parties in a complaint resolution. This sequence for businesses is as follows:

- Investigators of Complaints of Workplace Discrimination
- Counselors in Employees Assistance Program

- Trainers
- President and Vice Presidents
- Managers and Supervisors
- Employees

Levy and Paludi (2002) recommend establishing training programs for employees within certain departments because they each have unique responsibilities. Training programs should not separate employees by sex, race, disability, national origin, or other protected categories. For example, separate sessions for women and men on sexual harassment may perpetuate stereotypes that all women are victims and all men are perpetrators, which certainly is not supported by research. This type of training may be divisive. All employees have the same rights and responsibilities with respect to workplace discrimination and must be provided the identical information concerning their rights and responsibilities.

Temporary and seasonal workers, board members, volunteers, and long-term contract employees need to be included in discrimination and harassment training.

Qualifications of Trainers

Identifying the qualifications of trainers is important; in fact, California has identified what it considers to be a qualified trainer—that is, an individual who "either through formal education and training or substantial experience can effectively lead in person (training) or webinars." Courts (for example, *Cadena v. Pacesetter Corp.*, 2000) have stated that employers must ensure that trainers meet the following qualifications: "Completely understand the complex body of harassment and discrimination laws. . . . Keep up-to-date with new cases that change the interpretations of these laws."

Education qualifications of trainers for sexual harassment programs have been identified in the sexual harassment literature (Holladay & Quinones, 2008). We adapt this listing for trainers of all forms of workplace discrimination and harassment:

- Education and training in the psychological issues involved in sexual harassment;
- Education and training in the legal issues involved in sexual harassment;
- Publications and presentations on sexual harassment;

- Ability to work well with administrators and employees;
- Education and training in psychological issues involved in facilitating a training program.

One of the findings from empirical research on discrimination and harassment concerns the resistance of employees to talking about discrimination. These experiences are difficult to discuss. In addition, discrimination may be occurring to an employee who currently is being trained on discrimination awareness and their organization's policy. It is thus important to give legitimacy to the anxieties, confusion, and fears raised by trainees. In addition, some employees may want to joke about discrimination because of the sensitivity of the issue. It is important to establish a respectful atmosphere in the training session and to talk up front about the attitudes some employees brought with them to the training.

Therapeutic support staff (for example, Employees Assistance Program personnel) should be present during training programs to assist with flashbacks to incidents of discrimination and harassment that may occur (Contrada et al, 2000; Hamilton, Alagna, King, & Lloyd, 1987; Lundberg-Love & Marmion, 2006; Paludi & Paludi, 2003).

PEDAGOGICAL CONCERNS

Training should be facilitated in a formal training or meeting room where participants have sufficient space and are not crowded together. Ideally, the room should allow learners to be able to see each other to ensure that the flow of communication is among all participants in the training. This will facilitate the pedagogy of the training.

Several training methods are available for instructing employees about workplace discrimination, including the following: lectures, videos and films, simulation exercises, behavioral rehearsal, and Web-based training (DeCenzo & Robbins, 2007; Dessler, 2009; Smith & Mazin, 2004; Walker, 2000). The discipline of educational psychology applies the following principles of the psychology of learning to these types of training programs (Slavin, 2008):

- Gain the trainees' attention
- Maintain the trainees' attention
- Present material in an interesting way
- Use trainees' experiences as the basis for examples and applications

- Provide behavioral examples
- Make the content immediately applicable
- Structure the learning experience
- Allow opportunities for practicing information from the training program
- Provide feedback
- Provide visual images
- Emphasize importance of concepts
- Use realistic examples, not jargon
- Encourage trainees to learn from each other
- Model desired behavior

Human resource management research has identified benefits and weaknesses of pedagogical methods for training programs on discrimination and harassment (Callahan, Kiker, & Cross, 2003; Goldstein & Ford, 2002; Stockdale & Crosby, 2004; Wentling & Palma-Rivas, 2002). For example, lecture formats are ideal for disseminating information about the legal issues in discrimination, the organization's policy and procedures, and behavioral examples of discrimination. Trainees may become bored or impatient and consequently not pay attention, however. This is a serious issue because employees must understand their rights and responsibilities under Title VII and the organization's policy.

Case studies and scenarios encourage trainees to learn through guided discovery and teach individuals to think critically about discrimination (Carter, 2002). They do not, however, provide direct practice with issues in discrimination. In addition, trainers may not provide one right or wrong answer to the cases and consequently employees may not receive the best guidance in learning how to resolve cases of discrimination.

Behavioral rehearsal or role-playing techniques are a good method for teaching communication and interaction skills, they present opportunities for embarrassment and loss of self-confidence among the trainees. Furthermore, role-playing scenarios of sexual harassment or race discrimination may elicit laughter, which may be perceived negatively by employees who have experienced these forms of discrimination.

The use of videos in training program is beneficial for trainers because they can repeat part of the video or skip over material already presented (Blanchard, Thacker, & Blanchard, 2003; Dessler, 2009). Video training lacks personal contact, however, thus creating an opportunity for employees to become bored and not acquire knowledge about workplace discrimination.

Web-based training programs generate high levels of employee acqui-sition and retention of the material presented (Frisbie, 2002) as well as offers fast-paced learning. This pedagogical method can create frustra-tion in employees who are not computer literate or who would prefer learning from an individual, not a computer (Oddsson, 2001).

Inevitably, human resources professionals consider whether to use purchased antiharassment and discrimination training programs. Pur-chased programs are easy because development time is not required, the programs often are inexpensive compared with outside consultants or trainers, and all the training materials are conveniently packaged. These programs often are not customized (or only minimally customized) to organizations, and thus they (1) do not include an organization's perti-nent policies, (2) may be outdated by the time they are purchased because of changes in case law, and (3) are designed for anyone to use, including a novice who is not a subject matter expert. In all likelihood, these programs may not carry much protective weight by the courts.

The complexity of discrimination and harassment makes it unsuitable for asynchronous e-learning. This type of training lacks opportunities to (1) engage in discussion; (2) pose multifaceted or complex questions and receive (immediate) answers, particularly with questions about the more subtle nuanced types of behaviors; (3) share the social contact of interaction with peers and an instructor; and (4) partake in meaningful feedback. E-learning has been described as too simplistic, weak, dull, and monotonous. Learners are free to go through e-learning training at their own pace, which means they may be interrupted by phone calls and by co-workers, coffee and lunch breaks, and meetings, or they may engage in multitasking while progressing through the online program. All of these interruptions interfere with the employee's learning environ-ment. Classroom training is much more effective than asynchronous online learning in teaching about discrimination and harassment.

A study by Bingham and Scherer (2001) showed that participants who attended a short sexual harassment training knew more about sex-ual harassment and viewed the workplace misconduct as more improper than did a similar group of nonparticipants. Unfortunately, male partici-pants had an unfavorable response to the training, tended to blame the victim, were less tenable in perceiving coercive sexual harassment, and indicated that they were less apt to report sexual harassment. Addition-ally, men were more likely to perceive social sexual behavior at work as more amiable than were women. These gender differences were not apparent in the group of nonparticipants. Although the authors identified potential theories to explain the men's reactions, the most likely cause was the inadequacy of the training.

The training program lacked a strategic approach and lasted only 30 minutes (Bingham & Scherer, 2001). The authors did not discuss the objectives or teaching methodology of the program, nor the expertise of the presenter(s), all of which could influence the effectiveness of the training session. The results of this study should raise a red flag among human resources professionals when designing and implementing harassment and discrimination training programs. According to Bingham and Scherer (2001), attempts at cost reduction by minimizing the quality and quantity (length) of the training may create "inherent dangers . . . when developing sexual harassment programs" (p. 145). Organizations that believe the myth that something is better than nothing, actually may amplify potential trouble when implementing an inadequate program.

Research by York, Barclay, and Zajack (1997), demonstrated that combining two training methods, a videotape of five different vignettes and a case study analysis of each vignette, increased participant understanding of sexual harassment. Gender differences in perception and analysis were apparent in that women were more likely to identify sexual harassment in specific videos demonstrating more subtle misconduct; there was no difference in gender perception for the blatant misconduct.

Effective training methods must take into account learning styles of adults (Knowles, Holton, & Swanson, 2005), and thus will empower employees, help employees think strategically, and help employees communicate effectively. Interactive pedagogy encompasses adult learning principles. Research has identified that adults prefer learning situations which meet the following criteria:

- Are practical and problem centered
- Promote their positive self-esteem
- Integrate new ideas with existing knowledge
- Show respect for the individual learner
- Capitalize on their experience
- Allow choice and self-direction (Knowles et al, 2005; McNamara, 2008)

Thus, training programs on workplace discrimination must achieve the following:

- Provide overviews, summaries, case studies, and behavioral rehearsals to link research to practice;

- Use collaborative, authentic problem-solving activities;
- Assist individuals in becoming more effective and confident through guided practice and establishing routines;
- Ask individuals what they would like to know about the training topic;
- Provide a quality, well-organized, differentiated experience that uses time effectively and efficiently;
- Validate and respect participants' existing knowledge;
- Create activities that use individuals' experience and knowledge; and
- Be engaging and not repetitive.

The major objective of the training modules and pedagogical techniques is to facilitate transference to the workplace. Transference can be accomplished through the following:

- Association: having participants associate the new information with something with which they are already knowledgeable;
- Similarity: presenting information that is similar to material that participants already know; that is, it revisits a logical framework or pattern;
- Degree of original learning: the degree of original learning for the participants was high; and
- Critical attribute element: the information learned by the participants contains elements that are extremely beneficial and/or critical on the job.

RESOURCES TO BE DISTRIBUTED DURING TRAINING

Training sessions provide opportunities to disseminate information about the organization's policy against discrimination and to discuss discrimination in general. It is advisable for trainers to distribute pamphlets or handouts describing the following information to the trainees:

- Legal definitions
- Behavioral definitions
- Policy statements and procedures
- Name and phone numbers of investigators
- Locations where Information about discrimination may be obtained
- Information regarding the stress effects of discrimination

TRAINING PROGRAMS FOR EMPLOYEES WITH DISABILITIES

Training programs must take into consideration employees with disabilities who are being trained. A variety of pedagogies should be offered to employees with disabilities, including training options of Web-based training, assistive listening devices, and use of a reader or interpreter (DeCenzo & Robbins, 2005). Employers should include employees with disabilities in the design of the training program. This can be accomplished by conducting a needs assessment with employees with disabilities before the training program to inquire about the approach these employees would prefer. In addition, employers should provide a supportive learning environment by incorporating adult learning principles (Rothwell, 2008) to create a welcoming environment.

Furthermore, employers should ensure that the training site is accessible for all employees and that appropriate lighting and assisted listening devices are available and made known to the trainers.

ACKNOWLEDGMENT OF PARTICIPATION IN TRAINING

Following the completion of the training program, all employees and managers must sign an acknowledgment receipt that indicates they participated in the training program. A copy of this acknowledgment should be given to the participants; a copy should be retained in the human resources or personnel office (Smith & Mazin, 2004).

POST-TRAINING EVALUATIONS

Measuring the effectiveness of training programs in workplace discrimination is an important aspect of the training program so that the organization may determine whether the training delivered or failed to deliver the expected organizational benefits (Hoyle, 2006; Morgan & Casper, 2000; Tyler, 2002). The measures of success for the training programs in workplace discrimination are those identified during the needs assessment phase. Issues in the measurement phase can be discussed in two phases: (1) types of information about which to measure and (2) ways to measure whether the training effort achieved its goals. It is not enough to merely assume that any training an organization offers, even if it is legally mandated, is effective (Tyler, 2002). The transfer of knowledge from the training room to the workplace is the most important measure of success.

Information to Measure

The most well-known model for determining the effectiveness of training programs is the Kirkpatrick Model (Kirkpatrick, 1959, 1998), which includes four levels: results, behavior, learning, and reaction. Results concerns the benefits resulted from training. Behavior taps into what extent trainees change their behavior back in the workplace as a result of this training. The learning level asks to what extent trainees improved their knowledge and skills and changed their attitudes as a result of the training programs. The reaction component determines trainees' opinions about the structure of the training program, location of the program, trainer effectiveness, and so on.

The most commonly used level of the Kirkpatrick Model is the reactions level. This, however, is the least valid evaluation technique (Tan, Hall, & Boyce, 2003). Individuals' opinions are influenced heavily by factors that may have little to do with the training effectiveness. By measuring only reactions, organizations do not obtain information about employees' learning, how well they are integrating the new knowledge and skills on their job, whether training has reduced the incidence of workplace discrimination, or whether the reporting of post-training discrimination has increased (Stockdale & Crosby, 2004)

MEASUREMENT TECHNIQUES

Common performance-based evaluations that incorporate aspects of the Kirkpatrick Model are as follows: post-training survey, pre-post-training evaluations, pre-post-training evaluations with a control group, and the Solomon Four Group Design. We review some of these evaluations (for additional information, review Graziano & Raulin, 1996).

Performance-Based Evaluations

Employees' performance—for example, knowledge of the organization's policy, incidence of workplace discrimination, and Title VII provisions—is measured after they have attended the training program to determine whether they have increased their knowledge of this information. However, some trainees may have known this information before participating in the training program. Thus, to simply provide a "post-training survey or test" may overstate the benefits of the training program.

Pre-post-training evaluations can assist with this concern (Sadri & Snyder, 1995). The trainer administers a test or quiz before the beginning of the training program. Such a quiz may ask questions regarding the definition, incidence, and explanatory models of various forms of discrimination in the workplace, the firm's policy statement, and so on. Following the training program, the trainer readministers the quiz and determines whether scores on the post-test quiz are higher than those on the pretest version. This method can provide more reliable information about whether the training program contributed to increased scores on the post-test quizzes, which is what one would expect if the training program was effective.

To further answer the question regarding training effectiveness, a pre-post-training evaluation with a control group can be used. In this method, two groups of employees are established and evaluated on their knowledge, attitudes, and behavior. The control group is given no training. The other group receives training. Both groups are given a post-test evaluation. This method corrects for factors other than training that may have influenced employees' performance. The group that received training should have higher post-test scores than those in the control group.

Audits

In keeping with the human resource management literature (for example, Smith & Mazin, 2004), employers should conduct audits of their policies, procedures, and training programs. Audits provide information for administrators about how employers are preventing and reacting to discrimination complaints in their organization. As Greenberg-Pophal (2008) stated, a human resource audit is "an analysis by which an organization measures where it currently stands and determines what it has to accomplish to improve its human resource function" (in Dessler, 2009; p. 412). Audit questions include the following:

1. Does the company have policy statements dealing with equal employment opportunity issues (for example, nondiscrimination, sexual harassment, ADA, and the Age Discrimination in Employment Act of 1967 [ADEA])?

2. Do the policies prohibit discrimination and harassment from peers in addition to discrimination and harassment by managers?

3. Are the policy statements well publicized? Are they on the company's intranet? Posted in the human resources office?

4. Do employees know to whom they should report complaints related to equal employment opportunity?

5. Are remedies clear and commensurate with the level of discrimination or harassment?

6. Does the company have a new-employee orientation program that includes training on equal employment policies and procedures?

7. Does the company facilitate regular training programs on equal employment opportunity issues, including the company's policies and procedures?

8. Does the company have an Employees Assistance Program associated with the company that can provide support for employees?

9. Does the workplace foster an atmosphere of prevention by sensitizing individuals to the topic of equal employment opportunity?

10. Is the human resource department following state laws with respect to equal employment opportunity as well as federal laws?

Following the completion of the audit, the employer must then correct the omissions to meet their responsibility for ensuring reasonable care.

REFERENCES

Anand, R., & Winters, M. (2008). A retrospective view of corporate diversity training from 1964 to the present. *Academy of Management Learning and Education, 7,* 356–372.

Antecol, H., & Cobb-Clark, D. (2003). Does sexual harassment training change attitudes? A view from the federal level. *Social Science Quarterly, 84,* 826–842.

The Association of the Bar of the City of New York. (1993). *Law firm policies on workplace sexual harassment* (Report from the Committee on Labor and Employment Law). New York: The Association of the Bar of the City of New York.

Babcock, P. (2006). Watch out for the minefield of hidden bias. In Society for Human Resource Management (Ed.) *HR Magazine: Guide to managing people.* (pp. 44–47). Alexandria, VA: Society for Human Resource Management.

Barbazette, J. (2006). *Training needs assessment: Methods, tools and techniques.* New York: John Wiley & Sons.

Beauvais, K. (1985). Workshops to combat sexual harassment: A case study of changing attitudes. *Signs, 12,* 130–145.

Bell, M., & Kravitz, D. (2008). What do we know and need to learn about diversity education and training? *Academy of Management Learning and Education, 7,* 301–308.

Bingham, S., & Scherer, L. (2001). The unexpected effects of a sexual harassment educational program. *The Journal of Applied Behavioral Science, 37,* 125–153.

Blakely, G., Blakely, E., & Moorman, R. (1998). The effects of training on perceptions of sexual harassment allegations. *Journal of Applied Social Psychology, 28,* 71–83.

Blanchard, N., Thacker, J., & Blanchard, P. (2003). *Effective training: Systems strategies and practices.* Upper Saddle River, NJ: Prentice Hall.

Brown, J. (2002). Training needs assessment: A must for developing an effective training program. *Public Personnel Management, 31,* 569–578.

Burlington Industries, Inc., v. Ellerth, 524 U.S. 742 (1998).

Cadena v. Pacesetter Corp., 224 F. 3d 1203, 1215 (2000).

Callahan, J., Kiker, D., Montgomery, & Cross, T. (2003). Does method matter? A meta-analysis of the effects of training method on older learner training performance. *Journal of Management, 29,* 663–680.

Carter, S. (2002). Matching training methods and factors of cognitive ability: A means to improve training outcomes. *Human Resource Development Quarterly, 13,* 71–87.

Chavez, C., & Weisinger, J. (2008). Beyond diversity training: A social infusion for cultural inclusion. *Human Resource Management, 47,* 331–350.

Connell, D. (1991). Effective sexual harassment policies: Unexpected lessons from Jacksonville Shipyards. *Employee Relations, 17,* 191–206.

Contrada, R., Ashmore, R., Gary, M., Coups, E., Egeth, J., Sewell, et al. (2000). Ethnicity-related sources of stress and their effects on well being. *Current Directions in Psychological Science, 9,* 136–139.

DeCenzo, D., & Robbins, S. (2007). *Fundamentals of human resource management.* New York: Wiley.

De Meuse, K., & Hostager, T. (2001). Developing an instrument for measuring attitudes toward and perceptions of workplace diversity: An initial report. *Human Resources Development Quarterly, 12,* 33–51.

Dessler, G. (2009). *Fundamentals of human resource management.* Upper Saddle River, NJ: Prentice Hall.

Dwairy, M. (2004). Culturally sensitive education: Adapting self-oriented assertiveness training to collective minorities. *Journal of Social Issues, 60,* 423–436.

Ellis, C., & Sonnenfeld, J. (1994). Diverse approaches to managing diversity. *Human Resource Management, 33,* 79–109.

Equal Employment Opportunity Commission. (1990). *Policy Guidance on Sexual Harassment.* Washington, DC: U.S. Government Printing Office.

Equal Employment Opportunity Commission. (1999). *Enforcement Guidance: Vicarious Employer Liability for Unlawful Harassment by Supervisors.* Washington, DC: U.S. Government Printing Office.

Faragher v. City of Boca Raton, 524 U.S. 725 (1998).

Frisbie, S. (2002). *Sexual harassment: A comparison of on-line versus traditional training methods.* Ph.D. diss., Texas Tech University, Lubbock, TX.

Frederick v. Sprint/United Management Company, 246 F. 3d 1305 (2001).

Goldstein, I., & Ford, J. (2002). *Training in organizations: Needs assessment, development and evaluation* (4th ed.). Belmont, CA: Wadsworth.

Graziano, A., & Raulin, M. (1996). *Research methods: A process of inquiry.* White Plains, NY: Longman.

Gutek, B. (1997). Sexual harassment policy initiatives. In W. O'Donohue (Ed.), *Sexual harassment: Theory, research, and practice.* Boston, MA: Allyn & Bacon.

Hamilton, J., Alagna, S., King, L., & Lloyd, C. (1987). The emotional consequences of gender-based abuse in the workplace: New counseling programs for sex discrimination. *Women and Therapy,6,* 155–182.

Hedge, J., & Pulakos, E. (2002). *Implementing organizational interventions: Steps, processes and best practices.* San Francisco, CA: Jossey-Bass.

Holladay, C., & Quinones, M. (2008). The influence of training focus and trainer characteristics on diversity training effectiveness. *Academy of Management Learning and Education, 7,* 343–354.

Hoyle, A. (2006). Evaluation of training. A review of the literature. *Public Administration and Development, 4,* 275–282.

Jones, C. (2000). Levels of racism: A theoretical framework and a gardener's tale. *American Journal of Public Health, 90,* 1212–1215.

Kirkpatrick, D. (1959). Techniques for evaluating training programs. *Journal of the American Society for Training Development, 13,* 3–9.

Kirkpatrick, D. (1998). *Evaluating training programs: The four levels.* San Francisco, CA: Berrett-Koehler.

Kluge, A. (2008). What you train is what you get? Task requirements and training methods in complex problem-solving. *Computers in Human Behavior, 24,* 284–308.

Knowles, M., Holton, E., & Swanson, R. (2005). *The adult learner.* San Francisco, CA: Butterworth-Heinemann.

Kolstad v. American Dental Association, 527 U.S. 526 (1999).

Levy, A., & Paludi, M. (2002). *Workplace sexual harassment* (2nd ed.). Englewood Cliffs, NJ: Prentice Hall.

Lucier, K. (2008). A consultative training program: Collateral effect of a needs assessment. *Communication Education, 57,* 482–489.

Lundberg-Love, P., & Marmion, S. (2006). *Intimate violence against women.* Westport, CT: Praeger.

McNamara, C. (2008). *Effective employee training and development requires some knowledge of adult learning.* Retrieved May 30, 2009, from http://managementhelp.org/trng/dev/basics/adlt.lrn.htm.

Morgan, R., & Casper, W. (2000). Examining the factor structure of participant reactions to training: A multidimensional approach. *Human Resource Development Quarterly, 11,* 301–317.

Moyer, R., & Nath, A. (2006). Some effects of brief training interventions on perceptions of sexual harassment. *Journal of Applied Social Psychology, 28,* 333–356.

O'Connell, C. E., & Korabik, K. (2000). Sexual harassment: The relationship of personal vulnerability, work context, perpetrator status, and type of harassment to outcomes. *Journal of Vocational Behavior, 56,* 299–329.

Oddsson, F. (2001). Computerized training methods: Effects on retention and rate of responding. *Dissertation Abstracts International: 61,* 5546.

Paludi, M., & Paludi, C. (Eds.). (2003). *Academic and workplace sexual harassment.* Westport, CT: Praeger.

Pendry, L., Driscoll, D., & Field, S. (2007). Diversity training: Putting theory into practice. *Journal of Occupational and Organizational Psychology, 80,* 27–50.

Perry, E., Kulik, C., & Schmidtke, J. (2006). Individual differences in the effectiveness of sexual harassment awareness training. *Journal of Applied Social Psychology, 28,* 698–723.

Reese, L., & Lindenberg, K. (1999). *Implementing sexual harassment policy: Challenges for the public sector workplace.* Thousand Oaks, CA: Sage.

Riger, S. (1991). Gender dilemmas in sexual harassment policies and procedures. *American Psychologist, 46,* 497–505.

Roberson, L., Kulik, C., & Pepper, M. (2003). Using needs assessment to resolve controversies in diversity training design. *Group and Organization Management, 28,* 148–174.

Rothwell, W. (2008). *Adult learning basics.* Alexandria, VA: ASTD Press.

Rynes, S., & Rosen, B. (1995). A field survey of factors affecting the adoption and perceived success of diversity training. *Personnel Psychology,* 48, 247–270.

Sacco, J., & Schmitt, N. (2005). A dynamic multilevel model of demographic diversity and misfit effects. *Journal of Applied Psychology, 90,* 203–231.

Sadri, G., & Snyder, P. (1995). Methodological issues in assessing training effectiveness. *Journal of Managerial Psychology, 10,* 30–32.

Salisbury, J., & Jaffee, F. (1996). Individual training of sexual harassers. In M. Paludi (Ed.), *Sexual harassment on college campuse*s: Abusing the ivory power. (pp. 141–152). Albany, NY: SUNY Press.

Scheid, T. (1999). Employment of individuals with mental disabilities: Business response to the ADA's challenge. *Behavioral Sciences and the Law, 17,* 73–91.

Slavin, R. (2008). *Educational psychology: Theory and practice* (9th ed.). Boston, MA: Allyn & Bacon.

Smith, S., & Mazin, R. (2004). *The HR answer book.* New York: AMACOM.

Society for Human Resource Management. (2009). Retrieved September 11, 2009, from http://www.shrm.org.

Stockdale, M. S., & Crosby, F. J. (Eds.). (2004). *The psychology and management of workplace diversity.* Boston, MA: Blackwell Publishing.

Tan, A., Hall, J., & Boyce, C. (2003). The role of employee reactions in predicting training effectiveness. *Human Resource Development Quarterly, 14,* 397–411.

Trotter, R., & Zacur, S. (2004). Corporate sexual harassment policies: Effective strategic human resource management. *Journal of Business and Economics Research, 2,* 63–70.

Tsai, P., & Kleiner, B. (2001). Reasonable care of small business to prevent employee discrimination. *Equal Opportunities International, 20,* 24–26.

Tyler, K. (2002). Evaluating evaluations. *HR Magazine,* June, 47.

Walker, T. (2000). Effectiveness of multicultural training: Examination of expe-
riential and didactic teaching styles on multicultural awareness training
outcomes. *Dissertation Abstracts International: 06,* 5324.

Wentling, R., & Palma-Rivas, N. (2002). Components of effective diversity
training programs. *International Journal of Training and Development, 3,*
215–226.

York, K., Barclay, L., & Zajack, A. (1997). Preventing sexual harassment: The
effect of multiple training methods. *Employee Responsibilities and Rights
Journal, 10,* 277–289.

14

Conducting Workplace Investigations

Joanmarie M. Dowling

Workplace investigations are a common, and often critical, process for employers, especially in the context of employment discrimination or harassment claims. If done correctly, workplace investigations can reduce the likelihood that an internal problem becomes an external problem, can mitigate morale and productivity problems, and can prevent substantial legal problems and financial losses.

Few areas, however, are as fraught with peril as the workplace investigation. First, there is the practical and legal danger associated with the activity being investigated. For example, if you receive a report of sexual harassment, the need to investigate it becomes immediate and, if confirmed, the harassing behavior must stop before it continues or even spreads. Second, an employer must be mindful not to engage in illegal conduct in its response. Improper conduct during an investigation can, in and of itself, lead to claims of harassment, discrimination, retaliation, defamation, or violations of the Fair Credit Reporting Act, National Labor Relations Act, or other federal or state law.

Moreover, myriad unintended consequences stem from poorly conducted investigations—negative impacts on employee morale, adverse publicity, feeding an organization's rumor mills, distracting employees from their work, and cost. An investigation may create divisiveness when employees are asked to comment on activities of work colleagues or disclose information harmful to a colleague.

THE HALLMARKS OF A SUCCESSFUL WORKPLACE INVESTIGATION

Successful workplace investigations require careful planning and execution and include the following:

- recognizing the need for an investigation;
- selecting an appropriate investigator;
- creating an investigation plan;
- conducting a prompt and thorough investigation;
- making determinations supported by investigation findings;
- utilizing and consulting with counsel; and
- recommending appropriate action.

WHEN AN EMPLOYER SHOULD CONDUCT AN INVESTIGATION

Under federal and state antidiscrimination laws, an employer must conduct an investigation of complaints of discrimination, harassment, or retaliation. Sometimes the complainant will come to human resources and say, "I don't want anything to happen to this person, but I just want you to know that. . . . " If the complaint involves workplace harassment or discrimination, an investigation should be conducted regardless. In such situations, an employer should direct that an investigation be conducted, even where the complainant prefers to remain anonymous or has requested that the employer take no action.

SELECTING AN APPROPRIATE INVESTIGATOR

Selecting an appropriate investigator is key to the success of the investigation. Some options include human resources personnel, members of line management, private investigators and outside consultants, or legal counsel. Each group has particular benefits and limitations.

Human Resources Personnel

Many human resources personnel already have the knowledge and skills needed to conduct an efficient and effective investigation, such as experience as a neutral third party, ability to maintain confidentiality, knowledge of company policies, procedures, practices and rules, and knowledge of the people and places being investigated.

Members of Line Management

Many line managers possess the necessary skills and knowledge to be an appropriate choice to conduct investigation, such as familiarity with company polices and procedures and first-hand knowledge of the people and places being investigated. Witnesses, however, may be intimidated by line management or perceive that the line manager is biased because of past issues (for example, prior discipline). Additionally, line managers may be inclined to inadvertently interject bias into the investigation.

Private Investigator or Outside Consultant

Persons from outside the organization often are the most impartial investigators because they usually do not have any association with the organization, the employees, or witnesses, and therefore, have not developed any bias against the accused or the witnesses. However, a private investigator or outside consultant may lack important knowledge of the organization's policies or culture.

In-House or Outside Counsel

An attorney is often the most prudent and impartial investigator, but because of cost, timing, and other practicalities, an attorney may not always be an option. If that is the case, the investigation team should keep the following in mind:

- Any documents (including e-mail) or tapes generated during the investigation may become discoverable evidence in a lawsuit or a government inquiry.
- Counsel should be consulted both at the outset and end of the investigation to ensure that the investigation and its findings are in accordance with the law.

Above all, when selecting an investigator the employer should look for the following: (1) impartiality; (2) professionalism and credibility; (3) reputation among employees and management as honest, neutral, and fair; (4) knowledge of company policies, procedures, practices, and rules; (5) communication and interviewing skills; (6) ability to maintain confidentiality; (7) ability to adapt to and follow-up on unexpected or new information; and (8) effectiveness as a potential witness in an administrative or court proceeding.

CREATING AN INVESTIGATION PLAN

Creating an investigation plan is an often-overlooked step. While it is important to commence an investigation promptly, taking the time to create a plan can make the investigation more effective, efficient, and complete.

Identify Potential Witnesses

Before conducting interviews, develop a list of potential witnesses, all of whom are candidates to be interviewed. In addition to the complaining party and accused, consider co-workers who work in the area in which the alleged misconduct occurred, customers, suppliers, and others.

Anyone identified by either the complaining party or the accused should be considered for an interview. Keep in mind that not everyone who is named needs to be interviewed. The investigator should, however, be able to articulate sound reasons for not doing so (for example, redundancy). The investigator should supplement the lists of witnesses as necessary.

Schedule Witness Interviews For Maximum Effectiveness

Recognize that the chronology of interviews can effect the success of the investigation. For example, you may want to interview key Employee A before Employee B, so that Employee B cannot influence Employee A's statement. Also, the quicker the interviews begin, the better, because it prevents parties and witnesses from "getting their stories straight."

Once the interviews begin, the word will get out and travel fast. Be prepared to act accordingly. Contingency plans should be established for the occasional premature disclosure that may jeopardize your strategy from either a legal perspective or public relations point of view.

Schedule Witnesses to Ensure Appropriate Time

If you are planning to interview several witnesses in one day, schedule sufficient time to conduct a thorough interview and complete your notes after each interviewee leaves. Again, the order of the interviews is critical and needs to be determined on a case-by-case basis.

Identify Relevant Documentation to Review

Documents can play an important role in an investigation, as well as any subsequent litigation. Not only should the investigator be aware of the documents that exist before the investigation, but also the documents that may be created in anticipation of the investigation, during the investigation, and at the conclusion of the investigation. Bear in mind that many, if not all, of these documents may be discoverable in future potential litigation.

The following documents should be reviewed: rules, policies, or procedures, memoranda or notes about the incident, timecards, expense reports, logs, receipts, communications to employees, complaints, relevant employees' personnel files, relevant managers' notes and files, and samples of work of the employee and others in the group for comparison.

Consider Adopting Appropriate Interim Protective Measures

The employer may need to take interim protective steps to prevent or stop misconduct until conclusion of the investigation. For example, if work shifts or locations can be easily switched to avoid further contact between the accused and the complaining party, then it may be prudent to do so. The employer should, however, steer clear of any action that could be perceived as retaliation against the complaining party. Therefore, if someone is moved, it should *not* be the complaining party, unless the complaining party has been reassured that he or she does not need to move, but nevertheless requests such a move.

Conduct a Prompt and Thorough Investigation

An investigation should begin as soon as possible after learning of a complaint or concern giving rise to the need for an investigation. Although it is important to get the facts before witnesses and documents disappear, each case is different in this regard and there is no "cookie-cutter" approach. So, balance the need for preparation with the need to expedite the process.

It is not enough to initiate an investigation promptly, it must also be completed promptly. Again, the investigator must carefully balance the need for completeness with the need to complete the investigation in a timely manner.

Outline Questions in Advance

Prepare an outline of the questions for witness interviews to ensure a thorough and consistent line of questioning. Outlines should be tailored to the individual witnesses, although frequently many of the questions will be the same. Bear in mind that the investigator may need to modify the outline based on information gathered during the investigation itself.

Collect Relevant Documentation in Advance

Collect all relevant documents in advance of the interview. These documents will support and supplement your questions. You can use these documents to impeach a witness during an interview and otherwise make credibility determinations.

The investigator always should review relevant policies and procedures, as well as the accused's and complaining party's personnel files. In searching for additional relevant documents, look broadly: supervisor's files, contractor's files, witnesses' personnel files, purchasing records, travel history, policies and procedures, sign-in security sheets for building admittance, video security tapes, timecards, and reimbursement records. If possible, however, keep the number of individuals involved in this search limited. If the investigation later comes under attack, you do not want to implicate any more employees than necessary, nor do you want to give the impression the investigation was not kept as confidential as possible.

Federal or state law may affect an employer's ability to conduct a workplace search. For example, the federal Electronic Communications Privacy Act regulates access, use, disclosure, interception, and privacy protections of electronic and wire communications and may affect an employer's ability to access technological resources (for example, hard drives, network servers, cell phones, blackberries). In public sector employment, the federal constitution protects individuals from unreasonable searches conducted by the government, even when the government is the employer. Before accessing technological resources or conducting other workplace searches, the employer should consult with legal counsel to ensure that all legal requirements have been met.

Conducting the Interview

During interviews, the employer should utilize two management representatives. This provides the organization with two witnesses if the investigation becomes an issue in subsequent litigation. Additionally, one representative can be responsible for note-taking, leaving the other representative free to ask questions and develop a rapport with the witness.

Beginning the Investigation

To start the interview, the investigator should explain the purpose of the interview. It is important not to mislead witnesses about the investigation's purpose, as a misrepresentation may later taint the investigation findings.

When interviewing the "accused," tell him or her that the interview is designed to give him or her an opportunity to relate his or her version of the event and to advise management of any other information that should be considered during the investigation.

If the accused refuses to participate, management should tell the employee that the organization will be forced to base its decision on the other information gathered during the investigation, the inferences drawn from the evidence, and the accused's unwillingness to cooperate in the interview. Management should explain to the accused that such refusal may constitute insubordination and discipline may result. In a unionized work setting, the National Labor Relations Act allows employees to request the presence of a union representative in an investigatory interview that the employee reasonably believes might result in disciplinary action) ("Weingarten Rights").[1] Investigators should plan accordingly.

When interviewing other witnesses, the investigator should explain to the witness why he or she is present, indicate that the organization takes the allegation seriously, and express appreciation for the witness's cooperation.

Conducting a Complete Investigation

In investigations regarding specific events, inquire about all events that occurred during the relevant time frame, in chronological blocks of time. The investigator should have all of the details necessary to recreate each significant event, including the following:

- Exactly what occurred
- When it happened
- Where it happened
- Who was present

- Who else may know relevant information
- How it happened
- Who did or said what and in what order
- Why it happened and could it have been avoided
- Whether any notes, documents or other evidence exists

When interviewing the complaining party, you may also need to discuss his or her desired outcome and interim protective measures. If the complaining party discusses what type of action he or she would like to see taken, remember that you do not need to implement that action at the end of the investigation. Instead, ensure that whatever discipline you recommend is supported by the facts.

Where appropriate, do not be reluctant to follow up on answers with additional questions. Develop questions to corroborate or refute information provided by other witnesses or evidence, without disclosing the source if there is no need to disclose the source. If appropriate, ask questions such as, "If your position is accurate, then how would you explain the following?"

Questioning Styles

Remember not to abandon your conversational style in conducting interviews. Using a conversational tone can put the witness at ease. An investigator should avoid threats, coercion, or intimidation in questioning a witness.

It is best to avoid questions that are designed to elicit a "yes" or "no" answer, as open-ended questions can elicit better information. Also, an investigator should allow enough time for the interviewee to provide a complete response. Pausing between questions may be helpful, as an interviewee may offer additional information to "fill up the silence" if he or she believes you are waiting for them to complete their response.

Finally, save embarrassing or uncomfortable questions until the end of the interview,—if possible. If necessary, however, be sure to ask these questions. If the interview becomes confrontational or emotional, consider taking a break.

Address Confidentiality of Investigation

Do not promise confidentiality. An investigator may have an obligation to take immediate action that requires you to reveal confidences. Also, if a lawsuit or grievance is filed, you will probably not be able to keep a promise of confidentiality because disclosure could be compelled. You can tell the witness that you will attempt to share remarks only with those who have a need to know and keep the matter as confidential as reasonably possible.

Advise Witnesses of the Organization's Antiretaliation Policy

Advise the complaining party, the accused, and all other witnesses that retaliation will not be tolerated and provide a copy of the organization's antiretaliation policy or a separate notice setting forth the organization's policy that witnesses are required to sign. Remind witnesses that any perceived retaliation or continued harassment should be reported immediately.

Making Determinations Supported by Investigation Findings

Determining the credibility of all parties and witnesses may not always be an easy or straightforward task. Many times, it will require the investigator to make a "judgment call" as to whether or not a person is telling the truth. This is especially true where two witnesses' statements are contradictory and objective evidence is not able to verify either account. *Do not be afraid of being wrong and do not hold yourself to a standard of absolute certainty.*

The investigator should ensure that the conclusion and recommendation are reasonable. Conclusions should be supported by objective facts, stated in noninflammatory language.

Utilizing and Consulting with Counsel

When a conclusion is reached, legal counsel should review the investigation to ensure that it is consistent with company policy and applicable law.

Recommending Appropriate Action

Once the report has been completed, the investigator should determine what action to take and make a recommendation to the decision maker. Remember, in sexual and other types of harassment cases, the complainant should not suffer adverse employment actions unless the employer can prove that the allegations were made in bad faith. This standard is difficult to meet.

Possible actions against an offending employee include the following:

1. Discharge or suspension if a violation of policy or law definitely occurred and there are no mitigating circumstances. These actions may be limited, however, by federal or state law (for example, applicable civil service laws and rules) or discipline clauses in collective bargaining agreements.

2. Other forms of progressive discipline (for example, warnings and counseling), if no clear violation occurred or if evidence is inconsistent and cannot be reconciled.

3. If the claim cannot be substantiated and no disciplinary action is found to be appropriate, nonetheless, reiterate the organization's antiharassment and discrimination policies and document that the policy was disseminated.

4. Regardless of the outcome, use the investigation as an opportunity to reissue any applicable or relevant corporate policies, *for example*, antidiscrimination and antiharassment policies. Ensure that these policies are fully reviewed and updated by legal counsel before reissuing them.

Discipline should be consistent with the employer's prior practice and policies.

CONCLUSION

In litigation, an investigation can make the difference between success or disaster. A delayed, poorly planned, or poorly executed investigation can negatively affect the employer's credibility in the eyes of a judge, jury, or administrative agency fact-finder. In contrast, a timely and well-executed investigation can create a positive impression of the employer and underscore the employer's commitment to a workplace free from unlawful discrimination or harassment. Therefore, with appropriate resources and careful planning, an employer can greatly reduce the likelihood of legal liability for workplace discrimination or harassment.

NOTE

1. In 2001, the D.C. Circuit Court upheld the NLRB'S extension of Weingarten rights to the nonunionized setting. *Epilepsy Foundation of Northeast Ohio v. NLRB*, 268 F.3d 1095 (D.C. Cir. 2001). In 2004, the court overruled *Epilepsy Foundation* in *IBM Corp*, 341 NLRB 1288 (2004). As a result, nonunion employees are not currently entitled to representatives in investigatory interviews. However, with the Obama administration filling several NLRB vacancies, this rule may be changed again.

APPENDIX A

Equal Employment Opportunity Commission

Jennie D'Aiuto, Sara-Becca Smith, and Michele A. Paludi

INTRODUCTION

Throughout this volume of the handbook, contributors offered recommendations for effective policies, investigatory procedures, and training programs for the prevention of workplace discrimination. In addition, contributors provided suggestions for effective resolutions of complaints of workplace discrimination, taking into account case law, management theories and social science research.

One common goal of the chapters in this volume is to assist employers with resolving complaints of workplace discrimination internally. Employees who are not satisfied with the way their employer has resolved their complaints may seek resolution with the Equal Employment Opportunity Commission (EEOC). Except for complaints of wage disparity under the Equal Pay Act, this step occurs before filing a lawsuit in court. Individuals who file claims under the Equal Pay Act do not have to first file their claim with the EEOC in order to sue the employer in court.

A basic understanding of how the EEOC operates and the method with which complaints are processed is important to have a complete picture of the law and management of workplace discrimination. In this appendix, we provide an overview of the role of the EEOC in resolving complaints of workplace discrimination and summarize the process employees may follow in filing their complaint with the EEOC.

THE AUTHORITY OF THE EQUAL EMPLOYMENT OPPORTUNITY COMMISSION

The EEOC is a federal agency that was established by Title VII of the Civil Rights Act of 1964; it began operating on July 2, 1965. The EEOC coordinates all federal equal employment opportunity policies, practices, and regulations for applicants to jobs and employees. The EEOC enforces the following federal statutes:

* Title VII of the Civil Rights Act of 1964
* Age Discrimination in Employment Act
* Equal Pay Act
* Title I and Title V of the Americans with Disabilities Act
* Section 501 and 505 of the Rehabilitation Act of 1973
* Civil Rights Act of 1991

In 1972, Title VII was amended to grant the EEOC the power to bring court actions in certain cases on behalf of victims of discrimination. In addition, the EEOC has been instrumental in shaping laws of workplace discrimination (Levy & Paludi, 2002). For example, the EEOC has issued guidelines and policy statements to assist employers in understanding changes to laws regarding sexual harassment. Its *Guidelines on Discrimination on the Basis of Sex* (EEOC, 2009a) offers the basic definition cited in regard to sexual harassment. In addition, the EEOC has been quoted by the U.S. Supreme Court in its decisions in key cases in workplace discrimination, for example, *Meritor Savings Bank v. Vinson* and *Harris v. Forklift Systems.*

The EEOC is staffed by five commissioners and a general counsel that are appointed by the president of the United States and confirmed by the U.S. Senate. Each commissioner is appointed for a five-year, staggered term. The general counsel's term is four years. The five commissioners make policy and approve most litigation. The general counsel conducts EEOC enforcement litigation. In addition, the EEOC monitors cases to ensure that complainants are not retaliated against for filing a charge with them. The EEOC is headquartered in Washington, D.C., and has 51 field offices throughout the United States.

PROCESS OF FILING A COMPLAINT WITH THE EEOC

How to File a Complaint

According to the EEOC (2009b):

> Any individual who believes that his or her employment rights have been
> violated may file a charge of discrimination with the EEOC. In addition,

an individual, organization or agency may file a charge on behalf of another person in order to protect the aggrieved person's identity.

Complaints are filed with the EEOC in person, by mail, or by telephone. Individuals who need accommodations to file their complaint of discrimination (for example, interpreter) will be provided that assistance by the EEOC. A TTY device is available for hearing-impaired complainants (see EEOC, 2009c). In states or localities where there is an antidiscrimination law and an agency authorized to grant or seek relief, charges must be presented to the state or local agency.

Required Information in Complaint

In completing a complaint with the EEOC, the following information must be included (also see EEOC, 2009d):

1. Identifying information about the complainant, that is, name, address, telephone number.
2. Identifying information about the complainant's employer or union, that is, name, address, telephone number, and number of employees or union members if known.
3. A brief description of the alleged discrimination.
4. The date(s) the alleged discrimination occurred to the complainant.

Statute of Limitations in Filing a Complaint

Individuals must adhere to statutes of limitations to file complaints with the EEOC. Title VII specifies that a charge must be filed within 180 days of the alleged discrimination. If a charge is brought to the state or local agency initially, the EEOC complaint may be filed within 300 days of the discrimination.

For complaints involving age discrimination, state laws extend the filing limit to 300 days. These statutes of limitation do not apply under the Equal Pay Act. Employers should review the EEOC guidelines for employees and employers of multinational firms (EEOC, 2009b).

Previously, courts have heard complaints that occurred outside of the statute of limitations when the EEOC and courts decided that the situation involved a continuing violation, that is, several acts of discrimination but only one of the incidents of discrimination is within the statutory limits. The entire history of the alleged discrimination can become part of the claim under the continuing violation doctrine.

Investigating Complaints

Once charges are filed with the EEOC, the process proceeds in the following manner. The EEOC can ask to settle a complaint at any stage of their investigation if the complainant and employer want to do so.

The EEOC:

1. Notifies the company of the charge within 10 days of its filing and begins to investigate the charge to determine if the complaint is valid.
2. Requests information, interviews, documents, and visits the company where the alleged discriminatory conduct occurred.
3. Notifies the company in writing of its findings from the investigation within 120 days.
4. Selects the complaint for the EEOC mediation program if the complainant and employer agree. This program offers an alternative to a lengthy investigation. If the mediation is unsuccessful, the complaint is returned for investigation.
5. Stops the process if the charge is not sustained, notifies the individual of the outcome, and informs the complainant that they may still file charges against the company in civil court. The complainant has 90 days to file their suit following receipt of the right to sue letter.
6. Attempts to correct the problem through informal meetings with the employer if the charge is sustained. The case may settle at this point.
7. Begins a formal settlement meeting between the complainant and the company, if this informal process is not successful, that is, conciliation, mediation, or settlement meeting. The goal of this meeting is to reach a voluntary agreement between the parties.

We note that under the Equal Pay Act, complainants may file a lawsuit within two years of the alleged discrimination in cases of willful violations of the Equal Pay Act.

Once the complainant has filed a law suit in court the EEOC typically is no longer involved with the claim.

Remedies

Remedies available for employment discrimination include the following: back pay, hiring, promotion, reinstatement, front pay, reasonable accommodation, or other remedies to make the complainant "whole" ("in the condition s/he would have been but for the discrimination")

(EEOC, 2009d). In addition, remedies may include payment of attorney fees, court costs, and expert witness fees. Compensatory and punitive damages may be available as well.

Finally, the employer who violated Title VII may have to take preventive actions to minimize the recurrence of violations.

Summary

Three possible resolutions are satisfactory for an employer dealing with workplace discrimination (also see Levy and Paludi, 2002).

1. The EEOC or a state or local agency will never contact a company because the business's employees are satisfied with the internal investigation.
2. The EEOC gives notice to an employer of a complaint, and the employer responds calmly and confidently because it has done everything that is necessary to minimize liability.
3. An agency gives notice to the employer of a complaint and the employer, after responding calmly and confidently, determines that discrimination has occurred and remedies the problem immediately.

As Levy and Paludi (2002) concluded, "Any other scenario evidences an attitude that is foolish, time consuming, and costly, reflecting bad business judgment" (p. 153). Thus, it is important for employers to exercise "reasonable care" and enforce what is stated in its policies and procedures with respect to preventing workplace discrimination and investigating complaints.

EEOC AND POLICY DEVELOPMENT

The EEOC develops literature to provide guidance to interpreting the laws it enforces, including the following:

• Enforcement Guidance on Vicarious Employer Liability for Unlawful Harassment by Supervisors
• Enforcement Guidance on Disability-Related Injuries and Medical Examinations of Employees Under the Americans with Disabilities Act
• Enforcement Guidance: Unlawful Disparate Treatment of Workers with Caregiving Responsibilities

All of the EEOC's policy guidances are available at www.eeoc.gov.

ADDITIONAL EEOC ACTIVITIES

EEOC also offer employers the opportunity to participate in their Technical Assistance Program Seminars that deal with federal workplace discrimination laws. In addition, the EEOC facilitates customized training programs on workplace discrimination at companies. Additional information regarding these resources may be obtained from the EEOC (2009e). Resources for small businesses that do not have human resource departments also are offered by the EEOC (2009f).

The EEOC Training Institute facilitates seminars and courses on workplace discrimination. These are made available under the 1992 EEOC Education, Technical Assistance, and Training Revolving Fund Act. In accordance with this Act, the EEOC charges reasonable fees to defray the costs of education, training, and technical assistance for companies (EEOC, 2009g). The EEOC also has outreach programs, including providing information at job fairs, conferences, and community events (2009h).

REFERENCES

Equal Employment Opportunity Commission. (2009a). *Guidelines on discrimination on the basis of sex.* Retrieved September 20, 2009, from http://www.access.gop.gov/nara/cfr/waisidx_06/29cfr1604_06.

Equal Employment Opportunity Commission. (2009b). *Filing a charge of employment discrimination.* Retrieved September 20, 2009, from http://www.eeoc.gov/charge/overview_charge_filing.

Equal Employment Opportunity Commission. (2009c). *Contact EEOC.* Retrieved September 20, 2009, from http://www.eeoc.gov/contact.

Equal Employment Opportunity Commission. (2009d). EEOC's charge processing procedures. Retrieved September 20, 2009, from http://www.eeoc.gov/charge/overview_charge_processing.

Equal Employment Opportunity Commission. (2009e). Resources. Retrieved September 20, 2009, from http://www.eeoc.gov/employers/resources.

Equal Employment Opportunity Commission. (2009f). Information for small businesses. Retrieved September 20, 2009, from http://www.eeoc.gov/employers/smallbusinesses.

Equal Employment Opportunity Commission. (2009g). EEOC training institute. Retrieved September 20, 2009, from http://www.eotraining.eeoc.gov/viewpage.aspx?371bake8.

Equal Employment Opportunity Commission. (2009h). No-cost outreach programs. Retrieved September 20, 2009, from http://www.eeoc/gov/outreach/nocost.

Harris v. Forklift Systems, 510 U.S. 17 (1993).

Levy, A., & Paludi, M. (2002). *Workplace sexual harassment* (2nd ed.). Upper Saddle River, NJ: Prentice Hall.

Meritor Savings Bank v. Vinson, 477 U.S. 77 (1986).

APPENDIX B

State-Protected Categories

Michele A. Paludi

In addition to federal laws prohibiting workplace discrimination, some states have additional antidiscrimination laws. When state laws offer greater protection to employees, they are controlling. Otherwise, federal law is controlling. The following list presents protected categories not included in federal law. Federal and state government employees have additional protections against workplace discrimination. For a complete discussion of legislation passed and pending, we refer the reader to each state's nondiscrimination law, for example, D.C. Non-Discrimination Law (http://www.hrc.org/issues/workplace/837.htm).

State or Territory	Additional Protected Categories
Alaska	Parenthood Status
	Marital Status
California	Sexual Orientation
	Gender Identity
	Marital Status
	Medical Condition
Colorado	Sexual Orientation

(Continued)

State or Territory	Additional Protected Categories
	Gender Identity Any Lawful Activity
Connecticut	Sexual Orientation Gender Identity Marital Status
Delaware	Sexual Orientation Marital Status
District of Columbia	Sexual Orientation Gender Identity or Expression Marital Status (including Domestic Partnership) Political Affiliation Matriculation Personal Appearance Family Responsibilities
Florida	Marital Status
Hawaii	Sexual Orientation Marital Status
Illinois	Sexual Orientation Gender Identity Marital Status Unfavorable Discharge from Military Service
Indiana	Use of Tobacco
Iowa	Sexual Orientation Gender Identity
Kentucky	Smoker/Nonsmoker Status
Louisiana	Sickle Cell Trait
Maine	Sexual Orientation Gender Identity
Maryland	Sexual Orientation Marital Status
Massachusetts	Sexual Orientation Gender Identity
Michigan	Marital Status Height Weight
Minnesota	Sexual Orientation Gender Identity

State or Territory	Additional Protected Categories
	Marital Status
	Public Assistance Status
Montana	Marital Status
Nebraska	Marital Status
Nevada	Sexual Orientation
	Use of Lawful Product
New Hampshire	Sexual Orientation
	Marital Status
New Jersey	Sexual Orientation
	Gender Identity or Expression
	Marital, Civil Union, or Domestic Partnership Status
	Atypical Hereditary Cellular or Blood Trait
	Familial Status
New Mexico	Sexual Orientation
	Gender Identity
	Spousal Affiliation
	Serious Medical Condition
New York	Sexual Orientation
	Gender Identity
	Marital Status
	Political Activities
	Use of Lawful Product
North Carolina	Sickle Cell or Hemoglobin C Trait
	Use of Lawful Product
North Dakota	Marital Status
	Family Status
	Lawful Activity
Oregon	Sexual Orientation
	Gender Identity
	Marital Status
	Use of Tobacco
Rhode Island	Sexual Orientation
	Gender Identity or Expression
Texas	Participation in Emergency Evacuation Order
Vermont	Sexual Orientation

(Continued)

State or Territory	Additional Protected Categories
	Gender Identity
	Place of Birth
Washington	Sexual Orientation
	Gender Identity
	Marital Status
	Hepatitis C Status
Wisconsin	Sexual Orientation
	Marital Status
	Political Activity
	Unlawful Activity
Puerto Rico	Political Affiliation or Ideology

About the Editors
and Contributors

EDITORS

MICHELE A. PALUDI, Ph.D., is the series editor for Women's Psychology and for Women and Careers in Management for Praeger. She is the author/editor of 34 college textbooks, and more than 170 scholarly articles and conference presentations on sexual harassment, campus violence, women and leadership, workplace diversity, psychology of women, gender, and discrimination. Her book, *Ivory Power: Sexual Harassment on Campus* (1990, SUNY Press), received the 1992 Myers Center Award for Outstanding Book on Human Rights in the United States. Dr. Paludi served as Chair of the U.S. Department of Education's Subpanel on the Prevention of Violence, Sexual Harassment, and Alcohol and Other Drug Problems in Higher Education. She was one of six scholars in the United States to be selected for this subpanel. She also was a consultant to and a member of former New York State Governor Mario Cuomo's Task Force on Sexual Harassment. Dr. Paludi serves as an expert witness for court proceedings and administrative hearings on sexual harassment. She has had extensive experience in conducting training programs and investigations of sexual harassment and other Equal Employment Opportunity (EEO) issues for businesses and educational institutions. Dr. Paludi is President of Human Resources Management Solutions. In addition, she has held faculty positions at Franklin & Marshall College, Kent State University, Hunter College, Union College, and Union Graduate College, where she directs certificate programs in human resource management and leadership and management. She is on the faculty in the School of Management and was recently named "Woman of the Year" by the Business and Professional Women in Schenectady, New York.

CARMEN A. PALUDI, JR. holds advanced degrees in electrical engineering from Clarkson University and Syracuse University, and has conducted graduate studies in applied physics and electronics engineering at the University of Massachusetts, and engineering management at Kennedy Western University. His 32-year career spans work for the Department of Defense in federal civil service as well as the private sector. He has held positions as senior principle engineer, member of the technical staff, and senior scientific advisor for the United States Air Force, Sanders Associates, The MITRE Corporation, Titan Corporation, and L-3 Communications, Inc. He has over 20 technical publications in refereed journals, and presents at international symposia and conferences. Mr. Paludi was an adjunct faculty at New Hampshire Technical College and a guest lecturer at the Advanced Electronics Technology Center at the University of Massachusetts. He frequent lectures at the Union Graduate College. He is a capability maturity model integration (CMMI) trained and certified appraisal team member by the Software Engineering Institute at Carnegie Mellon University. He has developed and presented in-house training programs in requirements management, requirements development, and risk management. He has over 30 years of program management experience.

EROS R. DESOUZA, Ph.D., is currently a professor of psychology at Illinois State University. He earned his doctorate in community psychology from the University of Missouri at Kansas City. He has carried out qualitative and quantitative research on sexuality and gender issues, including sexual orientation and sexual harassment from a cross-cultural perspective. As of August 2009, he has written nine book chapters and over 40 scholarly articles; he has also co-authored 115 papers presented at conferences.

CONTRIBUTORS

BENJAMIN ADAMS is a graduate of Troy High School, Boston College (bachelor of arts in political science), Union Graduate College (master of business administration), and Albany Law School. Ben currently works for a Goldman Sachs subsidiary, in finance, and is pursuing a career in corporate management and corporate law.

LAURA G. BARRON, Ph.D., graduated with her bachelor of arts degree from Oberlin College and her doctorate in industrial/organizational psychology from Rice University in 2009. She is an assistant professor of psychology at University of Wisconsin—Stout. Her research focuses on diversity and discrimination and she is particularly interested in legal issues related to diversity. She recently was awarded two external grants to study these issues.

NICOLE T. BUCHANAN, Ph.D., is an associate professor in the Department of Psychology at Michigan State University and a core faculty affiliate in Michigan State University's Center for Multicultural Psychology Research, Center for Gender in Global Context, and the Violence against Women Research and Outreach Initiative. Her research examines the intersection of race and gender in harassment, racialized sexual harassment, health, coping, and resilience among women of color. Dr. Buchanan received the 2008 International Coalition Against Sexual Harassment Researcher Award, the 2008 Carolyn Payton Early Career Award for Research making "a significant contribution to the understanding of the role of gender in the lives of Black women," the Association of Women in Psychology's 2007 Women of Color Award for empirical research contributions, Michigan State University's 2007 Excellence in Diversity Award in the category of "'Individual Emerging Progress' for outstanding research and teaching accomplishments in the areas of diversity, pluralism, and social justice," and two Clinical Faculty Awards from the National Institutes of Health (NIH). Representative publications include: "The Effects of Racial and Sexual Harassment on Work and the Psychological Well-Being of African American Women," *Journal of Occupational Health Psychology*; "Comparing Sexual Harassment Subtypes for Black and White Women: Double Jeopardy, the Jezebel, and the Cult of True Womanhood," *Psychology of Women Quarterly*; "Sexual Harassment across the Color Line: Experiences and Outcomes of Cross- versus Intra-Racial Sexual Harassment among Black Women," *Cultural Diversity and Ethnic Minority Psychology*; and "Racialized Sexual Harassment in the Lives of African American Women," *Women & Therapy*.

JOAN C. CHRISLER, Ph.D., is a Class of 1943 Professor of Psychology at Connecticut College, where she teaches courses on the psychology of women and health psychology. She has published extensively on the psychology of women and gender, and is especially known for her work on women's health, menstruation, weight, and body image. She edited *Sex Roles: A Journal of Research* from 2002 to 2006, and is editor or co-editor of eight books, including *Women over 50: Psychological Perspectives* (2007, Springer), *From Menarche to Menopause: The Female Body in Feminist Therapy* (2004, Haworth), *Lectures on the Psychology of Women* (4th ed., 2008, McGraw-Hill), and the *Handbook of Gender Research in Psychology* (forthcoming, Springer).

JESSICA B. BRODSKY is a doctoral student in the school-clinical child psychology graduate program at Pace University. Jessica graduated with a bachelor of arts in psychology and a markets and management certificate from Duke University in 2005. After receiving her bachelor's degree, Jessica worked in marketing and promotions for three years before deciding to continue her studies in psychology. She volunteered on Project Real Adolescent Perspectives (RAP) at the New York University Center for Research on Culture, Development, and Education, assisting in various phases of the research process. Jessica later worked as an instructional aide in a first grade, mainstreamed classroom in Long Island, New York. She currently serves as a graduate assistant for Dr. Florence Denmark and is a member of Psi Chi and the American Psychological Association (APA).

PAUL COEN earned his bachelor of science degree in finance from Siena College and his master of business administration in 2009 from Union Graduate College, where he also earned a certificate in human resource management. He is a customer development account manager for Nestle USA.

JENNIE D'AIUTO graduated from Southern Vermont College located in Bennington, Vermont with her bachelor's degree in business administration and a concentration in criminal justice. She graduated from Union Graduate College, where she earned her MBA and human resources certificate. Her career goals include human resource management.

DARLENE C. DEFOUR, Ph.D., is a social psychologist/community psychologist. She is a graduate of Fisk University and received her doctorate from the University of Illinois at Urbana-Champaign. She is an associate professor of psychology at Hunter College of the City University of New York. There she teaches classes, including social psychology, personal adjustment, psychology of women, and psychological theories of ethnic and cultural identity. She is a currently a member of the board of directors of the New York Association of Black Psychologists and has served on the board of directors of the national association. She is also a member of several divisions of the American Psychological Association. The theme of her current research is the exploration of the various ways that violence in the form of racism and sexism as well as physical violence affects the everyday lives of adolescent and adult Black females.

FLORENCE L. DENMARK, Ph.D., is an internationally recognized scholar, researcher and policy maker. She received her doctorate from the University of Pennsylvania in social psychology and has five honorary degrees. Denmark is the Robert Scott Pace Distinguished Research Professor of Psychology at Pace University in New York. A past president of the American Psychological Association (APA) and the International Council of Psychologists (ICP), Denmark holds fellowship status in the APA and the Association for Psychological Science. She is also a member of the Society for Experimental Social Psychology (SESP) and a Fellow of the New York Academy of Sciences. She has received numerous national and international awards for her contributions to psychology. She received the 2004 American Psychological Foundation Gold Medal for Lifetime Achievement for Psychology in the Public Interest. In 2005, she received the Ernest R. Hilgard Award for Career Contribution to General Psychology. She is the recipient in 2007 of the Raymond Fowler Award for Outstanding Service to APA. Also in 2007, Denmark was elected to the National Academies of Practice as a distinguished scholar member. She received the Elder Award at the APA National Multicultural Conference in 2009. Denmark's most significant research and extensive publications have emphasized women's leadership and leadership styles, the interaction of status and gender, aging women in cross-cultural perspective, and the history of women in psychology. Denmark is the main nongovernmental organization (NGO) representative to the United Nations for the American Psychological Association and is also the main NGO representative for the International Council of Psychologists. She is currently Chair of the New York NGO Committee on Ageing and serves on the Executive Committee of the NGO Committee on Mental Health.

DEANNDRA E. DODD graduated *magna cum laude* from the University at Albany with a bachelor of science in business administration.

She attended Union Graduate College where she earned her master of business administration and also graduated *magna cum laude* from Albany Law School. She is currently living in Albany, New York.

JOANMARIE M. DOWLING, Esq., concentrates her practice in labor and employment law. She advises and represents employers on a wide array of labor and employment law issues, including employer recruiting, screening, and hiring practices; harassment and discrimination claims; union avoidance; collective bargaining; wage and hour law compliance; reasonable accommodations for employee disabilities and religion; and discipline and termination of employees.

J. HAROLD ELLENS is a retired university professor of philosophy and psychology, a retired US Army Colonel, a retired Presbyterian pastor and theologian, executive director emeritus of the Christian Association for Psychological Studies International; founder and editor-in-chief emeritus of the *Journal of Psychology and Christianity*, a clinical psychotherapist in private practice, the author, co-author, or editor of 175 volumes and author of 166 professional journal articles. He continues in his role as adjunct professor of philosophy and biblical studies at University of Detroit, Mercy, in classics at Wayne State University, and research scholar in the Department of Near Eastern Studies at the University of Michigan.

MARIE FUDA graduated from Siena College in 2008 with a bachelor of science in marketing and management. In 2009 she received her masters in business administration from Union Graduate College and will earn a certificate in human resource management from Union Graduate College in 2010.

WILLIAM GAEDDERT, Ph.D., is a professor in the psychology department at SUNY Plattsburgh. He has been at Plattsburgh State since receiving his doctorate from Iowa State University in 1981. Trained as a social psychologist, his research interests focus on gender and the psychology of justice. He teaches courses in industrial and organizational psychology, and research methods and statistics at both graduate and undergraduate levels.

THOMAS GERBER earned his master of business administration from Union Graduate College in 2009 and was elected to Beta Gamma

Sigma for his outstanding performance in the program. Since 2005, Mr. Gerber has been working toward the master of industrial engineering and management at Universitat Karlsruhe, from where he will graduate in 2010.

SHANNA T. GERMAN is a doctoral student in the school-clinical child psychology graduate program at Pace University. Shanna graduated with a bachelor of arts with honors in psychology and a minor in English from the University at Albany. There she served as vice president of Psi Chi-Albany Chapter. Shanna received her masters of arts from Yeshiva University in applied psychology and holds a certificate in group therapy from the Eastern Group Psychotherapy Society. After receiving her master's degree, she worked for two years as a research assistant at the New York University, Child Study Center, Department of Child and Adolescent Psychiatry, on a National Institute of Mental Health (NIMH)-funded intervention project working with at-risk, pre-kindergarten children and their families. There she co-authored a poster on predictors of parent involvement in school in a culturally diverse sample, as well as a paper symposium on overweight and elementary school functioning among Caucasian, African-American, Latino, and Asian children in the United States. Shanna currently serves as a graduate assistant to Dr. Florence Denmark.

MICHELLE HEBL, Ph.D., graduated with her bachelor of arts degree from Smith College and her doctorate from Dartmouth College. She joined the psychology faculty at Rice University in 1998, was given the endowed title of the Radoslav Tsanoff Assistant Professorship in 2000, and was promoted to associate professor in 2004. Her research focuses on the manifestation and remediation of discrimination against a variety of stigmatized groups. She currently has more than 75 publications and is a consulting editor for several applied journals.

INGRID JOHNSTON-ROBLEDO, Ph.D., is director of women's studies and associate professor of psychology at SUNY, Fredonia. She teaches courses on the psychology of women, women's health, and human sexuality. Her areas of expertise are women's health, reproductive health education, and women's experiences with pregnancy, childbirth, breastfeeding, postpartum adjustment, and motherhood.

JENNIFER L. MARTIN, Ph.D., is the department head of English at a public alternative high school for at-risk students in Michigan and a lecturer at Oakland University where she teaches graduate research methods in the Department of Educational Leadership; feminist methods and introduction to Women and Gender Studies (WGS) in the Department of Women and Gender Studies. She is not only a feminist teacher, but a feminist activist. She has volunteered as an assault responder and engaged in political action for feminist causes. Currently she is the Title IX Education Task Force Chair for the Michigan National Organization for Women in order to advocate for Title IX compliance in Michigan's schools. She has conducted research and written articles on the topics of peer sexual harassment, teaching for social justice, service learning, and the at-risk student.

DIANE E. SAMMONS, Esq., is an experienced litigator, who has practiced law for more than 25 years. She started her career as a criminal prosecutor in the Manhattan District Attorney's Office. After establishing an array of trial victories there, she began work at one of the largest commercial firms in New York state, focusing on mass complex tort cases (including the DES' litigation, tobacco litigation, and fetal-alcohol syndrome), commercial litigation, insurance, and white-collar criminal defense work. She came to work for Nagel Rice, LLP in 1990. In 2001, she became part of a team representing national and international victims in an Austrian ski train disaster against European companies. Her efforts have contributed to several significant jurisdictional victories over multinational corporations. She has also secured a successful result for her representation of several Austrian antinuclear organizations who sought to close a nuclear power station on the southern border of the Czech Republic. Her work in securing documentation through the Freedom of Information Act was a resource to her clients who had been struggling for years to secure basic safety documents from the Czech Republic.

ISIS H. SETTLES, Ph.D., is an associate professor in the Department of Psychology at Michigan State University (MSU) in the social-personality area. She is a core faculty affiliate of MSU's Center for Multicultural Psychology Research and MSU's Center for Gender in Global Context. Dr. Settles received her doctorate in personality psychology from the University of Michigan. Her research examines processes and outcomes associated with social group membership (for example, race and gender) and social group identification. In particular, she is interested in how individuals negotiate multiple identities, and how members of devalued social groups (especially women and people of color) perceive and cope with unfair treatment. Dr. Settles was the 2006 recipient of the Carolyn Payton Early Career Award for research making "a significant contribution to the understanding of the role of gender in the lives of Black women." Her research has been funded by grants from MSU's Office of Inclusion and Intercultural Initiatives and the National Institute of Mental Health.

SARA-BECCA SMITH completed her undergraduate degree at the College of Wooster in Wooster, Ohio. She graduated in 1999 with a bachelor of arts in sociology. She is currently attending Union Graduate College in Schenectady, New York in pursuit of a master of business administration. She will be graduating in the spring of 2010 with a certificate in management and leadership. In addition to her studies, Sara-Becca serves as the treasurer on the board of directors for a nonprofit organization serving the Capital Region of New York.

SUSAN STRAUSS, R.N., Ed.D., is a national and international speaker, trainer, and consultant. Her specialty areas include harassment, workplace bullying, organization development, and management/leadership development. Her clients are from business, education, health care, law, and government organizations, both public and private sectors. Dr. Strauss has authored book chapters, articles in professional journals, written curriculum and training manuals, and the book, *Sexual Harassment and Teens: A Program for Positive Change.* She has been featured on *The Donahue Show, CBS Evening News,* and other television and radio programs as well as interviewed for newspaper and journal articles by such publications as the *Times of London, Lawyers Weekly,* and *Harvard Education Newsletter.* She has presented at international conferences in Botswana, Egypt, Thailand, Israel, and the U.S., and conducted sex discrimination research in Poland. She has consulted with professionals from other countries such as England, Australia, Canada, and St. Martin.

STEVIE C. Y. YAP is a doctoral student in the Department of Psychology at Michigan State University. He obtained his bachelor of science degree at the University of Toronto. His current research interests are in examining the predictors and consequences of ethnic and gender identity and the psychological outcomes associated with the intersection of multiple identities.

Index